Olivi's Peaceable Kingdom

University of Pennsylvania Press
MIDDLE AGES SERIES
Edited by
Edward Peters
Henry Charles Lea Professor
of Medieval History
University of Pennsylvania

A listing of the available books
in the series appears at the
back of this volume

Olivi's Peaceable Kingdom

A Reading of the Apocalypse Commentary

David Burr

University of Pennsylvania Press

Philadelphia

Library of Congress Cataloging-in-Publication Data

Burr, David, 1934–
    Olivi's peaceable kingdom: a reading of the Apocalypse commentary /
David Burr.
      p.   cm. — (Middle Ages series)
    Includes bibliographical references and index.
    ISBN 0-8122-3227-5
    1. Olivi, Pierre Jean, 1248 or 9–1298. Lectura super Apocalypsim.
2. Bible. N.T. Revelation—Criticism, interpretation, etc.—
History—Middle Ages, 600–1500. I. Title. II. Series.
BS2825.A2B87   1993
228'.06—dc20   93-25557
                                                  CIP

Contents

Abbreviations

AF   *Analecta franciscana*. Quaracchi: College of Saint
          Bonaventure, 1885–1941.

AFH   *Archivum franciscanum historicum*.

BF   *Bullarium fransciscanum*. Rome: Vatican, 1759–1904.

Archiv   Heinrich Denifle and Franz Ehrle. *Archiv für Literatur- und
          Kirchengeschichte des Mittelalters*.

Berlin: Weidmannsche Buchhandlung, 1885–1900.

CCSL   *Corpus Christianorum*, series latina. Turnhout: Brepols, 1954–.

CSEL   *Corpus scriptorum ecclesiasticorum latinorum*. Vienna: Hoelder-
          Pichler-Tempsky, 1866–.

Lectura   Petrus Iohannis Olivi. *Lectura super apocalypsim*. In Warren
          Lewis, "Peter John Olivi: Prophet of the Year 2000."
          Doctoral dissertation, Tübingen University, 1972.

OFP   David Burr. *Olivi and Franciscan Poverty*. Philadelphia:
          University of Pennsylvania Press, 1989.

PL   J.-P. Migne. *Patrologiae Cursus Completus*. Series Latina.
          Paris: Migne, 1844–66.

Preface

Everyone who knows anything at all about Petrus Iohannis Olivi knows that his Apocalypse commentary was censured; yet opinions on that condemnation vary. The basic facts are clear. After Olivi's death in 1298, his writings were suppressed by the Franciscan order, yet his tomb at Narbonne became such a popular pilgrimage site that by the second decade of the fourteenth century the crowds were said to rival those at the Porziuncula in Assisi.

The hiatus between these two attitudes toward Olivi reflected a conflict within the order between the spiritual Franciscans and their leaders. Between 1309 and 1312, Pope Clement V tried to end the dispute through a compromise, but the arrangement barely outlived Clement. By 1316, when John XXII became Clement's successor after a two-year papal vacancy, some spiritual Franciscans, driven to extremes by their superiors, had forcibly taken control of several convents in France and Italy. They administered these convents as little islands of strict observance. John XXII, who saw the spirituals mainly as a disciplinary problem, cooperated with the Franciscan leaders in their attempt to crush dissent. The spirituals were told to submit, and those who refused were burned at the stake. In 1318 Olivi's body was unobtrusively exhumed and removed to an undisclosed location.

The attacks on Olivi had come to concentrate on his Revelation commentary, and with good reason. The spirituals found it increasingly relevant to their situation. By 1318 John had ordered an investigation which led to the report of an eight-man commission in 1319. He then submitted particular passages from Olivi's commentary to individual theologians before he himself condemned it in 1326.

These are the facts, but what can we make of them? The question has been asked and answered before, but the present seems an auspicious moment to reconsider it. It is in some ways a dangerous moment to do so, since circumstances have conspired to produce a more knowledgeable and therefore more critical set of readers than ever before. Until 1955 scholars who wanted to know something about Olivi's apocalyptic thought without wading through manuscripts tended to rely on the substantial extracts included in the report of the commission that judged the work in 1319. The report, published in Baluze's *Miscellenaea*, simply quoted a series of suspect passages and passed negative judgment on them. Scholars recognized that there were certain limitations attached to using this source—they were, after all, seeing Olivi at his worst—yet they understandably chose to work with what they had. The result was, as one might expect, a tendency to see Olivi as heretical.

In 1955 Raoul Manselli produced a revolution in Olivi scholarship with his book on the Apocalypse commentary. Manselli saw Olivi as a major reformer whose bold yet orthodox cry of warning the church would have done well to heed. He bolstered his case with ample citations from the commentary in his footnotes. The report of the eight-man commission was portrayed as a terrible misunderstanding. Manselli announced a critical edition as imminent, but years passed and the edition never appeared. Thus most scholars, still unwilling to read the manuscripts, simply transferred their allegiance from the excerpts in the 1319 commission report to those in Manselli's footnotes. When they mentioned Olivi, they usually accepted Manselli's contention that the commission had misrepresented him. The Mansellian hegemony began to dissolve in the 1970s. In 1972 Warren Lewis earned a doctorate at Tübingen by producing a remarkable analysis and critical edition of Olivi's commentary. While the Lewis edition filled an obvious need, a variety of factors have prevented its publication, and twenty-one years later there is still no critical edition in print. Paolo Vian is working on what promises to be a very solid edition, but it is impossible to say when it will appear. In the meantime, the photocopier is doing what the printing press has failed to do. As Robert Lerner once remarked to me, the Lewis edition is enjoying a tremendous career in *samizdat*. Easy access to Lewis's text has ushered in a new phase of Olivi research. Thus armed, scholars are no longer dependent on the excerpts fed them by Olivi specialists.

One might ask, of course, whether these scholars will simply discover that Manselli's reading was correct, thus obviating the need for any new book on the matter. I must say at the outset that there are few modern scholars I venerate as I do Manselli. He was quite simply one of the finest scholars I have ever read. Like Franz Ehrle, he made contributions to our knowledge of the spiritual Franciscans which will never be equaled. Having said so much, I must add that I still think a new book is desirable for at least three reasons. First, there is some need for a study in English.

During the last two or three decades, Olivi has become interesting to an ever-wider circle of American and British historians. A book in English would be valuable even if it did little except restate Manselli's view.

Nevertheless, there is reason to believe that a great deal more than that is required, and here we arrive at the second reason for a new study. It is possible to improve our understanding of Olivi by placing him more firmly within his historical context. Manselli did so ably in one sense, since he began his book with an analysis of apocalyptic thought before Olivi's time, paying considerable attention to the two exegetes whom Olivi continually cited, Joachim of Fiore and Richard of St. Victor; yet in another sense he provided very little context. Olivi was, after all, a student and later a lector in Franciscan *studia*. As such, he was exposed not only to a general apocalyptic ethos but also to a method of expositing scripture. As a student at Paris, he was presented with a way of reading the Bible much as he was presented with a way of reading Peter Lombard's *Sentences*. In the eyes of his contemporaries, Olivi's orthodoxy or heterodoxy was at least partly a function of his conformity or nonconformity with these acceptable ways of reading. We know something of the context that determined how contemporaries would view his work on the *Sentences* because modern scholars have devoted a great deal of attention to *Sentence* commentaries of that time; yet we are remarkably ignorant of the context in which they would have viewed his Apocalypse commentary, because we have spent very little time on any Franciscan Apocalypse commentary except Olivi's.

I have managed to find seventeen other Franciscan and Dominican Apocalypse commentaries written in the thirteenth and early fourteenth centuries. (The Dominicans are important because they were intellectually and institutionally close to the Franciscans, and these two mendicant orders seem to have read one another's commentaries.) Nine of these are published and eight remain in manuscript form, but of the former only two are in modern editions. The attribution problems are immense. In only eight cases can I name the author without feeling that my decision might someday be overturned. In some cases, I cannot name the author at all.

My inability to speak with much authority about the provenance of these commentaries, combined with the fact that my reading of some has been perforce more cursory than my reading of Olivi, inevitably makes my treatment of them the most vulnerable part of the present work. I fully expect to be subjected to heavy fire on their account. Nevertheless, even when used *grosso modo*, these commentaries make an important contribution. They offer a remarkable context in which to place Olivi's work. If my attributions are correct—and the law of averages suggests that they cannot *all* be wrong—then with three exceptions the authors either were educated in Paris or taught there, normally both. (Two of the exceptions were Oxford men, the third a German of indeterminate intellectual pedigree.) Thus the commentaries provide excellent insight into how the Apocalypse was interpreted by the most prestigious scholars of Olivi's time. Armed with this knowledge, we can see what was unique and what was traditional in his interpretation. Even if much of what I say about the commentaries is questionable, it will never be so questionable as to erase their fundamental value.

There is third reason, the simplest yet most important of all, why a new study of Olivi's commentary seems justified. Despite my profound respect for Manselli, I tend to disagree with him on some issues. Manselli's presentation was incisive but tendentious, not only an interpretation but a defense of Olivi, whom Manselli greatly admired. In the process, some genuine differences between Olivi and his contemporaries were obscured and some valid reasons for anxiety on the latter's part were underemphasized. It may seem odd and somewhat humorous that one who has been described in print as "Olivi's alter ego" should take it upon himself to accuse Manselli of excessive identification with his subject. I hasten to explain that my own ability to offer a corrective to his view stems not from any purported detachment but from a tendency to admire Olivi for an entirely different set of reasons. Obscure as this suggestion may seem, it will, I hope, become clear as the work progresses.

Having provided extensive biographical information on Olivi in two earlier works, I shall resist the temptation to repeat it all here. Nor will I pay much attention to any part of the extensive Olivi corpus except the Apocalypse commentary. The first three chapters will provide some background by examining early Franciscan apocalyptic thought and briefly surveying Olivi's career. The next five chapters will offer an interpretation of Olivi's commentary, and the last three will consider its subsequent condemnation.

This work was underwritten by several institutions. Summer grants from Virginia Tech and the American Philosophical Society offered me the opportunity to search for manuscripts, while a one-year grant from the National Endowment for the Humanities provided time to think and write. I was also supported by the advice and encouragement of more people than I can list here. Among American scholars, I offer special thanks to Randy Daniel, Bernard McGinn, and Robert Lerner for their good counsel. Above all, I thank Warren Lewis for appearing at my door almost two decades ago and presenting me with a copy of his dissertation. Both his edition and his introduction have been invaluable. I disagree with some of his views, but with great respect.

During my periods in England over the years, my research was aided by the remarkable openness and generosity of Decima Douie, Beryl Smalley, and Marjorie Reeves, who not only made me welcome at Oxford but were eager to share their own knowledge. I also owe a great deal to people I barely know. Extensive use of unpublished sources has meant that, like Blanche DuBois in *A Streetcar Named Desire*, I have often had to depend on the kindness of strangers. In England, Belgium, France, and Italy my personal and epistolary requests have been fulfilled by a series of knowledgeable, helpful librarians whom I know only as faces or as signatures on letters, yet on whom I depend as if they were my dearest friends. On the home front, among those I know very well indeed, I cannot thank my wife Annette for typing services or other free labor—she has her own career to pursue, as I have mine—but there is much else for which I am very grateful to her. I also thank Clare and Jessica, who have given me incredible support and have probably spent more time in my study than I have.

1. Joachism and the Eternal Gospel

In 1268 Peter Olivi sat with his fellow students at Paris and listened attentively while the minister general of his order, Bonaventure of Bagnoreggio, delivered his *Collations on the Seven Gifts of the Holy Spirit*.[1] Olivi was being treated to a large helping of Franciscan apocalyptic. There was already a discernible apocalyptic current in the order. While it would be erroneous to equate this current completely with Joachim of Fiore, he exerted such a strong effect that the Joachite tradition must be examined at some length.

The logical place to begin is with Joachim himself, but that would be a rather big project. The general outlines of his thought have been covered by a series of modern scholars.[2] Thus we will leave the task of extensive analysis to them and take only a general look at his view of history, although specific aspects of Joachim's thought will be mentioned throughout the book. Joachim's view of history rests on two bases. The first is his pattern of double sevens, according to which Old Testament and New Testament history are each divided into seven periods. He sees a *concordia* between the two in the sense that they parallel one another, at least in broad outline.[3] He is not unaware of Augustine's world week, seven periods of all history with the Christian era as the sixth and the seventh essentially in eternity; yet the double sevens are much more important to him.

The second basis is Joachim's trinitarian view of history, according to which the Old and New Testament eras are followed by a third age of peace, *spiritualis intellectus*, and spiritual jubilation characterized by a spiritual *concordia* of the Old and New Testaments. He ascribes the three ages to the Father, Son, and Holy Spirit, but does not mean to imply that each enjoys the attention of only one member of the Trinity. Nor does he mean to imply that the Christian era will end with the arrival of the third age. The two patterns fit together in such a way that the seventh period of church history corresponds with the third age in the threefold pattern, although the third age can also be said to begin in the sixth period.

Joachim was not the first person to see church history as divided into seven periods. By his time, that much was an exegetical commonplace among commentators on the Apocalypse, as we will see; yet his pattern of concordant double sevens was an innovation. Moreover, while other writers had occasionally imposed a threefold pattern on history, none had imposed the sort of pattern developed by Joachim or pursued the matter as zealously as he did.[4] In fact, it is hard to find much sense of dependence on other writers in Joachim, who saw his theology of history as developing out of insights gained through two visions.[5]

To describe Joachim thus baldly is to do violence to him. His work is much subtler than these neat divisions would suggest. In fact, some scholars have questioned whether the word "age," with its straightforward chronological implication, is an adequate translation for Joachim's more ambiguous *status*. It probably is not. The word *status* has qualitative implications and might often be rendered more adequately as "state of being," but the fact remains that it has strong chronological overtones as well.[6]

Hugh of Digne

Our earliest evidence of Franciscan Joachism is Salimbene's narrative of how a Florensian abbot, fearing that Frederick II would destroy his monastery and with it his collection of Joachim's writings, deposited the latter at the Franciscan house in Pisa. Rudolph of Saxony, the Franciscan lector there, was so taken by these recent acquisitions that he gave up other scholarly pursuits and became a *maximus Ioachita*.[7] These events must have occurred between ca. 1243 and 1247, since Salimbene places them during his own stay at Pisa. After that point, references to Franciscan Joachism fall thick and fast. In late 1247 and early 1248, Salimbene was in Provins, where he met Gerard of Borgo San Donnino and another friar, both *totaliter Ioachitae*.[8] By the summer of 1248, he was in Hyères, where Hugh of Digne, a *magnus Ioachita*, conducted what amounted to a Joachite study group for laymen and Franciscans alike.[9]

Are there any earlier traces? E. R. Daniel has attempted to trace Franciscan Joachism back to Naples in the 1240s. He suggests that John of Parma, another of Salimbene's "great Joachites," received his first exposure there before 1245.[10] This scenario seems possible, although there is little evidence for it. Nor, as Daniel himself recognizes, is there any significant evidence for his other claim that Hugh learned his Joachism from John;

yet Daniel seems quite justified in suggesting that Hugh became a Joachite between 1243, when Salimbene encountered him at Siena, and 1248, when they met again at Hyères.[11] What sort of Joachite had he become? Our knowledge of Hugh rests on three major sources: his writings, Joinville's life of Louis IX, and Salimbene. If we had only the first two, we would never believe he was any sort of Joachite at all. It is Salimbene who calls him a "great Joachite" no less than six times, and who gives us some aid in determining what that label meant.

Certainly it meant involvement with prophecy, but that might imply a number of things. When modern liberal churchmen speak of the prophetic function of Christianity, they are normally thinking of the Old Testament prophets' function as fearless critics of society. Hugh was such a critic. All three sources suggest that, when he thought correction was in order, Hugh could be quite uninhibited. Nevertheless, the Old Testament prophets were also "prophetic" in what has become the more popular sense of the term. They predicted the future, and so did Hugh. The real question is how he did so. Was he a visionary like the Old Testament prophets? Later tradition said as much,[12] and his sister Douceline certainly was,[13] but we never find Hugh actually claiming such gifts. In fact, we find him denying them. According to Salimbene, when the pope described Hugh as "Joachim's successor in prophecies," Hugh modestly replied that he was not a prophet himself, although he believed in prophecies.[14] One suspects that the real Hugh is speaking here. He did think that he could foretell the future, but not through visions. He did it primarily through biblical exegesis and secondarily through the prophecies of others like Joachim, Merlin, and the Sybil. The most illuminating passage in this respect is Salimbene's narration of an encounter between Hugh and a Dominican, Peter of Apulia, who came to the former's attention when he informed a friar at Hyères that he considered Joachim about as useful as a fifth wheel on a wagon. Hugh was immediately summoned, and the resulting confrontation tells us much of what we know about his Joachism. It also tells us a great deal about his personality and/or Salimbene's narrative skills. The opening exchanges could almost have been penned by a modern scriptwriter.

"You're the one who doubts Joachim?"

"I'm the one."

"Have you ever read Joachim?"

"I've read him, and I've read him well."

"I think you read him like a little old lady reads her Psalter. By the time she gets to the end she's forgotten what she saw at the beginning."

Right away we know there's going to be trouble. Fortunately Hugh and his adversary are consistent intellectuals and the clash will be one of ideas. Peter of Apulia challenges Hugh to prove from the book of Isaiah, in Joachite style, that the emperor Frederick II will die at the age of seventy by natural causes. Hugh does just that, in the process citing a prophecy of Merlin. When Peter suggests that it is heretical to cite a pagan like Merlin, Hugh notes that Augustine cited the Sybil and the church accepts prophecies by Balaam and Caiaphas. In answer to the objection that Christ himself told the disciples, "It is not yours to know the times or moments," Hugh observes that the apostles did not need to know many things we will profit from knowing now, since they would not live long enough to see them occur and in any case had other, more immediate concerns.

Salimbene informs us that Hugh had all of Joachim's writings, but we do not know what the term "all" included. Given Salimbene's own knowledge of the field, we can infer that Hugh must have possessed at least Joachim's *Liber de concordia* and commentary on the Apocalypse. Salimbene tells us that he also had the commentary on the four gospels. In addition to the authentic works, he undoubtedly owned a few of the more dubious ones. Certainly he must have had the commentary on Jeremiah, since it played an important role among Franciscan Joachites of that time.[15] Perhaps he also had the commentary on Isaiah and the commentary on Merlin and the Sybil, although these are normally dated in the next decade.[16]

Commenting on Salimbene's picture of Joachite discourse at Hyères, Marjorie Reeves observes,

> The curious thing about these conversations is that they turn entirely on Joachim's prophecies of the days of crisis and Antichrist, and not at all on the ushering in of the third *status*. Although Salimbene elsewhere claims the prophecies of new orders as a matter of course, the group around Hugh de Digne does not seem to have concerned itself openly with the Abbot's pattern of threes or the special role which his third *status* might give them. In his writings Hugh upholds the ideal of absolute poverty with all the passionate zeal of the later Spirituals, but, again, he makes no open claim that the strict Franciscan party holds the key to the third *status*. So far as the evidence goes, this group in Provence seems still to belong to what we have called the first phase of Joachimism, in which emphasis is placed on the pattern of twos and the crisis of history rather than on the pattern of threes and the *renovatio mundi*.[17]

This interpretation coheres with evidence from other quarters presented by Reeves.[18] It must be accepted with some caution, however, since it is based almost entirely on a single incident in which the topic of conversation was chosen by Hugh's adversary. Hugh is also depicted by Salimbene as referring on another occasion to the coming tribulation,[19] but otherwise we have little to work with. Moreover, while it is virtually unthinkable that Salimbene could have fabricated the whole story—why should he invent an episode in which, two years before Frederick's death, Hugh argued that he would live another sixteen years?—it is worth noting that the subject of this conversation, the only one at Hyères reported at length, accords with Salimbene's own preoccupations.[20] We will never know what else Hugh said that Salimbene did not see fit to remember.

The Jeremiah Commentary

Our knowledge of early Franciscan Joachism is clarified when we turn from Hugh to his reading material. The main target of our interest is not so much the authentic canon as the pseudepigrapha, and especially the commentary on Jeremiah, which is the earliest of the pseudo-Joachim commentaries. Most scholars believe that the Jeremiah commentary was written in southern Italy in the 1240s, certainly before 1248 and probably before 1243.[21] There is less agreement concerning its authors. The commentary was once generally seen as the product of Franciscan circles adapting Joachim for the purposes of minorite chauvinism, and there is much in it to support that view. Nevertheless, other passages seem to suggest either a Florensian or a Cistercian milieu.[22] Most recently, Robert Moynihan and Stephen Wessley have advanced the discussion by noting that the work exists in both a longer and a shorter version, and Moynihan has suggested an original by Joachim himself.[23] Unfortunately the manuscript evidence presented so far does not really solve the Franciscan/Florensian/Cistercian problem, and the evidence for an original version by Joachim can hardly be called convincing; yet research on the matter is in an infant stage and we will undoubtedly hear more. For the moment, the problem remains open and we must work with the printed editions, although they probably do not entirely coincide with the version read by thirteenth-century Franciscans.[24]

The commentary on Jeremiah is striking in a number of ways, and modern scholarly preoccupations have tended to highlight some points of interest while obscuring others. It is widely noted that the commentary celebrates the impending arrival of two new orders and describes them in such a way as to evoke the Franciscans and Dominicans. It is also generally observed that the commentary is preoccupied with the apocalyptic role of the empire, particularly with Frederick II, although it awards itself a theoretical composition date of 1197, purports to be addressed to Henry VI, and thus can refer to Frederick only obliquely. Scholars also regularly inform us that the Jeremiah commentary provides our first decent evidence of a growing interest in Joachim's threefold pattern as distinguished from his pattern of double sevens, and that it is the source of the date 1260, the passing of which without incident so disappointed Salimbene.[25]

Less attention has been paid to the fact that the Jeremiah commentary is a genuine jeremiad, and that its target is not only the empire but the church as well. The catalogue of charges features corruption, neglect of the faithful, and preeminently greed. The hierarchy is portrayed as intent upon gaining wealth at great spiritual cost. The quality of learning is also attacked.[26] The commentary is generous in spreading guilt out over the entire church. It is corrupt at all levels, and it is massively, almost totally corrupt.[27] The author unflinchingly heaps abuse on everyone from the pope down to the laity.[28] Only a few *spirituales* are acceptable before the Lord, but they are unsupported and even persecuted by the hierarchy.[29] Nevertheless—and here the logic of the text being exposed fits the commentator's predilections all too well—the church will soon be desolated by enemies who will serve up the just punishment of God, although they hardly recognize him as their employer. They in turn will then be destroyed. The author speaks of a threefold attack by the empire, the Cathari (always called, *modo italiano*, the Patarenes), and the Muslims; yet he is also heavily influenced by the imagery of Revelation 13 and repeatedly invokes the beasts from land and sea, normally seen as the empire and the Muslims. That leaves the Patarenes without any obvious totem, but they can be accommodated in various ways. They are often closely related to the emperor, a reflection of the widespread thirteenth-century view of the Ghibellines as protectors or even adherents of Catharism.[30] The empire plays an ambiguous role, however. It functions as both protector and victimizer. It is also ambiguous inasmuch as even the victimization has both a positive and negative side. The empire robs the church, yet robs it of wealth that the church should not love anyway. Desolation of the church by the empire and then the eastern power represents the means by which the church is purified.[31]

The Muslims play an important but unspecified role. The most commonly suggested scenario in the commentary calls upon them to destroy the Byzantine church, then the Latin one. The real question is what connection the author sees between the Muslims and the empire. He employs the image of the Euphrates to depict the empire in its role as protector and portrays the attack from the east as a result of imperial weakness.[32] We will later see the same symbolism utilized in some Franciscan Apocalypse commentaries. Nevertheless, on other occasions the author reflects the widespread Guelf image of Frederick as the friend of Muslims as well as heretics, and seems to predict an alliance.[33]

In any case, despite the desolation of the church, a group of faithful *spirituales* will quietly perdure without leaders, and from this righteous remnant will spring the new order to follow.[34] The church will be reborn uncorrupted by wealth, having been despoiled of it by its attackers. It will enjoy an *intellectus spiritualis*[35] of the faith and will convert widely among the Greeks, Jews, and infidels.

In the Jeremiah commentary, we find an apocalyptic scenario that resembles the genuine Joachim in some ways but differs markedly in others. The difference can be expressed best by reviewing Joachim's treatment of the beasts in Revelation 13 and 17, symbols that prove so meaningful to the Jeremiah commentary. Many elements accented in the Jeremiah commentary also appear in Joachim's Apocalypse commentary. He too is obsessed with the investiture controversy, the Cathari, and the Muslims; yet he is much less concerned about the church hierarchy. Joachim gives himself even more room than the Jeremiah commentary enjoyed to read a condemnation of the hierarchy into Revelation 13, since he identifies the beast from the land as a sect of pseudoprophets and consistently sees the land/sea distinction as one between religious and secular leaders; yet he never takes advantage of the opportunity. In fact, the pseudoprophets often look suspiciously like the Cathari.[36] Joachim is not immune to the idea that the coming desolation of the West by infidel armies will involve a just punishment of errant clerics,[37] but it is not a subject he particularly likes to discuss. The evil he prefers to describe is the kind that can be located safely outside the bounds of catholic orthodoxy.

John of Parma

By 1247 Salimbene was already being warned that the Joachites were a bad influence because they "stirred up" the brethren.[38] Thus Hugh of Digne's Joachism probably earned him enemies within the order.[39] It also earned him friends, and Salimbene tells us that he had four close ones.[40] The first was Jean de Bernin, archbishop of Vienne, who need not concern us since we have no reason to associate him with apocalyptic interests.[41] The second and third were Robert Grosseteste, bishop of Lincoln, and Adam Marsh, an English Franciscan. Adam's inclusion is understandable though hardly predictable. He visited the Continent from time to time and might be expected to have known another Franciscan as eminent as Hugh. Grosseteste is more surprising. He was closely related to the English Franciscans and may have been introduced to Hugh by Adam, perhaps at the Council of Lyon in 1245.[42] Their friendship must have been primarily an epistolary one, though, and if Jacques Paul is correct in identifying Hugh with the Hugh of Berions and the Hugh of Berioc mentioned in Adam's letters, then Hugh, Adam, and Grosseteste shared a broad range of cultural interests. Adam was the intermediary through which Grosseteste sent Hugh of Berions his translation of Aristotle's *Nichomachean Ethics*.[43] He was also the intermediary through which Grosseteste received "brief excerpts from various commentaries by the Abbot Joachim," which had been brought from Italy by a Franciscan.[44] Adam's letter forwarding the excerpts shows a clear but cautious interest in Joachim. He wants to hear Grosseteste's opinion before he makes up his mind. Perhaps he did eventually hear, but we never will. Nor is there any other significant evidence of either man's apocalyptic beliefs, although scattered comments by each show the extent to which apocalyptic reference was an accepted form of discourse in their day. What little we can glean from these comments suggests that their interest was measured and centered upon issues characteristic of Marjorie Reeves's "first phase" of Joachism.

The fourth friend was John of Parma, another "great Joachite." Here there is no doubt that enthusiasm over Joachite prophecy was an important element in the friendship. Salimbene makes this point very clearly.[45] He also informs us at some length that John, though much admired in other respects, compromised both himself and his order by his excessive Joachism.[46] In fact, though Salimbene hesitates to give us the whole story, it cost John his position as minister general. We know from other sources that disciplinary action taken against him afterward by Bonaventure, the new minister general, led to his retirement to a hermitage at Greccio, where he spent the next thirty-five years.[47]

John's tribulations in 1257 must wait until we have looked at the scandal of the eternal gospel. For the moment, we need only ask what we know of his apocalyptic views before that date. Salimbene links him closely with

Hugh, and Angelo Clareno informs us that the two agreed on all issues;[48] yet the scant evidence we have for John is quite different from the only slightly less meager data concerning Hugh. There is a more positive element in the evidence for John insofar as it deals not with Frederick and the coming tribulation, but with the providential role of the Franciscan order. The most trustworthy document in this regard is the joint letter published with Humbert of Romans, master general of the Dominican order, in 1255 when John was still minister general. It begins with the announcement that, in order to save the world, Christ has raised up these two new orders in the final days. The orders are characterized by a series of images which, though never directly quoting Joachim, evoke him nonetheless.[49] We must be cautious here, since John was at best co-author of this letter and we know that several Dominicans including Humbert saw their group as a providential new order of the final days.[50] Moreover, outside of the letter we have almost nothing to cite. Angelo Clareno speaks at length about John,[51] but he is writing over a half-century after the event and is extremely tendentious.

Mention of Angelo brings us to an important point about John. Salimbene assures us that he was a "great Joachite" in the late 1240s, but the evidence for his particular brand of Joachism begins with the joint letter of 1255. Thus, although John and Hugh were roughly the same age and Hugh may have been introduced to Joachism by John, our evidence for John is ten years later than our evidence for Hugh and reflects a much different situation. In Salimbene's narrative, we see Hugh speculating in southern France before Frederick's death. By the late 1250s, John was operating in a different context. Frederick was gone. The Franciscans were increasingly under attack from the secular clergy and Parisian masters. John was in charge of the order. In this situation, Joachite speculation had to perform slightly different functions. Heightened emphasis on the providential role of the order would be understandable.

It was at this moment that the scandal of the eternal gospel erupted. It brought disgrace to three Franciscans: John of Parma, Gerard of Borgo San Donnino, and a third brother named Leonard, who functioned in a supporting role and can be ignored. We will deal with the scandal itself later. Here we need only observe that it gave the secular masters precisely the ammunition they needed in their war against the mendicants. Most extant sources agree that John was told to resign in the wake of the scandal.[52] Several authors from the period actually attributed Gerard's edition to John.[53] According to Angelo, however, there were three reasons for

John's fall. The first was his uncompromising advocacy of poverty; the second his support of Joachim; and the third his associates Gerard and Leonard, who praised Joachim excessively.[54] Gerard will be accorded his own section. For the moment we will concentrate on the other two elements, beginning with the first, John's advocacy of poverty, and shifting unobtrusively to his Joachism as we go along.

Angelo portrays John as a man who stood for the highest level of observance, expected it from his brethren, and resigned in disgust when he saw that the majority of his order would not attain it. If they failed to do so, it was certainly not because John had been shy about bringing the matter to their attention. Angelo's narrative gives the impression that John spent a good deal of his time berating his colleagues. He also prophesied to them concerning the decline and eventual reformation of the order.[55] More specifically, he is said to have predicted the division of the order into those who wished to observe rule and *Testament* on the one hand and, on the other, those who wanted papal privileges and exemptions. This rift would be followed by the rise of a third group, "a congregation of holy poor men."[56] The chided brethren were kept silent by John's rank and eloquence, but they had a long memory and settled the score after he resigned.

One should approach this portrayal with caution. Salimbene too presents John as devoted to the sort of holy simplicity Francis would have appreciated,[57] and grants that John had enemies; yet he does not combine the two. In fact, he implies the opposite. If John had only curbed his Joachite enthusiasm, he would have exerted a significant influence on the church.[58] Moreover, the scolding speeches Angelo ascribes to John are essentially Italian spiritual polemics. John becomes one more witness to the complaints voiced by Angelo and Ubertino da Casale decades later at the Council of Vienne. He criticizes the practice of allowing a new brother to keep some of his wealth to buy books, or allowing him to give it to the order for new buildings "or other conveniences." He laments Franciscan involvement in legal battles with the secular clergy over burial, wills, and legacies. He insists that Francis's *Testament* and his rule are substantially the same and that the *Testament* should be followed as the definitive interpretation of the rule. He attacks those who grant legal force to papal declarations on the rule. He protests that those who observe the rule are considered disobedient troublemakers. He predicts an eventual split in the order.

The question is not whether John anticipated the later spirituals on

some of these issues. He did. He tried to limit the use of papal declarations, and Salimbene tells us of one occasion when he told brothers at a
general chapter that instead of passing new statutes they ought to try observing the ones they had.[59] Nevertheless, he did allow them to make new
statutes, and in his refusal to employ certain papal declarations he was part
of a group powerful enough to carry the day at general chapters throughout the 1250s.[60] Nor did this refusal end with John's demise. It survived the
advent of Bonaventure in 1257 and the general chapter of Narbonne in
1260. Much the same could be said of Franciscan wrangling over burial
rights. We know only from Angelo that John inveighed against them, but
we possess two letters in which Bonaventure complains about them, and
legislation from following years shows that a good part of the order was
also alarmed.[61]

The problem with Angelo's description lies not so much in discrete
items like John's attitude toward papal declarations and burial rights, but
in the *Gestalt*. He places John alongside Francis, the early companions,
Hugh of Digne, James of Massa, and others in a gallery of spiritual Franciscan saints. They may represent different moments—in Angelo's term,
different "tribulations"—in Franciscan history, but they all look very much
alike. This group is constantly opposed by the compromisers of Franciscan
perfection, a group which includes most of the Franciscan leadership including Bonaventure. Angelo goes out of his way to contrast John and
Bonaventure and to imply that the transition in leadership represented a
major decision on the part of the order, one in favor of laxity. He allows
us to infer that John recommended Bonaventure as his successor not because he particularly admired the latter's virtue, but because Bonaventure
was the sort of man who fit what the order seemed to want.[62] He represents Bonaventure as John's chief assailant during the hearing, and comes
close to suggesting that he was moved by something resembling demonic
possession.[63] Lest we miss the significance of this story, he presents it in
allegorical form through James of Massa's vision of Bonaventure attacking
John with iron talons.[64]

Certainly the total picture presented by Angelo is false. There is no
compelling historical basis for drawing this sort of line between John and
Bonaventure, whatever happened at the hearing. Nonetheless, we are left
with the question of whether individual details of the picture can be
trusted. Starting at the most basic level, we can say that John's dual interests, Franciscan perfection and apocalyptic speculation, were probably related. The same combination of enthusiasms is seen in Hugh of Digne. In

Hugh's case we never actually see how (or even whether) they are connected. Nor do we see their connection in John. Nevertheless, Salimbene's
reference to Hugh and John as "spiritual men" is suggestive.[65] The term is
double-edged. It has a solid Joachite foundation, since it reflects the vo-
cabulary used by Joachim to describe the third age, but it is also rooted in
Franciscan history and even in the rule. One suspects that Salimbene's use
of the label already reflects the union of these two traditions.[66] We see a
similar link in the 1255 joint letter, where the providential role of the two
orders is invoked to convince them that they ought to be nicer to one
another; and in Angelo's narrative, where John is reported to have defended his stance on Franciscan poverty by appealing to Joachim.[67] Moreover, another early fourteenth-century source, Ubertino da Casale, says he
himself heard John say at Greccio, four years before his death, "that the
sixth seal took its beginning from Francis and his state, and that the iniq-
uitous church would be consummated in the confusion of his life and rule
caused by his transgressing sons and those supporting bad superiors."[68]

These sources combine to suggest that John employed Joachite rhetoric to give the Franciscans an apocalyptic role, and that his belief in that
role encouraged him to guard the purity of his order. Thus they corroborate what historical experience and *a priori* reasoning might tell us anyway,
namely that a sense of eschatological immediacy makes men less open to
compromise. The sources also confirm Salimbene's statement that John
retained his Joachite leanings even after his fall;[69] yet they also reveal an
additional complication in determining what he said and believed as minister general. John spent another three decades of his life in Italy after 1257.
He may have retained his Joachite interests, but there is no reason to think
he applied them in precisely the same way. Ubertino's witness tells us what
John was saying in the early 1280s, not what he said in 1257. Angelo's picture depends on received tradition which may also reflect the later years.

So far we have avoided an event which might be expected to provide
us with excellent evidence of John's Joachism: his trial in 1257. Angelo
discusses it at length, but what he says makes it hard to take him very
seriously. He says that John, Gerard, and Leonard were attacked because
they defended Joachim's orthodoxy on the trinity, arguing that Innocent
III had censured not Joachim's own views on that subject, but his attack
on Peter Lombard. Their point was that Joachim was orthodox on the trinity but incorrect in his interpretation of Peter Lombard, who was orthodox as well.[70] This much all three defendants had in common. Angelo adds
that Leonard and Gerard were also prosecuted because of two writings.

The first praised Joachim and his views excessively and, I might say, untastefully. The second applied all the principal passages of sacred scripture to commend Francis's rule and describe the institution, decay, and renewal of his evangelical way of life, primarily blaming the leaders, especially the highest ones, for its decadence. It was said that Bonaventure sighed and shed tears when he read the work, for he recognized that it applied especially to him.[71]

Thus poverty was involved. It was involved in John's case, too. Angelo implies that the issue of Joachim was, if not a complete red herring, at least an excellent opportunity for lax brothers to take revenge upon John for his nagging. The defendants acquitted themselves well, as is to be expected when learned, pious men defend the truth, but it did them little good. Bonaventure himself admitted to John in private that he held the same opinion, but in public he continued his attack. Later he informed someone that, if he had not been concerned about the honor of the order, he would have had John openly punished as a heretic. "Bonaventure's wisdom and sanctity faded and his gentleness was changed by some agitating spirit into fury and anger."[72] All three were sentenced to perpetual imprisonment. John's sentence was confirmed by the cardinal protector of the order, but he was spared that fate when Cardinal Ottobuoni intervened, informing the order and cardinal protector that he shared John's beliefs and would take any punishment visited on John as an attack on himself. Thus John was allowed to pick a hermitage and chose Greccio.[73]

That is John's story as told by Angelo, and there are at least two reasons why we should be disinclined to accept it completely. First, it turns John into a protospiritual suffering unjustly at the hands of a hostile leadership and Bonaventure into (at best) a spokesman for laxity or (at worst) a pathological liar obsessed with the desire to destroy the man who gave him power. This scenario fits Angelo's theology of history better than it fits the facts. Here again, though, having decided that the tale is not totally accurate, we are left with the problem of whether any of its parts may be trustworthy. John did undergo some sort of hearing. That much is supported by other sources. The portion concerning Bonaventure's role may also contain some grain of truth. Perhaps he did accept John's apocalyptic perspective to some extent and told John so in private, but was pressured by the other ministers, the cardinal protector, or political necessity into proceeding against John anyway.[74] Perhaps Bonaventure, deeply involved in the Parisian secular-mendicant controversy, was angry at John for compromising the order and said some unfortunate things. We simply do not know.

Second, Angelo probably overstates the role of Joachim's trinitarian theology in the hearing. We know that he does so in the case of Gerard, as will become obvious in a moment. It is likely that John, like Gerard, was investigated because he applied Joachite apocalyptic in seemingly suspicious ways. That much is implied by Salimbene's comments, and Bernard of Bessa explicitly states that John found himself under investigation because he was "deceived by the Abbot Joachim's teachings concerning the final times."[75] Nevertheless, given Franciscan interest in the pseudo-Joachite commentary on Jeremiah (which expresses outrage at the attack on Joachim's trinitarian doctrine), one might hesitate before concluding that trinitarian theology played no role whatsoever.

Gerard of Borgo San Donnino

So far we have learned little about Franciscan Joachism in the mid-thirteenth century. Our sources for the next man, Gerard of Borgo San Donnino, are somewhat better, but he was probably so atypical that we cannot generalize from his case. Salimbene, who met him at Provins in 1247, says he taught grammar in Sicily before joining the order.[76] Sent by his province to study at Paris, he became a lector in theology. He was already a fervent Joachite in 1247 and incurred the wrath of French Franciscans by predicting, on the basis of the pseudo-Joachim commentary on Jeremiah, that Louis IX's crusade would turn out badly.[77] Salimbene describes him as a kind, decent, obliging man with one fatal flaw: his obstinate adherence to Joachism.

It was fatal to more people than Gerard. In 1254, in the middle of the secular-mendicant controversy at Paris, Gerard presented the secular masters with a remarkable gift. He published his *Evangelium aeternum*, or at least part of it. This work was supposed to combine Joachim's major writings—the *Liber de concordia, Expositio in apocalypsim*, and *Psalterium decem chordarum*—with glosses and an introductory essay by Gerard. Whether it ever did so is unclear. Booksellers were certainly peddling at least an abridged version consisting of the introduction and *Liber de concordia*, but that is all the Parisian masters seem to have possessed when they swung into action.[78] They quickly excerpted what they considered the more inflammatory ideas and made sure the pope was informed. He in turn established a three-man commission to look into the matter. The commission extracted its own list of offending passages, and the pope condemned Gerard's introduction in 1255. Of course it was not all that obvious to those who first read the introduction that it was Gerard's. The Parisian secular masters originally seem to have aimed their fire at the Dominicans. John of Parma, too, was accused of being the author. Thus Gerard's work caused great discomfort to the mendicants in general and to John in particular.

This fact raises the question of whether there was, in fact, a close relationship between John and Gerard. Angelo Clareno remarks that Gerard and Leonard were John's principal *socii*,[79] but it is unlikely that they were such in the technical sense of that word. Salimbene lists John's *socii* and does not include either of them, although he does include Bartholomeus Guiscolus, the other "total Joachite" whom Salimbene encountered in 1247 at Provins.[80] Moreover, Angelo offers an oddly garbled picture of Gerard. Rather than predicting Louis IX's crusading failure on the basis of scripture, Gerard becomes a visionary who announces Louis's capture at the moment it occurs. His theology is portrayed as entirely orthodox, and his trial is said to hinge on his defense of Joachite trinitarian doctrine.[81] One comes away from Angelo's description with the impression that he really knows little about the case.

Salimbene, who not only lived thrugh the period but knew Gerard personally, offers a much more credible narrative. Gerard was deprived of his position as lector and of the right to exercise pastoral duties, then was shipped back to Sicily. When Bonaventure began to clean house, he decided that Gerard should be investigated and ordered him back to Paris.[82] It was presumably en route to or from Sicily[83] that Gerard passed through Modena, where Salimbene was staying, and the two engaged in a final conversation. Salimbene asked Gerard if he wanted to dispute about Joachim, and Gerard replied, "Let's not dispute. Let's talk." They repaired to a secluded place behind the dormitory and Gerard proceeded to prove from Isaiah 18 that the Antichrist was already a living adult, King Alphonso of Castile.[84] Gerard expressed great interest in a certain Veronese living at Parma, a weaver who had the spirit of prophecy and wrote of the future. He asked Salimbene to get him a copy of these writings, since Gerard's *socii* would tolerate no detours.

Gerard left immediately thereafter and Salimbene never saw him again. Salimbene did attempt to carry out his commission, though. He visited the monastery where the visionary had been living, only to discover that the prophet had died and all the manuscripts containing his works had been erased in the process of training a new manuscript scraper. Salimbene's informant, the very scraper in question, noted that the writings had caused scandal to the monastery anyway. As a consolation prize, Salimbene was offered a complete set of Bernard of Clairvaux's works.

Salimbene says that Gerard refused to recant and was sentenced to prison. He continued to refuse, presumably until the end, since he was denied ecclesiastical burial.[85] Angelo tells us that Gerard entered prison quoting the Twenty-third Psalm, "He makes me lie down in green pastures," and that he happily spent eighteen years there, although he was deprived of books, communication with others, and the sacraments.[86] While Angelo, the fourteenth-century spiritual, presents Gerard as one link in the long chain of spiritual martyrs, Salimbene, who lived through the terrible embarrassment of the eternal gospel, feels that in the final analysis Gerard "composed a silly book and then spread his stupidity among the simpler brethren." Reflecting much the same anxiety that must have motivated Bonaventure, Salimbene welcomes Gerard's punishment as a sign that offenders are punished in the order and that the foolishness of one should not be imputed to all.[87] Despite Gerard's many virtues, in the end he acted foolishly because of his stubbornness.[88] Years later, while Salimbene was at Imola, the guardian brought him a copy of Gerard's work and asked about it. Salimbene advised him to burn it.[89]

The important question is what Gerard actually said in his introduction and glosses. Lacking his text, we must rely on the excerpts used in attacking and judging him. The Paris list included thirty-one propositions, seven from Gerard's introduction and the rest from Joachim's *Liber de concordia*. The list has come down to us in several forms, of which that offered by Matthew Paris is considered purest.[90] The seven relating to Gerard are: (1) that the eternal gospel, which is the same as Joachim's doctrine, excels the doctrine of Christ and the Old and New Testaments; (2) that the gospel of Christ is not the gospel of the kingdom or of the builders of the church; (3) that the New Testament will be superseded just as the Old Testament was; (4) that the New Testament will remain in force only until the year 1260; (5) that those living beyond that date will not be required to accept the New Testament; (6) that another gospel will succeed the gospel of Christ; and (7) that only those who travel about barefoot are fit to instruct people concerning spiritual matters.

Anyone who bothers to compare the twenty-four propositions supposedly taken from Joachim with the actual text of the *Liber de concordia* will recognize that the Paris compilers were not above distorting the original sense in order to make a case against Joachim and his mendicant supporters. Thus it is fortunate that we can compare the Paris list of Gerard's errors with the more objective treatment of the papal commission. The latter extracted a large number of statements from Gerard's introduction, of which the following are especially revealing:

1. Around the year 1200 the spirit of life departed from the two testaments so that there might be an eternal gospel.
2. Joachim's *Liber de concordia* should be considered the first book of the eternal gospel, the commentary on Revelation the second, and his *Psalterium decem chordarum* the third.
3. At the beginning of the first *status* three men appeared: Abraham, Isaac, and Jacob, the third of which had twelve sons. At the beginning of the second *status*, three more appeared: Zaracharias, John the Baptist, and Christ, the third of which had twelve disciples. Thus at the beginning of the third *status* three more appeared: the man in linen (Daniel 12:7), the angel with a sharp sickle (Revelation 14:14), and the angel bearing the sign of the living God (Revelation 7:2), who originally was one of twelve. Joachim is the man in linen, and the people of the third *status* are held to his writings. The angel bearing the sign of the living God is Francis.
4. The eternal gospel was especially committed to that order which proceeds equally from the order of laymen and clerics, a barefoot order.
5. While we do not know how long the generations of the third *status* will be, we know from scripture that they will be brief.

These basic ideas are buttressed with a wide range of threefold distinctions drawn more or less from Joachim's writings, such as that the first *status* was under the law, the second was under grace, and the third is under fuller grace; and that the first was in fear, the second was in faith, and the third is in love. The commission closes its section on Gerard's introduction by observing that the whole book is full of such "errors and fatuities," but they will quote no further, assuming that this much will offer a sufficient idea of what the book is like.[91] Indeed it does. We see from the list that Salimbene was right. Gerard was a "great Joachite," but he distorted Joachim in a dangerous way. Even while elevating Joachim's writings to the status of holy scripture, he twisted those writings in propounding "many falsities contrary to the doctrine of the Abbot Joachim, things which the abbot did not write, namely that the gospel of Christ and the doctrine of the New Testament did not lead to perfection and were to be superseded in 1260."[92]

The intended beneficiaries of this distortion were Joachim, Francis,

and the Franciscans, all of whom were written into the apocalyptic program. Nevertheless, in seeking to exalt them through what was clearly a
heretical prospectus, Gerard dealt them a serious blow. The Parisian secular scholars were primarily interested in seeing how much of the blame
would stick to the mendicants, but in the process they were willing to
implicate Joachim. Nor were they the only people willing to do so. When
Florentius, bishop of Acre and later of Arles, appeared before the Anagni
commission in July 1255 with a list of suspect passages from Joachim, he
seems to have been motivated not by any alliance with the Paris masters,
but by genuine concern about Joachism. The commission was armed with
a set of Joachim's works, yet in the end it seems they were content to
present Florentius's list with a few comments of their own.

The result of their deliberations on Joachim is enshrined in the second
and by far the larger section of the Anagni protocol, which, following
Florentius, begins by announcing that "the foundation of Joachim's teaching" is his theory of three *status*.[93] The parallel nature of these *status* encourages Joachim to predict the future and seems to suggest that, with the
coming of the third *status*, those things pertaining to the second will pass
away. The commission notes that, according to Joachim, the church will
be hard pressed by the forces of evil at the end of the second *status*, and
his reckoning places the end of that *status* in 1260.[94] Note that these are
not so much judgments as observations. Much of the section on Joachim
is, in fact, little more than an attempt to establish that he holds certain
ideas, without any serious effort to explain why these ideas are dangerous.
The commission members do consider them dangerous, however. They
are concerned about Joachim's doctrine of the three *status* because it seems
to prophesy the end of the church as they know it. It seems to identify the
Roman church with Babylon and to predict that it, too, will pass away as
the *ordo clericalis* of the second era is replaced with a new order of monks.
It also seems to predict the end of the New Testament sacraments at that
time. Moreover, it sees all this as occurring not in some distant future, but
almost immediately.[95]

This is not exactly a friendly reading of Joachim. While the commission does not simply accept Gerard's interpretation—indeed, the basic
outline of this section came from Florentius, whose concern about Joachim apparently transcended the eternal gospel scandal—Gerard's gloss is
cited on several occasions without any indication that his interpretation is
at variance with Joachim's intent.[96] One might hesitate before pronounc-
ing their view erroneous, since some modern scholars have read Joachim

in much the same way; yet their reading is certainly a distortion, since it concentrates exclusively on a few problematic elements without attempting to see them in the context of Joachim's total vision.

The commission's actual judgments vary. In the case of the imminent third order of monks, they observe that Joachim's exaltation of it is "incredible."[97] His timetable is judged to be inconsistent, since the same events are predicted for both the fortieth and forty-second generations.[98] So far we are in the realm of mere falsity, but the commission is willing to go further. Joachim's thoughts on the sacraments and certain of his comments in the prologue to the *De articulis fidei* are described as "suspect."[99] The latter are such because Joachim advises John, the individual to whom the work is addressed, to read it "in secret, in the manner of heretics, who spread their dogma in conventicles," and "he does not want his work to fall into the hands of masters, whom he impudently and proudly disparages."

In the process of berating Joachim, the commission says a bit more about Gerard. Mostly it tells us what we already knew from the first section of the protocol, but we also learn that he interpreted the abomination of desolation as a simoniacal pseudopope who would come toward the end of the sixth period.[100] We can assume that the sixth period in question is not that of Augustine's world week but the sixth period of church history. Thus Gerard recognized the other aspect of Joachim's thought, his system of double sevens, but we hear little about it because it was primarily the threefold system that bothered the commission. Gerard also seems to have predicted that a great corporeal and spiritual tribulation would take place around 1260. Then, after a short breathing space, a great, mostly spiritual tribulation would occur and the Antichrist would be revealed.[101]

The scandal of the eternal gospel had been brought to the pope's attention by secular masters hostile to the mendicants, but the Anagni commission was nothing of the sort. As Dufeil suggests,[102] it was composed of mendicants and their supporters. Thus the target was clearly defined: Gerard and, secondarily, Joachim. The pope's response was even more limited. In October 1255, Alexander IV condemned Gerard's introduction but not Joachim's writings.[103]

Florentius was apparently unsatisfied with this turn of events, and in 1263, after he became bishop of Arles, he took advantage of a provincial synod to forbid the use of Joachim's writings.[104] In the decree issued at that synod, he attacks those who accept the idea of three *status* and postulate a necessary concordance among them; maliciously venerate the

Holy Spirit, expecting the Son's role to end after some specific number of years; and, ignoring the descent of the Holy Spirit at Pentacost, assume that it will be infused in the course of the present period. These Joachites, he remarks, use their fictitious threes to predict when the time of the Holy Spirit will begin. They see the three successive *status* as involving three *ordines* as well as a threefold pattern of Old Testament, New Testament, and eternal gospel or gospel of the Holy Spirit. They blasphemously describe the spiritual gospel of the Son as literal. It follows from their position that the redemption made through Christ and the sacraments will be superseded, and these Joachites do not hesitate to suggest as much, since they say that all figures and signs will be removed and the truth revealed *absque sacramentorum velamine*.

Florentius explains that, while the pope condemned certain novelties stemming from Joachim's views, he left undiscussed and thus undamned the basic foundation of these novelties, namely "the books of concordances and other Joachite books." These works have lain hidden in the libraries of "certain religious" and thus have not been given the scholarly attention they should receive. If respectable scholars had only examined them carefully, these works would have been prevented from doing any more damage. Apparently unaware of any inconsistency, Florentius goes on to say that he considers it necessary to act because he sees how these errors are spreading, even among the learned.

Florentius's condemnation constituted a damaging precedent for future action, but for the moment it was not echoed on any higher level than his own province. Few people were willing to adopt Joachite views with Gerard's passionate enthusiasm, but many took his writings seriously. William of St. Amour suggested, probably correctly, that Joachim had powerful admirers in Rome. Even William himself was occasionally willing to cite him as an authority when it suited his advantage.[105] Nevertheless, the scandal of the eternal gospel had a direct and obvious impact on specific Franciscans like Gerard and John of Parma. It also had a diffuse effect on the entire order. Bonaventure was forced to begin his generalate in a defensive posture, working harder to show that the Franciscans were orthodox. Thus we find him distancing the order from the "great Joachites" by subjecting them to investigation, and we also find him more cooperative than his predecessor on issues like Franciscan involvement in the inquisition.[106] The order itself became more concerned with policing scholarship. Franciscans were forbidden to publish any new writing outside the order without first obtaining approval from the provincial ministers and diffinitors. Those who disobeyed would dine on bread and water for three days and lose the works in question.[107]

The scandal also marked not a turn away from Joachim, but a change in the books by him one cited. Franciscan commentators on the Apocalypse continued to evoke Joachim, but they cited his Apocalypse commentary, not the pseudo-Joachite commentary on Jeremiah. That observation may seem rather simple-minded, since these exegetes were, after all, commenting on the Apocalypse rather than Jeremiah; but the Jeremiah commentary relies so heavily on symbolism from the book of Revelation that it could almost be considered an honorary Apocalypse commentary. Franciscan commentators could have augmented their exegesis with references to the Jeremiah commentary, but they did not. Their silence is probably revealing. Nevertheless, before placing too much importance on this lack of explicit reference, we should read Olivi, compare the scenario he envisages with the one presented in the Jeremiah commentary, and ask if they do not look oddly similar.

Notes

1. For discussion of his time at Paris, see Chapter 3.

2. Marjorie Reeves, *Joachim of Fiore and the Prophetic Future* (New York, 1977), chapter 1, provides a succinct overview of Joachim's thought. Bernard McGinn, *The Calabrian Abbot* (New York, 1985) is an excellent recent study.

3. On Joachim's notion of *concordia* see McGinn, *Calabrian Abbot*, 130f.

4. On Joachim's originality see Marjorie Reeves, "The Originality and Influence of Joachim of Fiore," *Traditio* 36 (1980): 269–316.

5. On Joachim's visions see McGinn, *Calabrian Abbot*, 21f.; and Robert Lerner, "Joachim of Fiore's Breakthrough to Chiliasm," *Cristianesimo nella storia* 6 (1985): 489–512.

6. See, for example, Joachim, *Expositio in apocalypsim* (Frankfurt, 1964), 12va et passim. On this issue see Reeves, *Joachim of Fiore and the Prophetic Future*, 6f., and McGinn, *Calabrian Abbot*, 153f.

7. Salimbene, *Cronica* (Bari, 1966), 339.

8. Ibid., 339f.

9. Ibid., 339 and 343. The laymen were "notarii et iudices atque medici et alii litterati."

10. Daniel, "A Re-Examination of the Origins of Franciscan Joachitism," *Speculum* 43 (1968): 671–76.

11. Salimbene, *Cronica*, 339, says that, when he attended Hugh's Joachite colloquies in 1248, "prius eram edoctus et hanc doctrinam audieram." He then recounts his meetings with the Florensian abbot at Pisa and with Gerard of Borgo

San Donnino at Provins. One would think that, had he already heard Joachism from Hugh in Siena, he would have mentioned it at this point.

12. Angelo Clareno, *Historia septem tribulationum*, in *Archiv*, 2:282f.; *Chronica XXIV generalium*, in *AF*, 3:405.

13. Salimbene, *Cronica*, 805f.

14. Ibid., 332.

15. Salimbene, ibid., 340, says Gerard of Borgo San Donnino had it.

16. Marjorie Reeves, *Influence of Prophecy in the Later Middle Ages* (Oxford, 1969), 56f. and 519–21.

17. Ibid., 184f.

18. E.g., ibid., 45–53; Morton Bloomfield and Marjorie Reeves, "The Penetration of Joachism into Northern Europe," in *Joachim of Fiore*, ed. Delno West (New York, 1975), 1:107–28.

19. Salimbene, *Cronica*, 367.

20. See his disillusionment at Frederick's death as described in *Cronica*, 441, and the question about Antichrist he addressed to Gerard upon meeting him in 1256, an incident recounted in ibid., 661. It goes without saying that the actual course of Hugh's debate with the Dominican cannot be taken as a verbatim transcript.

21. See Reeves, *Influence of Prophecy*, 518f.

22. See Reeves, "The Abbot Joachim's Disciples and the Cistercian Order," *Sophia* 19 (1951): 355–71; and idem, *Influence of Prophecy*, 145–60. Her thesis is disputed by Bernhard Töpfer, *Das kommende Reich des Friedens* (Berlin, 1964), 108–15.

23. Moynihan, "Development of the 'Pseudo-Joachim' Commentary 'super Hieremiam,'" *Mélanges de l'école française de Rome. Moyen Âge, Temps Modernes* 98 (1986): 109–42; Stephen Wessley, *Joachim of Fiore and Monastic Reform* (New York, 1990), 116–24.

24. I will cite the Venice, 1525 edition. For Salimbene's text see Wessley, *Joachim*, 118.

25. Salimbene, *Cronica*, 441: "Audiens hec omnia frater Bartholomeus dixit michi, 'Et tu similiter Ioachita fuisti.' Cui dixi, 'Verum dicitis. Sed postquam mortuus est Fridericus, qui imperator iam fuit, et annus millesimus ducentesimus sexagesimus est elapsus, dimisi totaliter istam doctrinam et dispono non credere nisi que videro.'"

26. *Super Jeremiam*, 30vb, 43va, 44ra. In keeping with the Italian focus of the commentary, the main target is Bologna rather than Paris.

27. E.g., ibid., 51vb–52ra: "Nunc omnes corrupti sunt et abhominabiles, et non est qui faciat bonum, non est usque ad unum scilicet rarum, immo omnes infecti luxuria, omnes maledicti insana doctrina, omnes attracti irregulari disciplina."

28. Ibid., 56va–vb: "*Rex* Summus pontifex, *domina* Romana ecclesia quae est in cardinalibus, *principes Iuda* episcopi italici, *eunuchi* abbates religiosi, *faber* magistri eloquii mistici, *inclusi* sophisitici vel potius contemplativi omnis ordinis et officii capita, *captivantur* quia non crediderunt in deo nec in viis eius voluerunt ambulare. Et iccirco velut ficus malas abiiciet eos dominus in faces imperii comedentis."

29. Ibid., 44va: "Ego non dubito quod non affligantur viri evangelici a praelatis."

30. But see ibid., 2rb, where the dragon and two beasts of Rev. 12–13 are identified with empire, infidels, and Patarenes respectively.

31. E.g., ibid., 27ra: "Nota quod *mulier* ecclesia Romana est quae ob angustiam temporalem ex republica et heretica pressura et etiam gentium infidelium inundatione *parturiet*, temporalia amittendo. *Pariet* geminos ordines in utero fidei colluctantes."

32. Ibid., 45va. See also 46vb.

33. E.g., ibid., 39vb: "Revera federabitur Romanum imperium cum Saracenis et gentibus infidelibus designatis in portis, additis sibi pseudo prophetis et alii pseudo populis"; or ibid., 47va (re. Frederick II): "Aggregabit sibi bestialem catervam hereticorum et infidelium gentium."

34. See especially ibid., 53rb: "Anima Christi descendet ad inferos, populum utique de terrae finibus erumpentem fidem domino qua intus vivit, ut ex eis sublatis credentibus ascendat ad superos."

35. Ibid., 57vb. See also 51rb, which predicts a return to *studiis spiritualibus*.

36. Joachim, *Expositio in apocalypsim*, 167vb, where he speaks of the pact between the eleventh and last Saracen king and the false prophets, although the passage is ambiguous.

37. E.g., ibid., 198vb, where (expositing Rev. 17) he identifies the kings of the earth who will drink wrath as prelates and the merchants as false priests and hypocrites.

38. Salimbene, *Cronica*, 341.

39. He was not criticized for that reason alone, however. Salimbene, ibid., 367, says he had critics because of his Joachism and because some people blamed him for the creation of the order of Boscarioli, which he seems to have inspired inadvertently with an offhand remark. Presumably his reforming zeal and rough tongue earned him a few enemies, too.

40. Salimbene, *Cronica*, 334–36.

41. See Jacques Paul, "Hughes de Digne," in *Franciscains d'Oc* (Toulouse, 1975), 86f.

42. Paul, "Hughes de Digne," 87.

43. Adam Marsh, *Epistolae*, in *Rerum Britannicarum Medii Aevi scriptores* (in Rolls Series, London, 1858–82), no. 4, vol. 1, 114.

44. *Epistolae*, 146f.

45. Salimbene, *Cronica*, 334, 428. In the latter passage, we find Salimbene copying, for John, Hugh's manuscript of Joachim's commentary on the gospels.

46. Ibid., 439f.

47. Compare the various reports in Pelegrinus de Bononia, *Chronica abbreviatum*, in *Tractatus Fr. Thomae vulgo dicti de Eccleston de adventu fratrum minorum in Angliam* (Paris, 1909), 141–45; Thomas of Eccleston, *Liber de adventu minorum in Angliam*, in *Rerum Britannicarum Medii Aevi scriptores* (Rolls Series), no. 4, vol. 1, 50; Bernardus a Bessa, *Liber de laudibus*, in *AF*, 2:698; *Chronica XXIV generalium*, 287; Angelo Clareno, *Historia septem tribulationum*, 276–86; Luke

Wadding, *Annales minorum* (Rome, 1732), 4:2–6 and 6:12. Thomas of Eccleston simply says that John could no longer bear the heavy administrative burden and asked to be relieved.

48. *Historia septem tribulationum*, 282.

49. Published in Wadding, *Annales*, 3:380–83. See the analysis in Reeves, *Influence of Prophecy*, 146f., who notes that the passage also echoes Alexander of Bremen.

50. See Reeves, *Influence of Prophecy*, 147 and 161–74.

51. *Historia septem tribulationum*, 267–87. John's story begins during the third tribulation and extends throughout the fourth.

52. See the sources in note 47, above.

53. These included the *Croniques* of St. Denis, Bernard Gui, Nicholas Eymerich, and perhaps Jean de Meung. See Reeves, *Influence of Prophecy*, 63f. and 240. Some others attributed it to the Dominicans.

54. *Historia septem tribulationum*, 271–77, 283.

55. Ibid., 277–83.

56. Ibid., 282f. A parallel prediction attributed by Angelo to Hugh of Digne announced that the order would be divided, that the Dominicans would seek possessions, and that a new "order of fettered men" (*ordo catenatorum*) would appear incomparably more perfect than the Franciscans or Dominicans. Such predictions might seem to suggest a final order other than the Franciscans, but both the "holy poor men" and the "fettered men" are probably meant by Angelo to represent his own colleagues.

57. Salimbene, *Cronica*, 332 and 449f.

58. Ibid., 439f. characteristically sees that influence as directed toward the papal curia, not the order itself, but grants that John's Joachism brought complaints from some of the ministers.

59. Ibid., 438.

60. Thomas of Eccleston, *De adventu*, 32; "Diffinitiones capituli generalis Narbonnensis," *AFH* 3 (1910): 503; Rosalind Brooke, *Early Franciscan Government* (Cambridge, 1959), 264f.

61. For Bonaventure's letters see *Opera* (Quaracchi, 1882–1902), 8:468–71. For legislation see Michael Bihl, "Statuta generalia ordinis edita in capitulis generalibus celebratis Narbonae an. 1260, Assisii an. 1279 atque Parisiis an. 1292," *AFH* 34 (1941): 13–94, 284–358; Bonaventure, *Opera*, 8:467; Giuseppe Abate, "Memoriali, statuti ed atti di capitoli generali dei fratri minori," *Miscellanea franciscana* 33 (1933): 22; A. G. Little, "Statuta provincialia provinciarum Aquitaniae et Franciae (saec. XIII-XIV)," *AFH* 7 (1914): 472.

62. Angelo Clareno, *Historia septem tribulationum*, 270f.

63. Ibid., 285: "Tunc enim sapiencia et sanctitas fratris Bonaventurae eclipsata paluit et obscurata est, et eius manswetudo ab agitante spiritu in furorem et iram conversa defecit."

64. Ibid., 280f.

65. Salimbene, *Cronica*, 334.

66. Jacques Paul, "Le Joachimisme et les Joachimites au milieu du XIIIe siècle d'apres le temoignage de Fra Salimbene," in *1274: Année charniere* (Paris, 1977), 801,

observes that Salimbene uses the term *spiritualis* rarely, but when he does so it usually refers to one or more of the Joachites. Nevertheless, the term *viri spirituales* could be used without any hint of Joachite or zealot overtones. See the anonymous Apocalypse commentary beginning *Vox domini praeparantis cervos*, published in Aquinas, *Opera* (Parma, 1860–62), 23:573, where it means nothing more than "pious men."

67. Angelo Clareno, *Historia septem tribulationum*, 283. John's harangues as reported in ibid., 274–76, also suggest his willingness to defend the *Testament* by comparing Francis to Moses and Christ.

68. Ubertino da Casale, *Arbor vitae* (Torino, 1961), 422.

69. Salimbene, *Cronica*, 442.

70. Angelo Clareno, *Historia septem tribulationum*, 276.

71. Ibid., 277.

72. Ibid., 286.

73. Ibid., 276f., 285f.

74. Wadding, *Annales*, 4:4f., depends heavily on Angelo, yet portrays Bonaventure as moving against John unwillingly, because of heavy pressure from the latter's enemies in the order.

75. *Liber de laudibus*, 698. Thus also *Chronica XXIV generalium*, 350.

76. Salimbene, *Cronica*, 340 and 660.

77. Ibid., 340.

78. See Heinrich Denifle, "Das Evangelium aeternum und die Commission zu Anagni," in *Archiv*, 1:68f.; M.-M. Dufeil, *Guillaume de Saint-Amour et la polemique universitaire parisienne* (Paris, 1972), 124. Nevertheless, Bernhard Töpfer, "Eine Handschrift des Evangelium aeternum des Gerardino von Borgo San Donnino," *Zeitschrift für Geschictswissenschaft* 7 (1960): 156–60, describes a Dresden manuscript which, he claims, stems from Gerard's edition of the *Evangelium aeternum*, and if he is correct Gerard did eventually complete his project.

79. *Historia septem tribulationum*, 283.

80. *Cronica*, 804.

81. *Historia septem tribulationum*, 268f., 284.

82. *Cronica*, 341, 660.

83. Paul, "Joachimisme et les Joachimites," 806, places it in 1258 and presents Gerard as headed toward Sicily.

84. *Cronica*, 661f.

85. Ibid., 341.

86. *Historia septem tribulationum*, 284. Angelo, too, says he was denied ecclesiastical burial. Wadding, *Annales*, 4:4f., seems to be getting his material on Gerard from Angelo, yet announces that Bonaventure, at the end of his stint as minister general, freed Gerard after eighteen years in prison. He then cites not only Angelo but Bernardus a Bessa and Pelegrino da Bologna as authorities.

87. *Cronica*, 341, 660.

88. Ibid., 668.

89. Ibid., 663.

90. Thus Denifle, "Das Evangelium aeternum und die Commission zu Anagni," *Archiv* 1:71–74.

91. Ibid., 99–102.

92. Salimbene, *Cronica*, 660.

93. Denifle, "Evangelium aeternum," 102.

94. Ibid., 105.

95. Ibid., 106, 112, 115, 118–20, 126, 133–36.

96. Ibid., 109, 115, 123, 126f., 131, 133.

97. Ibid., 112, 115.

98. Ibid., 112.

99. Ibid., 133, 138.

100. Ibid., 109.

101. Ibid., 123. This is not inconsistent with what he is reported to have contended during his final interview with Salimbene.

102. *Guillaume de Saint-Amour*, 166.

103. *Chartularium universitatis parisiensis* (Paris, 1889), 257f.

104. J. D. Mansi, *Sacrorum conciliorum nova et amplissima collectio* (Venice, n.d.), 23:1002–4, with the correction by Denifle, "Evangelium Aeternum," 90.

105. See Reeves, *Influence of Prophecy*, 62f. for discussion and citations.

106. See Mariano d'Alatri, "San Bonaventura, l'eresia e l'inquisizione," *Miscellanea francescana* 75 (1975): 305–22.

107. Salimbene, *Cronica*, 670.

2. Respectable Apocalyptic

The scandal of the eternal gospel cast suspicion on Joachism. In its wake, one would expect Franciscans to treat apocalyptic thought in general and Joachim in particular with some caution. Thus it is important to emphasize that, however agonizing the reappraisal which occurred in the 1260s, neither apocalyptic nor Joachim were completely abandoned. Nor was an apocalyptic interpretation of the Franciscan order. Our immediate task is to clarify this point by examining Saint Bonaventure, the most eminent intellectual in the Franciscan order up to his death in 1274, as well as a series of Franciscan Apocalypse commentaries written in the thirteenth century.

Bonaventure's *Legenda Maior*

Given the role played by Bonaventure during the scandal of the eternal gospel, one might have expected him to distance himself as much as possible from apocalyptic speculation. He did nothing of the sort. Bernard McGinn and Joseph Ratzinger have explored his application of it to his own order in the *Collationes in hexaemeron*, while Stephanus Bihel and Stanislao da Campagnola have devoted substantial space to Bonaventure in their studies of a single apocalyptic theme, Francis as angel of the sixth seal.[1] Some scholars have attributed Bonaventure's interest more to political acumen than to intellectual commitment. They have argued that Bonaventure's espousal of notions like Francis as angel of the sixth seal must be seen as an attempt to moderate—one might say sanitize—the more radical claims of the spiritual Franciscan faction within the order. This explanation seems questionable for at least two reasons. First, it rests upon a rather anachronistic projection into the 1260s and early 1270s of a polarization which characterized the order only later.[2] Second, it ignores the genuine enthusiasm with which Bonaventure pursued such themes. To accord them merely tactical significance is to miss an important element in his piety.

In order to appreciate Bonaventure's contribution, we need advance the story only slightly beyond the point where we left it in the last chapter. In 1260, the Franciscan order gathered at Narbonne for a general chapter meeting. There it entrusted Bonaventure, its minister general, with the task of writing a new life of Saint Francis. Bonaventure's *Legenda maior* received official approval three years later, and in 1266 it was declared the sole acceptable life of the founder. All other biographies were to be burned.

Almost at the beginning of the *Legenda maior*, Bonaventure made a remarkable statement.

> Therefore there is every reason to believe that it is he who is designated under the image of an angel rising from the east with the seal of the living God. . . . "When the sixth seal was broken," John says in the Apocalypse, "I saw a second Angel rising from the east with the seal of the living God."[3]

In other words, Bonaventure identified Francis with the angel of Revelation 7:2, whom John saw "ascending from the east with the seal of the living God." Bonaventure repeated this identification in the final chapter of the *Legenda maior*. He would return to it in the *Legenda minor*, in sermons, and finally in the *Collationes in hexaemeron*,[4] but it was the *Legenda maior* that was bound to have the greatest impact in the future.

Bonaventure's Forerunners

It is one thing to recognize that Bonaventure accepted this identification and quite another to say where he got it or what he meant by it. We have seen that, according to the Protocol of Anagni, Gerard of Borgo San Donnino accepted it, while Ubertino da Casale tells us that John of Parma did too. Thus the identification seems to have been established among those enmeshed in the scandal of the eternal gospel, but was it voiced only by them before Bonaventure gave it respectability? The few Apocalypse commentaries at our disposal hint that most Franciscan exegetes did not see Francis as the angel of Revelation 7:2.

This conclusion is based on slender evidence: two commentaries written before or just after the *Legenda maior*. One of these can be attributed with some assurance to Guilelmus de Militona, whom I will call (with less assurance) William of Middleton.[5] The other, a commentary beginning *Vox domini praeparantis cervos*, is published in two editions of the Thomas Aquinas *Opera*. Its date and provenance have not been established, but one bit of evidence suggests a Franciscan author writing before 1266. The commentary refers to the life of a saint only three times. In one case the saint in question is Catherine of Alexandria, and in the other two it is Francis. In both references to Francis's life, the wording used is closer to that found in Thomas of Celano's first life of Saint Francis than to that found in Bonaventure's *Legenda maior*; yet in one of these two references the quotation from Francis, though closer to Celano's wording, is placed in the biographical context found in Bonaventure's life, not Celano's.[6] Thus it is tempting to place this commentary in a transitional period: after 1263, when Bonaventure's life was approved by the order, but before (or not long after) 1266, when it became the only allowable biography.

Both of these commentaries follow a basic approach which we will study in some detail when we examine Apocalypse commentaries after Bonaventure. It is an approach shared with all extant Dominican commentaries of the thirteenth century[7] and, as we will see, with all surviving Franciscan commentaries datable to the final third of the thirteenth century. It is an essentially conservative approach inasmuch as it accepts and develops an exegetical tradition going back to Richard of St. Victor, the *Glossa*, Haymo, and even Bede.[8] We need not worry much about Richard, Bede, et al., but in order to broaden our sample a bit we will include three Dominican commentaries of this era. One was published in 1890 under the name of Albert the Great, but is now attributed to Peter of Tarantaise;[9] while another, beginning *Aser pinguis*, is probably by Hugh of St. Cher, although Robert Lerner and others argue convincingly that it is the work not of Hugh alone, but of a team working under him.[10] The third commentary, beginning *Vidit Iacob in somniis*, has also been attributed to Hugh (more precisely, to his team) by Lerner.[11] These five commentaries, three Dominican and two Franciscan, offer a sample running from the 1230s into the 1260s.

According to the traditional approach followed by these commentators, the Apocalypse is divided into seven visions, some of them recapitulative in the sense that they cover church history as á whole. Thus the first vision (the letters to seven churches), the second (the seven seals), and the third (the seven trumpets) can each be seen as an outline of history from Christ to the eschaton. All commentators do not avail themselves equally of this opportunity. Only Peter of Tarantaise and *Aser pinguis* attempt to see the first vision in this way. Our five Franciscan and Dominican commentators are unanimous in granting such an interpretation to the second and third visions, however.

All but one distinguish between the first four visions, which deal with all of ecclesiastical history (or, as they often say, the *status generalis* of the church), and the last three, which deal only with the final times (the *status finalis*), comprising the time of Antichrist, the period after his death, final judgment, and eternal rewards or punishments. Having made this distinction, several commentators are then lured away from it by the fifth vision (the seven angels with vials), which they treat as another tour through church history.[12] *Aser pinguis* actually makes room for this interpretation by offering a five/two rather than a four/three division.[13]

Church history itself is seen by these commentaries as divided into seven periods (*status*): an initial period when the primitive church was attacked by the Jews; a second when it was persecuted by the Roman empire; a third when it was assaulted by the great heresies; and a fourth when it was subverted from within by hypocrites. The fifth period is harder to characterize, partly because the tradition itself offered different possibilities; but the fifth trumpet is unanimously identified as that of the precursors of Antichrist, sent to pave the way for him.[14] Many commentators also accept Richard of St. Victor's suggestion that in the fifth period the devil, having unsuccessfully used his temptations one at a time in the first four periods, now deploys them all at once.[15]

The sixth period is always seen as that of Antichrist, while the seventh is portrayed as an interval after the death of Antichrist in which there will be peace, holy men will be allowed to preach freely, humankind will receive a final chance to repent, and the Jews will be converted. This period is based not on the millenium of Revelation 20 but on Jerome's interpretation of Daniel 12, which allows a period of forty-five days.[16] Nevertheless, our commentators often follow the developing tradition in seeing that number as a minimum figure to which God can add more time if he wishes. As for the millenium of Revelation 20, these commentators follow Augustine in seeing it as the entire time from Christ to the coming of Antichrist, and thus they do not identify it with the seventh period at all.[17]

Closer analysis would reveal significant variations; yet the general similarites are so striking that we can speak with some confidence of a mendicant approach to the Apocalypse current at Paris during the early thirteenth century. Our consideration of Franciscan exegetes during the final third of the century will confirm that it was current then as well, and that it was accepted in more places than Paris. Nevertheless, one early thirteenth-century Franciscan pursued a notably different course. Alexander Minorita (sometimes identified as Alexander of Bremen) was not a Paris-trained exegete. In fact, he describes himself as having received his approach to the Apocalypse directly from God while taking communion.[18] The exegetical strategy so dramatically presented to Alexander sees the Apocalypse as a continuous reading of church history proceeding from the primitive church in chapter one to the eschaton in chapter twenty-two, a single voyage through church history rather than a series of voyages. The resultant commentary can thus afford to be substantially more detailed and specific. It is, in fact, packed with names and dates taken from a variety of sources, including patristic writings, papal letters, Joachim's Apocalypse commentary, the pseudo-Joachim commentary on Jeremiah, and contemporary German chronicles.

Alexander proceeds slowly and deliberately. By Revelation 7:2 he is only as far as Constantine, and by 20:2 he has just discussed the emperor Henry V. Thus 20:3 seems an awkward place to encounter the thousand-year binding of Satan. Alexander makes at least rough sense of it by suggesting, albeit obliquely, that the number cannot be taken literally, and by seeming to grant some validity to the Augustinian notion that it began with Christ; yet he also makes a slightly different sense of it by projecting a thousand-year reign of Christ after Pope Sylvester. He takes this latter notion seriously enough to note that there are at least seventy years of the reign left at present.[19] After that, we can expect Antichrist at any moment.

Divergent as Alexander's reading may be from the standard Parisian approach, they have one thing in common. Neither of them has a place for Francis as angel of the sixth seal. Alexander obviously cannot read Francis into Revelation 7:2 because his remorselessly historical exposition is only up to the fourth century by that point. The Franciscan Parisian exegetes—the Dominicans are irrelevant to this problem—cannot do so because they identify the opening of the sixth seal with the persecution of Antichrist and place that event in the future. These exegetes could theoretically see the passage as referring in a spiritual sense—more specifically, in the moral sense—to Francis, just as one might identify the angel with any good man who comforts and protects the church in time of affliction, but they fail to do so. They never even mention him in this context.

Do they mention him in any context? They do, and here the most significant document is *Vox domini praeparantis cervos*. The two references to Francis's life in that commentary both occur in chapter seven. It is hard to push this fact too far, since at that moment the commentator is dealing not with the angel of 7:2 but with the elect in 7:5–9. He interprets the twelve tribes in 7:4–8 as levels of justice in the elect and as a ladder up which all the elect should climb to attain beatitude. Benjamin, the highest rung of the ladder, is identified with solicitude in gaining merit. At this point, the commentator makes his first reference to Francis, noting that when near death he said, "let us begin to serve God, brothers, for up to now we have made little or no progress."[20] Shortly thereafter he turns to those standing before the throne in 7:9. Here his point is that "spiritual men (*viri spirituales*) continually strive to contemplate [God] through the eyes of love and meditation," a claim he substantiates by citing Celano's observation that "whether walking, sitting, eating or drinking, Francis was engaged in prayer."[21] In each case, the reference to Francis can be considered a moral interpretation. The major significance of these passages lies not only in the fact that they both occur in chapter seven, as if treatment of 7:2 had somehow reminded the author of Francis, but also in the parallel between what the author does in the first passage and what Bonaventure will do in the *Collationes in hexaemeron*.

Alexander Minorita, too, mentions Francis in another context, and here we find what is lacking in the Parisian exegetes: a literal, historical interpretation of a passage as referring to the Poverello and his order. Since Alexander is still in the twelfth century at 20:2 and allows the millennium to expire at 20:7, it is inevitable that his own period should fall between these two verses. Sure enough, Francis, Dominic, and their orders arrive at 20:6. Alexander notes that at the very moment when dark shadows were falling over the world, God chased them away with two great lights, Dominic and Francis. He explicitly cites the prediction of two new orders in the pseudo-Joachim *Super Hieremiam*.[22]

Expiration of the millennium clears the way for Gog, Magog, and Antichrist,[23] but by 20:10 they have been consigned to the lake of fire, followed in 20:15 by those not included in the book of life. Alexander is now ready for the new heaven and earth. He sees the descent of the heavenly Jerusalem at the opening of chapter twenty-one as a description of souls returning from heaven to reanimate their bodies for final judgment.[24] Thus the end of chapter twenty seems to close the books on a great deal more than the mendicants. It seems to mark the end of history itself. One would thus expect Alexander to interpret the twenty-first and twenty-second chapters as a sustained description of judgment and heavenly bliss. That expectation remains strikingly unfulfilled. When he arrives at Revelation 21:9 and the angel who leads the tour of the holy city, he notes that, while this section speaks of the city after final judgment, Jerusalem must be built by the elect with good works before the last day. Then he leaps back to his own time and interprets the new Jerusalem as a prediction of the Franciscan and Dominican orders.[25]

His commentary on the last two chapters deals almost exclusively with the mendicants. The heavenly city has descended and will be present among us throughout the temptation of Antichrist, until judgment day. Does Alexander anticipate an interval between Antichrist and judgment day when the elect will enjoy peace, an equivalent of the seventh period offered by other exegetes? The question simply does not interest him. What does matter is that the heavenly Jerusalem, the community of the elect, is being built in his own time under the guidance of the mendicants, who will provide a model of constancy in the coming battle with Antichrist.[26] Thus Alexander provides precisely what is lacking in the Parisian exegetes: a sustained effort to read the mendicants into the Apocalypse as part of its literal interpretation. Nevertheless, his way of doing so lay well outside the accepted boundaries of current exegesis and made no significant mark on thirteenth-century commentaries, although, as we will see, his exegetical strategy enjoyed a remarkable renaissance in the fourteenth century.[27]

This excursus into early thirteenth-century exegesis may seem out of place in its present position, thrust rudely between Bonaventure's *Legenda maior* and his *Collationes in hexaemeron*. It fulfills its role, however. Some knowledge of Franciscan exegesis is helpful in answering not only the question of whether Bonaventure was atypical in identifying Francis with the angel of 7:2, but also the other question posed earlier, what he meant by this identification, for the latter problem cannot be solved without asking whether Bonaventure's assertion is based upon a definable approach to biblical interpretation. His *Legenda maior* raises that question, and the *Collationes*, viewed in the light of current exegesis, help to answer it.

Bonaventure's *Collationes in hexaemeron*

The *Collationes in hexaemeron* were written less than a year before Bonaventure's death. They are an index of where his thought was tending during his final months, and we can gather from them that the tendency was in a decidedly apocalyptic direction. This is not entirely surprising to anyone who examines his work during the preceding decade. We have seen that even the *Legenda maior* has its apocalyptic dimension. In the *Collationes de septem donis de spiritus sancti*, delivered at Paris in 1268 and apparently heard there by Olivi, that dimension is striking. In fact, the 1268 *collationes* anticipate the 1273 ones in their apocalyptic interpretation of heterodox Aristotelianism, a phenomenon which increasingly concerned Bonaventure in his final years.[28]

It is reassuring to be able to see the *Collationes in hexaemeron* as part of a continuing tendency, because it is a work that presents serious problems to the textual scholar. It has survived in *reportationes* by listeners, not in a definitive form prepared by Bonaventure himself. Comparison of the Siena manuscript published by Ferdinand Delorme with the text found in the Bonaventure *Opera* shows that all listeners did not hear the same thing.[29] Nor were these *collationes* completed even in oral form. Bonaventure was called away on other matters, then died before he could produce a complete, polished work, if indeed he intended to do so.

Although not an Apocalypse commentary, the *Collationes in hexaemeron* are very much about the Apocalypse. References to that book punctuate the work and help Bonaventure to create a theology of history that is both reminiscent of and different from the one offered by preceding Franciscan exegetes. It reflects standard Parisian exegesis in dividing history into seven periods, but Bonaventure's periods differ significantly from those offered by the commentators.[30] His first three are much the same, featuring the primitive church, the martyrs, and the doctrinal disputes of the fourth and fifth centuries. His fourth period differs somewhat, since he identifies it with the production of laws, including the Benedictine rule, the code of Justinian, and canon law; yet even here the traditional element of combatting laxity is evident. His fifth period, which includes the confrontation between eastern and western churches as well as the rise of Islam, never quite coalesces into a coherent pattern and seems hard to reconcile with the traditional identification of that period with the precursors of Antichrist, although there are obvious parallels.

It is with the sixth period, however, that we sense something very different occurring. Bonaventure describes it primarily as a time of clear doctrine. This period is marked by the advancement of learning and peace within the church, but it is also marred by persecution and temptation. These negative elements belong not only to the past—he especially mentions the emperors Henry IV and Frederick I[31]—but to the future as well, leading to the persecution of Antichrist. At least one highly reputed churchman will be enmeshed in error and those who stand firm will do so at the cost of their reputations. Violence, convincing arguments, and even miracles will be deployed against the godly, and the temptation will be so keen as to lead even the elect astray if such were possible. Rational investigation will avail little, and the elect will have to rely on authority alone.

Bonaventure sets no date for these events, but seems to expect them soon. He declines to speculate on how long the sixth period will last, but—and here we have the other major difference between him and the Parisian exegetes—he feels it has already been underway for five centuries, having begun with Charlemagne.[32] The sixth period will be followed by a seventh of peace and enlightenment in which the church militant "will be conformed with the triumphant as far as is possible on the pilgrim way." This final age will mirror the original state of the church to some extent. "But how long it will last," Bonaventure says, "God only knows."[33]

We must return to the first of the two central differences between Bonaventure and the Parisian exegetes. Whereas the exegetes identify the sixth period with one phenomenon, the temptation of Antichrist, Bonaventure identifies it with two, one positive and one negative. The negative event of Antichrist is balanced by gains in doctrine, prophecy, and the expansion of Christianity.[34] The twofold nature of the period corresponds with the passion of Christ, in which there was first light, then darkness, then light again. This comparison is interesting in a number of ways. Obviously the dark should correspond to Antichrist, but what about the first and second light? There is some reason to believe that the first is a reference to the time of Charlemagne, for the period began in his time. Bonaventure alludes to his conquests and his encouragement of learning. He adds somewhat obscurely that "there must necessarily arise one prince, a zealot for the church, who either will be or already has been," but immediately adds, "would that he had not already been," and again mentions Charlemagne's accomplishment. He notes that Charlemagne exalted the church while his successors attacked it.[35]

Bonaventure's reference to the second light is more problematic, perhaps even a bit misleading. He observes that some of the evil princes who succeeded Charlemagne "wished to destroy the church, but the angel ascending from the place of the sun cried to the four angels, 'Do not harm the earth and sea until we seal the servants of our God on their foreheads.'" We are back to the angel of Revelation 7:2. The light/dark/ light progression may be misleading because the Antichrist is still to come—good and evil seem combined in a very complex way in Bonaven-

ture's view of the sixth period—but one must take the reference to Revelation 7 : 2 very seriously. Are we, then, back to the *Legenda maior*? Is the
angel Francis? In order to answer that question we must look very closely
at a series of passages in the *Collationes in hexaemeron*. In one of these,
Bonaventure states that

> the contemplative soul is sealed by God. Hence, in reference to the sixth
> angel, it is said that there appeared an angel having the seal of the living God.
> This was in the sealing of Jerusalem standing in heaven. To this angel there
> appeared an expressive seal regarding the mode of life consonant with this
> seal. . . . From the tribe of Judah, twelve thousand sealed, etc.[36]

The angel with the seal of the living God is obviously that of Revelation 7 : 2, but that passage contains no reference to Jerusalem standing in
heaven. Bonaventure is combining 7 : 2 with Revelation 21. Elsewhere the
combinations are even more impressive. For example, take the following
passage, in which Bonaventure begins with Revelation 21 : 10, "He took
me up in the spirit to a great, high mountain and showed me the holy city,
Jerusalem." Bonaventure then says,

> How can this be? See what is said at the end of the Apocalypse. Around the
> middle, however, it is said, "I saw the lamb standing on Mount Sion, and
> with him 144,000 having his name and the name of his father written on
> their foreheads." But in the opening of the sixth seal it is said in the Apoca-
> lypse, "I saw another angel ascending from the rising of the sun, having the
> seal of the living God, and he cried to the four angels authorized to harm
> the earth and sea, saying, 'Do not harm the earth, sea or trees until we seal
> the servants of our God on their foreheads.' " This passage establishes, first,
> that it was those who were upon Mount Sion who were sealed and, later,
> that one of the angels pouring out the vials—it must be the sixth—showed
> him the city the size of which was one hundred forty-four cubits. Around the
> beginning of the Apocalypse it is said to the sixth angel, that of Philadelphia,
> "I shall make him who overcomes a pillar in the temple of my God and write
> on him my name and the name of the city, the new Jerusalem," which was
> mentioned only at the end. There are six periods with rest. And just as Christ
> came in the sixth period, thus it is necessary that the contemplative church be
> born at the end.[37]

Here again we find reference to the angel of Revelation 7 : 2, but the
seal and the 144,000 are now connected not only with Revelation 7 but
also with Revelation 14, which finds the 144,000 standing on Mount Sion
with the names of lamb and father written on their foreheads. Revelation
14 actually refers to six angels, but Bonaventure ignores them, leaping

instead to Revelation 16 and 21:9. In the latter, the angel who shows John the heavenly city is indeed one of the seven vial-pouring angels of Revelation 16, but is not more specifically identified in the Bible. Bonaventure simply assumes that he must be the sixth.

Having merged Revelation 7, 14, 16, and 21, Bonaventure turns to still another sixth angel, the angel of Philadelphia found in Revelation 3:7. Here again there is a reference to the new Jerusalem seen at the end of time. Here again, too, there seems to be a reference to the sixth period of church history, but now with an implied correlation between Christ coming in the sixth period of world history (the long-accepted Augustinian pattern) and the emergence of the contemplative church "at the end." At any rate, Bonaventure has tied five chapters of the Apocalypse together. He is is not simply interested in "the angel of the sixth seal" of 7:2 but in "the sixth angel" as seen in 3:7, 7:2, and (rather hypothetically) in 21:9.

The angel of Philadelphia is a favorite subject in the *Collationes in hexaemeron*. In discussing the sixth period of church history, Bonaventure recalls the persecutions under Frederick I and Henry IV and notes that there were two popes in the time of each.

> And it is certain that one of them wanted to exterminate the church, but the angel ascending from the rising of the sun cried to the four angels, "Do not harm the earth and sea until we seal the servants of our God on their foreheads." Thus the church's tribulation continues up to this time. And it was said to the angel of Philadelphia, who is the sixth one, "Thus says the holy and true one who has the key of David, he who opens and no one shuts, he who shuts and no one opens. I know your works. Behold, I have set an open door before you." And he said that now understanding of scripture or revelation or the key of David would be given to a person or to a multitude, and I believe rather to a multitude.[38]

Here again we have the angel of 7:2, now clearly associated with the persecutions and spiritual achievements of the sixth period. The angel of 3:7 turns up, too, this time in connection with the key of David and the open door, images which in turn refer to the understanding of scripture given in the sixth period. The angels of 7:2 and 3:7 are combined again in a passage that connects them with yet another angel whom we have not as yet encountered. Bonaventure identifies the sealing of the twelve tribes in 7:5–9 with twelve mysteries which are to be unlocked. He then observes,

> Note that the twelve sealings, the measuring of the city, the showing of the city and the opening of the book are under the sixth seal and under the sixth

angel. And the key of David is spoken about to the sixth angel, the one of Philadelphia (which is interpreted "preserving the inheritance"), of whom it is said, "I will write upon him who overcomes my name and that of the city, the new Jerusalem." . . . This means, I will give knowledge of scripture to this sixth angel, but it will be bitter to his stomach, and in his mouth it will be sweet as honey. And this order is understood through John, to whom it was said, "Thus I wish him to remain, until I come."[39]

Here the "sixth angel" is partly that of Revelation 3:7–13, the angel of Philadelphia. He is connected, as before, with the key of David (an improved knowledge of scripture) and with the new Jerusalem (a complex symbol tying together the ordered human mind, the summit of contemplative experience, and the community of the final age). By quoting 3:12 at length, Bonaventure relates all these things to the sealing of the elect. The sixth angel in this passage is also that of Revelation 7:2, as Bonaventure's reference to the opening of the sixth seal suggests; yet the "sixth angel" mentioned immediately thereafter is not that of 7:2 or 3:7. He is at least partly that of 21:9, who guides John on his tour of the new Jerusalem and whom, as we have seen, Bonaventure chooses to see as identical with the sixth angel of 16:12.

Beyond that point, however, we move into new territory. The "sixth angel" described here is also that of Revelation 10, who comes from heaven bearing an open book which John proceeds to eat. Thus John becomes a symbol of the new order to whom knowledge of scripture is given in the final age. The reference to John 21:22, "I wish him to remain until I come," suggests that this order will be the final one, apparently emerging in the sixth period of church history and lasting until the eschaton. If the "sixth angel" Bonaventure has in mind is Francis, the founder of this new order, it is understandable why Bonaventure twists the text a bit and portrays the angel himself as eating the book.

There are other relevant passages. At one point, Bonaventure describes the sixth period as "a time of clear doctrine" when there should appear "a single order . . . similar to the order of Jesus Christ," the head of which would be "an angel ascending from the rising of the sun, having the seal of the living God and conforming to Christ. And he said that he had already come."[40] At another point, he speaks in the future tense of a new understanding of scripture, predicting a time when "our lion from the tribe of Judah will arise and open the book, when there will be a consummation of the passions of Christ which the body of Christ now suffers."[41] Here the allusion is to Revelation 5:5.

In short, Bonaventure is not primarily interested in the angel of the sixth seal, but rather in the "sixth angel," and his references to that figure move well beyond the themes derived from Revelation 7 : 2. The "sixth angel" arises from a combination of several passages into a rich, complex image uniting various elements important for Bonaventure's evaluation of Francis and his historical role.[42] That image includes two different types of wisdom, namely increased understanding of scripture and an ecstatic knowledge which transcends the intellect. It also allows for historical development since, as we shall see, Francis's apocalyptic role begins in the sixth period of church history and is consummated in the seventh. In effect, he stands at both ends of a major historical development. He stands in the middle as well, since the stigmatized Francis is related to the tribulation and purgative suffering that will occur in the sixth period, as we will also see.

Does Bonaventure identify Francis with the sixth angel, however? He never does so explicitly in the *Collationes in hexaemeron*, and this fact led Stanislao da Campagnola to conclude that by 1273 Bonaventure was retreating from his earlier position, probably because he thought it necessary to delimit Joachite tendencies within the order.[43] This position is hard to accept for at least three reasons. First, the very fact that Bonaventure explicitly identifies Francis with the apocalyptic angel elsewhere seems to strengthen rather than weaken the possibility that he is doing so here, although it sharpens the question of why he does not do so explicitly. Second, Bonaventure's "sixth angel" passages are thematically related to Francis through the fact that some of what is said in them regarding the sixth angel is explicitly said of Francis elsewhere in the work.[44] Third, Bonaventure says certain things concerning the "sixth angel" that one would be hard put to apply to anyone except Francis. For example, if Bonaventure speaks of an emerging order "similar to that of Jesus Christ, the head of which should be an angel . . . with the seal of the living God and in conformity with Christ," then announces that this angel "had already come,"[45] whom else besides Francis could he have in mind?

Thus it seems preferable to believe that Bonaventure did identify Francis with the "sixth angel" but, for reasons of his own, preferred to do so implicitly rather than explicitly. Whatever these reasons may have been, it seems unlikely that they had anything to do with putative dangers surrounding the identification. As we will see, this identification was commonly accepted in the later thirteenth century. Moreover, what we know of Bonaventure makes it extremely hard to imagine him imparting to young Franciscans, in coded form, an idea with which they were largely familiar but which he thought perilous in some way. This image simply does not make much sense. But does he identify Francis with *all* the sixth angels or only with the angel of 7:2? In view of what has been said so far about how the various references interlock, it seems impossible to separate them. To be sure, the resultant image is conceptually muddier than we might have hoped, but Bonaventure may well have preferred it that way.[46]

Note that Bonaventure's reflections on the "sixth angel" are reminiscent of earlier Franciscan exegesis in some ways but quite different in others. Two obvious similarities are that he too sees church history as divided into seven ages and the Apocalypse as divided into seven visions. As Bonaventure himself succinctly puts it, "John covers the seven periods [of church history] in seven visions, each of which is sevenfold."[47] The differences are equally important. First, whereas earlier exegetes portrayed only the first four or five visions as recapitulating church history as a whole, Bonaventure seems to have seen them all as doing so. Second, whereas the exegetes saw the sixth period as that of Antichrist, Bonaventure gave it a double significance, positive and negative. Third, whereas the exegetes saw the sixth period as still to come, Bonaventure thought it had been in progress for close to five hundred years. Thus he was able to locate Francis within it. That allowed him to read Francis into the Apocalypse wherever a "sixth angel" appeared. In fact, he could see this identification as the literal interpretation if he chose to do so.

Ubertino da Casale reports that Bonaventure did present it as the literal interpretation. Ubertino claims to have heard as much from Olivi, who was present at Paris when Bonaventure said just that.[48] Olivi describes the same event in his Apocalypse commentary but does not mention whether Bonaventure advanced this interpretation as the literal meaning of the passage.[49] One cannot conclude from this fact that Ubertino has it wrong, since he says Olivi told him about it personally, not that he read it in Olivi's commentary. It is not impossible that Bonaventure did present it as such and that Olivi said as much to Ubertino when they were together at Santa Croce in Florence between 1287 and 1289. The truth of the matter escapes us.

Our interest in the "sixth angel" has encouraged us to speak largely of the sixth period. In fact, Francis is also related to the seventh in Bonaventure's theology of history. He is an early manifestation of the contemplative order which will bloom in that period. Thus Francis seems to link the sixth and seventh periods together in a single development. That fact, combined with Bonaventure's acceptance of the Joachite notion of *concordia*,[50] might be expected to make him more confident than others in predicting the shape of the seventh period; yet he says little about it beyond what we have seen: it will be a time of peace, contemplation, and increased knowledge.

Nevertheless, what he does say raises a question modern scholars have been notably unable to answer, at least to one another's satisfaction: What is the connection between the Franciscan order and the new contemplative order of the seventh period? Francis founded the former and is a member of the latter, but does that make them the same? Most modern scholars have followed Ratzinger, who suggests that Bonaventure's scholarly activities and compromises as minister general can be explained by his recognition that Francis anticipated a manner of life unattainable by any thirteenth-century institution.[51] Bonaventure, he says,

> could set aside the *sine glossa* which he knew from the Testament of Francis to be the real will of the founder . . . because the proper historical hour for such a form of life had not yet struck. . . . Bonaventure realized that Francis's own eschatological form of life could not exist as an institution in this world; it could be realized only as a break-through of grace in the individual until such a time as the God-given hour would arrive at which the world would be transformed into its final form of existence.[52]

Ratzinger acknowledges that some evidence points in a much different direction. He suggests that Bonaventure may originally have identified the Franciscans with the future order. Moreover,

> many texts seem to indicate that Bonaventure believed that the Franciscan order was originally determined to be the final, eschatological order immediately, and was to bring about the beginning of a new era. In this case, it would have been the failure of its members that impeded the realization of this. Now the order would have to be purged by another final tribulation before it would be able to find its true and final form.[53]

Ratzinger's main reason for positing a disjuncture between the Franciscans and the final order of the seventh age lies in a passage in which Bonaventure develops various ninefold orders, all correlated with the angelic hierarchy. Here he divides the church into laymen, clerics and contemplatives, each containing three orders. The contemplatives are divided into those who devote themselves entirely to prayer; those who strive "in a speculative way, . . . as do those who engage in the examination of scripture"; and "those who attend to God in an elevative way, that is, an ecstatic and rapturous way."[54] The first, corresponding to the thrones, are the monastic orders such as the Cistercians, Premonstratensians, and so forth. The second, corresponding to the Cherubim, are the Dominicans and Franciscans. The third correspond to the Seraphim. "It seems that Francis belonged to it," Bonaventure says, "but what it is to be or already is, it is hard to know."

Ratzinger's view has its difficulties. E. R. Daniel rightly finds it odd that the decision to place Francis and the Franciscans in two different orders should hinge upon the interpretation of a single passage.[55] Certainly Ratzinger is correct in emphasizing the element of historical change in the *Collationes in hexaemeron*. As he neatly observes, Bonaventure sets the Dionysian cosmic hierarchy on its side, producing "not only a static hierarchy structured from above to below, but . . . a hierarchical development of history."[56] Nevertheless, one might ask whether, in the process of sensitizing us to the theme of historical change, he has not undervalued the element of continuity within that change. As I have observed elsewhere,[57] this continuity is seen in the twofold knowledge Bonaventure assigns to the new age. On the one hand, it is what he calls *sapientia nulliformis*, the wisdom through which, in Ratzinger's words, "the mystic approaches in silence to the very threshold of the mystery of the eternal God in the night of the intellect whose light is extinguished at such heights."[58] Bonaventure speaks of this wisdom in terms like "rapture" and "ecstasy," and identifies it with Francis's experience on Mount Alverna. Thus it seems to stand at the top of the mystical ladder, and to be fittingly attributed to the seraphic order.

On the other hand, the knowledge of the new age includes a fuller understanding of scripture somewhat reminiscent of Joachim's *intellectus spiritualis*.[59] There is ample reference to this phenomenon in passages dealing with the "sixth angel," as a review of those quoted earlier will demonstrate. This sort of knowledge seems quite different from *sapientia nulliformis*. In fact, it seems to resemble what Bonaventure describes as *sapientia multiformis*.[60] Bonaventure does not explicitly identify this type of knowledge with the cherubic order, yet he does describe the latter as that order which proceeds through *speculatio*, "as is the case with those who engage in the *speculatio* of scripture."[61]

The former, ecstatic type of knowledge was seen in Francis, and will flourish in the seventh period. The second, scriptural variety is associated with the sixth period, the "time of clear doctrine," but the passages referring to the "sixth angel" also point forward to a new understanding of scripture in the seventh period. The knowledge of scripture given to the "sixth angel" is identified with that granted in Revelation 10 to the apostle John, symbol of the future order that will remain until the end.[62] Thus both types of knowledge are associated with both the sixth and seventh periods, just as Francis himself is. One might object that this observation does little to advance the discussion, since it is the Franciscans who are at issue, not Francis. Yet Francis, after all, was a Franciscan. That fact, like the twofold nature of his knowledge, seems to suggest that he holds dual citizenship in the cherubic and seraphic orders, or, more precisely, that his attainment of the seraphic order does not entail rejection of virtues characteristic of the cherubic order. Can other Franciscans not go and do likewise? Bonaventure seems to call upon them to do just that.

> And he added, consider your own call, for it is great. . . . Contemplation cannot come about except in the greatest simplicity; and the greatest simplicity cannot exist except in the greatest poverty. And this is proper to this order. The intention of blessed Francis was to live in the greatest poverty. And he said that we had receded a lot from our state, and therefore God permitted that we be afflicted so that by these means we may be led back to our state that must possess the promised land. God promised great things to Israel, and the greatest among them were chosen, as were his apostles. The Jews became blind. These were enlightened. The former gave themselves to the flesh. Some chose to give their purses to Christ. Note also that only a few entered the promised land, and that those who discouraged the people did not go in.[63]

It seems obvious that Bonaventure is referring to the Franciscans when he says "this order." Like the ancient Israelites, they are both recipients of a great call and notorious backsliders. Thus they must be purified by affliction before they can enter into their inheritance. All will not enter, but some can, and woe to him who discourages them.[64] All of this accords ill with the notion that the Franciscans must wait for a new age before moving beyond their present state.

Another passage seems equally important. In discussing the order which corresponds to the Seraphim, the order of those who attend to God through ecstasy, Bonaventure says,

> This order will not flourish unless Christ appears and suffers in his mystical body. And he said that this apparition of the seraph to blessed Francis, which was both expressive and impressed, showed that this order was to correspond to that one, but was to attain to this through tribulations [*iste ordo illi respondere debeat, sed tamen pervenire ad hoc per tribulationes*].[65]

It is not entirely clear what the *illi* and *hoc*, or even the *iste ordo* refer to here, but the *illi* and *hoc* would seem to refer either to the seraphic order or to Saint Francis, and the *iste ordo* to the Franciscan order. If so, then we find roughly the same pattern suggested in the preceding passage, except that here the promised land becomes the seraphic order, the ultimate stage of the religious life on earth. Thus Bonaventure is telling his fellow sons of Saint Francis about the great developments in progress and inviting them to participate. Levels of piety and knowledge already attained by a few people in the past will be more widely attained in the future. He invites them to share in that attainment.

Subsequent Exegesis

Once Bonaventure had offered Franciscans his vision of an apocalyptic Francis, they must have found it hard to ignore. Bonaventure's reputation alone would have insured as much, but the status of the *Legenda maior* as the official biography made its avoidance doubly difficult. The Bonaventuran legacy would obtrude on two different levels, popular piety and scholarly exegesis, and would do so in two different ways. It is primarily the exegetical response that concerns us here. We will study it by examining six Franciscan commentaries which are probably characteristic of Franciscan interpretation during the later thirteenth century. Four are complete. The other two exist in large fragments. Of the complete commentaries, one can be attributed with confidence to John Russel.[66] Another is probably by John of Wales, but that attribution is far from unshakable.[67] Still another may well be by Vital du Four, though there are suggestions to the contrary.[68]

The most problematic of the four is a commentary published in 1647 under Alexander of Hales's name, then in 1773 among Bonaventure's works.[69] Modern scholars have been unwilling to assign it to either Alexander or Bonaventure.[70] We will call the author "Alexander" here simply because we must call him something, but the quotation marks suggest willingness to accept further illumination on the matter. Some manuscripts insinuate, albeit vaguely, that Vital du Four is the author, and the suggestion can hardly be dismissed out of hand, since this commentary shares a surprising amount of material with the one tentatively assigned to him above. One is reminded of the situation with the commentaries beginning *Aser pinguis* and *Vidit Iacob*, both of which Robert Lerner persuasively assigns to Hugh of St. Cher and his associates.[71] Here we enter an intriguing area, however. Much of the common material in the Vital and "Alexander" commentaries is also shared by *Vidit Iacob*. Since the common material in the two Franciscan commentaries is interspersed with other material reflecting two very different minds, it seems likely that the shared material reflects not a common author but the influence of some parent commentary.[72] The question of who is influencing whom cannot be answered at this point, since it demands a more careful analysis than anyone has provided so far.

We are left with the two large fragments of commentaries. The first is by Matthew of Aquasparta, and it survives in two manuscripts, the largest of which contains exegesis of the first nine chapters.[73] The second fragmentary commentary is found in a single manuscript entitled *Distinctiones super apocalypsim* and attributed to Raymond Rigaud.[74] It seems to contain excerpts from a complete commentary, run together without any interest in continuity.

Obviously, not all of these commentaries can be dated accurately. Beryl Smalley dates John Russel's in the academic year 1292–93.[75] It is likely that Vital du Four's commentary—if it is indeed by Vital—was written after 1292, when he began his teaching career, and before 1307, when he became a provincial minister. Raymond Rigaud's would belong after 1287, when he became a master, and before his death in 1296. Matthew of Aquasparta's would be slightly older, perhaps in the early 1280s. John of Wales's commentary could be of roughly the same vintage as Matthew's, since he taught at Paris in the early 1280s, serving on the commission that censured Olivi's works in 1283; yet it could also be substantially earlier, since John's teaching career stretched over a very long period. In fact, he was teaching at Oxford before Bonaventure's *Legenda maior* was adopted as the sole official biography. The date of the "Alexander" commentary is equally unclear. The important thing for our purposes is that the first four commentaries can be dated toward the end of the thirteenth century, while the last two may be late, but may also be early, so early as to escape the impact of Bonaventure's later works and even perhaps his *Legenda maior*. This is an area in desperate need of research.

In any case, all of these commentators adopt what we have termed the standard Parisian approach to the Apocalypse. Obviously its influence extended well beyond Paris. In these commentaries, we find the Apocalypse divided into seven visions, some of them recapitulative in the sense that they cover all of church history. Here too we find the four/three division already seen in earlier exegetes, with those visions concerning the *status generalis* opposed to those dealing with the *status finalis*. Here again we find church history divided into seven periods, and the periods are precisely the ones seen in earlier commentaries. Nevertheless, while all six commentators recognize this structure, not all are equally anxious to use it. John of Wales lies at one end of the spectrum. One gets the impression that he accepts this historical reading of the Apocalypse largely because his chosen authorities (Bede, Haymo, the *Glossa*, and Richard of St. Victor) do so, but he is much happier pursuing a course of atemporal, moral interpretation. On the other hand, Vital and "Alexander" show their kinship with *Vidit Iacob* precisely in their commitment to a historical reading, although they too do a great deal else.

So far we have said nothing about these scholars' debt to Bonaventure. In fact it is rather slight. Their periodization, indeed their whole general approach to the Apocalypse, is based upon the exegetical tradition inherited from the previous century and shared with the Dominicans. There is no trace of Bonaventure's Janus-like sixth period, with its positive and negative aspects. Like the mendicant exegetes examined earlier, they identify the sixth period entirely with the reign of Antichrist. Thus it follows that they also reject Bonaventure's decision to place himself in the sixth period. Like earlier exegetes, they see it as yet to come. At least two of them, "Alexander" and Vital, specifically place themselves in the early fifth period, that of the precursors of Antichrist, and they are willing to back their claim with a thorough indictment of contemporary decadence in the secular and sacred spheres. Here again they are showing their relationship with *Vidit Iacob*.[76]

They point to heresy and corruption. As for the former, both Vital and "Alexander" complain that they are entering a time in which falsity, subtlety, and novelty are valued more than Christian truth.[77] "Alexander" says a great deal about the matter and alludes to a rich variety of heresies,[78] but like many of his contemporaries he often leaves us uncertain as to whether he is citing some contemporary aberration or simply dredging up an idea from the pages of doctrinal history. While on the whole Vital says less about heresy, his commentary shows a definite interest in the connection between Christianity and pagan philosophy.[79] As for corruption, "Alexander" criticizes both ecclesiastical and secular leaders at some length. He attacks the latter not only for their oppression of the church but for grinding the faces of the poor.[80] Vital concentrates almost exclusively on ecclesiastical vices, although he does mention secular oppression of the church at one point.[81] In the ecclesiastical sphere, both writers attack corrupt *prelati* at length,[82] especially complaining of their simony, neglect of pastoral duties, and corruption of the laity through their own bad example.[83] The lower clergy are also chastized, but less fulsomely.[84]

Criticism of the *prelati* inevitably stops at the water's edge. There is no effort to attack the prelate of prelates. Commentators on the Apocalypse could hardly avoid the criticism of Rome built into their text, but this could be handled without causing offense, or at any rate without causing much offense. For example, "Alexander" comments that the city of Rome is called a whore in Revelation 17:1 because of the sale of benefices.[85] Later, however, he identifies Rome with "some prelates of the church" who corrupt others through their bad example.[86] The total effect is to identify Rome with bad prelates wherever they might be found rather than with the Roman curia in particular.

Vital is in some ways more interesting. He too is intelligent enough to realize that Rome is the target of chapters 17–18 and includes the city of Rome as one of four possible interpretations of the great whore at 17:1, but does not specify what period he has in mind. His most surprising comment is reserved for Revelation 17:18, "The woman that you see is a great city." He begins safely enough, but then his exegesis takes a surprising turn. He explains that John "speaks for that time in which Roman idolatry was in force, or for a future time when perhaps heresy and all perfidy will thus reign." Then he cites Joachim. He goes on to say that

> in that time kings will be gathered to fight with it and to strike at the sons of Babylon, who call themselves sons of Christ and are not, but are rather the synagogue of Satan; and indeed their intention will be evil, but they will nevertheless ignorantly and unknowingly perform God's will, whether killing the just who will thus be crowned with martydom or bringing judgment upon the evil by whom the earth has been stained with blood. Thus after this blow, which has now begun in part, there will be victory for the Christians and joy for those fearing the true God.[87]

Vital's thought here is—to say the least—undeveloped, but it is oddly evocative of the pseudo-Joachite Jeremiah commentary. We will see these ideas further developed in the exegesis offered by Olivi and later by Henry of Cossey. Such connections make it doubly interesting that the passage should be found in a commentary attributed to Vital, who studied theology at Paris in the late 1280s and perhaps the early 1290s as well. By the fall of 1295 he was a lector at Montpellier, where Olivi himself had recently taught. At the time of Olivi's death at Narbonne in 1298 Vital was a lector at Toulouse, not far away. Vital's doctrinal solidity is suggested both by his teaching career and by the administrative positions with which he was eventually entrusted. Provincial of Aquitaine from 1307 to 1312, he was appointed a cardinal in the latter year and became bishop of Albano in 1321. During these years he was a determined opponent of the spiritual Franciscans in general and Olivi in particular, as we will see.

An equally intriguing comment on Rome is offered by the third member of the triumvirate, *Vidit Iacob*, which is withering in its criticism of the clergy. The author regards church leaders with genuine contempt, constantly emphasizing that only a few remain uncorrupted.[88] He mentions Rome in nine passages.[89] Four of these contain negative allusions to Rome, the Romans, or the Roman empire, without any attempt to specify the precise meaning or even the period in question. Another passage is so ambiguous that one could not even call it a negative comment. The remaining four are more thought-provoking. In one, the author comments that, whereas Christian blood was once shed in Rome through killing, it is now shed there though exaction.[90] In the remaining three cases, all falling within his consideration of the beast with ten horns of Daniel 7 and Revelation 17, he applies the image to the future Roman empire in the time of Antichrist.[91] In one of these cases, he refers the image backward to pagan Rome as well. The ten horns are kings who will be under the Roman empire at that time. The little horn of Daniel 7:8 is "Antichrist, who will be born in the time of the Roman kingdom, and then will occur that falling away of the Roman empire, temporal *or eccelsiastical*, mentioned in II Thessalonians 2."[92] Thus *Vidit Iacob* and Vital both hint at the possibility that the great "falling away" in the time of Antichrist may compromise the papacy itself, although each does so fleetingly.

If these commentators simply identified the sixth period with Antichrist, what did they do with the angel of the sixth seal? Every one of them must have approached Revelation 7:2 with Bonaventure's identification echoing through his mind. How could they possibly ignore it? Some did. John of Wales, "Alexander," and John Russel manage to get through Revelation 7 without even mentioning Francis. In fact, of the three, only "Alexander" mentions Francis at all in his commentary, and neither of his two references credits Francis with any apocalyptic signifiance. It is intriguing that John of Wales and "Alexander" are the two authors whom we mentioned as possibly antedating the *Legenda maior*, and it would be tempting to read a great deal into this circumstance were it not for the fact that John Russel wrote in the 1290s.

The other three commentators do mention Francis, and just where one would expect them to do so. All three identify him with the angel of 7:2. The problem is not whether they do so but what they could possibly mean by it. Here again, we are back to the fact that the angel of 7:2 is the angel of the sixth seal and is thus identified with the sixth period. These scholars identify the sixth period with Antichrist, placing it in the future. Francis, however, belongs in the early fifth or even the late fourth period. It is therefore hard to see how they could take Revelation 7:2 as a literal reference to Francis.

All three approach the passage in an analogous way. Matthew of Aquasparta simply announces that, while the passage refers principally to Christ, it can be understood also of Saint Francis and offers an excellent theme for preaching about him.[93] Raymond Rigaud applies the passage to Christ, then says,

> Or it can be applied to Blessed Francis, and then it will be taken in this way: Blessed Francis, sent by Christ (*legatus a latere Christi*), is introduced in four ways through these words: Blessed Francis was an angel *propter agilitatem expeditionis*, ascending *propter virilitatem executionis*, from the place of the sun *propter serenitatem conversationis*, and having the seal of the living God *propter auctoritatem legationis*.[94]

Vital du Four has almost precisely the same passage. He says,

> Blessed Francis is described here *ut fidelis legatus, quantum ad agilitatem expeditionis* because he is described as an angel; *quantum ad virilitatem executionis* because he is described as ascending; *quantum ad serenitatem conversationis* because he is described as "from the rising of the sun"; and *quantum ad austeritatem legationis* because he bears the seal of the living God.[95]

In both of these cases, what we are given is essentially a preaching outline. The sort of preaching they have in mind is perhaps not a sermon but a *collatio*, which would be delivered to fellow-Franciscans. It might be one of a series of *collationes* on a given subject presented over a period of several days, like Bonaventure's *Collationes in hexaemeron* or his *Collationes de septem donis spiritus sancti*.

Manuscripts of Vital's commentary show that either he or his readers explicitly acknowledged the homiletical uses of this identification. In two Assisi manuscripts (MSS 71 and 358), a marginal notation identifies it as pertaining to a *collatio*. In two other Assisi manuscripts (MSS 46 and 66), the identification is found in the text itself. In MS 46 the passage in question begins with the words *Collatio pro beato Francisco*, while in MS 66 it is prefaced with the announcement *Accipiamus pro collatione*. Until further study of the manuscripts is undertaken, it will be impossible to say whether the reference to a *collatio* should be considered a later addition or part of the original text.

Another indication of the Franciscan commitment to preaching on this theme can be found in a Florentine manuscript of John of Wales's commentary.[96] Here a hand other than that of the scribe has added comments in the margin and, at the top of the page throughout the work, has listed topics for a series of *collationes*. There are a great many of these topics. (He numbers them through forty-two, then simply gives the topics without numeration.) In any case, at the top of the page where the commentary on chapter seven begins, he writes, *Collatio 19 de beato Francisco vidi alterum angelum, etc.* The most significant thing about this rubric is, of course, that John of Wales's commentary does not even mention Francis in connection with Revelation 7. Thus the writer is reflecting not what he sees before him in the commentary but what he recognizes as an accepted preaching topic.

If we were to end our examination right here, we might be tempted to close with the firm conclusion: Franciscans after Bonaventure were influenced by his identification of Francis with the Angel of Revelation 7:2 and incorporated it in their preaching; yet Franciscan exegetes of the later thirteenth century could not accept such an identification as the literal meaning of the passage, since they differed from Bonaventure in their reading of the sixth period and in the way they located themselves in history. Thus these exegetes either avoided mention of Francis or admitted the identifiction as a handy preaching theme without taking it literally. In reality, such a conclusion is a bit too facile. In the first place, all four manuscripts of the Vital commentary mentioned above also say that one could base a *collatio* on the identification of the angel of Revelation 7:2 with Christ. Thus, when exegetes announce that identification of the angel with Francis would make a good *collatio*, we can certainly infer from their words that the identification with Francis could have a devotional function even if it was not taken literally; but we cannot infer that it was not also taken literally.

The preceding observation rests on the assumption that Vital took the identification with Christ literally, however he took the identification with Francis. Unfortunately, even this much cannot be demonstrated, and that brings us to a second reason why it is hard to say precisely what these writers had in mind: thirteenth-century Apocalypse commentaries devote remarkably little space to basic hermeneutical questions. Exegetes normally proceed as if they assumed that the seven periods of church history constituted the literal sense of the Apocalypse, but they avoid saying so. Their choice of words offers a rough-hewn method for separating the literal from the spiritual sense. When they interpret a passage in what is apparently its literal sense they use words like "signifies" or "refers to." When they suggest a spiritual sense they tend to use phrases like "can be applied to." The word *potest* provides the key. It normally suggests a spiritual application. The distinction here is not necessarily one between a historical and moral application. A passage may have a single, literal historical application and secondary, spiritual historical applications. For example, Vital's interpretation of the seven vials in Revelation 16 is determined by his assumption that the Apocalypse offers four visions about the whole church and three more about the period from Antichrist to eschaton. Since the seven vials constitute the fifth vision, Vital concludes that the vision refers literally to preaching against the seven deadly sins to be carried out in the time of Antichrist, but he also suggests that "we can exposit it allegorically" (*possumus exponere primo allegorice*) of preaching against the seven enemies of the church in the seven periods.[97] Here we have two historical applications, one literal and the other spiritual. We also have one of those rare passages in which the "signifies"/"can be applied to" dichotomy is explicitly linked to the literal and spiritual senses, thus clarifying what is implied elsewhere.

When we apply all of this to exegesis of Revelation 7:2, we encounter a problem. Matthew of Aquasparta and Raymond Rigaud say precisely what we might expect them to say. They affirm that the passage refers to Christ but can be (*potest*) applied to Francis. It is Vital who betrays us. He simply announces that Francis "is described," a term which might be expected to accompany the literal meaning.

Moreover, Vital refers to Francis not only at Revelation 7:2, but six other times as well. Three cases are relatively unimportant. For example, in expositing the eagle of Revelation 4:7 he suggests that "these words can be taken in commendation of either John the Evangelist or Blessed Francis," then shows how it could be done.[98] Here he is using that evocative term *potest*, and doing nothing more than he does with other saints: he is suggesting how a text might be appropriated for preaching purposes. What he offers is essentially a moral interpretation with Francis as an example. He can be identified with the eagle because he possesses certain qualities symbolized by the eagle. So did the apostle John and so, presumably, did others.

Other passages seem to offer a somewhat stronger claim. In one, Vital applies Revelation 2:17 first to Christ in the eucharist, then to Christ as the price of our redemption. "Or," he adds, it can be applied to "Christ promising to the blessed Francis that singular privilege of the seraphic vision and sealing."[99] In another passage, Vital suggests that the book with seven seals (Revelation 5:1) "can be said to be the divine plan, Christ's life, the church militant, the church triumphant, the blessed virgin, the Apocalypse, Christ in the sacrament, and the blessed Francis." Francis is included because he "is a book written inside spiritually through compassion and outside physically through the stigmata of Christ's passion, the seven seals of which the lion of the tribe of Judah opened."[100] In these cases, the claim being made is stronger in the sense that the vision on Mount Alverna and consequent stigmata are emphasized in such a way as to suggest that Francis is particularly and perhaps uniquely revelatory of Christ. Nevertheless, use of the word *potest* again seems to imply that we are dealing with spiritual interpretation.

Another passage is more perplexing. Vital remarks that Francis is "designated" through Elijah, one of the two witnesses of Revelation 11. He then offers an extended parallel between Elijah and Francis. Francis's animals are compared with Elijah's raven; his witness before the sultan with Elijah's firmness in the face of a hostile king; and his ride in a fiery chariot with Elijah's own.[101] It is hard to read the passage without wondering whether something on the order of a Joachite concordance is lurking in the background. Moreover, one is struck by the fact that, in describing the two witnesses of 11:6, Vital says *designatur pater Franciscus*.[102] The word *designatur* is particularly interesting because, in the *Legenda maior*, Bonaventure uses the word *designatus* when referring to Francis's credentials as angel of Revelation 7:2.

Can we conclude, then, that Vital saw Revelation 7:2 and 11:6 as literal references to Francis? Probably not. It seems more likely that we are simply encountering the limits of the "refers to"/"can be applied to" dichotomy as a way of distinguishing the literal and spiritual senses. It is worth noting that when Vital, in dealing with 7:2, says *describitur hic Franciscus*, he is using precisely the same verb employed by Matthew of Aquasparta in a sermon on that passage,[103] and, as we have seen, Matthew apparently did not think that the angel of the sixth seal was literally Francis. It is also worth noting that Revelation 11:6 presents the same difficulty as 7:2, inasmuch as Vital's historical structure demands that the two witnesses of 11:6 should appear during the reign of Antichrist and therefore in the sixth period.

The conclusion to be drawn from these facts is perhaps that, even though Vital lacked the exegetical assumptions to read Francis into any chapter of the Apocalypse as its literal significance, he was very enthusiastic about employing that book as a vehicle for preaching about Francis, and he was not overly concerned with the precise meaning of the language used in the process. It is hard to dig much deeper than that, because Vital was not really preoccupied with or even very interested in analyzing the precise level of significance any particular statement might possess. In fact, like other thirteenth-century exegetes, he was often willing to let his categorization of the senses of scripture float with the material being analyzed.[104] The more general conclusion to be drawn from all six commentators is that, while three of them tried to work Bonaventure's apocalyptic reading of Francis into their exegesis in some way, none of them accepted the Bonaventuran periodization, which would have allowed them to accept Francis as the literal meaning of Revelation 7:2. Here they chose to follow the main stream of exegetical tradition rather than Bonaventure.

Granting this much, it is still worth asking whether any of these commentators at least managed to suggest some apocalyptic role for future Franciscans. All of them affirm that each period contains a new assault of Satan countered by a new order of preachers. That much is traditional. Some commentators go slightly beyond tradition and describe the preachers of the fourth period in a way that evokes the Franciscans. Vital gently suggests that perhaps the same order will oversee the defense in the fourth and fifth periods.[105] John Russel is more emphatic: "I firmly believe," he declares, "that the order of preachers in the fifth period will be the same as that in the fourth, that is, the order of the poor of Christ, sowing the word of God throughout the world."[106] One might detect here a discreet reference to the mendicants. Nevertheless, according to these commentators the fourth period began around the time of Saint Benedict and includes within it the entire history of monasticism down to the brink of their own age. From this perspective, all *regulares* including the mendicants become the order of the fourth and fifth periods.

William of Middleton seems to offer a more promising anticipation of Olivi when, in his discussion of Enoch and Elijah, he notes that the church of the last days will return to the humility of the first period. He then speaks of Enoch and Elijah as two orders and mentions their *vilitas habitus*.[107] Nevertheless, his comments are so brief and imprecise that one is hard put to decide how much weight should be given to them.

It should be added that these commentators can manage only a very limited acceptance of Joachim. On the whole, they accomodate him as a part of exegetical tradition without ever coming to terms with what was unique about his theology of history. Joachim tends to be included within a list of *auctoritates* in the introduction or made to function as one more *auctoritas* to be cited concerning the meaning of a particular word or passage.[108] There are exceptions. For example, "Alexander's" celebration of the seventh period creeps just far enough beyond the normal description to suggest that he has been reading Joachim or is borrowing from someone who did;[109] the lengthy *concordia* between the Old Testament period and the New Testament period through the death of John the Evangelist offered by Vital seems dependent on Joachim's *Liber de concordia*;[110] discussions of the seven heads and ten horns of the beast in Revelation 13 as offered by Vital, "Alexander," and *Vidit Iacob* clearly echo Joachim's commentary on the Apocalypse;[111] and Vital explicitly cites Joachim during his ruminations on the impending destruction of Babylon by a kingly coalition. On one issue, however, there are no exceptions: Joachim's threefold division of history is resolutely ignored.

Having examined these commentaries, we can form some idea of what were considered the normal parameters of Franciscan exegesis when Olivi began to compose his Apocalypse commentary. How he respected or rejected those parameters will be the subject of subsequent chapters.

Notes

1. McGinn, *Calabrian Abbot*, 205–34; Joseph Ratzinger, *Die Geschichtestheologie des heiligen Bonaventura* (Munich, 1959), cited here in its English translation, *The Theology of History in St. Bonaventure* (Chicago, 1971); Stephanus Bihel, "S. Franciscus fuitne Angelus sexti sigilli?" *Antonianum* 2 (1927): 29–70; Stanislao da Campagnola, *L'Angelo del sesto sigillo e l'"alter Christus"* (Rome, 1971).

2. See my *OFP*, ch. 1.

3. Bonaventure, *Legenda maior*, prologus:1, in *Opera* (Quaracchi, 1882–1902), vol. 8.

4. *Legenda maior*, 13:3–10; *Legenda minor*, 1:1 and 1:9, in *Opera*, vol. 8; *Sermones*, in *Opera*, vol. 9 (see especially 574f., 582, 586f.). In *Sermones*, 586f., Rev. 7:2 is combined with Rev. 3:7. See footnotes 48 and 49 below for references by Olivi and Ubertino da Casale to a sermon at Paris in which Bonaventure identified

Francis with the angel of Rev. 7:2. For the *Collationes in hexaemeron*, see the following discussion.

5. Guilelmus de Militona, *Expositio super apocalypsim*, MSS Assisi 82 and 321. For scholary opinion on what town is designated by *Militona* see Guillelmus de Militona, *Quaestiones de sacramentis* (Quaracchi, 1961), 6*-13*; Ignatius Brady, "Sacred Scripture in the Early Franciscan School," in *La Sacra scrittura e i francescani* (Rome, 1973), 81.

6. Aquinas, *Opera* (Parma, 1860–62), 23:570, 573. The work is also published in *Opera* (Paris, 1871–80). On the two passages see notes twenty and twenty-one below.

7. I have seen those by Hugo de Sancto Caro, Nicholas Gorranus, and Petrus de Tarantasia. The Nicholas Gorranus commentary is published under his name in *In Acta Apostolorum . . . et Apocalypsim Commentarii* (Antwerp, 1620). For the others see below.

8. On this tradition see Robert Lerner, "Refreshment of the Saints," *Traditio* 32 (1976): 97–144.

9. *In Apocalypsim B. Joannis Apostoli Luculenta Expositio*, in Albertus Magnus, *Opera* (Paris, 1890), 38:465–792. See Robert Lerner, "Poverty, Preaching and Eschatology in the Revelation Commentaries of 'Hugh of St. Cher,'" in *The Bible in the Medieval World* (Oxford, 1985), 160f.

10. Lerner, "Poverty, Preaching and Eschatology," 157–89. For the "team" theory and its pedigree see Beryl Smalley, *The Gospels in the Schools* (London, 1985), 120. I shall refer to the commentary as *Aser pinguis* and cite the edition found in Hugo de Sancto Caro, *Biblia latina cum postilla* (Paris, 1545).

11. Lerner, "Poverty, Preaching and Eschatology," 157–89. Lerner's claim is supported by attributions offered in various manuscripts and the commentary fits well into Hugh's chronology. I shall refer to it here as *Vidit Iacob*. It is published in Thomas Aquinas, *Opera* (Parma, 1860–62), 23:325–511; and *Opera* (Paris, 1871–80), 31:469–661 and 32:1–86. I shall cite the former.

12. They do not necessarily abandon the first view. As we will see (in Vital's case), one could apply the vision both to the sixth period and to all of church history.

13. *Aser pinguis*, 378ra.

14. *Aser pinguis* is an exception, since it is too vague to be categorized in this way.

15. Richardus de Sancto Victore, *In apocalypsim Ioannis*, in *PL*, 196:783.

16. See Lerner, "Refreshment of the Saints" for this tradition. By the time these commentators wrote, the tradition had spawned variants on this number, and thus *Vox domini praeparantis cervos*, 564 and 578, speaks of forty-two rather than forty-five.

17. See the discussion of Augustine in chapter seven.

18. Alexander Minorita, *Expositio in apocalypsim* (Weimar, 1955). His description reminds one of Joachim's narrative in *Expositio in apocalypsim*, f. 36va. Described in one manuscript as *simplex et laicus*, he himself uses the word *laicus* twice (pp. 7, 11). It is less certain how one should take this. On the successive redactions of this commentary see Sabina Schmolinsky, "Expositio Apocalypsis intellectum

historicum: Der Kommentar des Alexander Minorita im Rahmen der deutschen Rezeptionsgeschichte Joachims von Fiore," doctoral dissertation, University of Munich, 1987.

19. *Expositio*, pp. 443, 450. His message is hardly clear, though. Moreover, he sees the millennium as a minimum figure to which God can add a space for conversion if he wishes.

20. *Vox domini praeparantis cervos*, 570. Almost exactly these words are attributed to Francis in just this context in Bonaventure, *Legenda maior*, 14:1; yet the wording is even closer to that found in Thomas of Celano, *Vita prima, vita secunda, et tractatus de miraculis: Vita prima*, 103, in *AF*, vol. 10, although here it is found in a different context.

21. *Vox domini praeparantis cervos*, 573. See Thomas of Celano, *Vita prima*, 71. Compare Bonaventure, *Legenda maior*, 10:1, where the words are slightly different, though very close. The situation in which they are delivered is the same in each case.

22. *Expositio*, 436–37, 493–95; *Super Hieremiam*, 8, 76–79.

23. Ibid., 450–58.

24. Ibid., 462.

25. Ibid., 469–501, already anticipated on pp. 453–54.

26. Ibid., 454, 467, 501.

27. Bonaventure reflects Alexander's approach in *Sermones de S. Patre Nostro Francesco*, sermo IV, in *Opera*, 9:386–87, when he identifies the angel of 7:2 with Constantine as well as with Francis. Olivi's treatment of the millennium and his general way of interpreting the seven visions (combining recapitulative with successive elements) might be said to effect a partial harmonization of Alexander's view with the dominant Parisian one.

28. See *Collationes de septem donis spiritus sancti*, 8:16, in *Opera*, vol. 5, where he identifies the three major errors of heterodox Aristotelianism with the number of the beast. This passage so impressed Olivi that he echoed it at least twice in his own writings. For his references and mention of his own presence, see David Burr, "The Apocalyptic Element in Olivi's Critique of Aristotle," *Church History* 40 (1971): 15–29.

29. *Collationes in hexaemeron et Bonaventuriana quaedam selecta* (Quaracchi, 1934); *Collationes in hexaemeron*, in *Opera*, 5. Nevertheless, Delorme (p. XVI) thinks it likely that Bonaventure inspected and corrected the version printed in *Opera*. For another possible member of the audience see David d'Avray, "A Franciscan and History," *AFH* 74 (1981): 456–82.

30. *Collationes in hexaemeron*, 16.

31. Ibid., 16:29.In Delorme, *Collationes*, 192, Frederick II is also mentioned.

32. *Collationes in hexaemeron*, 9:8, 13:33, 14:17, 15:1–9, 15:28, 16:20, 18:28.

33. Ibid., 16:19,22,30.

34. Ibid., 16:29. Bonaventure speaks of *praeclaritas victoriae, praeclaritas doctrinae*, and *praeclaritas vitae propheticae*.

35. Ibid., 16:29.

36. Ibid., 23:14: "Sic anima contemplativa signatur a Deo. Unde sub sexto angelo dicitur, quod apparuit angelus habens signum dei vivi, hoc fuit in assigna-

tione Ierusalem ut in caelo consistentis. Huic angelo apparuit signum expressivum, quantum ad modum vivendi consonum isti signo, quod est, quod signatur: Ex tribu Iuda duodecim millia signati etc.; et hoc est: qui habet hanc triplicem lucem elevantem, triplicem oportet quod habeat perfectionem, respondentem caritati. Unde signare hoc modo est per professionem ad hoc alligare et imprimere signum, ut respondeat illi signo caritatis."

37. Ibid., 23:3–4: "Quomodo potest hoc esse? Vide illud, quod dictum est, in fine Apocalypsis; circa medium autem dictum est: Vidi supra montem Sion agnum stantem, et cum eo centum quadraginta quatuor millia, habentes nomen eius et nomen patris eius scriptum in frontibus suis. In apertione autem sexti sigilli dictum est in Apocalypsi: Vidi alterum angelum ascendentem ab ortu solis, habentem signum Dei vivi, et clamavit quatuor angelis, quibus datum est nocere terrae et mari, dicens: Nolite nocere terrae et mari neque arboribus, quoadusque signemus servos Dei nostri in frontibus eorum. Et audivi numerum signatorum, centum quadraginta quatuor millia, signati ex omni tribu filiorum Israel. . . . Primo ponit signatos, qui erant supra montem Sion, et postea, quod angelus unus de effundentibus phialas, qui oportet, quod sit sextus, ostendit ei civitatem, cuius mensura centum quadraginta quatuor cubitorum erat. Circa principium Apocalypsis dicitur sexto angelo, scilicet Philadelphiae: Qui vicerit, faciam illum columnam in templo Dei mei et scribam super eum nomen meum et nomen civitatis novae Ierusalem, de qua locutus non fuit nisi in fine. Sex sunt tempora, quorum sextum tempus habet tria tempora cum quiete. Et sicut Christus in sexto tempore venit, ita oportet, quod in fine generetur ecclesia contemplativa."

38. Ibid., 16:29: "Et certum est, quod aliquis inter eos voluit exterminare ecclesiam; sed angelus ascendens ab ortu solis clamavit quatuor angelis: Nolite nocere terrae et mari, quousque signemus servos Dei nostri in frontibus eorum. Unde adhuc restat ecclesiae tribulatio. Et dictum est angel Philadelphiae, qui sextus est: Haec dicit sanctus et verus, qui habet clavem David; qui aperit, et nemo claudit; claudit, et nemo aperit. Scio opera tua, quia ecce, dedi coram te ostium apertum. Et dixit, quod adhuc intelligentia scripturae daretur vel revelatio vel clavis David personae vel multitudini; et magis credo, quod multitudini." Obviously the *dixit* refers to Bonaventure. The reporter is speaking. The *credo* is apparently Bonaventure speaking. This is part of what he said (*dixit*).

39. Ibid., 20:29: "Nota, quod duodecim signationes sunt sub sexto sigillo et sub sexto angelo, et mensuratio civitatis et apertio libri; et sexto angelo, scilicet Philadelphiae, qui interpretur, conservans hereditatem, dictum est de clave David, et de quo dicitur: qui vicerit scribam super eum nomen meum et nomen civitatis novae Ierusalem. . . . Hoc est, dabo notitiam scripturarum isti sexto angelo; sed amaricabitur venter eius, et in ore eius erit dulce tanquam mel. Et iste ordo intelligitur per Ioannem, cui dictum est: Sic eum volo manere donec veniam." See Jn. 21:22.

40. *Collationes in hexaemeron*, 16:16.

41. Ibid., 20:15. In 13:7 there is another reference in the future tense to the new understanding of scripture.

42. If Bonaventure is eclectic in developing his image of the "sixth angel," he is hardly all-inclusive. He does not refer to the sixth angel mentioned in Rev. 14,

even though he makes use of that chapter. Nor does he refer directly to 9:14, where one actually finds the words "sixth angel," this time referring to the sixth one to blow his trumpet.

43. *L'Angelo*, 194–97.

44. See, for example, *Collationes in hexaemeron*, 22:23: "Et isti sunt propinqui Ierusalem et non habent nisi evolare. Iste ordo non florebit, nisi Christus appareat et patiatur in corpore suo mystico. Et dicebat, quod illa apparitio Seraph beato Francisco, quae fuit expressiva et impressa, ostendebat, quod iste ordo illi respondere debeat, sed tamen pervenire ad hoc per tribulationes." (Note that the reporter again becomes a narrator, speaking of Bonaventure in the third person.) Here we find the "expressive seal" and "Jerusalem" themes, applied elsewhere to the "sixth angel," explicitly linked with Francis.

45. Ibid., 16:16.

46. Ratzinger, *The Theology of History in Saint Bonaventure*, 27f., recognizes the interlocking pattern of sixth angels, yet does not apply it *in toto* to Francis. His discussion of Francis as apocalyptic angel (pp. 33–37) is carried out entirely in terms of Rev. 7:2, moving along the same path traveled by Bihel and Stanislao da Campagnola; yet in *Origins of Papal Infallibility* (Leiden, 1972), 78, Brian Tierney recognizes the significance of Bonaventure's image of Francis as "sixth angel" as opposed to "angel of the sixth seal." He says, "We must remember that there were several angels in the Apocalypse who could be designated as the sixth angel. Of these, two especially interested Bonaventure. One was the angel of the sixth seal. . . . The other was the angel of the sixth church at Philadelphia." Robert Lerner, "An 'Angel of Philadelphia' in the Reign of Philip the Fair," in *Order and Innovation in the Middle Ages* (Princeton, 1976), 253, agrees.

47. *Collationes in hexaemeron*, 16:20.

48. Ubertino, *Arbor vitae crucifixae Jesu* (Torino, 1961), lib. 5, c. 3.

49. *Lectura super apocalypsim*, 393f. See later discussion of this passage.

50. *Collationes in hexaemeron*, 15:22–28 and 16:1–31.

51. *Theology of History*, especially 46–71 and 155–63.

52. Ibid., 50f.

53. Ibid., 53f.

54. *Collationes in hexaemeron*, 22:20–22.

55. E. R. Daniel, "St. Bonaventure: Defender of Franciscan Eschatology," in *S. Bonaventura, 1247–1974* (Grottaferrata, 1974), 4:804. Bernard McGinn sides with Ratzinger against Daniel in "The Significance of Bonaventure's Theology of History," *Journal of Religion Supplement* 58 (1978): 571, and *Calabrian Abbot*, 231 n.92.

56. *Theology of History*, 92.

57. "Bonaventure, Olivi, and Franciscan Eschatology," *Collectanea franciscana* 53 (1983): 31–35.

58. *Theology of History*, 60f. See *Collationes in hexaemeron*, 2:8–34, 3:24–30, 22:22.

59. *Collationes in hexaemeron*, 13:7, 16:16, 16:29, 20:15, 20:29.

60. Ibid., 2:11, in which *sapientia multiformis* is explicitly identified with scripture.

61. Ibid., 22:21.

62. Ibid., 20:2; see also 13:7, 20:15. See Jn. 21:22.

63. *Collationes in hexaemeron*, 20:30. The words "he said" refer to Bonaventure.

64. See Ibid., 9:8, 22:23. Even in their affliction they are conforming with the stigmatized Francis.

65. Ibid., 21:23.

66. Iohannes Russel, *Expositio super apocalypsim*, MS Oxford Merton 122. See Beryl Smalley, "John Russel," in *Studies in Medieval Thought and Learning* (London, 1981), 205–48.

67. Iohannes Gallensis, *Expositio in apocalypsim*, MSS Assisi 50, Todi 68, Breslau Univ. 83 (I.F. 78) and elsewhere. See Dionisio Pacetti, "L'Expositio super Apocalypsim' di Mattia di Svezia," *AFH* 54 (1961): 297–99. Balduinus ab Amsterdam, "The Commentary on St. John's Gospel edited in 1589 under the Name of St. Bonaventure," *Collectanea franciscana* 40 (1970): 71–96, uses still another manuscript of the work. The commentary is attributed to Iohannes by the Todi and Breslau manuscripts but assigned to Vitalis de Furno by Assisi 50.

68. See Pacetti, "L'Expositio super Apocalypsim' di Mattia di Svezia," 297–99. It is attributed to Vital by MSS Assisi 66 and 71, and to both Vital and *fratre Petro doctore sacrosante romane ecclesie* (by different hands) in Assisi 358. A note inside the front cover of 358 argues for authorship by "Petrus," blaming the Vital attribution on confusion caused by the common *incipit*; yet the note appeals for support to the Vitalis attribution in Assisi 50, which we have assigned here to Iohannes Gallensis.

Most of the work found in Assisi 66, etc. is published in Bernardinus Senensis, *Commentarii in apocalypsim*, in *Opera* (Paris, 1635), vol. 3, but the edition turns to a completely different work at Rev. 20:12 and thereafter echoes various authors including Guilelmus de Militona and Nicholas de Lyra. In fact, it differs from the work in Assisi 66, etc. at specific points throughout. I shall cite from MS Assisi 66.

69. Alexander Halensis, *Commentarii in apocalypsim* (Paris, 1647); Bonaventura, *Sancti Bonaventurae . . . Operum . . . Supplementum* (Trent, 1773), 2:1–1037. I shall cite the former.

70. For manuscript evidence and comments on style and date see the analysis by the Quaracchi editors in their prolegomena to Bonaventure's Bible commentaries in *Opera*, 6:ix–xiii.

71. See notes 10 and 11 above.

72. These two Franciscan commentaries and *Vidit Iacob* are apparently bound together by dependence upon a common source, since each finds the other two in agreement against it at some point. Lerner, "Poverty, Preaching and Eschatology," 160–65, shows another web of dependency connecting *Vidit Iacob, Aser pinguis*, Petrus de Tarantasia, and Nicholas Gorranus.

73. Matthaeus de Aquasparta, *Expositio super apocalypsim*, MS Assisi 51. Assisi 57 contains only Rev. 2:13–5:9.

74. Raymundus Rigaldi, *Distinctiones super apocalypsim*, MS Hereford Cathedral P 3.3 (XIV).

75. Smalley, "John Russel O.F.M.," in *Studies in Medieval Thought and Learning* (London, 1981), 212.

76. *Aser pinguis* contains an equally vehement attack, but it is *Vidit Iacob* which "Alexander" and Vital constantly echo. Vital and "Alexander" both describe themselves at one point as in the fourth period, but affirm at another that the time of the predecessors of Antichrist has come "in part."

77. Vital, *Expositio*, 77rb; "Alexander," *Commentarii*, 159; *Vidit Iacob*, 397, says the same.

78. "Alexander," *Commentarii*, 159, 162, 174, 237, 241, 267, 286, 313. *Vidit Iacob*, 364, 367, 408, 435, 445, 483, 489, 492 does the same.

79. *Expositio*, 60va–vb, 63rb–64va, 74ra–vb, 106rb, 117rb–va. This interest is also seen in *Vidit Iacob*, 405 and "Alexander," *Commentarii*, 176 (which reflect the common source) and in "Alexander," *Commentarii*, 301.

80. *Commentarii*, 153, 161, 230, 234, 237, 243, 311, 375. Here again he resembles *Vidit Iacob*, who vigorously attacks victimization of the poor at 345, 395, 469, 482. *Commentarii*, 153, and *Vidit Iacob*, 395, reflect the common source.

81. *Expositio*, 99ra. The text of Assisi 66 is corrupt here, but the edition of the Bernardino *Opera* is correct.

82. E.g. "Alexander," *Commentarii*, 147f., 151, 213, 243, 301, 310, 311., 336, 338; Vital, *Expositio*, 60vb–61rb, 71va–vb, 75va, 127vb, 133rb. See also *Vidit Iacob*, 345, 348, 356, 361, 369, 377, 380, 395, 442, 443, 451, 456, 482, 487, 501.

83. *Vidit Iacob* is particularly concrete and wide-ranging in his criticisms, noting among other things (p. 442): "Mirum est quomodo sacerdos vel clericus eisdem manibus audet tangere corpus Christi, quibus paulo ante tractaverat pudenda meretricis."

84. E.g. "Alexander," *Commentarii*, 151–53; Vital, *Expositio*, 75va; *Vidit Iacob*, 395, 442, 443, 451, 482.

85. *Commentarii*, 310.

86. Ibid., 311.

87. Vital, *Expositio*, 130ra–rb: "*Et mulier quam vidisti est civitas magna*, idest reproborum universitas, vel romana civitas, que habet regnum super reges terre. In quo dominum est imperii universalis et loquitur pro tempore illo in quo vigebat romana ydolatria, vel pro tempore futuro, quando forte ita regnabunt hereses et omnis perfidia, secundum Ioachim, ex omnibus datur intelligi, quod per istum primum quidem regem intelligimus sextum de quo dictum est, *unus est*, sollum illo tempore, oportet congregari reges ad pugnandum cum illo, et ad percutiendum fillios babilonis, qui dicunt se fillios christi et non sunt, sed sunt sinagoga sathane, et quidem illorum intentio, per omnia et in omnibus prava erit, sed tamen inscii et nescientes, facient in utroque volluntatem dei sive occidendo iustos quos oportet coronari martirio, sive iudiciis impiis, a quibus corrupta in sanguibus est terra. Post plagam igitur istam, que iam ex parte inchoata est, erit victoria christianis, et gaudium timentibus verum deum, prostrato capite isto super quo regnat unus rex, et usque ad consumationem de draco." The mention of Rome in connection with 17 : 1 is at *Expositio*, 126r. At 133va, "this great city" in 18 : 17 is identified as "the world or Rome" without further comment.

88. *Vidit Iacob*, 348, 356, 361, 380, 395, 501. At times, he goes well beyond excepting a few. Thus at 380 he says, "Ecclesia tota facta est ut carnalis, fundata in sanguine non Apostolorum, sed nepotulorum et consanguineorum procedens et

per successionem sanguinis; quia fere ubique nepos, avunculus et consanguineus consanguineo succedit in beneficio."

89. *Vidit Iacob*, 414, 452, 471, 475, 476, 482, 485. In some of these passages, the word is used more than once.

90. Ibid., 485.

91. Ibid., 414, 475, 476.

92. Ibid., 414.

93. *Expositio*, 336v. One of Matthew's sermons on Francis uses the passage in precisely this way. See *Sermones de sancto Francisco* (Quaracchi, 1962), 1.

94. *Distinctiones*, 134rb–va.

95. *Expositio*, 64rb. The parallel with Raymond is not surprising if, as seems likely, Vital studied with him at Paris.

96. Florence Bibl. Laur. Conv. Sopp. 239 (Santa Croce 885), 40vb.

97. *Expositio*, 112ra, 116vb–119va. He also offers what he labels as a moral interpretation, applying the passage to all preachers in all ages who preach against the seven deadly sins.

98. *Expositio*, 48ra–rb. Vital mentions no names after the first sentence. "Alexander," *Commentarii*, 79, has almost the same passage but applies it only to John. The other two insignificant references in Vital are at 27va regarding 2:13, where he alludes to Francis's conformity with Christ as a form of martyrdom; and perhaps later when he cites Francis's warning against procrastination (p. 45 in the 1635 edition, although explicit mention of Francis is absent in Assisi 66, 40vb).

99. Ibid., 29vb–30ra.

100. Ibid., 50vb.

101. Ibid., 86va–vb.

102. The 1635 edition (p. 96f.) says "designatur proprie beatissimus pater noster Franciscus," and this reading has some manuscript support. See MS Florence, Bibl. Laur. Conv. Sopp. 547 (Santa Croce 812), 60rb. Assisi 46 says "designatur verissimus pater noster Franciscus." I have not checked the others.

103. *Sermones*, 1: "Describitur autem beatus Franciscus in verbo proposito. . . .Describitur enim . . ."

104. Thus, for example, in *Expositio*, 50rb, when he identifies the seven seals with scripture, he affirms seven senses of scripture.

105. Ibid., f. 73rb.

106. Ibid., f. 118vb: "Firmiter autem estimo quod idem erit ordo predicatorum in quinto statu qui et in quarto, hoc est ordo Christi pauperum, verbum Dei per mundum seminantium." *Vidit Iacob*, 397, makes the same point in similar words: "Nam bene potest fieri ut idem sint predicatores in quinto statu, qui fuerunt in quarto, qui ita sunt de quarto et de quinto ordine. Nam magis attenditur diversitas et ordo statuum ecclesiae, quam diversitas praedicatorum sibi adinvicem succedentium: Apostoli enim multi et suo primo ordine et secundo fuerunt, sicut et multi sub quarto et sub quinto potuerunt simul esse. Non determino tamen quod ita sit." The Parma edition has *desint* instead of *idem sint*, but MS Oxford Bodleian 444, 81ra, uses the latter, and it makes more sense. The connection is noted by Smalley, "John Russel," 237.

107. *Expositio*, MS Assisi 82, ff. 69vb–70vb.

108. John of Wales, *Expositio*, MS Todi 68, 24ra, provides an example of how Joachim edged his way into prefaces as part of a list of *auctoritates*, each with his own particular trait. Ibid., 63rb, offers an example of how Joachim's interpretation could be cited without looking too closely at its special qualities.

109. *Expositio*, 204–206.

110. *Expositio*, 40vb–41ra, which reflects Joachim, *Liber de concordia novi ac veteris testamenti* (Philadelphia, 1983), 139, 286, 409.

111. Compare the treatment of the seven heads of the beast from the sea in Rev. 13 as found in Vital, *Expositio*, 98vb-ra; "Alexander," 236f. (as corrected by Bonelli edition, 574, which offers a more accurate text); and *Vidit Iacob*, 432f.; with Joachim, *Expositio*, 10r–v (actually speaking of the ten heads of the dragon). Or compare the treatment of the ten crowns of the beast in Rev. 13 in concert with the four beasts of Dan. 7 as found in Vital, *Expositio*, 98vb–99ra and *Vidit Iacob*, 433f. with Joachim, *Expositio*, 162r–163v. See also the list of opposites sent by the devil in *Vidit Iacob*, 443, reflecting Joachim, *Expositio in apocalypsim*, 10v. Reeves, *Influence of Prophecy*, 87, notes several of these parallels.

3. Olivi before 1298

So far we have been laying a foundation of sorts by sketching the state of Franciscan apocalyptic thought in Olivi's time. In order to complete the foundation we must say something of Olivi's career up to the moment when he completed the Apocalypse commentary. That is roughly equivalent to describing his entire life, since he was still working on the commentary in 1297, perhaps even early 1298, and died in March 1298.[1]

A Beguin reference to Olivi recorded in Bernard Gui's *Practica inquisitionis* says that Olivi died in the fiftieth year of his life and the thirty-eighth of his vocation as a Franciscan.[2] Thus he must have been born in 1247 or 1248 and entered the order in 1259 or 1260 at the age of twelve, one year before youths were normally admitted.[3] He performed his novitiate at Béziers[4] and eventually was sent to Paris as a student. We cannot say when he arrived in Paris, but the 1260 statutes prohibit provinces from sending students to Paris until they have spent two or three years in a *studium* within their own province, unless they are already so far advanced that they can profit from a Paris education immediately after their novitiates.[5] Olivi must have received some sort of education in Serignan before entering the order—otherwise they would not have let him in at all[6]—but it is hard to believe that at age twelve he would have qualified as the sort of exception foreseen by the 1260 statute. Thus one would not expect him to have arrived in Paris much before the mid-1260s. We know that he heard Bonaventure deliver his *Collationes de septem donis spiritus sancti* in 1268, because Olivi himself tells us so.[7] He may also have been present in 1266 for the Paris general chapter meeting, but that is harder to determine. In his *Tractatus de usu paupere*, Olivi reports that "at Paris in full chapter, with me present," Bonaventure bewailed the laxity prevalent in the order; and in the Apocalypse commentary he announces that "at Paris in the chapter of our brothers, with me listening," Bonaventure preached that Francis's identity as angel of the sixth seal was established "through a revelation that is clear and worthy of faith."[8]

Since the phrase "in full chapter" could simply refer to a meeting of all the brothers at Paris in the chapter house—and in this sense the *Collationes* might be said to have been delivered "in chapter"—these passages do not require one to believe that Olivi is referring to the 1266 general chapter meeting. Nor is there any reason to rule that possibility out. The former passage is the only occasion I can recall when Olivi alludes to an event as occurring "in full chapter," and the sentiments reported there sound like something Bonaventure could have directed to a general chapter meeting. Participation in such a meeting was restricted and Olivi would not have been one of the official delegates; yet even if he could not take part in the deliberations, it seems possible that Paris students would have been allowed to hear the minister general address the full chapter. On the other hand, there is no reason to assume that Olivi's opportunity to hear Bonaventure was limited to general chapter meetings. The minister general must have passed through Paris on other occasions, often enough at any rate for Olivi, reporting on Bonaventure's fleshly weaknesses, to add the words, "as I myself often heard him confess."[9]

Olivi's departure from Paris is equally undocumented. The 1260 statutes say that Parisian studies should continue at least four years unless the brother is already advanced enough to merit a position as lector.[10] Here again Olivi probably did not qualify as an exception, but if he was one of the few exceptional students tapped to work for the *magisterium* he might have stayed substantially longer. He did not become a master, but his comments lead one to believe that he was destined for that end until suspicions concerning his doctrinal soundness interrupted the process and led him to the 1283 censure instead.[11] By that time he had long since left Paris and was functioning as a lector in one or more houses in southern France. That in itself would not suggest that he had been denied the *magisterium*, since it was not unheard of for a Franciscan scholar to study at Paris, become a lector elsewhere, then eventually return to Paris and teach there. Vital du Four seems to have done so. Nor would the sheer length of time involved in Olivi's case suggest derailment. Richard of Middleton, born one year after Olivi, did not become a master until 1284. The most one can say of Olivi's Parisian experience is that it extended to 1268, when he heard Bonaventure deliver the *Collationes de septem donis spiritus sancti*, and probably continued until at least the end of the 1260s. It is unlikely that his stay extended until 1273, since he never mentions having heard Bonaventure deliver his *Collationes in hexaemeron*, nor does he even allude explicitly to them. This is all the more notable in that, as we will see, Olivi's apocalyptic thought shows strong parallels with this work.

Our earliest solid evidence of Olivi's teaching career places him in southern France in the late 1270s. A letter written before his 1283 censure puts him in Montpellier, but another passage suggests that he taught at Narbonne.[12] He was writing long before that, however. In the early 1280s, reacting to two charges against him, he observes that he said something on each subject "before the time of Brother Jerome."[13] Jerome of Ascoli became minister general in 1274. His generalate, which extended to 1279, was not an easy period for Olivi. Jerome presided over a censure of Olivi's views on the Virgin Mary and probably on other topics as well.[14] In 1279 Olivi was in good enough odor with his provincial minister to be asked to write something on Franciscan poverty in connection with the deliberations leading up to the bull *Exiit qui seminat*,[15] but he was soon in trouble again, and this time it escalated until, in 1283, Olivi was censured by seven Parisian scholars who had been assigned the task of evaluating his work.

The story of this censure has been told and need not be rehearsed here.[16] The important thing is that it included no reference to Olivi's apocalyptic thought. We know that even at that time he was already heavily engaged in such speculation, that his bent was already Joachite, and that his Joachism included the threefold division of history as well as the sevenfold division.[17] Something will be said about this early apocalyptic thought in the process of dealing with specific elements in the Apocalypse commentary, but detailed study of it must be reserved for another occasion. For the moment it is sufficient to note that the apocalyptic speculation ignored by the 1283 commission can be found not only in Olivi's Bible commentaries (which they show no sign of having read), but also in the very documents from which they extracted passages for censure. Thus they did not ignore his apocalyptic thought simply because they were unaware of it.

In fact, Olivi specifically informs us that some critics did try to make his apocalyptic speculation an issue. In the letter mentioned earlier, he discusses this topic even though, as he remarks, his correspondents have not asked him about it. He does so, he says, "because some people accuse me of following dreams and fantastic visions like a soothsayer, and of rashly busying myself with the prediction of future events."[18] Olivi begins with the dreams and visions, offering a few ground rules for testing the spirits.[19] Next he considers the predictions, and he is obviously speaking of apocalyptic thought. He insists that he has shunned specificity, never asserting "that this or that would happen during that day or year, or this or that person would do this or that thing." He is certain that the Franciscans, after being purged by innumerable temptations, will reform divine worship throughout the world, but he does not presume to suggest a detailed scenario for this process.

If the censure contains no reference to Olivi's apocalyptic thought, that is partly because the elements that would later cause alarm, though present in earlier works, were not as obvious there as they would be in the Apocalypse commentary. Olivi was censured for a rich variety of philosophical and theological assertions ranging from the nature of quantity to the sacramentality of marriage, and in most cases one is hardly surprised to discover no discernible apocalyptic connection. The one exception is in the realm of Franciscan poverty. The censure contained several items relating to this matter. The earliest of Olivi's *Questions on Evangelical Perfection* to deal with poverty, the eighth (probably written in 1278 or early 1279), does contain several references to the Antichrist. Moreover, it crowns the argument for poverty with an explanation of its apocalyptic significance, using both Joachim's sevenfold and threefold patterns.[20] This section is hardly minor, constituting as it does about 7 percent of a very long question. Nevertheless, question eight deals with the value of poverty and is a late installment in the secular-mendicant controversy, not the intrafraternal battle over *usus pauper* which partly inspired Olivi's censure. In question eight Olivi's thesis is essentially the one defended by his order as a whole. The statements concerning poverty actually censured in 1283 are found in the ninth question, which asks explicitly whether *usus pauper* is an essential part of the vow. Here Olivi, defending the view rejected by leaders of his order, cites most of the arguments already used in question eight to defend poverty, suggesting their relevance to the present subject and often arguing that their efficacy hinges on the assumption that poverty includes restricted use as well as lack of ownership. At times his repetition of the material in question eight is extensive; yet when he arrives at the apocalyptic section he simply remarks that the comments made there are applicable to *usus pauper* and goes on to other matters.[21] Another work on poverty, his *Treatise on Usus Pauper*, does make an explicit connection by saying that the current attack on *usus pauper* as part of the vow is a preparation for the sect of Antichrist, but it says little else about the matter.[22]

Olivi's Bible commentaries from the same period are a slightly different matter. They are rich in apocalyptic speculation, and it is arguable that most of the elements later attacked in the Apocalypse commentary are already present there;[23] yet these elements are not emphasized as they would be in the Apocalypse commentary, and there is no evidence that the 1283 commission had even seen these works.

A second reason why Olivi's apocalyptic speculation escaped censure at this point is that, while ecclesiastical leaders might have wondered whether this aspect of his thought was incorrect, they had not yet been given any reason to see it as subversive. Concrete events had not yet encouraged them to see apocalyptic speculation as an invitation to disorder and rebellion. That would occur only in the 1290s, as we will see in a moment. Of course, given the oddly heterogeneous nature of the assertions censured in 1283, none of the considerations offered so far can completely explain why Olivi's apocalyptic views were not represented there. Such considerations simply suggest why it was more likely to become a target after the 1290s than before.

The 1283 censure ended Olivi's academic prospects for a while, but in 1287 he was rehabilitated and sent to Florence, where he taught at Santa Croce until 1289. Then he was transferred to Montpellier. Eventually he returned to Narbonne, where he was living and presumably teaching when he died in 1298. He seems to have avoided further censures during these years. Others were less fortunate. I have argued elsewhere that the 1290s were a watershed period. They marked the point at which zealots found themselves being persecuted—or simply prosecuted, depending on one's perspective—by their own leaders at the pope's request. In 1290 Nicholas IV ordered the minister general, Raymond Geoffroi, to investigate "certain brothers who seemed to introduce schism into the province of Provence, condemning the state of the other brethren and considering themselves to be more spiritual than the others." This inquiry resulted in the punishment of several brothers at the 1292 general chapter held in Paris.[24] While Olivi was not included in the censure, he had to attend the chapter and explain his view of *usus pauper*.[25] Thus *usus pauper* was clearly an issue, although there is no evidence that apocalyptic thought was also involved.

An even more significant investigation was initiated by Boniface VIII. A hazy but instructive picture of his target can be derived from a series of letters written by Boniface in 1296 and 1297; from a letter by King Charles II of Naples referring to another of Boniface's letters, now unfortunately missing; from a much later letter by Angelo Clareno responding to charges contained in that missing document; and from still another letter by Olivi written in 1295.[26] From this multifarious collection of documents we gather that the pope had become concerned about unauthorized groups that dressed and acted like religious orders, mainly like the Franciscan order. These groups, composed of laymen and renegade *religiosi* (also mainly Franciscan), often claimed to observe the Franciscan rule. Some of them felt that they were, in effect, the only priests and leaders left in the church, since God had withdrawn all spiritual authority from the pope and his underlings. Their condemnation was aimed particularly at Boniface, whose election they saw as invalid not only on moral grounds (since he, like several popes before him, had encouraged the Franciscan order to compromise the rule), but on legal grounds as well (because his predecessor's resignation was illegal). The group that opposed Boniface was willing to make this issue a test of faith. Those who accepted him as pope were portrayed as part of the synagogue of Satan and thus outside the true church. The words of Revelation 18:4, "Come out of her, my people," were being taken by the rebels as a call to separate from the corrupt institution loyal to Boniface.

The roots of this crisis are not hard to discern. While Olivi was negotiating his career in France, a parallel rigorist movement had been growing in Italy. In the 1270s and 1280s it had precipitated a serious clash in the March of Ancona and several leaders were imprisoned. They were freed in 1290 by order of Raymond Geoffroi, who had just been elected minister general, but the continued hostility of their Italian superiors led Raymond to send the zealots to Armenia. There they eventually encountered more hostility and returned to Italy. With Raymond's encouragement, they appealed to Pope Celestine V, who established them as a separate group, the Poor Hermits of Pope Celestine, thus leaving them free to observe the Franciscan rule as strictly as they wished, but outside the Franciscan order. When Celestine resigned in December 1294 after about four months in office and was succeeded by Boniface VIII, one of Boniface's first official acts was to rescind most of Celestine's legislation. Thus, rather than saving the zealots from their superiors, Celestine had given the superiors one more grievance against them and then left the zealots open to their wrath.[27]

For the moment, the superiors could not expect to use their position to full advantage. Franciscan zealots were not the only people upset by Boniface's election. In the following months an odd coalition of enemies kept the pope busy, and persecuting superiors could hardly expect to get his undivided attention, let alone his full cooperation. Moreover, the zealots found in Raymond Geoffroi as sympathetic a minister general as they would ever encounter. Thus their Italian superiors could apply only limited pressure for a while. One gets the impression from the letters mentioned earlier (and from other evidence like the career of Jacopone da Todi during this period)[28] that the zealots entered upon paths that were diverse and occasionally exotic.[29] Some, including Angelo Clareno, discretely departed for Greece. Others remained in Italy and threw themselves into the campaign against Boniface. Still others remained but attempted to be apolitical.

Olivi's response to these events was not only a *quaestio* defending the legitimacy of Celestine's resignation but a letter to Conrad of Offida, an Italian zealot leader, condemning those who repudiated Boniface.[30] The letter has provoked charges of hypocrisy from several scholars, but it is quite consistent with Olivi's general attitude toward reform and his apocalyptic timetable as well[31] The reform he sought was less radical than the one being furthered by these Italian zealots, and—as we shall see—his apocalyptic program, while it envisioned an inevitable moment of confrontation between the elect and the carnal church in the relatively near future, did not affirm that the moment was already at hand in 1297, much less 1295.

We will deal with the apocalyptic timetable later. For the moment it is his reform program that bears examination. The difference between Olivi and the recalcitrant Italians is that a large number of the latter accepted not only the rule but Francis's *Testament* as binding, and took their image of Francis and the early order not from Bonaventure's *Legenda maior* but from extracanonical material like the so-called Leo sources and a variety of oral traditions purporting to reflect the reminiscences of Francis's early companions.[32] The Italian zealots tended to see papal declarations concerning the rule, scholarly rule commentaries on it, and most thirteenth-century Franciscan legislation elaborating it as dilutions of the authentic Franciscan life. They also felt that their struggle with their superiors was simply the latest chapter in a long history of conflict going back to Francis's own time, when Brother Elias had taken control of the order and begun to steer it off course.

Olivi, on the other hand, accepted most of the developments that had transformed the Franciscan order in previous decades. His reforming ideals, like Bonaventure's, were directed at negative aspects of that transformation, not at the transformation itself. He insisted that Franciscan bishops were required to observe *usus pauper*, but he did not reject the notion of Franciscan bishops. He wanted to limit the control Franciscans exercised over procurators, who received donations for them and saw to their needs; but he accepted the idea of procurators. He was clearly uncomfortable with what he found in some papal declarations, rule commentaries, and legislation, but he accepted the validity of all three, citing them as authorities when they supported his position and discretely ignoring them when they did not.

Of course it is hard to find the representative Italian zealot just described. Some would nominate Angelo Clareno for the role, but it is difficult to equate the man we encounter in Angelo's letters and in *Historia septem tribulationum* with the position opposed by Olivi in his letter to Conrad of Offida. In fact, we have no reason to assume that Angelo was saying in 1295 precisely what he later said in the letters and *Historia*.[33] Moreover, the Italian spirituals were hardly an organized body and it is clear that some—Conrad of Offida comes to mind—probably stood slightly to Angelo's right, others (like the rebels attacked by Olivi) substantially to his left. Nevertheless, when we compare Angelo with Olivi the contrast is instructive. During the years when Angelo was moving in and out of Italy, in and out of confinement, Olivi was occupying a moderately prestigious role as lector in a series of unexceptional convents. He probably grumbled about decline in the order, but it is plausible that he passed his later life in Montpellier and Narbonne without ever feeling that his acceptance of living standards there constituted a violation of his vows.

However that may be, the events of the 1290s must have had a profound effect on the pope's attitude toward both apocalyptic speculation and the *usus pauper* controversy. In his letter to Conrad of Offida, Olivi predicted that the radical Italian zealots would give enemies of reform a convincing argument to use in gaining papal support, and he was probably right. Olivi wrote in September 1295. In October Boniface removed Raymond Geoffroi from his position as minister general. In May of the following year, in an election held at Anagni and undoubtedly supervised by the pope, John of Murrovalle became Raymond's successor.[34] We cannot assume that that Boniface's sole motive was to secure a minister general who would act with greater vigor against the zealots, for there were other factors which might have made the change seem desirable;[35] yet the fact remains that, two years after taking office, John did launch a concerted attack on the zealots, and with papal support. It would be understandable if the behavior of Italian zealots during the period after Celestine's resignation led Boniface to see the *usus pauper* controversy as a disciplinary problem calling for decisive action, and Franciscan apocalyptic thought as a volatile element in that problem.

In other words, the climate of opinion within the higher leadership of both church and order may have shifted in the middle and later 1290s in such a way as to make it much more attentive to and suspicious of Franciscan apocalyptic, just as it was less tolerant of dissenting views on *usus pauper*. The disruptive possibilities of both had been revealed. Conversely, the events of the 1290s may have caused a hardening of attitude on the part of the dissenters as well. As we will see in dealing with the fourteenth-century condemnation of Olivi's commentary, apocalyptic interpretation of the *usus pauper* controversy often functioned as a self-fulfilling prophecy. It not only encouraged dissenters to take a strong stand but provided a context in which punishment of dissent functioned as evidence that the dissenters were righteous and the persecutors minions of Antichrist. Thus such punishment was more likely to corroborate the dissenters' views than to alter them.

It was in this altered atmosphere that Olivi wrote his Apocalypse commentary. The new situation would affect the way both zealots and leaders read his commentary; but how did it affect the author himself? Was his own situation becoming more precarious? Our only evidence suggesting as much comes from his letter to the three sons of King Charles II of Naples, who were currently being held as hostages in Catalonia.[36] They had invited Olivi to come and administer spiritual counsel. In May 1295, only four months before his letter to Conrad of Offida, Olivi replied. He offered three reasons why it might not be a good idea: his habitual avoidance of worldly glory; the problem of getting permission; and their father's fear that he might "beguinize" (*inbeguiniri*) them, an early reference to the pious laypersons who supported the Franciscan rigorists and would themselves become the target of inquisitorial investigation. This much sounds negative, yet the total impression one receives is that Olivi really wants to go. He states no less than three times that he is willing to make the trip, and on one occasion he suggests that if the princes really want him, they should do what they can to get the necessary travel authority from secular authorities. He reveals that he himself has gained the conditional assent of Raymond Geoffroi, who was still minister general at that date. Most intriguing, he suggests that if they want him they should send word soon, since "if I do not come to you I may have to hurry off somewhere else."[37] This sounds ominous. Perhaps he simply means that he might die, but the letter does not give that impression. May 1295 seems early for French rigorists to have felt the effect of events in Italy, but perhaps their situation had continued to deteriorate since the early 1290s.

Of course, four months after writing the princes, Olivi penned his letter to Conrad of Offida defending Boniface's election. Warren Lewis suggests that the real change in Olivi's perspective actually began one month later when Boniface removed Raymond Geoffroi, who was sympathetic toward Olivi's aims and may have been a personal friend.[38] His pessimism deepened the following May when, probably thanks to Boniface, John of Murrovalle was elected. John had served on the commission that censured Olivi in 1283. Olivi began to ask whether his acceptance of Boniface might have been premature, and it was in this mood that he began his Apocalypse commentary. Lewis's suggestion is intriguing, but consideration of it must be delayed until the chapter on Antichrist.

Notes

1. For his date of death see David Burr, *The Persecution of Peter Olivi* (Philadelphia, 1976), 5.
2. Bernardus Guidonis, *Practica inquisitionis heretice pravitatis* (Paris, 1886), 287.
3. See Olivi's comments on the proper age of admission in *Lectura super Matthaeum*, MS Oxford New College 49, 118va–vb and *Lectura super Marcum*, MS Rome Vat. Ottob. lat. 3302, 32v.
4. *Lectura super Lucam*, MS Rome Vat. Ottab. lat. 3302, 32v.
5. Bihl, "Statuta generalia ordinis," 72.
6. H. Felder, *Geschichte des wissenschaftlichen Studien im Franziskanerorden bis um Mitte des 13. Jahrhunderts* (Freiburg i. Br., 1904), 332–42 discusses minimum educational requirements for entrance into the order.
7. In the sixteenth of his *Quaestiones de perfectione evangelica* as edited in David Burr and David Flood, "Peter Olivi: On Poverty and Revenue," *Franciscan Studies* 40 (1980): 47, Olivi narrates that "frater Bonaventura me audiente optime exposuit" concerning the number of the beast. What follows is essentially the interpretation given by Bonaventure in the *Collationes* in question. See *Opera*, 5:497. Olivi had cited the same passage in his *Quaestiones in secundum librum sententiarum* (Quaracchi, 1921–26), 1:98, but incorrectly. See David Burr, "The Apocalyptic Element in Olivi's Critique of Aristotle," 21–23. Bonaventure could have offered the same interpretation on some other occasion, but we do not know about it.
8. *Quaestio de usu paupere and Tractatus de usu paupere*, (Florence, 1992), 138: "Nichilominus tamen in tantum dolebat de communibus laxationibus huius temporis quod parisius in pleno capitulo me astante dixit quod ex quo fuit generalis nunquam fuit quin vellet esse pulverizatus ut ordo ad puritatem beati Francisci et sotiorum eius et ad illud quod ipse de ordine suo intendebat perveniret"; *Lectura*, 393f.: "Et hoc ipsum per claram et fide dignam revelationem est habitum, prout a fratre Bonaventura solemnissimo sacre theologie magistro ac nostri ordinis quondam generali ministro fuit Parisius in fratrum nostrorum capitulo, me audiente, solemniter predicatum."

9. Ibid.: "Fragilis tamen fuit secundum corpus et forte in hoc aliquid humanum sapiens quod et ipse humiliter sicut ego ipse ab eo sepius audivi confitebatur."

10. Bihl, "Statuta," 72.

11. This seems the underlying message of his opening comments in his letter to the unidentified "R," in *Quodlibeta* (Venice, 1509), 51(63)v. On the comments and their meaning, see Burr, *Persecution*, 32.

12. For reference to Montpellier in the letter to "R" see *Quodlibeta*, 53(65)r. For the date of this letter see Burr, *OFP*, 40–42. For reference to Narbonne see *Questiones in secundum librum sententiarum* (Quaracchi, 1922–24), 1:633. The *Series condemnationum factarum de erroribus quos frater Petrus Iohannis docuit*, a fourteenth-century document, says that some of Olivi's errors were condemned at a meeting in Montpellier during Jerome of Ascoli's generalate. See Leo Amoròs, "Series condemnationum et processuum contra doctrinam et sequaces Petri Ioannis Olivi," *AFH* 24 (1931): 502. That does not place Olivi in Montpellier, but it does place him in southern France sometime during Jerome's generalate (1274–79).

13. *Quodlibeta*, 51(63)v and 52(64)r.

14. See the evidence in my *Persecution*, 35–37.

15. See ibid., 11.

16. On the censure see ibid., 35–66. For a closer look at the poverty issue in the censure see my *OFP*, 88–105.

17. Kevin Madigan, "Peter Olivi's *Lectura super Matthaeum* in Medieval Exegetical Context" (doctoral dissertation, University of Chicago, 1992), demonstrates as much for that work. See also my *OFP*, 172–83, and my "Apokalyptische Erwartung und die Entstehung der Usus-pauper Kontroverse," *Wissenschaft und Weisheit* 47 (1984): 84–99.

18. *Quodlibeta*, 53(65)r.

19. On Olivi's attitude toward visions see Burr, "Olivi, Apocalyptic Expectation, and Visionary Experience," *Traditio* 41 (1985): 273–85.

20. *Das Heil der Armen und das Verderben der Reichen* (Werl/Westfalen, 1989), especially 148–61.

21. *De usu paupere*, 32.

22. Ibid., 148.

23. See especially Madigan, "Peter Olivi's *Lectura super Matthaeum*," ch. 5.

24. *Chronica XXIV generalium*, 420–22.

25. See Burr, *OFP*, 108f.

26. On these sources see ibid., 112–24.

27. On Celestine see Peter Herde, *Cölestin V* (Stuttgart, 1981).

28. On Jacopone see George Peck, *The Fool of God* (University, Ala., 1980).

29. See my discussion in *OFP*, 112–24.

30. *Quaestio* and letter published in Livarius Oliger, "Petri Iohannis Olivi de renuntiatione papae Coelestini V quaestio et epistola," *AFH*, 11 (1918): 309–73 (letter at 366–73).

31. *OFP*, 155f.

32. See Rosalind Brooke, *Scripta Leonis* (Oxford, 1970).

33. On this subject see my passing comments in *OFP*, 122–24 and the exten-

sive remarks of Gian Luca Potestà, *Angelo Clareno* (Rome, 1990). Potestà agrees that Angelo is not the target of Olivi's letter, emphasizes that Angelo's writings reflect a later time, and detects a progression of thought even within the letters. For a biography see Lydia von Auw, *Angelo Clareno* (Rome, 1979).

34. Luke Wadding, *Annales minorum*, 5:348.

35. On the John-Boniface relationship see my *OFP*, 125–28.

36. Published in *Archiv*, 3:534–540.

37. Ibid., 539: "Si super meo adventu aliquid imperare et providere dignamini, placeat vobis michi cito mandare, quia si ad vos non venio, ad locum alterum forsitan festinare habebo." Warren Lewis, "Peter John Olivi: Prophet of the Year 2000" (doctoral dissertation, Tübingen University, 1972), introduction, 66f., brought this line to my attention. Lewis, 382 n.257 remarks, "I think Olivi wanted very badly to get away from Narbonne."

38. "Peter John Olivi," introduction, 72–74, 227–29. On Raymond see my *Persecution*, 37; Pierre Péano, "Raymond Geoffroi, ministre général et défenseur des spirituels," *Picenum seraphicum* 11 (1974): 190–203.

4. The Fifth Period

We are finally ready to examine the Apocalypse commentary. The fifth period might seem an odd place to begin, though. What happened to the first four? They certainly exist, but they are much less important for our purposes and for Olivi himself than the last three. Nevertheless, at least some attention should be given to them, and the simplest way to do so is to look briefly at the preface to Olivi's commentary, in which he describes the basic pattern of church history and lays down a few hermeneutical principles. That Olivi's Apocalypse commentary should begin with a preface is not in itself unusual, since most thirteenth-century commentaries began with general observations concerning the work. What is unusual about Olivi's preface is the extent to which it provides the principles actually used in the rest of the commentary and summarizes the basic historical pattern depicted there. Olivi's commentary is a remarkably coherent document.

The Seven Visions and Periods

Within the first few lines of his preface, Olivi makes two basic assertions that place him within the main line of thirteenth-century mendicant exegesis: the Apocalypse contains seven visions, and it describes seven periods of church history. Nevertheless, Olivi goes on to define both his agreement and disagreement with this tradition by considering twelve questions; then, as an encore of sorts, he adds a thirteenth. Some of these questions are more important than others, and even some of the more important ones can be ignored at present, since they deal with matters to be covered later in this work. For the moment we will examine only the most basic issues.

Olivi begins by laying out the seven periods. The first four are essentially those offered by what we have described as the accepted exegetical strategy among mendicant scholars during Olivi's time as a student. They are the periods of the apostles, the martyrs, the doctors, and the anchorites. The last three periods are also much the same, but with significant alterations. Whereas other exegetes see the fifth period as that of the precursors of Antichrist, Olivi views it as a time of condescension in which the church has grown in size and wealth but simultaneously become more lax until, by the end of the period, "practically the whole church from head to foot is corrupted and thrown into disorder and turned, as it were, into a new Babylon."[1] Note the shift in tense. Olivi is speaking of his own time. Among the scholarly exegetes mentioned so far (here as elsewhere we exclude Alexander Minorita), the few who make any attempt to place themselves in history opt for the beginning of the fifth period. Olivi puts himself at its end, so late that (as we will see) the sixth period already has dawned. As far as he is concerned, the fifth period began in the eighth century with the Carolingians. Normally he dates it from Charlemagne, but he is also willing to begin with Pepin.[2]

In dealing with the sixth period, too, Olivi makes a significant adjustment. He agrees with preceding commentators that it will be the period of Antichrist, but insists that it is already one of renewal. This renewal began to some extent in the time of Saint Francis, but will begin in a fuller sense after the destruction of Babylon.[3] It involves "renewal of the evangelical life, destruction of Antichrist's sect, and final conversion of the Jews and Gentiles, or rebuilding of the church as it originally was."[4] It also entails new knowledge.[5]

Much of what Olivi says about the sixth period suggests that its significance can be seen only in the light of the seventh. In fact, the peace and illumination of the seventh period will be a continuation and fulfillment of the renewal appearing in the sixth. In effect, he joins the two periods into a single age in which the church militant will gradually conform to the church triumphant as much as is possible in this life. The development will not be unopposed. It is, in fact, already being opposed by the carnal church and will eventually be assaulted by Antichrist. Thus, rather than anticipating a future pattern of decline in the fifth period leading to Antichrist in the sixth and then a brief respite in the seventh, Olivi projects a more complex pattern in which the contemporary reform of the dawning sixth period is first opposed by the lingering vestiges of the fifth period, then will be attacked by the Antichrist, but will finally emerge triumphant and blossom into the seventh period.

The seventh period contains a progression within itself, since it pertains both to the final stage of history and to eternal bliss. "Insofar as it pertains to this life, it is a certain quietus and a marvelous participation in the future glory, as if the heavenly Jerusalem had descended to earth. According as it pertains to the next life, however, it is the period of the general resurrection, the glorification of the saints, and the final consummation of all things." The seventh period can also be identified with the state of holy souls before they reclaim their bodies.[6]

At first glance, this might all seem rather indefinite. The dawn of the sixth period is identified with one event which happened close to a century earlier, and with another that has not yet occurred. The seventh period is identified with three different things. Nevertheless, Olivi's basic vision is clear. He takes the notion of historical development seriously. The church is progressing through a series of stages, each of which makes some contribution. Even the condescensive fifth period has a positive role to play. Olivi's sixth period represents another link in the historical process, but it represents more than just another link. It is the hinge on which all of later church history turns. It is organically related to the fifth period in much the same way it was for other mendicant commentators. Antichrist in the sixth period is the culmination of a long decline already underway in the fifth. Nevertheless, because Olivi parts company from other commentators in seeing the sixth period as a time of renewal, he can also see it as organically related to the seventh period of peace and contemplation. The seventh period witnesses a fulfillment of the renewal born in the sixth.

Olivi is aware that historical periods do not change like stoplights, but rather fade out gradually like the smile on the Cheshire cat. Or, to use the image Olivi himself employs, each period is nurtured in the womb of the preceding one.[7] Sometimes it can be a very long gestation period indeed. In the case of the second and third periods, we find an early doctor like Clement of Alexandria writing a century before Constantine brought the period of the martyrs to a close. In the case of the third and fourth, we discover that Athanasius and Anthony were contemporaries. In the case of the fifth and sixth, the overlap already has lasted a century in Olivi's time.[8]

Like other mendicant commentators, Olivi sees each period as characterized by a specific evil assaulting the church and by a specific group called into being to combat that evil. Thus the first period pitted the apostles against the Jews, the second the martyrs against the pagan Roman empire, the third the doctors against the heretics, the fourth the anchorites against the lax, and so on. This dialectical relationship between good and evil provides part of the dynamic through which the church progresses.

The Three Ages

Like Joachim of Fiore, Olivi combines his pattern of double sevens with a threefold division of world history into the ages of Father, Son, and Holy Spirit.[9] He begins his commentary with a quotation from Isaiah 30:26: "The light of the moon will be like the light of the sun, and the light of the sun will be sevenfold, like the light of seven days, on the day when the Lord binds up the wound of his people and heals the blow struck against them." These words, Olivi says, literally prophesy the illumination to come at the end of history, but they refer allegorically to Christ and the New Testament. Somewhat later, he returns to the Isaiah passage in the process of explaining why the sixth period is always described as preeminent over the first five. Here he applies Isaiah's prediction to two moments in church history, the beginning of the church and the sixth and seventh periods. He comments that, "just as in Christ's first advent the sun shone seven times brighter than before, so will it in the sixth period and more fully in the seventh."[10]

Shortly thereafter Olivi cites the Isaiah passage once again, noting that "in the sixth period the sun of Christian knowledge will shine sevenfold, like the light of seven days."[11] In these later evocations of the passage, Olivi makes it clear that he envisages a threefold division of history, and in one case he identifies it as "a solemn and admirable representation of God's supreme trinity and unity."[12]

While Olivi's threefold division is essentially Joachite, his chronological division of the periods is more straightforward than Joachim's.[13] The age of the Father ran to the birth of Christ, while that of the Son extended from Christ to the time of Saint Francis and included the first five periods of church history. The age of the Holy Spirit comprises the sixth and seventh periods. Like Joachim, Olivi occasionally seems to identify it with the seventh period alone, but that is understandable. The third age is in the process of formation throughout the sixth period, and will be completely realized (in an earthly way) only in the seventh.

The Principle of *Concordia*

If Olivi accepts both the Joachite sevenfold and threefold patterns, does he also follow Joachim (and, more immediately, Saint Bonaventure) in positing a *concordia* between Old and New Testament events? He does, but not very systematically or at any great length. It is significant that his discussion of this matter appears in the thirteenth topic proposed by him for consideration in the preface. He begins by saying that he will address twelve topics, but then, after listing them, throws in a thirteenth.[14] Thus his discussion inevitably strikes one as somewhat of an afterthought. To be sure, it is a rather prolix afterthought. Olivi demonstrates how the seven periods of the church can be related to the seven ecclesiastical sacraments, seven days of creation, seven ages of world history, and seven periods of Old Testament history.[15] He concludes with a tribute to the virtues of *concordia*: "If you match the various sevenfold patterns in scripture with those in this book, innumerable mysteries will be clarified as long as you diligently attend to their *concordia* and parallel meaning."[16] Nevertheless, it is not a task Olivi himself pursues with any great resolution. His lack of interest does not mean that the Joachite concordances are unimportant to him. On the contrary, they are very important indeed. The reason he says so little about them is that he is commenting on the Apocalypse and, like Joachim himself, concentrates on what that work can tell him about church history.

Olivi's Debt to Joachim

What we have said so far about Olivi's acceptance of the three ages and the principle of *concordia* suggests that he was heavily indebted to Joachim of Fiore. This point is worth emphasizing because, in his study of the Apocalypse commentary, Raoul Manselli maintains that Olivi "considers Joachim an authority like all the others," values Richard of St. Victor just as highly, and eschews Joachim's trinitarian reading of history.[17] The final assertion is, as we have seen, incorrect. Olivi not only accepts but makes substantial use of Joachim's pattern of threes as well as his pattern of sevens. Nevertheless, the first two comments, concerning Olivi's view of Joachim simply as one more authority and his equal respect for Richard, demand further analysis.

Manselli is correct in suggesting that Olivi is willing to reject Joachim's views on occasion and that he cites Richard as much as he does Joachim; yet such observations take us only part of the way toward understanding Olivi's position. His attitude toward Joachim separates him from the mainstream of thirteenth-century mendicant exegesis.[18] Many of the commentators mentioned in chapter two are willing to mention Joachim and even cite him as an authority. He is treated as one of many authorities, and certainly not one of the most prominent. Compared, for example, with Bede, Haymo, or the *Glossa*, he receives little attention. Commentators are occasionally willing to try their hand at a Joachite *concordia* or echo his interpretation of a particular passage; yet they normally introduce him in contexts which do not force serious consideration of what is distinctive in his theology of history.[19] His trinitarian view of history is discretely omitted.

Olivi proceeds in a strikingly different manner. He apparently writes with three books before him: the Apocalypse itself, Joachim's commentary, and Richard of St. Victor's commentary. One gets the impression that he is proceeding methodically through all three works. Joachim and Richard are cited constantly. These are almost the only commentaries he mentions. Whereas other Franciscan commentators make ample use of Bede, Haymo, and the *Glossa*, Olivi cites the *Glossa* only twice and does not mention Bede or Haymo at all. Other Franciscan exegetes depend upon Augustine's *City of God* for their interpretation of Revelation 20. Olivi discusses Augustine at that point but largely rejects him, as we will see.

One might ask, of course, whether Olivi's limited set of *auctoritates* reveals his preferences or his library. It may reflect the latter, but it certainly reflects the former. Olivi has chosen to explore the Apocalypse with two scholars whom he respects. Nevertheless, he does not respect them equally or even in the same way. Richard is an intelligent man to whom Olivi listens carefully, but whom he is willing to reject, occasionally rather sharply.[20] Joachim is a prophet. Olivi remarks that the third age had "a certain prophetic beginning" in "the revelation accorded to the abbot Joachim and perhaps to certain others of his time."[21] He is quite serious about the word "revelation." In his Isaiah commentary, in the process of asking whether the prophets could have been given certain knowledge of future contingents, Olivi surveys the varieties of prophetic experience as seen in Isaiah, Balaam, Daniel, John the Divine, Nebuchadnezzar, the pharaoh who *did* know Joseph, Joseph himself, Caiaphas, the Virgin Mary, and Joachim. He argues that Daniel was given "some habitual knowledge or wisdom concerning the general laws or rules of divine providence, by which God rules all things and especially human affairs." Daniel used this knowledge to judge the meaning of the king's dream in much the same way we draw conclusions from universal principles. We know these principles without any argumentation whatsoever, and from them we draw some conclusions necessarily and others only probably.

In this way Joachim, in his *Concordia* and commentary on the Apocalypse, says he suddenly received the entire concordance of the Old and New Testaments in the form of certain general rules, from which he now deduces certain things through argumentation in such a way that he considers some of his conclusions to be certain and others to be nothing more than probable conjecture which might often be incorrect.[22]

Our natural reason works in the same way. Without any argumentation, we know certain first principles from which we draw some conclusions necessarily and others only probably. Thus, even if Joachim's writings contain error, it does not follow that he received no divine illumination. Olivi explains that he is belaboring this point because some people have wished to argue from Joachim's mistakes that his views came entirely from human conjecture or even from the devil.

Olivi returns to this theme in the Apocalypse commentary, commenting that

on this and similar matters Joachim was offering opinions, not making assertions. For just as, through the natural light of our intellects, we know some things unquestionably as first principles, know others as conclusions necessarily deduced from these principles, and hold still others only as opinions formed on the basis of probable argument; and in the latter case we are often wrong, yet the concreated light granted to us is not on that account false, nor are we incorrect insofar as we recognize that our opinions are not infallible; thus the light given freely to us through revelation knows certain things as first and unquestionable revealed principles, knows others as conclusions necessarily deduced from those principles, and holds certain views merely as probable and conjectural opinions formed on the basis of these [first principles and necessary conclusions]. This is what seems to have occurred in the case of the knowledge of scripture and the concordance of New and Old Testaments given by revelation to the Abbot Joachim, as he himself asserts.[23]

To state the matter in this way is to reveal part of Joachim's advantage over other *auctoritates*, but not all of it. His advantage lies not only in the special revelation granted him but in his historical position, as we will see in the next chapter. On the other hand, that same historical position explains some of his errors. Olivi remarks that "the great light given to [Joachim] in the dawn, as it were, of the third age was mixed with shadows in the knowledge of future events, particularly since the night shadows of the fifth period engulfed his time." For that reason we inevitably find mistakes in his work, but we can be sure that such erroneous statements were offered, not as assertions, but merely as opinions.[24]

Thus Olivi maps out a view of Joachim that raises him above the mass of human exegetes, yet not so far as to make him unquestionable. It is noteworthy that Olivi consistently identifies Joachim's illumination with his principle of *concordia*. One suspects that in Olivi's eyes the *concordia* revealed to Joachim involves more than the principle of double sevens relating the New and Old Testaments. It also involves the various threefold patterns and the relationship between the sevenfold and threefold patterns. These aspects of Joachite thought are fundamental to Olivi's exegesis and comprise the way in which he can be called profoundly Joachite. Eclectic and inventive, he does not relate his patterns in precisely the same way as Joachim, or even offer precisely the same patterns. He interprets Joachim in the light of Franciscan tradition and thirteenth-century history.

The Seven Periods as Subject of All Seven Visions

Olivi also seems to depart from previous mendicant commentators (and to embrace the unstated premise of Bonaventure's *Collationes in hexaeme-ron*) in asserting that all seven periods of church history are the subject of all seven visions in the Apocalypse. Whereas most mendicant exegetes before him had referred to four visions concerning the *status generalis* of the church followed by three on the *status finalis*, Olivi argues that the seven periods are the literal meaning of visions two through seven, while the first vision is allegorically about the seven periods and literally about the seven churches to which the letters are addressed.[25] This sevenfold pattern in each vision is underscored by Olivi's suggestion that one can learn about the seventh period by studying not only the seventh vision, but the seventh member of each preceding vision, just as one can learn about the sixth period by studying the sixth vision and the sixth part of each vision.[26]

To state the matter thus suggests that Olivi sees each of the six visions as emphasizing the corresponding period, so that the first vision is principally about the first period and secondarily about all the rest, and so forth; yet that is not the way things actually work in his commentary. The first vision, the letters to the seven churches (Revelation 1:1–8), is special inasmuch as according to Olivi it is literally about those particular seven churches and only spiritually about the seven periods. Thus one would expect him to pay more attention to the early church in expositing it, but he does not.[27] Nor can his exegesis of the second vision, the opening of the seven seals (4:1–8:1), be said to favor the second period in any obvious way. Over half of it deals with the sixth seal, which is interpreted in connection with the sixth period. His treatment of the third vision, that of the seven trumpets (8 : 2–11 : 18), proceeds through the seven periods of church history, in the process devoting five pages to the third period and eighty-six to the sixth. The fourth vision—covering the woman pursued by a dragon into the wilderness, the beasts arising from land and sea, and the angels announcing the fall of Babylon (11 : 19–14 : 20)—provides Olivi with a major text for his treatment of the two Antichrists, which belong to the late fifth and the sixth periods. In examining the fifth vision, the pouring out of the seven vials (15 : 1–16 : 17), Olivi distributes his attention evenly across church history. His exegesis of the sixth vision, the judgment of Babylon (16 : 18–?),[28] does concentrate heavily on the sixth period, however, and his commentary on the seventh vision, the new heaven and earth (?–22 : 15), deals almost exclusively with the seventh, thus conforming to his announcement in the preface that the seven periods are not distinguished in the seventh vision as they are in the first six.[29] This concentration on the sixth and seventh periods in dealing with the last two visions serves to decrease the actual distance between Olivi and other exegetes, since it moves him closer to the standard mendicant 4/3 pattern. He does explicitly present the fifth vision as a trip through all seven periods, but, as we have seen, so did most mendicant commentators. Hugh of St. Cher explicitly acknowledged as much by speaking of a 5/2 pattern rather than a 4/3 pattern.

The hermeneutical web spun in Olivi's preface is an intricate one. We have seen that, in addition to speaking of seven periods within seven visions, he suggests briefly how the seven periods of church history conform to the seven sacraments, the seven days of creation, the seven ages of world history, and the seven periods of Old Testament history in such a way that an understanding of one illuminates the others.[30] He also describes seven offices or activities performed in the church and insists that all seven are present in each period, although one is preeminent in each period. Moreover, each vision relates primarily to one office.[31] All of these elements appear within his exegesis, although all do not deserve equal attention. The sacraments and days of creation are of minor concern, and the offices, though more important, are not an essential datum in understanding Olivi's exegetical strategy. The parallel with Old Testament history is seldom explicitly mentioned but, as we will see, is very important indeed. So is the parallel with world history. These last two are basic elements in Olivi's notion of *concordia*.

The resultant commentary is not easy reading. It is long (1,002 pages in the Lewis edition) and very dense. Two ordering principles render service: Olivi works consecutively, line by line, through the text; and in ex-positing the sevenfold visions he explicitly relates each letter, seal, trumpet, or vial to a period of church history. The other ordering principles mentioned above are present but often work implicitly, lying slightly beneath the surface. Thus, initially at least, they offer little aid to the reader. Moreover, like other commentators, Olivi relates the text to history, theology, and spirituality, and may switch without warning from one to the other. The same passage may be related to a period, an individual, a particular virtue or sin, the human soul, Christ, and so forth. Olivi shifts the balance, devoting more of his commentary to history than the other mendicant exegetes mentioned so far; yet a substantial part of his commentary is still devoted not to the literal sense but to the spiritual senses.

Mention of the spiritual senses prepares us for the last general point to be made about Olivi's hermeneutical principles. Whatever else they contain, they do not address the standard four senses of scripture—the literal, allegorical, anagogical, and moral—familiar to students of medieval thought. He refers to them in dealing with the four beasts of Revelation 4: 66, the book written within and without (Revelation 5:11), and the four beasts of Revelation 6:6,[32] but they play no significant role in his exegesis. Neither he nor other mendicant exegetes think of themselves as systematically applying the four senses to their text. Nevertheless, Olivi is very conscious of applying a twofold distinction between the literal sense and another which he terms the mystical or spiritual.[33] Sometimes he distinguishes between what should be taken literally and what should be taken "spiritually and allegorically,"[34] without bothering to explain how the latter two differ. We must return to this matter in our discussion of the sixth period. The important point for the moment is that Olivi proceeds from a twofold rather than a fourfold distinction.

The Preface and Mendicant Exegetical Tradition

We turn from Olivi's preface to the rest of his commentary already aware that his relation to previous Franciscan thought is complex and rather ambiguous. In positing seven visions and seven periods of church history, he is simply following the main line of exegetical tradition. In suggesting that all seven visions deal with all seven periods, he is departing from previous exegetes and reflecting Bonaventure, although in actual procedure Olivi and his fellow exegetes are closer than this theoretical difference might suggest. His view of the sixth period as both positive and negative, his belief that he himself is in the sixth period, and his dependence on the Joachite principle of *concordia* distinguish him from previous Franciscan commentators but place him in step with Bonaventure. His explicit and enthusiastic acceptance of the Joachite threefold division of history into ages of Father, Son, and Holy Spirit separates him from Bonaventure and the commentators alike.

The Fifth Period: Peace and Laxity

In considering the fifth period, Olivi departs from previous mendicant exegetical tradition in a way that seems minor yet has enormous repercussions. Somewhat like his predecessors, he sees the fifth period as a time of peace and laxity, or peace leading to laxity. After the Muslims swept away a good part of the Christian world in the fourth period, the rest of that world retrenched in the fifth. From the time of the Carolingians, Islam was held in check and the West achieved some degree of internal order, thus leaving many of its inhabitants free to concentrate on achieving moral decay.[35] This is not to say that the fifth period was an unrelieved disaster. Olivi recognizes the value of peace, and he recognizes that general decadence was balanced by notable zeal within cenobitic monasticism.[36] Nor are the evils that have plagued this era entirely unique to it. They are, on the whole, those common to the human race throughout history.

Nevertheless, these evils combine in the fifth period in such a way as to make its decline a stunning one. We have seen that as far as Olivi is concerned "practically the whole church from head to foot is corrupted and thrown into disorder and turned, as it were, into a new Babylon."[37] He feels that the late fifth period is characterized by three specific forms of corruption. The first is widespread laxity among clergy, monks, and laity, occasioned by the bad example of bishops and abbots, who not only sin themselves and fail to correct the sins of subordinates, but who actually favor such sinners.[38] He is quite clear as to what sort of sin is involved. On one occasion he speaks of "pride, luxury, simony, litigation, fraud, and rapine," while on another he refers to "the simony through which all ecclesiastical things are bought and sold by practically everyone, . . . the abuses of ecclesiastical possessions and legacies, and the innumerable and horrendous fornications perpetrated in connection with the divine sacraments."[39]

Olivi does not mean to imply that ecclesiastical possessions are in themselves evil. That view is not entirely absent from thirteenth-century Apocalypse commentaries. *Aser pinguis* and *Vidit Iacob* are willing to cite the legend according to which the donation of Constantine was greeted by angelic voices announcing that "today poison has been poured into the church."[40] Olivi, however, says nothing of the kind. Given his periodization, one might expect that the odds would be slightly better of hearing him criticize a "donation of Charlemagne" than a donation of Constantine, but that does not occur either. He remarks that the pontificate granted to Peter and the apostles "was usefully and rationally commuted to a state allowing temporal possessions, at least from the time of Constantine to the end of the fifth period."[41] Thus ecclesiastical possessions have their place in the divine economy, but Olivi's very way of saying as much suggests that their place is temporary. "It is fitting that at the end [the priesthood] should return completely to the original order, which pertains to it by virtue of primogeniture, greater perfection, and greater conformity with Christ."[42] More of that later, however.

The second besetting form of corruption is the rise and remarkable progress of Catharism. Olivi sees its success as occasioned and facilitated by the first evil, but also as a punishment for it. He follows Joachim in taking the Cathari very seriously—one could hardly expect a native of Languedoc to do otherwise—but draws the line at linking them with the temptation of Antichrist. That temptation should be so subtle that even the more educated among the elect are almost seduced into accepting it, and the Cathar heresy simply is not up to the job. It "contains so many stupid and patently absurd errors that the wise can in no way be seduced by it," and has already been refuted by a series of scholars, including Augustine. In fact, it has been opposed so successfully since the early thirteenth century that it is "badly damaged and now just about buried."[43] Thus Olivi sees the Cathari as the major enemies of the fifth period and the two Antichrists as the major enemy of the sixth.[44] Olivi's pluralization of Antichrist will be discussed at length in another chapter. For the moment we need only note that he speaks of the temptation of Antichrist just as his predecessors did, but actually divides it into two separate entities presided over by the mystical and great Antichrists.

Olivi has his own ideas on what the temptation of Antichrist should look like, and that brings us to the third evil stalking the later fifth period. Olivi first describes it simply as "an attack on the life and spirit of Christ by those in the first group and other religious as well," an assault so convincing that it will almost trap the elect.[45] Later, however, he refers to it as "the fall of certain higher, more learned, and more recent religious into worldly desires and the curious learning of worldly philosophers." In fact, this third evil comprises what Olivi sees as the potent double temptation facing his own day: on the one hand, an Islamicized Aristotelianism striking at the roots of Christian doctrine; on the other, an attack on Franciscan poverty. The latter attack is, in turn, twofold. Carnal elements outside the order insist that evangelical perfection is achieved, not by renouncing all possessions, but by having them in common, while carnal elements within it argue that *usus pauper* is not an essential element in the highest poverty.[46]

These twin evils can hardly be termed a late discovery on Olivi's part. They were, in fact, major concerns throughout his scholarly career. Neither represented an exclusively apocalyptic preoccupation—Olivi could discuss both Aristotelian philosophy and Franciscan poverty at length without even mentioning the Antichrist—yet he decided quite early that each issue had an apocalyptic dimension. Both topics demonstrate the remarkable unity of Olivi's thought. His apocalyptic preoccupations were not a sideshow developed apart from his philosophical and theological concerns. They represented his effort to see the historical significance of those concerns.

The main target of Olivi's philosophical strictures is not Aristotle in particular but "worldly philosophy," a more general phenomenon which includes not only Plato and other pre-Christian philosophers but Islamic thinkers like Avicenna and Averroës. Olivi is not interested in playing Aristotle off against Plato as Bonaventure occasionally did. Both philosophers went astray, though in slightly different ways, for both proceeded in ignorance of Christian revelation. Nevertheless, Aristotle is granted substantially more attention by Olivi because he apparently considers Aristotle the more intellectually interesting of the two and because he expects Aristotelian philosophy to play an important role in the apocalyptic drama being played out during the thirteenth century.

Olivi's apparent coolness toward Aristotle, a constant element throughout his scholarly career, has been considered elsewhere and need not be examined at length.[47] Let it suffice to say that, while Olivi did not reject Aristotelian philosophy in all its aspects—that would, indeed, be a bit like rejecting rational thought itself—and occasionally sided with him even when it meant disagreeing with Bonaventure, in the final analysis he agreed with Bonaventure that Aristotelian thought represented a coherent system proceeding from non-Christian assumptions to non-Christian conclusions. Aristotle's knowledge of grammar, logic, and rhetoric was impressive, and his forays into the physical sciences were fruitful in some particulars; yet the inherent limitations of human reason, combined with the depredations of original sin and lack of access to divine revelation, assured that he would go astray on the most important questions, such as the nature and destiny of humankind and God's nature.

Thus the prudent Christian might employ Aristotle piecemeal, accepting some elements and rejecting others, but there could be no question of a synthesis between Christian doctrine and Aristotelian philosophy as a whole. As Olivi surveyed the academic scene in his own time, he saw a number of major scholars defying these guidelines. They were, he felt, accepting Aristotle on faith, treating him as "the infallible measure of all truth" and "the god of this world."[48] Moreover, they were reading their Aristotle with the aid of commentaries by Islamic philosophers.[49] Olivi did not find that combination very surprising. In fact, it made a great deal of sense to him.

This brings us to the second great error Olivi thought was stalking his time, the rejection of Franciscan poverty. Here again we find a preoccupation which characterized Olivi's thought beginning with his earliest writings. Here again it has received enough study elsewhere to be given only passing attention at this juncture.[50] As he scanned the attacks on his order during the secular-mendicant controversy, subsequent criticism of the Franciscan rule by Dominicans, and recent arguments by certain Franciscan theologians that *usus pauper* was not an essential part of the Franciscan vow, Olivi concluded that they were all aspects of a sustained assault on evangelical perfection by carnal elements in the late fifth period. The same elements might be expected to emulate Islamic philosophers by according Aristotelian philosophy an uncritical acceptance. The thread linking these phenomena is noted by Olivi in one of his earliest works, the eighth of his *Questions on Evangelical Perfection*. There, while enumerating the virtues of poverty, he suggests that it protects us from the dangers of heresy,

> since it removes in marvelous fashion those things from which errors in the faith arise. For almost all of them arise from excessive attention to and curious quest of temporal and sensible things. For the wisdom of the philosophers and particularly Aristotle took all its principles from the experience of the senses or from the sensible elements of the world, and thus considered simply impossible whatever seemed contrary to sense experience. . . . But the

lover of poverty cannot be a curious investigator or valuer of the world and hence cannot be deceived by the elements of the world, for he counts all temporal things as nothing.[51]

Olivi adds that "overvaluation of common or private wealth is the singular foundation and doorway of the sect of the Antichrist as well as of the whole Jewish error, not to mention the Saracen," for if one denies that poverty is superior to any form of temporal possessions, "it necessarily follows that Christ was not the true Christ promised by the law and prophets."[52] Olivi's point is a complex one. If Jesus was really the messiah, he must have lived the best possible life. Since Olivi never doubts for an instant that he and his fellow Franciscans are correct in claiming that Jesus led a life of the highest poverty, it follows that Jesus' credentials as messiah depend upon whether poverty is the best form of life. So, in fact, does the validity of Christian exegesis. Olivi observes that the law and prophets attribute wealth and power to the messiah. While Christians give these passages spiritual meaning, the Jews accord them a literal or carnal interpretation. The Christian approach assumes that spiritual riches are the essential thing and material ones are unimportant, while the Jewish view attributes importance to material wealth.

In other words, Olivi sees the glorification of Aristotelian philosophy and the denigration of Franciscan poverty as two sides of the same coin. Both are evidence of a tendency to see the world in carnal rather than spiritual terms. Viewed from this angle, all the great contemporary enemies of Christianity display the same profile. The Jews demand a carnal interpretation of the Bible and thus await a rich and powerful messiah who will bring them earthly success. The Muslims look forward to a heaven of carnal pleasures. Aristotle bases his philosophy on sense experience and thus cannot penetrate the surface of reality to discover the true nature and destiny of humankind. One might object that the other great contemporary threat, Catharism, does not accord well with this basic profile, since its major flaw from a Catholic perspective lies in its extreme repudiation of carnality; yet Olivi is convinced that even the Cathari must fit the pattern to some extent. He insists that all heresies, no matter how they may feign chastity and austerity, must eventually turn to carnal pleasures either publicly or secretly, for whoever does not taste true spiritual delights will eventually seek solace in carnal ones. Thus the apparent sanctity of the Cathar *perfecti* must eventually be unmasked as hypocritical.[53]

Like several other mendicant exegetes, Olivi thinks that the problems of the fifth period are the result of a combined assault by the same evils that characterized the third and fourth periods, heresy and laxity. He notes that even in these earlier times the two were not chronologically distinct, since the doctors and anchorites, the two orders called into being to combat these evils, were partly coeval and were closely related to one another.[54] Moreover, he suggests that in the third period, too, heresy was closely related to involvement with "worldly philosophy," although the philosophy in question was not Aristotelian but Platonic. Olivi—like several other mendicant exegetes—sees Arianism as the key heresy of the third period; yet, unlike others, he considers it to be derived from Origen's thought, and he recognizes the latter as a Platonist. Moreover, he is able to make a direct connection between heresy in the third period and the major anti-Christian political force in the fourth, since he holds that Mohammed denied Christ's divinity because he had been taught by Arians.[55]

Although Aristotelianism and the assault on poverty represent complementary aspects of the same carnal orientation during the fifth period, poverty necessarily enjoys a certain priority in the order of events. It is only right, Olivi observes, that Christ's life should be attacked first, then his deity and other aspects of Christian doctrine.[56] This distinction does more than describe the actual chain of events in the thirteenth century. It also points toward the distinction between Olivi's two Antichrists, the mystical and the great. This distinction will be explored more fully in another chapter, where we will see that the persecution by the mystical Antichrist takes place within the church and involves an attack on Franciscan poverty by purported Christians. The persecution by the great Antichrist strikes more openly at the faith itself. Olivi links it with an Islamicized Aristotelianism, but in a rather complex way. Rather than identifying Aristotelianism with the temptation carried out by the great Antichrist, Olivi normally describes it as preparing the way for that temptation by introducing essentially non-Christian elements into Christian theology.[57] Thus, although Aristotelianism is a preparation for the great Antichrist, both it and the attack on poverty actually belong more properly to the time of the mystical Antichrist.[58]

Even this formulation has its difficulties, since the Antichrist has traditionally been placed in the sixth period, but Olivi has introduced his double temptation as the third element to bedevil the late fifth period. In reality, Olivi is not quite sure where to place it. He occasionally offers the possibility that the mystical Antichrist should be tucked in with other carnal elements of the fifth period rather than being assigned to the sixth along with the great Antichrist. He is sometimes equally willing to place the entire double temptation squarely in the sixth period.[59] He can afford to be imprecise on these matters because he is already in both periods. He remarks that in his own day the sixth period has been running concurrently with the fifth for a century.[60] While the great Antichrist will not appear until after the fifth period has completely ended and the world is entirely in the sixth, the mystical Antichrist will appear toward the end of the overlap, and thus he can be seen as belonging to either period.

Olivi's Departure from Tradition

We will turn to the sixth period in a moment, but before doing so we must remark that Olivi's conception of the fifth period resembles that of other Franciscan commentators in some basic ways, yet differs sharply in others. Other commentators regularly see the fifth period as an era of decline preparing the way for Antichrist. They speak of it as that of "the precursors of Antichrist" and portray the temptations of the fifth period as a combination of those already featured in earlier periods, mainly heresy and laxity. Olivi differs from the rest, however, in his decision to place his own time near the end of the period rather than at its beginning. Whereas others see the church in their time as starting down a long slide, Olivi thinks it is already near the bottom.

He also differs from other commentators in his reading of what has gone wrong. When we examine other mendicant commentators, we discover that those who explicitly place themselves in the fifth period, that of the precursors of Antichrist, are willing to document their choice with what amounts to a frontal assault on contemporary corruption. They pay particular attention to corrupt prelates. Their inclination is understandable in the light of the secular-mendicant controversy. Given the opposition Franciscans had encountered from ecclesiastics in trying to establish themselves, one can see why they felt inclined to the settle the score. Olivi's strictures against *prelati* fit this pattern to some extent, yet he differs from other mendicant commentators in two important ways. First, the others do not give the Franciscan movement major apocalyptic significance. Thus their discussion of contemporary evils does not center on specifically Franciscan issues. The corruption they bewail is a traditional variety that was already being lamented over a century earlier by Saint Bernard. Olivi, however, sees the assault on Franciscan poverty as a major enormity of the declining fifth age. He includes within that attack the attempt of secular clergy and masters to protect their turf against mendicant interlopers, the interorder sniping of Dominican friars at Franciscans, and the controversy among Franciscans over the role of *usus pauper*.

This last element is particularly important, because it involves an argument that Olivi and his faction were destined to lose. Thus it had a much different long-term significance. When Hugh of St. Cher, "Alexander," and other mendicants attacked lax prelates in their commentaries, the polemical overtones of their criticism gave their apocalyptical speculation a lively relevance but did not make it dangerous, because the mendicants were destined to triumph over secular opposition with the pope's assistance. Much the same thing can be said about the threat of heterodox Aristotelianism. Here again we have a danger recognized by other mendicants besides Olivi. It was reflected in some mendicant Apocalypse commentaries and comprised a major element in Bonaventure's critique of his age. It, too, represented an apocalyptic issue which, however relevant to contemporary experience, could be advanced without risk, since the Averroist *bête noir* was soon be hunted to its lair by the bishop of Paris, the archbishop of Canterbury, and the pope himself. We know that the beast actually made its escape, lived to frighten Petrarch in the following century, and was still alive (if not particularly well) at Padua in the early sixteenth century; yet that was not because the pope had given it any succor.

The outcome of the *usus pauper* controversy proved strikingly different. By depicting it as an important battleground in the war between spiritual and carnal forces that would characterize the declining fifth period, Olivi was proposing adherence to his own definition of Franciscan poverty as a litmus test of membership in the elect. It was, unfortunately, a test the pope himself would eventually fail, since Olivi's formulation of *usus pauper* was destined for rejection. Thus the pope was doomed to identify himself as leader of the carnal element.

The historical effect of this papal self-disclosure might have been less pronounced had it contradicted Olivi's expectations and thus represented a clear inaccuracy in his predictions. Instead it confirmed those predictions. This brings us to the other way in which Olivi differed from his fellow mendicant commentators. However acrimoniously these other commentators attacked the *prelati* of their time, they studiously avoided any notion that the prelate of prelates, the pope himself, might be involved. Of earlier mendicant commentators, only *Vidit Iacob* and Vital suggest that the coming temptation of Antichrist might capture the papacy, and they do it so briefly, so tentatively, as to have barely done it at all. Olivi's attitude is very different. He takes the temptation of Antichrist seriously. If it is to be the *non plus ultra* of temptations, then it must place the elect absolutely alone. It must force them to defend the truth in opposition to those very institutions that normally defend the truth. The elect will have to defend theological orthodoxy in defiance of the university masters, defend Franciscan poverty in defiance of their own Franciscan leaders, and defend both in defiance of the pope.

It is the last element that is most striking. Thirteenth-century Franciscans were quite open to the possibility that they might have to oppose some bishops and some university masters. They had already done so, because the former had denied them permission to preach and the latter had denied them permission to teach. Franciscans were even open to the possibility that they might have to disobey some of their own superiors if ordered to violate the rule. That much was written into the rule itself.[61] It was quite another thing to foresee a time in the near future when the elect would have to defy an ungodly system of bishops, masters, and Franciscan superiors led by the pope himself. That is, however, precisely what Olivi foresaw, and he did so in such a way as to project that vision not only onto a distant temptation of the great Antichrist in the sixth period, but onto the impending temptation to be led by the mystical Antichrist within the overlap between the fifth and sixth periods.

Olivi's notion of the mystical Antichrist must remain undefined until a future chapter, but the general outlines of the temptation attributed to him can be discussed here. It is, in effect, a story of how "Babylon" or "the carnal church" grows in the fifth period until it practically swallows up the entire church. Olivi's references to "Babylon" and "carnal church" have inspired interest ever since his Apocalypse commentary was written. We will see that, when the commentary was in the process of being condemned during the early fourteenth century, ecclesiastical judges tended to read both terms as straightforward references to the Catholic hierarchy. Manselli and others have argued persuasively that such an interpretation is too simplistic, but it remains questionable whether even a subtler reading will change the outcome much.

The *locus classicus* for Olivi's use of "Babylon" is his comment, already cited in part, that the the final return to apostolic poverty will be aided, although accidentally, not only by the great imperfection in possession and dispensation of temporals witnessed in the church, but also by the great pride, luxury, simony, litigation, fraud, and rapine occasioned by it, through which around the end of the fifth period practically the whole church from bottom to top is infected, disordered, and turned, as it were, into a new Babylon.[62]

Elsewhere he refers to the "horrendous laxity and blindness around the end of the fifth period, so that [the church] seems to be Babylon rather than Jerusalem, and more a synagogue of the reprobate persecuting Christ and his spirit than the church of Christ."[63] In yet another passage he notes that in the fifth period "the seat of the beast (that is, of the beastly crowd) is raised up, so that it prevails in numbers and power and nearly absorbs the seat of Christ, with which it is mixed in place and name." It is this crowd that is also called Babylon the whore.[64]

In such passages, words like *quasi, videatur,* and *fere* keep Olivi from actually identifying the institutional church with Babylon but let him come very close to doing so. His actual intention is partially clarified when we add to the notion of Babylon another key idea, that of the carnal church. Here again Olivi avoids any simple assertion that the carnal church is nothing more or less than the institutional church. It is tempting to say that, for Olivi, the carnal church represents carnal tendencies in the church throughout the ages. These tendencies have grown more virulent in the fifth period and have come to exert a powerful influence on the institutional church, but they cannot simply be identified with it. The important thing is that Olivi recognizes another element within the church, a spiritual element which, though hardly dominant during the late fifth and sixth periods, is destined to endure and finally triumph in the seventh.

Much the same thing should be said about another term seized upon by Olivi's fourteenth-century critics, "Rome." Here again they were inclined to see a straightforward reference to the hierarchical church. Obviously we are dealing with a term which was almost guaranteed to give exegetes some trouble, since, in fulminating against Babylon, the author of the Apocalypse was clearly aiming at the Roman empire and its capital city. Most mendicant commentators were on their guard in dealing with references to Rome. They avoided any suggestion that one could read these passages as a denunciation of the papacy. Olivi too treats them with care. He observes that when the catholic fathers called the great whore of Revelation 17 "Rome," they referred not to the church of the just sojourning within it, but to the reprobate who attack that same pilgrim church. Thus one should seek neither the whore nor the elect in one place, but rather throughout the Roman empire. The whore stands for the Roman people and the Roman empire as they were in a pagan state and also as they later were in a state of Christianity, but sullied with many crimes.[65]

Nevertheless, it would be unwise to become too abstract in discussing terms like "Babylon," "carnal church," and "Rome." At times Olivi does seem to apply all of them very concretely. For example, at one point he refers to "the carnal church, not only in Rome but diffused throughout the entire kingdom of the Romans," then says that it will be divided into the elect, those carnal elements in rebellion against Antichrist, and those carnal elements who support Antichrist.[66] Such a comment could make sense only if, at least for the moment, Olivi was identifying the carnal church with the church itself in an institutional sense as it exists at a particular moment.

Moreover, the entity represented by "the carnal church," "Babylon," and "Rome" will soon be destroyed by a pagan army. There are many future events which Olivi discusses without being sure about them, but he is very sure about this one. He refers to it again and again.[67] The precise scenario is less clear—it is, after all, a contingent future event—but Olivi provides some hints. He seems relatively confident in expecting carnal elements to control the institutional church in the near future. Indeed, he feels they are already on the way to doing so, and speaks of the "seat of the beast" as the "carnal clergy reigning and presiding over the entire church in this fifth period, for the bestial life transcendently and singularly reigns and finds its principal seat there far more than among the laity subjected to them."[68] Even as he writes, "almost all clergy and regulars who possess common goods think incorrectly about evangelical renunciation of such goods," and "many who renounce common goods say that *usus pauper* is not included in the vow."[69]

Persecution of the Elect

Things will get even worse. In the near future the pope, who has hitherto protected proponents of evangelical poverty from their enemies, will probably turn against them.[70] As we will see in a future chapter, Olivi thinks that an evil secular-spiritual alliance will attempt to suppress defenders of evangelical poverty.[71] He refers to the spiritual leader as a pseudopope "who will indeed be 'pseudo' because he errs in a heretical way against the truth of evangelical poverty and perfection, and perhaps also because he will not be canonically elected but schismatically introduced." This will be the temptation of the mystical Antichrist. It is impossible to say for sure whether the chief secular leader or the pseudopope will be the mystical Antichrist, but we will see that Olivi clearly favors the pseudopope's candidacy. The resultant temptation will be so seductive that even the elect will almost be led into error. The faithful will be faced with a situation in which all the standard authority figures are united in error. Major ecclesiastical leaders, university professors, and superiors of religious orders will attempt to divert the faithful toward cupidity, carnality, and earthly glory. Should any dare to disobey, they will be turned over to the secular authorities, who will be more than happy to punish them.

Faced with this wall of opposition, the small group who remain faithful will turn in other directions. They will find the Greeks, Muslims, Tartars, and Jews more receptive to the gospel than the carnal Latin church, and will gain a number of converts. Within the church, they will find the laity more receptive than the clergy.[72] We will see that Olivi refuses to identify these religious refugees entirely with the Franciscan order, but nevertheless defines them largely in Franciscan terms. He also sees them as the first fruits of a new age that has developed within the womb of the old one.

The Destruction of Babylon

Thus the closing days of the fifth period will witness a desperate but apparently uneven battle within the Latin church. A small number of evangelical preachers, supported by a few laymen, will announce the new dispensation of the dawning sixth period; yet all of the major authorities, whom the church had spent the entire high Middle Ages teaching the faithful to obey, will use their impressive arsenal of persuasive and coercive powers to defend the worst aspects of the declining fifth period. Against all odds, the handful of evangelical preachers will emerge triumphant, but with the aid of an unexpected and unlikely ally. Babylon will be destroyed by a non-Christian army that has aimed its blow not at corrupt elements within the church, but at Christianity itself. It will succeed in a purely physical sense. Rome will lie in ruins, and with it the carnal church. The elect will be liberated from one great oppressor, but will fall into the hands of another.

Olivi is not very communicative as to how all this will come about.

There are few things of which he seems surer than the destruction of Babylon, and he clearly thinks of this event as a successful military attack that will end the power of a corrupt ecclesiastical hierarchy and, in the process, wreak havoc on the city of Rome.[73] He is less clear about who will do the destroying and how, but he does suggest that conflict among Christian kings will weaken their armies to the point that the Latin world will be open to such an attack and, as a later chapter will show, he is very open to the possibility that the non-Christian army in question will be Muslim. He suspects that, after inadvertently solving a major Christian problem by demolishing the carnal church, the Muslims themselves will be somehow confounded and the church will experience a brief period of peace. At one point Olivi refers to this brief Islamic eclipse as the result of "Christ triumphing in his soldiers," yet he also cites—without comment but, one suspects, with approval—Joachim of Fiore's suggestion that victory will come about "by preaching more than by fighting," through the agency of a new order. After a short time, however, Islam will regain strength and the stage will be set for the temptation of the great Antichrist, in which the Muslims will also play a major role.[74]

The destruction of Babylon is an important event for Olivi. It signals the end of the fifth period, but it also signals the end of the church as he knows it. While the temptation of the mystical Antichrist is seen by him as a future event, it is also a present reality, at least in nuclear form. The attack on evangelical poverty is already underway. Ecclesiastical leadership is already decadent. The flight of spiritual men from the carnal church and the resultant evangelization of non-Christians has been going on since Francis's time. The worst is yet to come, but things are already bad enough. The temptation of the mystical Antichrist can be seen to some extent as nothing more than present tendencies carried to the point where, *the present hierarchical structure remaining intact*, the church hierarchy is dominated by carnal leaders *from the top down*, openly rejects evangelical poverty, and is supported in its campaign by secular power. The two italicized phrases are crucial. The first suggests why the scenario is relatively easy to imagine—all one needs to do is envisage the present ecclesiastical structure in a somewhat more decrepit state—and the second points to a major factor separating the present from the future. The pope has hitherto backed supporters of evangelical poverty against their enemies, but in the future he too will oppose them.

Once one proceeds beyond the destruction of Babylon, however, one has a great deal less to fall back on. During the brief respite between mystical and great Antichrist, will there be anything resembling the present church government? Rome will lie in ruins. What *will* be left? One pseudo-pope will have been destroyed, and another will hold sway during the persecution of the great Antichrist; yet will there be any popes in between? Will those spiritual men who continue to preach the gospel be controlled by anything resembling an organizational structure? Can anything what-soever be said about life after the destruction of Babylon? Olivi does not say. He is remarkably unwilling to say much about ecclesiastical organi-zation in the sixth period, but he is willing to say quite a bit about the major forces that shape that period. It is to these that we must now turn.

Notes

1. *Lectura*, 52: "Circa finem quinti temporis a planta pedis usque ad verticem est fere tota ecclesia infecta et confusa et quasi nova Babilon effecta."
2. Ibid., 11f., 28, 72, 79.
3. Ibid., 12, 75, and elsewhere.
4. Ibid., 10.
5. Ibid., 58.
6. Ibid., 11.
7. Ibid., 73f.
8. Ibid., 74f.
9. In Olivi's commentary the chronological associations of *status* are even stronger than in Joachim's. He actually uses the word *status* to designate both the three "ages" of world history and the seven "periods" of church history, but for clarity I will consistently translate the word in these two different ways.
10. Ibid., 46.
11. Ibid., 58.
12. Ibid., 47.
13. Reeves, *Joachim of Fiore and the Prophetic Future*, chapter 1, offers a suc-cinct description of Joachim's divisions.
14. *Lectura*, 6, 9.
15. Ibid., 89–99.
16. Ibid., 99.
17. Manselli, *La Lectura*, 164f., 186.
18. They separate him from Alexander Minorita as well, but in a different way, as we saw in chapter 3.
19. See the exceptions to this statement noted in Chapter 2, note 111, above.
20. For example, *Lectura*, 843, describes one of Richard's views as *valde ab-surdum*, and ibid., 642, rejects another as *nimis extorta seu violenta*.
21. Ibid., 395f.
22. *Lectura super Isaiam*, MS Paris Bibl. Nat. nouv. acq. lat. 774, 54r: "Et hoc modo Ioachim in libro de concordia et in expositione apocalypsis dicit se subito

accepisse totam concordiam veteris et novi testamenti quantum ad quasdam generales regulas, ex quibus ipse postmodum aliqua quasi argumentando deducit et ut sibi videtur aliquando sic quod ex hoc estimat se habere certam intelligentiam conclusionis sic deducte, aliquando vero non nisi probabilem coniecturam in qua plerumque potuit falli."

23. *Lectura*, 512: "Super quo et consimilibus advertendum quod ipse plura dicit non assertorie sed opinative. Sicut enim ex naturali lumine intellectus nostri quedam scimus indubitabiliter ut prima principia, quedam vero ut conclusiones ex ipsis necessario deductas, quedam vero nescimus sed solum opinamur per probabiles rationes et in hoc tertio sepe fallimur et possumus falli, nec tamen ex hoc lumen nobis concreatum est falsum nec pro tanto fallimur pro quanto opiniones nostras scimus non esse sententias infallibiles; sic lumen per gratuitam revelationem datum quedam scit ut prima et indubitabilia principia revelata, quedam vero ut conclusiones ex ipsis necessario deductas; quedam vero ex utrisque solum probabiliter et conjecturaliter opinatur; et sic videtur fuisse in intelligentia scripturarum et concordie novi et veteris testamenti per revelationem abbati Ioachim, ut ipsemet asserit, data."

24. Ibid., 658: "Non mireris si cum magna luce sibi data quasi in aurora tertii status habuerit permixtas tenebras in notitia futurorum, et maxime cum nocturne tenebre quinti temporis suo tempore inundarent. Quod autem non assertorie sed opinative talia dixerit, patet ex pluribus superius a me tactis super quinta tuba et super sexta."

25. Ibid., 24–26.

26. Ibid., 56f., 61f.

27. In expositing the fifth and sixth letters, he deals largely with the corresponding periods, and would undoubtedly have done so with the seventh as well if the text had been more cooperative.

28. *Lectura*, 5, explains that it may be taken as ending at Rev. 20:1, 20:11, or 21:1, depending on whether one begins the seventh vision with the damnation of the dragon, the general judgment, or the final glorification of the universe.

29. Ibid., 22f.

30. Ibid., 89–103.

31. Ibid., 15–21. He also argues that each office has seven parts, one corresponding with each of the seven periods.

32. Ibid., 286, 306, 367–70. In two of these three cases their mention is obviously rendered *de rigeur* by the material exposited.

33. E.g. ibid., 430, "potius misticus quam litteralis."

34. E.g., ibid., 567, "spirituales et allegoricas voces." See also ibid., 429, "mistice et allegorice."

35. Ibid., 66, observes that the fifth and seventh periods are alike in this respect. See also ibid., 314, 391, on the temporal peace of the fifth period.

36. Ibid., 10. Ibid., 787, et passim, suggest that Olivi sees the fourth period as that of eremitical monasticism and the fifth as that of cenobitic.

37. Ibid., 52: "Circa finem quinti temporis a planta pedis usque ad verticem est fere tota ecclesia infecta et confusa et quasi nova Babilon effecta."

38. Ibid., 493–96.

39. Ibid., 29, 52.
40. *Aser pinguis*, 403ra; *Vidit Iacob*, 430f.
41. *Lectura*, 51.
42. Ibid., 51.
43. Ibid., 493f., 506–15, 524. Olivi mentions the Waldensians as well, but he is mainly interested in the Cathari. His announcement that the latter were "just about buried" proved premature, since they enjoyed a brief revival in the early fourteenth century.
44. Ibid., 17–19.
45. Ibid., 494.
46. Ibid., 516f.
47. See my "Petrus Ioannis Olivi and the Philosophers," *Franciscan Studies* 31 (1971): 41–71, and "Apocalyptic Element," 15–29.
48. For references from other Olivian works see Burr, "Apocalyptic Element," 17; Burr, "Petrus Ioannis Olivi and the Philosophers," 59.
49. *Lectura*, 359, 378.
50. See Burr, *OFP*, especially chapter seven; Burr, "Apokalyptische Erwartung."
51. *Das Heil der Armen*, 104: "Hoc ipsum potest ostendi ex eo quod miro modo tollit et evacuat illa unde errores fidei sunt exorti et oriri possunt. Nam omnes fere sunt exorti ex aestimatione nimia et conquisitione curiosa rerum temporalium et sensibilium. Sapientia enim philosophorum et maxime Aristotelis omnia principia sua sumpsit ab experientia sensuum seu a sensibilibus mundi elementis et propterea iudicat simpliciter impossibile quicquid videtur esse contrarium experimentis sensuum."
52. Ibid., 105.
53. *Lectura*, 216f., 521f. The Cathari too are described as following a literal or carnal interpretation of scripture and as placing high value on sense experience.
54. Ibid., 73–75; 373–75.
55. Ibid., 376f., 481–83. See also the passages from other works quoted in Burr, "Apocalyptic Element," 19. The importance of Arianism in Olivi's (and others') theology of history derived largely from the political clout it gained through its brief acceptance within the empire during the fourth century and its remarkable subsequent popularity among the Germanic tribes.
56. Ibid., 425f.
57. Ibid., 378f., 656.
58. Thus ibid., 513, 656.
59. Ibid., 19, 633.
60. Ibid., 75.
61. On disobedience of superiors see Burr, *OFP*, 163–66.
62. *Lectura*, 52: "Ad istum autem reditum valde, quamvis per accidens, cooperabitur non solum multiplex imperfectio in possessione et dispensatione temporalium ecclesie in pluribus comprobata, sed etiam multiplex enormitas superbie et luxurie et simoniarum et causidicationum et litigiorum et fraudum et rapinarum ex ipsis occasionaliter accepta, ex quibus circa finem quinti temporis a planta pedis

usque ad verticem est fere tota ecclesia infecta et confusa et quasi nova Babilon effecta."

63. Ibid., 492: "Et nota quod prima harum trium est horrenda laxatio et excecatio circa finem quinti temporis. Ita ut potius videatur esse Babilon quam Ierusalem et potius synagoga reproborum persequens Christum et spiritum eius quam ecclesia Christi."

64. Ibid., 801: "Sublimata est sedes bestie, id est bestialis caterve, ita ut numero et potestate prevaleat et fere absorbeat sedem Christi, cui localiter et nominaliter est commixta."

65. Ibid., 825f., 831.

66. Ibid., 819: "Hec ergo est ecclesia carnalis tam Rome quam in toto regno Romanorum seu Christianorum diffusa. Trium autem partium eius erit una electorum de solo Christo et eius spiritu curantium et ad omnem tribulationem pacienter sustinendam preparatorum. Secunda erit carnalium antichristo seu decem regibus rebellare conantium. Tertia erit aliorum reproborum ad antichristum confugientium seu confugere disponentium."

67. E.g., ibid., 401, 492f., 805f., 837f., 853, 856.

68. Ibid., 802: "Per hanc autem sedem bestie principaliter designatur carnalis clerus in hoc quinto tempore regnans et toti ecclesie presidens, in quo quidem bestialis vita transcendenter et singulariter regnat et sedet, sicut in sua principali sede et longe plus quam in laicis plebibus sibi subiectis."

69. Ibid., 427: "Fere omnes clerici et regulares possidentes aliquid in communi videntur minus bene sentire de evangelica abrenuntiatione huiuscemodi communium. Multi etiam abrenuntiationem hanc secundum rem vel secundum apparentiam preferentes sic amant et estimant laxam vitam, quod usum pauperem seu moderate restrictum a voto professionis evangelice dicunt esse exclusum et etiam debere excludi."

70. Ibid., 538, regarding the drying up of the Euphrates: "Designatur per hoc aut discessio fere omnium ab obedientia summi pontificis, de qua dicit apostolus secunda ad Thessalonicenses, 'Nisi venerit discessio primum,' et cetera; aut cessatio favoris eius ad statum evangelicum, per quem eius emuli sunt usque nunc impediti in ipsum irruere iuxta votum." This passage might suggest that "perhaps" would be more suitable than "probably," but the scenario offered elsewhere makes it clear that Olivi expects papal defection. See the more extended analysis in the chapter on the mystical Antichrist.

71. See Chapter 6 for citations and further discussion of what is said in this paragraph.

72. *Lectura*, 565, 664f.

73. E.g., ibid., 401, 492f., 805f., 838, 853, 856, 858. We have seen this suggestion already in the pseudo-Joachim Jeremiah commentary and in Vital du Four.

74. Ibid., 709, 837f., 853.

5. The Dawning Sixth Period

We noted in the last chapter that once Olivi's projection of the future moves beyond the destruction of Babylon, and with it the close of the fifth period, he can no longer fall back on familiar models of church government in attempting to flesh out his vision. Thus one would expect him to proceed cautiously in describing the sixth period. That expectation is in some ways fulfilled. His suggestions are punctuated with warnings that he can assert nothing and that such matters can only be left up to God. How these warnings should be taken is a problem that we can defer to a later chapter. For the moment the important thing is that, despite the unfamiliar landscape and periodical warnings, Olivi actually says a great deal about the sixth period. At times he is surprisingly sanguine about his ability to do so.

Olivi's Progressive View of History

In fact, Olivi tells us that the meaning of passages in the Apocalypse dealing with the sixth and seventh periods is more easily demonstrated than that of passages dealing with earlier periods. It would have to be so if we were to know much about anything, for our understanding of those earlier periods really depends upon our grasp of the sixth, just as our understanding of those things that are ordained to an end depends upon our knowledge of the end itself.[1] Here we arrive at the central point to be made about the sixth period: it is the goal toward which church history has been striving. Unless we understand that goal, we will not discern the shape of church history. One could dismiss this observation as rather standard. The Judeo-Christian tradition normally sees history as going somewhere. Olivi is saying a great deal more, however. He has a strongly progressive notion of history. "Just as there are many grades of perfection between the least and the greatest, it was fitting that the church should ascend from the least to the greatest through intermediate grades."[2] He draws a parallel between the seven periods of church history and the seven steps of contemplation,[3] and he encapsulates his progressive vision of church history in a series of images including those of flowing water, a growing tree, and a long journey.[4] His most striking and suggestive image appears at the end of the preface.

> Three mountains separated by two valleys will strike a man who sees them from a great distance as a single mountain. . . . Then, when he stands on the first mountain, he will see the first valley and two mountains, and when he stands on the second mountain he will see two valleys and three mountains. Just so, the Jews before Christ's first advent, like one standing before the first mountain, did not distinguish the first from the later ones, but took the whole for a single [advent]. Christians before the sixth period of the church distinguished between the first and the others because they stood on the first and saw an intervening space . . . between the first and final advents, but did not commonly distinguish between the advent in the sixth period and the one at final judgment. . . . Those, however, who shall be placed in the sixth period or who see it in the spirit distinguish it from the first and last. Then they see this distinction in the prophetic books, and also in those things said by Christ and the apostles about Christ's final advent and the final age of the world. Then they also see the concordance of various events in the first five ages of the world with those in the first five periods of the church, as well as the concordance of the seven periods under the law with the seven periods of church history.[5]

Olivi's mixture of tenses reflects his conviction that the sixth period, though still not completely realized, was born nearly a century earlier in the time of Saint Francis. Thus, although Olivi himself is not standing at the top of the second mountain, he is high enough to have a general sense of what lies beyond. Here we see the importance of his decision to place himself in the sixth period, to see Francis as a major founder of that period, and to see that period as one of renewal which will blossom into a seventh period of peace and enlightenment. He is in a relatively good position to know what the new age will be like, because he sees it already dawning around him. What he sees is, to be sure, the developing sixth period, but its connection with the seventh insures insight into the latter as well.

One might protest that Olivi's progressive notion of church history accords ill with his negative portrayal of the fifth period. He deals with this problem in a number of ways,[6] but we need not concern ourselves with them here except to note that the progress he discerns is not a steady one, with the world every day in every way getting better and better.

Instead he sees the first five periods of church history as aimed at the sixth in the sense that the virtues and vices characterizing these periods all worked to produce the sixth. Thus the sixth is not only the beginning of a new age but the culmination of what has gone before.[7] The running battle that has characterized all history will now be resolved in a major confrontation.

Olivi and Previous Franciscan Exegesis

Here we arrive at one of the elements separating Olivi from other Franciscan commentators. All accept the traditional notion that Antichrist will reign in the sixth period. Moreover, all concur in seeing a close tie between the fifth and sixth periods. The fifth is that of the precursors of Antichrist and prepares the way for the sixth. There is also widespread interest in Richard of St. Victor's presentation of the fifth period as a grand finale of sorts in which the devil, having failed in his attempt to subvert the church with heresy in the third period and laxity in the fourth, now attempts to do the job with both combined.[8] Thus there is a strong sense of direction on the negative side. One might almost refer to a law of cumulative evil. Nevertheless, precisely because they move in the exegetical tradition running through Richard of St. Victor all the way back to Bede, other mendicant commentators lack the positive element so prominent in the Olivian reading of the sixth period. They see it as a period of great temptation but not as one of stunning renewal. Nor do they place themselves in the sixth period as Olivi does. Nor do they see the sixth period as closely connected with the seventh. Nor, finally, do they see Saint Francis as the inaugurator of the sixth period. These are important differences with major repercussions for Olivi's thought.

We must investigate these repercussions, but before doing so it would be wise to recall that, although Olivi is atypical in these respects, he is not entirely without antecedents. Bonaventure takes an analogous position in the *Collationes in hexaemeron*.[9] Olivi is much more willing to speculate on the shape of things to come, and his scenario displays a concreteness lacking in Bonaventure's brief, evocative discussion, but in some ways they are remarkably alike in their reading of the sixth period. They both place themselves within the period, although they differ as to how far into it they actually are. This difference is part of a more general one in their periodization. They agree on the first three periods of church history, but they then diverge to such a degree that Bonaventure begins his sixth period where Olivi begins his fifth, around the time of Charlemagne.[10] Olivi is reflecting Joachim, not Bonaventure, when he portrays his own time as suspended between the fifth and sixth periods. Nevertheless, he and Bonaventure both see the sixth period in positive as well as negative terms. Bonaventure describes it as a time of "clear doctrine" characterized by the progress of learning and peace within the church, but marked also by persecution and temptation. His temptations are past as well as present and future, including the German emperors' attacks on the papacy and the advent of Antichrist.[11] He does not set a date for the latter event, but the tone of his work suggests that he expects no great delay. Insofar as he sees any harbinger of it in his own time, he is especially exercised about heterodox Aristotelianism.[12]

Because Bonaventure, like Olivi, sees the sixth period as a time of renewal, he can see it as linked, not only with the preceding period, but with the following one as well. He does not speculate on the length of the seventh period as Olivi does, but agrees with Olivi in presenting it as a time of enlightenment in which the church militant "will be conformed with the triumphant as far as is possible on the pilgrim way," a formulation similar to Olivi's. Their common positive reading of the sixth period, their willingness to put themselves in it, and their linkage of it with the seventh period allow both Bonaventure and Olivi to see Saint Francis's appearance as a major apocalyptic event. Bonaventure, of course, begins the sixth period too early to see Francis as its founder, but does manage to read him into the Apocalypse as the angel of the sixth seal.

There are some ways in which Olivi is very unlike Bonaventure, however. First, while Bonaventure places Franciscan poverty within an apocalyptic context, he does so in a much different way. He suggests that, like Israel, the order must pay for its backsliding by wandering in the wilderness until, purified by tribulation, it is finally fit to enter the promised land of its apocalyptic destiny.[13] There is no suggestion in the *Collationes* that the coming apocalyptic persecution will feature a frontal assault on evangelical poverty. Second, Bonaventure does not share Olivi's fear that ecclesiastical authority at the highest levels will soon stop defending evangelical poverty and begin to attack it instead. These are important differences, especially in combination. In both of these respects, Bonaventure is closer to the main line of mendicant exegesis than he is to Olivi.

There is another way in which Bonaventure differs from Olivi. While both accept not only the sevenfold division of church history common among exegetes but the Joachite notion of concordance which sees that division as reflecting another sevenfold Old Testament pattern, only Olivi accepts the Joachite threefold division of history into the ages of Father, Son, and Holy Spirit. Joseph Ratzinger, whose study of the Bonaventuran *Collationes in hexaemeron* revolutionized the modern view of Bonaventure as apocalyptic thinker, argues that the complex patterns found there contain a trinitarian structure of history that "implies both yes and no to Joachim."[14] If such is the case, then Bonaventure's silence concerning the Joachite three ages constitutes an important part of the "no"; yet his love for numerical patterns and trinitarian formulations makes one cautious about interpreting the threefold patterns offered by him as a quiet debate with Joachim.

Olivi has no difficulty whatsoever accepting the Joachite three ages. His allusions to them so pervade his Apocalypse commentary that it hardly seems necessary to provide an example. Moreover, he often interprets them much as Joachim did. In his commentary on Matthew, he echoes Joachim's suggestion that the third age will be analogous to the procession of the Trinity in that, after the "letter" of the Old and New Testaments, there will follow a *concordia* and spiritual interpretation of both.[15] In the Revelation commentary, he echoes Joachim by announcing that

> just as in the first age of the world, before Christ, the fathers were involved in expounding the great works of the Lord carried out from the beginning of the world, and in the second age running from Christ to the third age the sons were involved in seeking the wisdom of mystical things and the mysteries hidden from immemorial times, so in the third age nothing remains except to sing to God and rejoice in him, praising his great works and great wisdom, as well as the goodness clearly manifested in his works and the words of his scriptures. For just as in the first age God the Father revealed himself as terrible and to be feared, and the fear of him shone forth, even so, in the second age, God the Son revealed himself as teacher, preserver, and expressive word of his father's wisdom. Therefore in the third age the Holy Spirit will reveal himself as a flame and furnace of divine love, a cellarer of divine inebriation, a storeroom of divine aromas and spiritual unctions and unguents, and a dance of spiritual jubilations and jocundities, through which all truth concerning the wisdom of the incarnate word of God and concerning the power of God the Father will be known, not only by simple understanding, but also by gustatory and tactile experience.[16]

Some of this is taken directly from Joachim's Apocalypse commentary, and much of the rest has a distinctly Joachite flavor. Olivi continues in an equally Joachite vein, noting that, just as the first age was characterized by the corporal works which are more fitting to laymen, and the second by the knowledge of scripture more fitting to clerics, "so in the third, a chaste and sweet contemplation more fitting to monks or religious should dominate."[17]

Here too, however, there are significant differences. The Joachite and Olivian periodizations can be seen as generally similar: The age of the Father extends roughly from Adam to Christ; that of the Son from Christ to the thirteenth century; and that of the Holy Spirit from the thirteenth century to the end of time. But on a more complex level, the patterns begin to diverge. Each man projects an overlap between the second and third ages, but Joachim sees a much greater one stretching from the time of St. Benedict to the mid-thirteenth century, while Olivi begins his with the time of Joachim and St. Francis and thinks it will last for about a century.[18] In the final analysis, while Olivi is heavily indebted to Joachim, and while his interpretation of the Apocalypse can be described as an attempt to combine Bonaventuran Franciscan apocalyptic with a much more radical appropriation of Joachite exegesis than Bonaventure himself countenanced, there are important ways in which he departed from both.

The Sixth Period and the Third Age

Such a remark obviously invites us to return to the text, asking precisely what Olivi did say about the sixth period and third age. The first observation to be made is that the three ages and seven periods fit together rather neatly on one level, but they produce some ambiguity on another. They are quite harmonious in the sense that the first five periods of church history belong to the second age, that of the Son, while the last two belong to the third, the age of the Holy Spirit. But, examined more carefully, the pattern is more complex. There are overlaps between the fifth and sixth periods and between the second and third ages, and these overlaps coincide to some extent, but not completely. Both begin around the time of Saint Francis, but the overlap between the fifth and sixth periods continues until the destruction of Babylon, while that between the second and third ages seems to run all the way to the death of Antichrist. Thus this second overlap comprises the entire sixth period. That is why Olivi occasionally seems to identify the third age with the seventh period alone. It is the third age *par excellence*, the point at which, Antichrist having been defeated, the spiritual pleasures already tasted in the sixth period can be fully enjoyed.

On the other hand, we will see that Olivi occasionally suggests, at least implicitly, some difference in the form spirituality can be expected to take in the sixth and seventh periods. In fact, he implicitly distinguishes three stages: the overlap between the fifth and sixth periods; the interval between the fall of Babylon and the fall of Antichrist; and the period after the fall of Antichrist. His comments on church government in the third age are sketchy at best, but here too there may be a similar distinction. In each case one might ask whether Olivi is suggesting a progressive development rather than a series of abrupt changes, but whichever option is chosen, we are left with the fact that the third age is not all of a piece. This would not be a problem if some of Olivi's most interesting comments about the third age were not addressed to that age *tout simple*, without specifying the degree of applicability to the period before Antichrist's demise. The best one can do with such statements is assume that they are certainly true of the seventh period and probably applicable in some sense to the sixth as well. We will ignore these statements for the moment and concentrate on those that specifically mention the sixth period.

The first question to be asked is when the sixth period begins. The answer is hardly a simple one. In commenting on the opening of the sixth seal in Revelation 6:12–7:13, Olivi observes that some people date the beginning of the sixth period from "the solemn revelation made to the Abbot Joachim and perhaps to some of his contemporaries concerning the third general age," which contains the sixth and seventh periods of the church. Others favor different moments, such as the birth of the Franciscan order, the later period of attack on the rule by the carnal church, or the destruction of that carnal church. Sensibly considered, Olivi remarks, all of these opinions could be taken as true, just as each of the four evangelists portrays the gospel of Christ as beginning with a different event, and just as the beginning of the Babylonian captivity alters according to which prophet one reads.[19] These examples are hardly fortuitous. Olivi is assuming a double *concordia*. The events of the early sixth period of church history parallel those of Old Testament history in its sixth period, but they also parallel the birth, death, and resurrection of Christ, who ushered in the sixth period of world history.

Note, too, Olivi's assumption that the same passage of scripture refers simultaneously to several different events. There is nothing unique about this multiple reference. Olivi tells us on several occasions that it is a characteristic of prophetic scripture. On the one hand, such scripture combines the general with the particular. It speaks of a specific case and yet "ascends and expands" to a wider reference. For example, the beast from the sea in Revelation 13:1 refers specifically to the Saracens, but it also refers to the whole beastly crowd of reprobate fighting against the elect from the beginning of the world to its end.[20] On the other hand, prophetic scripture can refer simultaneously to several specific events. That is the case with the passage concerning the opening of the sixth seal, and, we will see, it is also true of those passages simultaneously referring to both of the two Antichrists.

Olivi's interpretation of the earthquake in Revelation 6:12 demonstrates how this multiple reference functions. He is not very interested in the first beginning of the sixth period with Joachim of Fiore (which he describes merely as a "prophetic beginning"), and makes no effort to apply the earthquake to it. In the case of the second beginning in the time of Francis, however, the earthquake can be applied to the spiritual upheaval represented in conversions to the Franciscan way on the one hand and carnal opposition to it on the other; to the Albigensian crusade; to "commotions and subversions" in Italy; and to the Tartar invasions, especially the devastation of Hungary. In the third beginning, it refers to the attack on the Franciscan rule and consequent upsets in the church in the time of the mystical Antichrist. In regard to the fourth beginning, it refers to events surrounding the great Antichrist's death.[21]

These applications are all valid, but they are not all equal. Olivi grants that there is a single "more literal" interpretation. What is said in the Apocalypse concerning the opening of the sixth seal will not be completely fulfilled before the carnal church is destroyed. Thus the passage applies "more literally and more principally" to the fourth beginning and the earthquake refers more literally to the great Antichrist's death, although it can be applied to the other beginnings "in various respects and senses."[22]

The sixth period will witness the birth of the third great age of history. In it, "the singular perfection of the life and wisdom of Christ is to be revealed and the senility of the prior period so universally repelled that it seems as if a certain new age or new church is then formed, the old one being rejected, just as, in Christ's first advent, a new church was formed and the old synagogue rejected."[23] Here we encounter both the essence and the apparent dangers of Olivi's expectation. Let us begin with its essence.

The Novelty of the Sixth Period

Olivi identifies the sixth period with a new revelation of Christ's life and wisdom. It is a revelation of his life in the sense that it involves a new appreciation of evangelical perfection. That means evangelical poverty, but it also means a great deal else. Olivi observes that in the sixth period not only Christ's precepts but his counsels are to be observed.[24] The *viri spiri-tuales* of the sixth period will be contemplatives endowed with a humility and patience surpassing previous ages. They will prefer to suffer rather than to act, yet will be graced with the ability to stir hearts through their preaching.[25]

Olivi has no difficulty finding a model for the new *vir spiritualis*. It is Francis of Assisi, the "principal founder, initiator and exemplar of the sixth period and its evangelical rule."[26] Nor is he in doubt as to where one might discover that evangelical rule. It is stated in the Franciscan rule, which itself is nothing less than the gospel observed by Christ and imposed on the apostles.[27] Thus Olivi's focus is not only on Francis but also on his rule and, by extension, on its adherents. In fact, much of the struggle that characterizes the sixth period up to the destruction of Babylon concerns the rule. It is so intimately related to the new life of the sixth period that the forces of carnality have countered by attempting to discredit and destroy the rule, while spiritual men have rallied to defend it.

Intellectus spiritualis

The sixth period also witnesses an impressive advance in knowledge. Here we have the "wisdom of Christ" alluded to by Olivi. His Apocalypse commentary begins with the words of Isaiah 30:26: "The light of the moon will be like that of the sun, and the light of the sun will be sevenfold like the light of seven days, on the day when the Lord binds the wound of his people and heals the wound of his people and heals the injury inflicted by his blow." He first applies the passage to Christ's work in the first century, but later refers it to the events of the sixth and seventh periods.[28]

Olivi refers to this increased knowledge of the third age as an *intellectus spiritualis*. What, then, does he mean by the term? It is important to emphasize once again that the third age represents a progression beyond the second, but it is also a progressive development in itself, commencing with the sixth period and leading to worldly fulfillment in the seventh,

then celestial fulfillment in eternity. It is also important to underscore that
the third age begins with Saint Francis and Joachim of Fiore. Olivi can
thus see himself as a beneficiary of the new era. For that reason, when we
ask ourselves what sort of thing this *intellectus spiritualis* of the third age
really is, we might do worse than to examine what Olivi is doing in his
Lectura super apocalypsim. When Olivi speaks of *intellectus spiritualis* in the
sixth period, he normally discusses it in the context of exegesis. Whatever
else it may be, it is an improved understanding of the Bible.[29]

In his Matthew commentary, Olivi accepts Joachim's notion that the
third age will mirror the procession of the Holy Spirit within the Trinity.
After the letter of Old Testament and the letter of the New Testament, we
discover a *concordia* and a spiritual interpretation of both.[30] Such statements seem to imply that the *intellectus spiritualis* of the third age involves
an understanding of the spiritual senses of scripture as medieval exegetes
normally understood that term. Other passages seem to support this assumption, as when Olivi identifies eating the book in Revelation 10:10
with tasting "the spiritual senses and meanings" of the Apocalypse.[31]

Nevertheless, one might hesitate before concluding that the new
knowledge is identical with the spiritual senses. In the first place, Olivi
recognizes that these senses antedate the third age. Like Joachim, he accepts the traditional identification of the literal sense with the stone rolled
away from Christ's tomb.[32] Viewed from this perspective, literal interpretation becomes characteristic of pre-Christian, Jewish exegesis, while spiritual interpretation is identified with the Christian era. At the same time,
Olivi seems to see Joachim's importance as an exegete largely in terms of
his contribution to the literal interpretation of the Apocalypse. Olivi is
clear on this point. All seven visions of the Apocalypse except the first deal
literally with church history. The *intellectus spiritualis* of the new age seems
to include an improved understanding of this literal sense, not just of the
spiritual senses. Olivi remarks that the literal significance of a passage can
sometimes be more spiritual than the allegorical one.[33]

Granting this much, one might ask whether it is a mistake to assume
that Olivi's use of the term "spiritual" follows the one normal among exegetes. The answer seems to be that he entered the Apocalypse commentary
bearing a number of traditional ideas, and not all of them were entirely
consistent with his program there. Ideally he should have reserved the
word "spiritual" for that interpretation of scripture employed by spiritual
exegetes of the third age. Thus employed, it would not stand in opposition
to literal interpretation, but rather would include it. Its legitimate opposite

would be carnal interpretation. Unfortunately, what Olivi should have done is not precisely what he did. He occasionally seems to cooperate with this scenario, comparing the literal interpretation not with the spiritual meaning but with the mystical one; yet at other times he compares it with the spiritual sense.[34]

However muddy Olivi's terminology, it is clear that the new *intellectus spiritualis* includes an improved understanding of the literal sense. This fact fits nicely with Olivi's repeated assertions that the sixth age brings a clearer understanding of the Apocalypse itself.

> Just as the solemn beginning of the New Testament, occurring in the sixth age of the world and prepared for by the five preceding ages, clarified the prophets' meaning in regard to Christ's first advent and the times leading up to it, so the solemn beginning of the sixth period of the church, prepared for by the preceding five, clarifies the meaning of this book and other prophetic books in regard to Christ's threefold advent and the times leading up to both the first and second advents. Because of this, in the sixth period the sun of Christian wisdom will cast a sevenfold light, like the light of seven days.[35]

Olivi's identification of the sixth period with an improved understanding of prophecy explains why he sees Joachim as one point at which the period can be said to have begun. Olivi feels that the Joachite theory of concordance is central for the new wisdom of the third age. When we ask precisely what its value for that era may be, the answer is that it will help us to unravel prophetic works, especially the Apocalypse. In answer to those who shy away from such a project, Olivi suggests that at this juncture we need all the help we can get. In commenting on the opening of the book in Revelation 5:5, he remarks that it particularly applies to three moments in history when the saints call for more information. The first was the time just before Pentecost; the second was that of the great heresies; and the third will be the time of Antichrist.[36] Elsewhere he remarks that "great wisdom and watching and attentive consideration will be needed if we are to understand the name and number of the beast and the properties of his seven heads."[37] It is pointless to take Paul's warning against undue apocalyptic speculation as a prohibition of present investigation. Paul did not have to prepare for the Antichrist's imminent arrival, as those in the dawning sixth period do. Thus the Joachite theory of concordance, which offers a predictive tool enabling us to see deeper into biblical prophecy, becomes an invaluable aid in preparing for the apocalyptic onslaught. In his commentary on Job, Olivi endows it with even greater importance by suggesting that the Antichrist himself will employ concordances, supporting his authority with a collection of bogus ones.[38]

Francis, *Intellectus*, and *Gustus*

Important as Joachim may be for an understanding of the new era, he pales to insignificance when compared with the other great initiator of that era, Francis of Assisi. We have seen that Olivi's image of Francis is central to his understanding of how the life of Christ is fulfilled in the third age. (A great deal more will be said about the matter in a moment.) It might seem less helpful to present Francis, the little simpleton, as a key figure in the fulfillment of Christ's wisdom, particularly in the light of what has been said concerning the role of biblical exegesis in the sixth period; yet Olivi's attempt to portray him in this way is in some ways analogous to the picture of Francis's scriptural knowledge offered by Thomas of Celano and Bonaventure: Francis's knowledge is the result of divine inspiration; it rests more directly upon love and prayer than upon intellect and study; and it is closely related to knowledge of the future.[39] In the *Legenda maior*, Bonaventure moves smoothly from Francis's knowledge of scripture to his prophetic gifts.

On the whole, Francis's connection with the new wisdom ties him more with what Olivi will say of the seventh period than with the picture he offers of the sixth, for in depicting the seventh he speaks less of exegesis and more of mystical vision or contemplation, as we will see. In a larger sense, however, Francis is relevant to both periods, for he represents a type of wisdom in accordance with Olivi's characteristically Franciscan insistence that contemplation, which includes both conceptual understanding and love, is principally an activity of the will rather than the intellect.[40]

Wisdom lies more in *gustus* and *affectus* than in *rationalis aspectus*.[41] God's secrets can be penetrated fully only by *gustus*.[42] We are not speaking simply of appreciation as opposed to knowledge, but rather of a special type of knowledge. In his Genesis commentary, in the middle of a passage dealing with how Joseph could interpret dreams, Olivi remarks that, while one cannot have in oneself a *lumen creatum* sufficient for knowledge of all things, one can have a certain spiritual *intellectus et gustus* capable of *degustandam et discernendam* accurately truths proportionate to such a gift. The saints were accorded a certain high and supermundane taste and sense (*gustum et sensum*) of divine eternity and its eternal truth and goodness.

Olivi compares this gift to the way in which "someone who has become knowledgeable about wines through constant exercise of his taste can tell by taste alone whether a wine is good or bad, sweet or bitter." God has not distributed such abilities equally among his saints. Some have a livelier sense (*vivaciorem sensum*) for discerning human behavior, others for discerning good from evil angels, and still others for discerning visions sent by God.[43]

Contemplative wisdom involves *gustus*. Olivi seeks in contemplation a deeper sort of knowledge in which simple intellectual apprehension is transcended through an affective experience given directly by the Holy Spirit. God, he says, is seen in the threefold light of natural reason, holy scripture, and devout experience, and the third consummates the first two.[44] Discussing Job's encounter with God, he remarks that

> just as contemplatives see clearly and explicitly through divine illumination what they once held implicitly and enigmatically through faith, so Job now sees more clearly and explicitly what he saw earlier through faith and through some contemplation, though not as explicitly or intensely nor with such perfect *sensus* or *gustus*.[45]

Thus we have a scale of knowledge running from faith through contemplation to direct vision. The scale is to some extent a continuum. Olivi may comment that Job's vision was as different from ordinary contemplative experience as sight is from hearing, but he still speaks of more or less clarity, more or less *gustus*. Moreover, he recognizes that even Job will get a more satisfactory answer in heaven.

Olivi's preoccupation with contemplative *degustatio* is related to his sense of the limitations inherent in human speech about sacred things. Commenting on John 16 : 25 he says,

> Note that all external and sensible speech concerning divine things, however literal it may be, is obscure and parabolic when compared with that internal and superintellectual speech through which Christ's spirit clearly illumines and instructs the mind concerning divine things. Similarly, all internal speech of the Holy Spirit concerning this life, however high and clear it may be, is enigmatic and parabolic when compared with that given through the beatific vision of God. Concerning the first mode, Christ wishes to say that all his external doctrine, according to which he has taught them about divine things as a man up to now, is more or less parabolic and enigmatic or metaphorical and obscure when compared with what he will do shortly after through his spirit.[46]

The words "shortly after" remind us that, although Olivi's scale of knowledge can be seen as a historical progression, he does not intend to imply that specific types of knowledge are limited to those periods with which they are particularly identified. The significance of Pentecost is not lost on him. He knows that the Holy Spirit operates in all ages, that the seven grades of perfection can be realized by individuals at any time, and that spiritual knowledge is in some sense characteristic of the entire Christian era.[47] When he speaks of the sixth and seventh periods as the age of the Holy Spirit, he is speaking relatively. The third age is not appropriated to the Holy Spirit because the spirit begins to operate only then, but because the contemplative experience granted through the spirit is then given more generally and with greater intensity.

Christ's Centrality

It is, of course, Christ's spirit. The point is so obvious that perhaps it need not be made at this juncture, but there is no harm in belaboring the obvious when Olivi's orthodoxy is at stake. Given the long-standing debate over whether Joachim's notion of the three ages so identifies Christ and the New Testament dispensation with the second age as to imply that they will become obsolete in the near future, it is worth noting that, however difficult such a charge is to substantiate in Joachim's case, it is even harder to prove in Olivi's. To be sure, he lays heavy emphasis on the novelty of the third age, when "the antiquity of the former time is so universally renounced that a new church might seem to be formed, old things being rejected, just as in Christ's first advent a new church was formed, the old synagogue being rejected."[48] This sounds dangerously like Gerard of Borgo San Donnino, but Olivi is careful to place the third age within the Christian dispensation. Like Joachim, he develops his threefold pattern in conjunction with his twofold pattern of double sevens, and the latter pattern clearly assumes that the Christian era will perdure until the end of time. Thus the age of the Holy Spirit will fulfill the Christian dispensation, not replace it. He observes that "in order to make the end [*finis*] of the church concordant with the end of the synagogue or of the previous age, in the sixth period of which Christ came as the end of the prior age, God chose the sixth period of the church to more perfectly express his form and life in Christ."[49] Shortly thereafter he makes the same point in slightly different words:

> Just as in the sixth age, carnal Judaism and the senility of the prior time
> having been rejected, the new man Christ came with a new law, life and cross,
> so in the sixth period, the carnal church and the senility of the prior time
> having been rejected, the law, life and cross of Christ will be renewed, and
> for this reason at its beginning there appeared Francis, marked with Christ's
> wounds and totally crucified with as well as configured to Christ.[50]

In both cases he is developing a *concordia* between the old Augustinian
division of world history into seven "days" and the seven periods of church
history. According to the former, Christ came to usher in the sixth age,
which represents the entire Christian dispensation down to the final judgment. Thus Olivi's parallel is not between two consecutive periods but
between a period and one of its subperiods. The sixth period of church
history ushered in by Francis unfolds within the sixth period of world
history inaugurated by Christ. In this context, *finis* seems to mean not
"conclusion" but "fulfillment."

Olivi underlines the same point by speaking of Christ's three advents:
in the flesh, to inaugurate the first period of the church; in the spirit in the
sixth period; and in judgment at the end of time.[51] This notion has been
described as unique to Olivi, but here again there is a parallel in Bonaventure's *Collationes in hexaemeron*, at least in the Delorme version.[52] Bonaventure remarks that after Antichrist's death there will be more peace and
tranquillity than at any time since the beginning of the world. There will
be men whose sanctity equals that of apostolic times, "for those opposing
Antichrist will be given the spirit in the highest degree." Thus "the time
will be called that of Christ's advent in the spirit, allegorically speaking."
Since Bonaventure would also acknowledge Christ's first advent in the
flesh and his final one in judgment, that gives us the requisite three. The
passage might lead one to believe that Bonaventure is more interested in
the Joachite threefold pattern than we have suggested, but it is worth
noting that he places this advent after Antichrist's death. Thus his observation is actually an extension of the statements already seen in some Franciscan Apocalypse commentaries concerning the seventh period. He seems
to see it as a short interval, since he adds that those who followed Antichrist will be given forty-two days to repent, reflecting the forty-two years
given the Jews after Christ's death.

In any case, it is clear that for Olivi, Christ is lord of all periods of
church history,[53] yet he is present in a special way in the sixth and seventh.
The perfection attained by the *viri evangelici* will be evangelical perfection
or the perfect life of Christ. Their poverty will be apostolic poverty, and

their sufferings will be an imitation of Christ's passion. The spirit that illumines them and aids them in attaining new insight into prophetic literature will be Christ's spirit. It will not be a different spirit of Christ than the one given to previous generations. Olivi is careful to note that Christ's second advent in the spirit is in one sense characteristic of the entire Christian era, not just its latter part.[54] Here again the distinction is ultimately one of degree. The sixth period will witness such an increase in the gifts of the spirit that it can be described as a second coming of Christ in the spirit.

The Role of Historical Perspective

So far we have dealt with the new knowledge of the third age almost exclusively in terms of a new infusion of Christ's spirit. There is another side of it, however. To some extent it can be seen as the result of sheer historical perspective, the product of being further down the path of historical development. Here Olivi's use of river, tree, and voyager images is instructive. In the extended journey image cited earlier in this chapter, he compares the three advents of Christ with a succession of three mountains separated by two valleys. His goal is to explain why Jews living before the incarnation expected only the coming of the messiah, while Christians during the first five periods of church history recognized only two advents of Christ. After the birth of the sixth period, people can finally be expected to see all three advents, but at that point they can also gain new insight into the concordance of church history with the seven ages of world history on the one hand and the seven periods of Old Testament history on the other.[55]

Elsewhere he uses a tree image with similar effect. Considering the gates of Revelation 21:21, he remarks that

> although a multitude of people entered in to Christ through the apostles and other saints of the second general age of the church, as if through gates of the city of God, this passage is nevertheless more appropriately applied to the principal doctors of the third general age, through whom all Israel and the whole world will enter in to Christ. For just as it more befitted the apostles to be the foundations of the entire church and Christian faith, so it more befits these others to be the open gates and the openers or explicators of Christian wisdom. For just as a tree, when it is nothing but a root, cannot be totally explicated or explicitly demonstrated to all so well as when it is fulfilled in branches, leaves, flowers and fruits, so the tree or fabric of the church and

divine providence and the wisdom shining forth and shared in its diverse parts could not and should not have been as well explicated from the beginning as it can and should be at its fulfillment. Thus just as, from the beginning of the world to the birth of Christ, the illumination of the people of God and explication of the order and procession of the entire Old Testament and providence of God in the establishment and governance of the world increased successively, so it is with the illuminations and explications of Christian wisdom in the time of the New Testament.[56]

This is an extraordinary statement. Along with the voyager image, it shows the combination of contemplative enlightenment and historical perspective involved in our improved understanding. We see what previous ages could not see, partly because of the greater spiritual gifts with which our age is endowed and partly because the events are there before us, enabling us to reinterpret not only our own time, but the entire shape of history.

Such passages explain why Olivi sees knowledge of the sixth period as a prerequisite for understanding the first five. They also explain why he is prepared to challenge standard authorities like Augustine. The bishop of Hippo was a saintly and intelligent man, but he did not have much Christian history to work with and thus could not see the pattern of development that has since gradually emerged. It is understandable that his reading of the Apocalypse was in some ways erroneous.[57] Joachim wrote eight hundred years later and basked in the early rays of the new enlightenment, so it is not surprising that he should have seen truths unnoticed by Augustine; yet even he was a victim of his historical position. Olivi applies the tree image not only to Christian history as a whole, but to the sixth period in particular.[58]

Olivi's acceptance of a progressive development in the sixth period itself may at least partially explain some of his differences with the Italian spirituals. His expectation of positive change within the sixth period may have discouraged him from canonizing the early Franciscan situation as normative and encouraged him to accept some of the remarkable changes which transformed his order during the thirteenth century. In any case, it enabled him to seek a Franciscan renewal which would be something more than a return to the standards of early Franciscanism.

Francis as Apocalyptic Angel

This brings us to an issue largely evaded so far: Francis's role as an apocalyptic figure. We saw earlier that Bonaventure's identification of Francis with the angel of the sixth seal proved hard for later Franciscans to ignore. We also saw that exegetes like Vital du Four and Matthew of Aquasparta might follow Bonaventure in this respect, but they lacked the basic assumptions that would have enabled them to view Revelation 7:2 as a literal reference to Francis. Olivi shared precisely those assumptions, and he knew of Bonaventure's identification not only because he had read the *Legenda maior*, but also because, as he tells us in the Apocalypse commentary, he had heard Bonaventure say the same thing at Paris. He does not mention whether Bonaventure presented the identification as the literal meaning of the passage, although, as we saw in the second chapter, Ubertino da Casale says in his *Arbor vitae* that Olivi told him precisely that. We simply do not know. As we have seen, Bonaventure had the necessary presuppositions to accept Francis as literally designated by Revelation 7:2, and Olivi certainly accepted him as such.

In dealing with Revelation 7:2, Olivi begins by quoting Joachim's suggestion that the angel mentioned there is a man who will come at the beginning of the third age.[59] He then works carefully through the passage, displaying Francis's credentials as that man. Olivi describes him as "the renewer of the evangelical life and rule to be propagated and glorified in the sixth and seventh periods, and its greatest observer after Christ and his mother." He ascends from the rising of the sun, "that is, from the beginning of the opening of the solar sixth and seventh day or the third general age of the world." Through him is also signified "the crowd of his disciples to come in the third and fourth beginning of the sixth opening and similarly to ascend from the rising of the sun, in whom his example, merit, and virtual rule from heaven will be so singularly present that whatever good he does through them should be ascribed to him rather than to them."[60] Of course, the passage gives him an opportunity to speak of Francis's configuration with the passion of Christ through the stigmata. More surprisingly, it encourages him to raise the question of whether Francis will imitate Christ, not only in passion, but in resurrection as well, a problem which must be examined in a moment.

Since Revelation 7:2 offers Olivi so many possibilities, and since it comes to him with such a rich Franciscan heritage, it is surprising to discover that his most sustained treatment of Francis as apocalyptic figure is actually in his exegesis of Revelation 10:1–3.[61] It makes good exegetical sense for him to consider Francis at this point, however, since the passage belongs within the vision of the seven trumpets, which Olivi, like others, sees as a history of the preaching office. The angel of 10:1 falls within the blowing of the sixth trumpet and thus within the sixth period. Olivi acknowledges that some commentators have identified this angel, who descends from heaven holding an open book, as Christ. Certainly Christ, who illumines our minds, is our principal teacher, but he nonetheless ordains angelic men and spirits to teach others. The angels in this vision represent such men and spirits. Again Olivi quotes Joachim at length, this time to the effect that Revelation 10 : 1 literally represents a single powerful preacher, a practitioner of both the active and contemplative life, a man endowed with spiritual understanding of scripture; yet it can also be applied spiritually to many spiritual men in the future.[62] "It should be known," Olivi says,

> that just as our most holy father Francis is, after Christ and under Christ, the first and principal founder and initiator and exemplar of the sixth period and its evangelical rule, so he, after Christ, is primarily designated by this angel. Thus as a sign of this fact he appeared transfigured in a fiery chariot in the sun in order to show that he had come in the spirit and in the image of Elijah, as well as to bear the perfect image of the true sun, Christ.

Olivi goes on with a close reading of the passage which stresses Francis's poverty, humility, contemplative wisdom, and missionary zeal. In the process of exploring the latter element, he notes that Francis tried to preach to the Saracens three times. One occasion was in the sixth year of his conversion, symbolizing his status as angel of the sixth seal. This effort also served as a sign of the conversions to be effected by his order in the sixth period of the church. He tried again in the thirteenth year of his conversion, as a sign that the Saracens and other infidels would begin to be converted by his order in the thirteenth century. Olivi observes that just as on the thirteenth day from his birth Christ appeared before the kings of the East, and in his thirteenth year he disappeared from his mother and was found in the temple, so in the thirteenth century from Christ's birth Francis and his evangelical order appeared, and in the thirteenth century from his death "he will be exalted upon the cross and ascend in glory over the whole world." There follows here another comment that we must consider in a moment when dealing with the peculiar problem of Francis's resurrection. It is followed by one of Olivi's most pointed remarks about how spiritual men will turn away from the Latin church in the sixth period.

> He will place his right foot upon the sea of infidel nations and his left upon the land of the faithful, because his principal impetus and progress will be toward conversion of the whole world to Christ, yet not in such a way as to

desert the early church of the faithful. For just as, in the time of the apostles, their principal (and, as it were, right) progress was toward conversion of the pagans, and their secondary (or, as it were, left) progress was toward the Jews, because they sensed that they would not prosper so much by fishing on the land of the Jews as by fishing in the sea of the pagans, so this angel will sense that he will not prosper as much in the carnal church of the Latins as among the Greeks, Saracens, and Tartars, and at last the Jews. . . . Moreover, from Francis's time until now this angel has fished more in the sea of the laity tossed about by secular cares than on the land of the regulars and clerics. For simple, uneducated men are more easily brought to penance than great clerics or monks.[63]

Francis's Resurrection

Finally, we must look at Olivi's comments concerning a possible resurrection of Saint Francis. The matter is raised as an addendum to his discussion of Francis as angel of the sixth seal. Obviously it arises in the context of his effort to see Francis as conformed with the life, death, and resurrection of Christ, but it is also related to (in fact, it immediately follows) his words about how Francis will work through his disciples during the third and fourth beginnings of the sixth period. Having shared his thoughts on that subject, Olivi goes on to say,

> I have also heard from a very spiritual man, very worthy of belief and very intimate with Brother Leo, confessor and companion of blessed Francis, something that is consonant with this scripture but which I neither assert nor know nor think should be asserted, namely that both through the words of Brother Leo and through revelation made to him personally, he learned that during the pressure of that Babylonian temptation in which Francis's state and rule will be crucified, as it were, in the place of Christ himself, he will rise again glorious, so that just as he was singularly assimilated to Christ in his life and in the stigmata of the cross, so he will be assimilated to him in a resurrection necessary for confirming and informing his disciples, just as Christ's resurrection was necessary for confirming the apostles and informing them concerning the foundation and governance of the future church. In order that the resurrection of the servant should be distinguished clearly in degree of dignity from the resurrection of Christ and his mother, however, it is said by certain people who are not entirely to be rejected that Christ was resurrected immediately after three days, his mother after forty, and this man after the whole duration of his order up to its crucifixion (assimilated to the cross of Christ and prefigured in Francis's stigmata).[64]

Some modern historians have been tempted to discount this passage, suggesting that Olivi is simply reporting a view concerning which he himself is unenthusiastic. Such an interpretation is hard to accept. Olivi grants that the view is not to be asserted, but he is careful to lay out his source's credentials and explicitly warns us that the "certain people" of whom he speaks should not be rejected without consideration. Far from being dismissive, these characterizations seem rather bold when one considers that Olivi is speaking as a Paris-trained intellectual addressing his fellow Franciscans in pursuit of his duties as lector in a relatively prominent convent. The amazing thing is not that Olivi would discuss a point like this so tentatively, but that he would discuss it at all in an essentially academic context. One searches in vain for anything quite like this in other Franciscan commentaries, but there are parallels outside the realm of exegesis. Bonaventure speaks of resurrection in one of his sermons on Saint Francis, and one can even find a reference to the subject—albeit a more oblique one—in his *Legenda maior*.[65] Nevertheless, Bonaventure gives the word a highly metaphorical sense in these contexts and does not refer it to any future occurrence.

The real parallels with Olivi's remark would seem to be found in the literature of the Italian spirituals. In the two passages from that literature which shed light on the matter, the trail leads back to Conrad of Offida by way of Ubertino da Casale.[66] Olivi knew Ubertino at Florence in 1287–89, but his 1295 letter shows that he also knew Conrad. It is intriguing that Olivi and Ubertino use almost the same words in describing him. Olivi says, "Audivi etiam a viro spirituali valde fide digno." In the *Arbor vitae* Ubertino says, "Ego . . . audivi a sancto viro Conrado et a quampluribus fide dignis." Ubertino differs from Olivi in announcing that the idea was revealed "to Brother Leo and to some others" and was simply told to Conrad, but he agrees with Olivi in suggesting that the purpose of the revelation will be to comfort Francis's sons at a time when their rule is being universally assaulted. Ubertino insists that this can be "devoutly awaited but not temerariously asserted." He is a bit more specific about the nature of Francis's resurrection, however. He says Francis will arise *in corpore glorioso* and appear visibly to his followers.

The passage in the Revelation commentary is not Olivi's only allusion to this matter, or even to the "spiritual man" in question. Close to two decades earlier in his Matthew commentary, he served notice that he was already aware of the prediction.

> It has been revealed (as I have heard from a very spiritual man) that this will be fulfilled by the angel of the sixth seal with certain of his confreres in order

that he should conform to Christ in his resurrection as well as in his passion, and in order that his disciples at that time, nearly enticed into error, should have an instructor and comforter as the apostles had the risen Christ.[67]

Thus if the spiritual man was indeed Conrad of Offida (and he certainly seems the most likely candidate), Olivi must have met him very early, presumably during his trip to Italy in 1279.[68]

There are two problems here that bear further exploration. One is the question of precisely what Olivi really meant to say in speaking of Francis's resurrection. Perhaps the most significant passage in this respect is one which does not even mention resurrection. Remember that, in his exegesis of Revelation 10:1-3, Olivi announces that in the thirteenth century after Christ's death "he will be exalted upon the cross and ascend in glory over the whole world." In context, "he" seems to refer to Christ, but in the preceding part of the sentence Olivi has referred to the appearance of "Francis and his evangelical order." In this latter part the idea makes a great deal more sense if here as well "he" actually stands for them as well as Christ. Olivi is referring one more time to the coming tribulation of the *viri spirituales*, Francis's sons.

It is the next few lines that are most significant. Olivi predicts that "from the time the evangelical life and rule is solemnly attacked and condemned (beginning under the mystical Antichrist and more fully under the great one), Christ, his servant Francis, and the angelic crowd of his disciples will spiritually descend against the errors and malicious actions of the world and against the whole army of demons and wicked men." Olivi goes on to say that "he will descend from heaven, and he will be clothed as by a cloud with a knowledge of scriptures that is not earthly and false but heavenly and pure." He will have this knowledge not only for himself but in order to convey it to others. Next comes the passage cited earlier, in which he is said to "place his right foot on the sea of the infidel nations," and so forth.

Who, then, is the "he" in question? Olivi has granted that such passages refer both to Christ and to those through whom he works. In the present case, the situation is even more complex because the servant through whom he works, Francis, has his own followers. Thus the "he" seems to have a triple reference. It applies principally to Christ, and then to Francis, but also to the *viri spirituales* inspired by Christ and Francis. Obviously what we have here in the exegesis of 10:1 is structurally similar to the interpretation of 7:2. The basic message in each case is that Francis was, is, and will be conformed with Christ's life, death, and resurrection.

In each case the passion and resurrection are largely projected into the future, thanks to an identification of Francis with his rule and followers. In each case the essential point is that the rule will be attacked and the followers will be hard-pressed, but Francis will aid them in their hour of need. The particulars vary. In one case he comes alone, in another with some of his followers, and in a third with Christ and some followers. In two cases his appearance is described as resurrection, in a third as descent. One begins to get the impression that the specific scenario is not terribly important. Olivi finds the idea of Francis's resurrection unproved and un-provable, yet intriguing. He is capable of shifting the details a bit every time he entertains the idea; yet he sees behind them an idea that appeals to him and which he enjoys pondering. Even his particulars remain oddly general, never attaining the precision suggested by Ubertino's visual ap-pearance of a glorified body.

The Role of Visionary Experience

We are left with the other question inspired by these passages: Why would an intelligent scholar like Olivi have shown such interest in a vision? Viewed from one angle, the matter seems easily resolved. Olivi liked the idea of Francis's resurrection because it fit nicely into his general expec-tations for the future. It went beyond anything he could find in more traditional (and less questionable) authorities, but it supported and fleshed out what he read into those other authorities. There is more to the prob-lem than this, however. The disappointment registered by some modern historians when faced with evidence of Olivi's interest in visions serves to remind us that, while Olivi is remarkably accessible to us in some ways, he is very foreign in others. He moved in circles that not only accepted the existence of visions but placed some value on them. We are familiar with those circles as described by Ubertino da Casale, who acknowledges that he was influenced by his contact with people like Pier Pettinaio, Cecilia da Firenze, Margherita da Cortona, Angela da Foligno, and Chiara da Mon-tefalco.[69] The *Fioretti* show us how important visionary experience was in validating the sanctity of Conrad of Offida and other like-minded Francis-cans in the Marches, and Ubertino's reference to Conrad offers further evidence of this connection.

Olivi's circles are less easy to document. Obviously during his sojourn in Florence he would have received at least some exposure to the ethos described by Ubertino, but one suspects that he already had encountered something analogous in southern France. Certainly the sort of connection between Franciscans and pious laity described by Ubertino—a mutual enrichment in which Franciscans reached outside the order to give and receive spiritual support—existed in southern France by the fourteenth century and served to protect spiritual Franciscans when the pope and Franciscan leadership turned on them. Scattered comments by Olivi (like his observation that spiritual men have found the fishing better among laymen) suggest that the connection already existed in his time. Moreover, it is significant that of the several visionaries whom Olivi seems to have known personally, at least two were apparently women.[70]

Nevertheless, Olivi had a special reason to find visions interesting: They supported his theory of history and were in turn supported by it. His expectation of increased spiritual illumination in the third age probably led him to give more attention to visionary experience than would have been the case had he placed himself in the early fifth period of church history, as some of his fellow exegetes did. Naturally a denizen of the sixth period had to be careful. We have seen that, in a letter written in the early 1280s, Olivi admits that he is already subject to criticism for following "dreams and fantastic visions." He replies that he thinks no dream or vision should be followed unless we can establish infallibly that it is sent by God and we can be sure we know what it means. A list of criteria for testing the spirits follows.[71] A fuller set of criteria is offered in still another work, a treatise aimed at warning the faithful against certain spiritual temptations, tricks played by the devil on those who might prize visions.[72] Both sets of criteria emphasize the danger of accepting false visions, but both sets leave room for the reader to assume that there are indeed genuine ones. This message is reinforced elsewhere in Olivi's writings, as in the Job commentary, where he argues against those who insist that the time of prophecy and visions has passed,[73] or in his commentary on Mark and Luke, where he lists the right and wrong reasons for doubting a vision.[74]

Of course the sixth period was not scheduled to last forever. When we turn to the contemplative knowledge enjoyed in the seventh period, we will see why visionary experience in his own time might have struck Olivi as a foretaste of things to come.

Notes

1. *Lectura*, 61: "Ex predictis autem patet quod principalis intelligentia sexti et septimi membri visionum huius libri fortius probatur et probari potest quam intelligentia membrorum intermediorum inter primum et sextum seu inter radicem et sextum. Unde et clara intelligentia ipsorum dependet ab intelligentia sexti, sicut et ratio eorum, que sunt ad finem, dependet a fine." He is really talking about the sixth part of each vision, not the sixth period, but we have seen that the former is primarily about the latter.

2. Ibid., 48: "Sicut enim multi sunt gradus perfectionum inter infimum et supremum, sic decuit quod ecclesia ab infimo ad supremum ascenderet per gradus intermedios tanquam per preambulas dispositiones precurrentes ultimam formam."

3. Ibid., 155.

4. Ibid., 41, 76, 100–102, 116, 395, 661, 969. The tree image on p. 41 is of particular interest because it seems to reflect an image in Joachim's *Liber figurarum*: "Sextus vero status describitur quasi per modum late et multe expansionis ramorum fructuosorum, reiectis virgultis et ramis inutilibus."

5. Ibid., 101f.: "Sicut enim viro distanti a monte magno, duas magnas valles seu planities intra se continente ac per consequens et trino, videtur mons ille non ut trinus sed tantum ut unus mons, nullis vallibus distinctus; ex quo vero vir ille stat super primum montem videt primam vallem et duos montes vallem illam concludentes; ex quo vero stat in monte secundo seu medio videt duas valles cum montium ipsas includentium trinitate, sic Iudei, qui fuerunt ante primum Christi adventum quasi ante primum montem, non distinxerunt inter primum et postremos, sed sumpserunt totum pro uno. Christiani vero sextum statum ecclesie preeuntes distinguunt quidem inter primum et ultimum, tanquam iam positi super primum et tanquam videntes medium spatium conversionis gentium, quod est et fuit inter primum adventum et ultimum. Communiter tamen non distinguunt inter illum, qui erit in extremo iudicio, et inter illum, qui erit in statu sexto, quando, secundum apostolum, Christus illustratione sui adventus interficiet antichristum. Qui autem statuentur in sexto vel in spiritu vident ipsum, distinguunt ipsum a primo et postremo. Videntque tunc hanc distinctionem in libris propheticis, et etiam in hiis que a Christo et apostolis dicta sunt de finali Christi adventu et de finali statu mundi. Tunc etiam vident, quotlibet opera quinque priorum etatum concordet cum quinque primis ecclesie statibus et septem prelia seu signacula sub lege completa concordent cum septem ecclesie statibus."

6. Ibid., 48–50, attempts to find some sense in which the fifth period might be considered better than the first four.

7. Ibid., 76: "Sicut tota virtus priorum temporum intendit generationem sexti et septimi status, sic tota malitia eis contraposita cooperabitur malitie antichristi et reliquorum exercentium electos sexti et septimi status." See also ibid., 55: "In sexto et septimo statu est solemnis finis priorum temporum et quoddam novum et solemne seculum."

8. *In apocalypsim Ioannis*, 783.

9. See the comparison in Burr, "Bonaventure, Olivi and Franciscan Eschatology," 23–40.

10. *Collationes in hexaemeron*, 16.

11. Ibid., 16:29. See also Delorme, *Collationes in hexaemeron et Bonaventuriana quaedam selecta*, 192.

12. On the Antichrist see *Collationes in hexaemeron*, 13:33, 14:17, 15:1–9. On Aristotelianism see 4:8–13, 6:2–10, 7:1–12, 19:12–15. In the *Collationes de septem donis spiritus sancti*, 8:16, Bonaventure identifies the number of the beast with what he considers to be three basic Aristotelian errors.

13. *Collationes in hexaemeron*, 9:8, 20:30, 21:23, 22:23.

14. *The Theology of History in Saint Bonaventure*, 48.

15. *Lectura super Matthaeum*, MS Oxford New College 49, 107vb. See also ibid., 58va, and *Lectura super Isaiam*, MS Paris Bibl. Nat. nouv. acq. lat. 774, 58v.

16. *Lectura*, 230: "Sicut enim in primo statu seculi ante Christum studium fuit patribus enarrare magna opera domini inchoata ab origine mundi, in secundo vero statu a Christo usque ad tertium statum cura fuit filiis querere sapientiam misticarum rerum et misteria occulta a generationibus seculorum, sic in tertio nil restat nisi ut psallamus et iubilemus deo laudantes eius opera magna et eius multiformem sapientiam et bonitatem in suis operibus et scripturarum sermonibus clare manifestatam. Sicut etiam in primo tempore exhibuit se deus pater ut terribilem et metuendum, unde tunc claruit eius timor, sic in secundo exhibuit se deus filius ut magistrum et reservatorem et ut verbum expressivum sapientie sui patris. Ergo in tertio tempore spiritus sanctus exhibebit se ut flammam et fornacem divini amoris et ut cellarium spirituale ebrietatis et ut apothecam divinorum aromatum et spiritualium unctionum et unguentorum et ut tripudium spiritualium iubilationum et iocunditatum, per quam non solum simplici intelligentia sed etiam gustativa et palpativa experientia videbitur omnis veritas sapientie verbi dei incarnati et potentie dei patris." Compare with Joachim, *Expositio in Apocalypsim*, 84v–85v. Marjorie Reeves, *Influence of Prophecy*, 197, quotes this passage with the direct borrowings from Joachim in italics.

17. *Lectura*, 231: "Sicut etiam in primo tempore fuit per quandam appropriationem et antonomasiam labor corporalium operum, qui magis competit laicis, in secundo vero lectio et eruditio scripturarum, que plus competit clericis, sic in tertio debet praebundare casta et suavis contemplatio, que plus competit monachis seu religiosis."

18. Ibid., 918f., suggests dating the third age from the first crusade. See Chapter 7 below for further discussion.

19. Ibid., 394–96.

20. Ibid., 698f.: "Mos est scripture prophetice, dum de uno speciali agit sub quo spiritus propheticus invenit locum idoneum ad exeundum et dilatandum se, a specialibus ad generalia ascendere et expandi ad illa. . . . Sic ergo in proposito occasione bestie sarracenice dilatatur spiritus propheticus ad totam bestialem catervam reproborum, que ab initio mundi usque ad finem pugnat contra corpus seu ecclesiam electorum et per septem etates seculi habet capita septem."

21. Ibid., 394–408, 817.

22. Ibid., 396, 407f. At ibid., 429, he observes that fulfillment of the allegorical meaning sometimes precedes that of the literal.

23. Ibid., 57: "Sextum vero membrum ipsarum visionum et sexta visio huius libri declarat, quod in sexto tempore ecclesie est revelanda singularis perfectio vite et sapientie Christi et quod vetustas prioris temporis est sic universaliter repellenda, ut videatur quoddam novum seculum seu nova ecclesia tunc formari veteribus iam reiectis, sicut in primo Christi adventu formata est nova ecclesia veteri synagoga reiecta."

24. Ibid., 238.

25. Ibid., 235f., 241.

26. Ibid., 560: "Sanctissimus pater noster Franciscus est post Christum et sub Christo primus et principalis fundator et initiator et exemplator sexti status et evangelice regule eius."

27. Ibid., 393: "Ex quo igitur per romane ecclesie auctenticam testificationem et confirmationem constat regulam minorum per beatum Franciscum editam esse vere et proprie illam evangelicam, quam Christus in seipso servavit et apostolis imposuit et in evangeliis suis conscribi fecit."

28. Ibid., 1–3, 46, 58.

29. For example, Ibid., 563: "Eritque scientia scripturarum non terrestrium et falsarum sed celestium et purissimarum."

30. Olivi, *Lectura super Matthaeum*, 107vb.

31. *Lectura*, 575.

32. Ibid., 132, 272.

33. Ibid., 430: "Attamen quando litteralior sensus sic respicit finaliora bona vel facta, tunc ipse est spiritualior quam sint allegorici ipsum precurrentes, iuxta quod litteralius et magis proprie dicitur Deus esse vita et sapientia et summum bonum quam dictatur esse leo vel sol vel ros vel mel."

34. For the first see ibid., 430f.: "potius misticus quam litteralis"; "non ad litteram sed solum mistice." For the second, ibid., 366f., 781.

35. Ibid., 58: "Et ideo, sicut solemnis initiatio novi testamenti, facta in sexta mundi etate cum precursione quinque etatum, elucidat intellectum prophetarum quoad primum Christi adventum et quoad tempora ipsum precurrentia, sic solemnis initiatio sexti status ecclesie cum precursione quinque priorum elucidat intelligentiam huius libri et ceterorum prophetalium quoad trinum Christi adventum et quoad tempora precurrentia tam primum quam secundum adventum. Propter quod in ipso sexto tempore erit sol sapientie christiane septempliciter lucens sicut lux septem dierum."

36. Ibid., 325–27.

37. Ibid., 846.

38. *Lectura super Iob*, MS Florence Bibl. Laur. conv. soppr. 240, 65ra.

39. Celano, *Vita secunda*, 102–5; Bonaventure, *Legenda maior*, II:1–2.

40. Olivi, *Quaestiones de perfectione evangelica*, qq. 1 and 2, published in *Studi francescani* 60 (1963): 382–445; 61 (1964): 108–40; *Lectura super Ioannem*, MS Florence Bibl. Laur. Plut. 10 dext. 8, 80ra.

41. Olivi, *De studio divinarum literarum*, printed in *Sancti Bonaventurae . . . Operum . . . Supplementum* (Trent, 1755), 8:39f.

42. Olivi, *Expositio super Dionysii de angelica hierarchia*, MS Rome Vat. lat. 899, 22vb.

43. Olivi, *Lectura super Genesim*, MS Florence Bibl. Naz. Conv. Sopp. G 1 671, 122rb.

44. *De studio divinarum literarum*, 49.

45. *Lectura super Iob*, 65va: "Sciendum tamen quod sicut contemplativi ea vident clare et explicite per divinam illustrationem que prius implicite et enigmatice tenebant per fidem, sic et Iob ea que nunc vidit in maiori claritate magisque explicite prius videbat per fidem et per aliquam contemplationem sed non ita claram nec ita explicitam nec ita intense nec cum sensu aut gustu ita perfecto."

46. *Lectura super Ioannem*, 73vb: "Nota quod omnis exterior et sensibilis locutio de divinis quantumcumque fiat per nomina propria est obscura et parabolica respectu interioris et superintellectualis locutionis qua spiritus Christi mentem interius de divinis clare illustrat et docet. Et consimile omnis interior locutio spiritus sancti spectans ad statum huius vite quantumcumque sit alta et clara est enigmatica et parabolica respectu illius que sit per dei visionem beatificam et beatam. Christus secundum primum modum vult dicere quod tota doctrina sua exterior secundum quam eos ut homo de divinis usque nunc docuit est quasi parabolica et enigmatica seu similitudinaria et obscura respectu illius quam paulo post faciet per spiritum suum."

47. *Lectura*, 132, 272, 791.

48. *Lectura*, 57.

49. Ibid., 48.

50. Ibid., 96: "Sicut etiam in sexta etate, reiecto carnali Iudaismo et vetustate prioris seculi, venit nobis homo Christus cum nova lege et vita et cruce, sic in sexto statu, reiecta carnali ecclesia et vetustate prioris seculi, renovabitur Christi lex et vita et crux, propter quod in eius primo initio Franciscus apparuit, Christi plagis characterizatus et Christo totus concrucifixus et configuratus." See also ibid., 48, quoted in the preceding chapter. A similar argument concerning Olivi's early works is offered by me in "Apokalyptische Erwartung," 90f.

51. *Lectura*, 46, 57, 101f. See also pp. 40–42, where Christ is presented as efficient, exemplary, and containing cause of all seven periods.

52. *Collationes in hexaemeron et Bonaventuriana quaedam selecta*, visio III, collatio IV, p. 185.

53. *Lectura*, 330.

54. Ibid., 57

55. Ibid., 100–102.

56. Ibid., 968f.: "Sciendum igitur quod licet per apostolos et alios sanctos secundi generalis status ecclesie intraverit multitudo populorum ad Christum tanquam per portas civitatis dei, nihilominus magis appropriate competit hoc principalibus doctoribus tertii generalis status, per quos omnis Israel et iterum totus orbis intrabit ad Christum. Sicut enim apostolis magis competit esse cum Christo fundamenta totius ecclesie et fidei christiane, sic istis plus competit esse portas

apertas et apertores seu explicatores sapientie christiane. Nam sicut arbor, dum est in sola radice, non potest sic tota omnibus explicari seu explicite monstrari, sicut quando est in ramis et foliis ac floribus et fructibus consummata, sic arbor seu fabrica ecclesie et divine providentie ac sapientie in eius partibus diversimode refulgentis et participate non sic potuit nec debuit ab initio explicari, sicut in sua consummatione poterit et debebit. Et ideo sicut ab initio mundi usque ad Christum crevit successive illuminatio populi dei et explicatio ordinis et processus totius veteris testamenti et providentie dei in fabricatione et gubernatione ipsius, sic est de illuminationibus et explicationibus christiane sapientie in statu novi testamenti."

57. In Ibid., 564, Olivi remarks, "Nam in prioribus quinque ecclesie statibus non fuit concessum sanctis, quantumcumque illuminatis, aperire illa secreta huius libri, que in solo sexto et septimo statu erant apertius reseranda, sicut nec in primis quinque etatibus veteris testamenti fuit prophetis concessum clare aperire secreta Christi et novi testamenti in sexta etate seculi reserandis et reseratis."

58. Ibid., 395, where in describing the various beginnings he says it "sumpsit sue generationis et plantationis initium" in Francis; "sumet initium refloritionis seu repullulationis" from the preaching of spiritual men against the new Babylon; and "sumet initium sue clare distinctionis" from the destruction of Babylon.

59. Ibid., 414–16, presenting Joachim, *Expositio in apocalypsim*, 120va–21ra.

60. *Lectura*, 416f.: "Ascendit etiam ab ortu solis, id est circa initium solaris diei sexte et septime apertionis seu tertii generalis status mundi. Item per ipsum intelligitur cetus discipulorum eius in tertio et quarto initio sexte apertionis futurus et consimiliter ab ortu solis ascensurus, quibus eius exemplar et meritum et virtuale de celo regimen singulariter coassistet, ita ut quidquid boni per eos fiet, sit sibi potius ascribendum quam eis."

61. Ibid., 560–88.

62. Joachim, *Expositio super apocalypsim*, 137rb. In this section Olivi makes extensive use not only of Joachim's *Expositio*, but also of the *Liber de concordia*.

63. *Lectura*, 564f.: "Ponet etiam pedem suum dextrum super mare nationum infidelium et sinistrum super terram fidelium, quia principalis impetus et processus eius erit ad totum orbem convertendum ad Christum, sic tamen quod ex hoc non deseret priorem ecclesiam fidelium. Sicut enim tempore apostolorum fuit principalis et quasi dexter processus eorum ad conversionem paganorum, secundarius vero et quasi sinister ad plebem Iudeorum, quia senserunt non se ita prosperaturos seu prospere piscaturos in terra Iudeorum sicut in mari paganorum, sic et iste angelus sentiet non se ita prosperaturum in carnali ecclesia Latinorum sicut in Grecis et Sarracenis et Tartaris et tandem in Iudeis. Ponet etiam pedem dextrum super mare, quia promptior erit ad adversa tolleranda et ad antichristi prelia invadenda quam ad prospera temporalis pacis et glorie asumenda. Pro tempore etiam quod a Francisco usque nunc cucurrit, plus piscatus est hic angelus in mari laicorum secularibus curis fluctantium quam in terra regularium et clericalium. Simplices enim idiote facilius trahuntur ad penitentiam quam magni clerici vel monachi." See also ibid., 578: "In tempore medio inter misticum antichristum et magnum predicaturus est ordo ille multis linguis et gentibus."

64. Ibid., 417f.: "Audivi etiam a viro spirituali valde fide digno et fratri Leoni confessori et socio beato Francisci valde familiari quoddam huic scripture con-

sonum, quod nec assero nec scio nec censeo asserendum, scilicet quod tam per verba fratris Leonis quam per propriam revelationem sibi factam, perceperat Franciscum in illa pressura temptationis babilonice, in qua eius status et regula quasi instar Christi crucifigetur, resurget gloriosus, ut sicut in vita et in crucis stigmatibus est Christo singulariter assimilatus, sic et in resurrectione Christo assimiletur, necessaria tunc suis discipulis confirmandis et informandis, sicut Christi resurrectio fuit necessaria appostolis confirmandis et super fundatione et gubernatione future ecclesie informandis. Ut autem resurrectio servi patenti gradu dignitatis distaret a resurrectione Christi et sue matris, Christus statim post triduum resurrexit, et mater eius post quadraginta dies resurrexisse dicitur a quibusdam non omnino spernendis, iste vero post totum tempus sui ordinis usque ad crucifixionem ipsius cruci Christi assimilatam et Francisci stigmatibus presignatam."

    65. *Sermones de S. patre nostro Francisco*, sermo 3; *Legenda maior*, cap. 15.

    66. Ubertino da Casale, *Arbor vitae*, 442f; *Speculum vitae*, in A. G. Little, P. Mandonnet, and P. Sabatier, *Opuscules de critique historique* (Paris, 1903), 378f. Both documents show Ubertino announcing the view as he heard it from Conrad.

    67. *Lectura super Mattheum*, 155rb–va: "A viro valde spirituali audivi revelatum esse quod in angelo [angulo in Oxford MS, angelo in others] sexti signaculi cum quibusdam consociis suis de illo implebitur istud, ut sicut est conformis Christo in passione, sic sit in resurrectione. Et ut discipuli illius temporis qui fere in errorem ducentur de celis habeant instructorem et comfortatorem sicut apostoli habuerunt Christum resurgentem."

    68. On this trip see Burr, *OFP*, 39.

    69. *Arbor vitae*, prologue. Ties between Franciscans and lay mystics, particularly Clare of Montefalco and her circle, are also revealed in documents relating to the heresy of the *spiritus libertatis*. See Livarius Oliger, *De secta spiritus libertatis in Umbria saec. XIV* (Rome, 1943).

    70. One was the second of the two visionaries whose reports influenced his attempt to find some way of reconciling the notion that Christ died after he was wounded in the side with the passion narrative in the gospel of John, which clearly states that he died before. On this problem see my "Olivi, Apocalyptic Expectation, and Visionary Experience," 273–75. The relevant passage from Olivi's commentary on John is published as an appendix in Ferdinand Doucet, "De operibus mss. Petri Io. Olivi Patavii," *AFH* 28 (1935): 428–41. The other female mystic was the recipient of a vision narrated in an anonymous treatise found in MS Capestrano XXI, 118r–120r and usually attributed to Olivi. Other visionaries mentioned by Olivi are the "very spiritual man" from whom he received the idea of Francis's resurrection; the first visionary who reported on Christ's side wound (but whom Olivi does not explicitly claim to know personally); and perhaps still others implied by a casual reference in *Lectura super Isaiam*, 59r.

    71. *Quodlibeta* 53(65)r. For fuller discussion of Olivi's criteria see my "Olivi, Apocalyptic Expectation, and Visionary Experience."

    72. Published in Raoul Manselli, *Spirituali e Beghini in Provenza* (Rome, 1959), 282–90.

    73. *Lectura super Iob*, 12vb.

    74. *Lectura super Marcum et Lucam*, 7v–8r.

6. The Double Antichrist

So far we have paid substantial attention to the positive aspects of the dawning sixth period and offered a general overview of the negative aspects. To put it briefly, Olivi feels that the thirteenth century is witnessing a Christian renewal characterized by increased knowledge and a return to evangelical poverty. This renewal marks the beginning of the sixth period of church history and the third age of history in general. Nevertheless, the thirteenth century belongs not only to the rising sixth period but to the declining fifth as well. The tension between the *viri spirituales* of the sixth period and the carnal elements that have risen to power in the fifth will finally blossom into the temptation of the mystical Antichrist, a genuine persecution of the elect. This persecution will end when a pagan army destroys the city of Rome, the carnal church, and presumably much else besides. The elect, finding themselves free from oppression, will succeed admirably in their missionary efforts and Islam will be seriously weakened, but it will soon revive. The elect will be in for another persecution, the temptation of the great Antichrist. His death will usher in a seventh period of peace and contemplation. The third age will then be fully established.

Having said so much about the sixth period, we are left with the feeling that there is still a good deal to be said. One might wish to know more about the two Antichrists. Who are they and how did the idea of a double Antichrist come about? It would also be instructive to look more closely at the timetable for these events. When will each of the two Antichrists arrive and when will each be destroyed? In this and the following chapter we will examine such matters, beginning with the double Antichrist. In considering this problem we will begin to solve the chronological problem as well.

Recent Opinion

It has not escaped historians' attention that the arrival of Antichrist was a much-considered topic in the thirteenth and early fourteenth centuries.[1]

Nor has it gone unnoticed that Olivi made an important contribution to this topic when he distinguished between the mystical and the great Antichrist; yet there is little agreement as to what he meant by these terms. Clearly his double Antichrist is not derived from 1 John 2:18 or the related passages in John's letters (1 John 2:22, 1 John 4:3, 2 John 1:7), although he is aware of these passages and willing to acknowledge that in one sense history is teeming with antichrists. Nor is he simply accepting Joachim of Fiore's two Antichrists, which are a different matter arising from a completely different problem, that of what to make of Gog and his eschatological cameo appearance in Revelation 20:9.[2] His notion of the double Antichrist seems *sui generis*.

The closest thing to an established opinion on the matter is the one offered by Raoul Manselli. Manselli remarks that "we will not stray far from the truth if we say that Olivi sees the mystical Antichrist as a pseudo-pope who will place himself, in opposition to the true pope, at the head of the wicked and ally himself with political forces favorable to the carnal church." He will, in fact, be head of the carnal church, perhaps with his seat in Rome, toward the end of the overlap between the fifth and sixth periods of church history.[3] In dealing with the great Antichrist, Manselli says, Olivi kept his distance from the various traditions that had sprung up in the Middle Ages. He excluded all that could not be supported directly from the Bible. Olivi was aware that some Franciscans in Italy treasured so-called "revelations" which offered specific predictions, but he treated such things in "a dry, cautious, critical manner which barely disguised genuine disapproval."[4] Certainly he never intended to identify the Antichrist with a current pope, although he did tend to feel that the mystical Antichrist would be a false pope. He also thought the church in his own time had begun the descent that would eventually land it in the mystical Antichrist's arms.

Warren Lewis argues for a strikingly different view. Like Manselli, he sees the mystical Antichrist as a precursor to the great one, but concludes that "one remains more a demonic ideal at work in the minds and hearts of men whereas the other is a concrete being in time and space. What must be said to have been fulfilled allegorically during the time of the Mystical Antichrist can be said to be fulfilled literally with reference to the Great Antichrist."[5] Like Manselli, Lewis observes that Olivi was hesitant to state a future scenario too precisely and was notably unenthusiastic about current speculation that the Antichrist would be a resuscitated Frederick II or one of his descendents;[6] yet Lewis goes substantially further than Manselli in another direction. "It is clear," he says, "that Olivi 'thinks' of the Antichrist as a heretical pseudopope, although he hesitates—perhaps out of respect for the divinely ordained office of Petrine primacy in the sixth age of the church—to name Boniface VIII by name."[7] Here we arrive at what is obviously the most striking aspect of Lewis's argument, his conviction that Olivi engaged in precisely the sort of speculation Manselli is sure he avoided. Notice, however, that for Lewis the Antichrist in question is the great one, since the mystical Antichrist is, in his view, not an individual at all. By and large, modern scholars have tended to follow Manselli rather than Lewis, but in doing so they simply ignore Lewis rather than refuting him.[8] Their neglect is unfortunate, because Lewis presents the fullest case yet for a position that has existed more as a suspicion than as a conviction in the minds of several medievalists during the last few decades.

Lewis acknowledges that as late as September 1295 Olivi was willing to argue for the validity of Pope Celestine V's resignation and Boniface VIII's subsequent election. During the following month, however, Boniface removed Olivi's friend Raymond Geoffroi from his post as minister general, eventually replacing him with Olivi's old antagonist, John of Murrovalle. These events inspired Olivi to reconsider his position. He decided that Boniface could not yet be identified as Antichrist, but he was at least auditioning for the role, though not for the entire role. Olivi's notion of the Antichrist was, Lewis says,

> too grand, too all-inclusive to be applied to just one man. The mythical, miraculous, magnificent being whom Olivi had in mind combines in himself both the qualities of a political world ruler of the Frederick-type as well as the apostasy and immorality and christian scandal of a false and heretical pope. . . . The Antichrist is *per se* a spiritual category, a mystical concept. His public appearance would possibly take the form of not one but two human beings—a world ruler putting himself in the place of God and a pseudopope, the chief of all false prophets and the "image of the beast," whom the antichristian ruler establishes in his false papacy.[9]

Olivi, Lewis says, saw no one on the horizon who qualified for the role of world ruler, but Boniface was acting very much as if he might be the pseudopope.

Who is correct, Manselli or Lewis? In order to answer this question, we will examine a few key passages and try to draw some conclusions from them.

The Earthquake

The earliest significant passage in which Olivi ponders the two Antichrists is his exegesis of Revelation 6:12–7:13, the opening of the sixth seal, a passage already examined in the last chapter.[10] In it, we recall, Olivi proceeds on the assumption that the same passage in scripture can refer to several discrete future events. He interprets the earthquake (Revelation 6:12) in that way, relating it to four separate beginnings of the sixth period. In regard to the third beginning, it refers to the attack on the Franciscan rule and consequent troubles during the time of the mystical Antichrist. In regard to the fourth beginning, it alludes to the events surrounding the great Antichrist's death. Olivi acknowledges that there is, in fact, a single "more literal" interpretation. Since what is said here concerning the opening of the sixth seal will not be completely fulfilled before the carnal church is destroyed, the passage refers "more literally and more principally" to the fourth beginning. The earthquake applies "more literally" to the great Antichrist's death, although it can be applied to the other three beginnings "in various respects and senses."[11]

The Dragon

Olivi considers the Antichrist again in discussing the seven-headed dragon introduced at Revelation 12:3.[12] The passage, he says, is mainly about the seven battles of the church throughout its history. The dragon itself is the devil. What, then, of the seven heads? According to Joachim, he reports, they are allegorically seven kings who serve as the principal leaders of seven battles against the church in the seven periods of church history. These are Herod, Nero, Constantius, Cosroes or Mohammed, the first German emperor to infringe upon the liberties of the church, he who will strike Babylon (a.k.a. the carnal church), and the leader of the beast ascending from the earth (Revelation 13:11). The tail is Gog, and the ten horns are ten kings who will destroy Babylon.[13]

Having stated the basic interpretation, Olivi expands it. Caiaphas is no less qualified than Herod to be the first head, and all ten pagan emperors who persecuted the church deserve to be the second. All the Arian emperors, kings, and religious leaders form the third head; the Saracens and their leaders the fourth; and the carnal and lax of the fifth time are the fifth.[14] The mystical Antichrist will be the sixth head, while the great

Antichrist and the king who supports him will be the seventh. Gog will be the tail. If, however, one prefers to place the mystical Antichrist in the fifth head along with the others who belong there, then the great Antichrist will be the sixth and Gog the seventh. Olivi offers no guidance as to what we should do with the tail in this case.

He offers the same list of rulers in dealing with the seven kings of 17:9, but here he notes that in the *Liber de Concordia* Joachim identifies the fifth as Henry, king of the Germans, and the sixth as the king who will destroy the new Babylon. When the latter is struck down, the seventh head (Islam) will be wounded almost to death. The church will then have internal and external peace, for both the carnal church and Islam will be missing; yet after a brief time the seventh head will arise again as the other who "has not yet come"(17:10) and will be a receptacle of all the errors seen in the seven heads. The mystical Antichrist should be identified with the sixth king if the great one is taken as the seventh, but if the great Antichrist is taken as the sixth and Gog as the seventh, the mystical Antichrist should either be associated with the great in the sixth period or taken for the collected dregs of all laxations and other evils in the fifth. Here Olivi briefly considers the beast in Daniel 2:34, identifying it as both the Saracens in particular and paganism in general since Constantine (as well as heresy since its expulsion from the church in the fifth period).[15] Here again we see multiple reference, but this time of a more complex type including both particular and general applications.

The Woman in the Desert

In expositing the birth of the child and flight into the wilderness of Revelation 12:1–6, Olivi applies it entirely to the first century until he arrives at the 1,260 days in Revelation 12:6. He identifies the latter with the duration of the mission to the Gentiles following the rejection of Christianity by the Jews,[16] but remarks that "Joachim built his entire *concordia* of the Old and New Testaments on this number." Olivi then reports at length on how Joachim employs the idea of forty-two generations. He includes the latter's conviction that the generations in the second age of the world, the age of the Son (running essentially from Christ to Antichrist), should be reckoned at thirty years each.[17]

Having summarized Joachim, Olivi suggests a few adjustments. Joachim, he notes, began the forty-two generations of the second age with

Christ's birth, while later writers have chosen to begin them from his ascension. "To one who studies the words of this chapter more diligently,
however, it is clear that they should be counted from the flight of the
woman—that is, the church—into the desert of the Gentiles." That in
itself is hardly a clear notion. Olivi observes that this flight could be seen
as commencing with the conversion of Cornelius; the departure of some
disciples after Stephen's martyrdom; the growth of a Christian community
in Antioch; the mission of Paul and Barnabas; the total abandonment of
Jewish ceremonial law; or the destruction of Jerusalem. On the other end
of the development, the forty-two generations could be seen as ending
with either the mystical or the great Antichrist.[18]

Once again, Olivi concludes that each of these views can be considered correct in some respect. There is "great rationality and notable truth"
in the way Joachim, beginning with the incarnation, carries the forty-two
generations through to his own time. "For the third age, overlapping with
the second age, fundamentally began in the sixth year of the forty-first
generation" when Francis underwent his conversion. "From that point on,
all persecution of his evangelical state pertains to the persecution of Antichrist." Thus the attack on the mendicants began at Paris in the forty-
second generation, while in the same generation Frederick II and his
followers persecuted the church.

If we begin the reckoning with Christ's baptism, in the forty-first
generation "the evangelical order began to be famous in doctrine throughout the Latin church." The forty-second witnessed repeated attacks on the
mendicant orders culminating in their defense by Nicholas III in *Exiit qui
seminat*. In the same generation there appeared at Paris "those philosophical or rather pagan errors which are considered by the doctors to be great
seedbeds of the great Antichrist's sect, just as the preceding were seedbeds
and indeed plants of the error of the mystical Antichrist." If we begin with
Christ's death and ascension, the forty-first generation witnessed a comet
as well as Charles of Anjou's victory over first Manfred and then Conradin,
while the forty-second saw Peter of Aragon invade Sicily. "From that point
on there followed many discords among kings and kingdoms which seem
to some not-unlearned people to prepare the way for great evil." At the
end of the forty-second generation "there occurred the novelty of Pope
Celestine's election and that of his successor, and certain other burden-
some events." If we begin counting from the time Peter abandoned the
first *cathedra* at Jerusalem for a second among the Gentiles (just as he
would later accept a third at Rome), then "the forty-two generations or

1,260 years will be completed at the end of this . . . century, which has only three more years to go."[19] It is because of this passage that historians date the Apocalypse commentary in A.D. 1297 or early 1298.[20]

At this point Olivi pauses to observe that Joachim himself did not see his concordances as a precision instrument that could measure events of the New Dispensation exactly against those of the Old, but wished them to be applied with a degree of flexibility, even to the point of inserting or subtracting generations when it seemed necessary.[21] In the process of establishing this point, Olivi observes that, according to Jerome, the persecution carried out by Haman in the time of Esther occurred more than a century after the destruction of Babylon.[22] According to Peter Comester, the persecution in the time of Judith was carried out under Cambyses, whose father, Cyrus, destroyed Babylon.[23] The principle of concordance dictates that this double Old Testament persecution must be balanced by a similar double persecution occurring later than the forty-two generations that begin with the incarnation. Moreover, the transmigration of the Jews occasioned by the Babylonians preceded the destruction of Babylon by forty years if we count from the transmigration of Jeconiah, by twenty-nine if we count from that of Zedechiah, or even by seventy if we count from the point at which Jeremiah began to prophesy the event; and the transmigration of the church from the synagogue preceded the destruction of the synagogue by forty-two years from Christ's baptism or thirty-eight from his ascension. Thus "the transmigration of evangelical men from the synagogue of pseudo-Christians precedes the destruction of the new Babylon, whether you date that transmigration from the beginnings of their state, the first persecution of them already undertaken by certain pseudo-masters, that to be undertaken by the mystical Antichrist, or intermediate persecutions."[24]

This passage is interesting for a number of reasons. In the first place, it shows how the effort to insert the books of Esther and Judith into Jewish history produced a double or even triple persecution—one before the destruction of Babylon and one or two after—which necessitated a roughly parallel proliferation in church history and thus paved the way for a double Antichrist. It also suggests that the insertion produced a chronological incoherence that could not be entirely repaired. The point it most obviously demonstrates, however, is the importance of *concordia* for Olivi's idea of a double Antichrist.

So far Olivi has not carried the investigation to its logical conclusion, forty-two generations starting with the destruction of Jerusalem, nor has he included the arrival of either Antichrist, although he has suggested that the persecution of Antichrist is already underway. Nevertheless, if we accept his assumption that the second age can be measured at least approximately in generations of thirty years each and date the destruction of Jerusalem at ca. A.D. 72 (as Olivi seems to do), then the requisite 1,260 years should occur around the A.D. 1332. It is tempting to carry the parallel to what seems its logical conclusion, take the 1,260 years as running from destruction to destruction, and read Olivi as suggesting that the destruction of the carnal church should thus occur around A.D. 1332. It would then follow that the mystical Antichrist should appear before that date and the great Antichrist after it. Nevertheless, Olivi has not said exactly that. He has given us reason to assume that he is right on the verge of saying it, first with an observation that the birth of Christ (when the sixth age began *fundamentaliter*) occurred 1,206 years before the conversion of Francis (when the sixth period began *fundamentaliter*), then with his comment that the migration of the church from the synagogue preceded the destruction of Jerusalem, just as the migration of spiritual men from the carnal church precedes the destruction of the new Babylon.

On the other hand, the whole chain of associations was begun by Olivi's suggestion of a 1,260 year lapse, not between the two migrations, but between the first migration and the conversion of the Jews, a harder thing to reduce to a single date.[25] Olivi's multiple references to this conversion seem to suggest that he sees it as beginning from the time of the second migration but continuing, in effect, until after the death of Antichrist. If we assume that Olivi is thinking of the *full* conversion of the Jews, then the year 1332 represents the *terminus ad quem* for the death of the great Antichrist. If, however, we take him as thinking of the beginning of the process, when the spiritual men turn to the world after being rejected by the Latin church, then his reference to the two migrations is germane and the year 1332 can be accepted as *terminus ad quem* for the destruction of Babylon.

The matter is further clarified or confused by Olivi's comments on Daniel 12:11f., which follow immediately.[26] Some people, he says, have concluded from this passage that the great Antichrist will appear 1,290 years after Christ's death at the latest, and that the seventh period, the great jubilee of peace, will begin no later than 1,335 years after the crucifixion. He himself thinks this approach too simple. If we recognize that there are various beginning and ending dates, we will recognize that there is no reason to begin counting with Christ's death. Olivi derives no hard dates from these considerations, but they would seem to suggest that, if the anonymous *quidam* are correct in counting from the death of Christ, then the great Antichrist should be with us by 1324 at the latest and we can count on tasting the full bliss of the seventh period by 1369. If, however, we take the destruction of Jerusalem as the latest point from which one might count, the great Antichrist might not arrive until 1362 and the seventh period will dawn by 1407 at the latest. Unfortunately, Olivi notes that there is a different way of interpreting these numbers. They can be seen as days and applied only to the period of Antichrist's persecution, not to the entire scope of church history leading up to it.

The Two Beasts

Olivi's next significant comments on the Antichrist come in his consideration of Revelation 13 and the two beasts, which, he says, prefigure the battle against Christ's church in the time of Antichrist. The beast from the sea is from an infidel nation.[27] Its ascent signifies the battles through which it conquered those lands that the Saracens still occupy today as well as those that it won and lost.[28] Since it is the custom of prophetic scripture to speak of one special case but generalize from it, the beast stands particularly for the Saracens but more generally for the whole beastly crowd of reprobates fighting against the elect from the beginning of the world to its end.[29]

The beast from the sea is superlatively equipped with seven heads, ten horns, and ten crowns. Olivi remarks that, according to Joachim, the heads of this beast differ from those of the dragon as the metropolitan churches, which are the heads of others, differ from their bishops, who are their heads and rule in Christ's place. In short, the heads of the dragon are individuals, while those of the beast are groups. The first was the Jewish people; the second the pagans and especially the Romans; the next four the Greeks, Goths, Vandals, and Lombards, the principal kingdoms of the Arians; and the seventh the Saracens. Thus these heads are not precisely correlated with those of the dragon.

Joachim, Olivi observes, argues that the ten kings who will destroy the carnal church (Revelation 7:12−14) and the sixth king of Revelation 17:10, of whom it is said "one is," all represent the Saracens. This conclusion may perhaps be true, Olivi says, but it is not sufficiently proven, for by the same reasoning all seven heads could be of the Saracen sect (which

Joachim denies).[30] After exploring the issue for a moment, Olivi says, "I don't care what the truth of this matter may be. It's sufficient for me to know that [the Antichrist] will be contrary to Christ and his people."[31] Nevertheless, he remains quite interested in the Saracens. He affirms that, while what is said of the beast applies in general to the reprobate as a whole, it can be referred particularly to the beast arising "from the fourth period through the end of the church."[32] Seen in this way, it has seven heads because of the seven centuries during which the Saracens have ruled and will continue to rule until Antichrist comes, and because there were seven key Islamic leaders starting with Mohammed.[33] The head that seemed mortally wounded but recovered (Revelation 13:3) refers to the war that will occur in the sixth period under the sixth head and tenth horn. Returning to Joachim's theory, which sees the seventh head alone as Muslim but identifies it with the Muslims as a whole, Olivi observes that Joachim tends to identify the head's apparent death and recovery not with defeat in the first crusade followed by victory in the following century, but with future success by a new order in converting the Muslims through preaching, followed by a resurgence of Islam.[34] Obviously the order in question is that part of the *ordo fratrum minorum* that has not bowed the knee to Baal; yet, as we will see, it is not only they.

Olivi now gives briefer and less sympathetic attention to Richard of St. Victor's view that the slain and recovered head refers to Antichrist's pretended death and resurrection.[35] Olivi acknowledges that Simon Magus is said to have acted thus, but states his ignorance as to whether Antichrist will make a similar attempt. He notes Joachim's suggestion in the *Liber de concordia*[36] that in the first year of Antichrist's reign he will lose his kingdom but obtain it again through fraud. Olivi remarks that this interpretation allows another way of applying the notion of death and resurrection to Antichrist.[37]

Following an uneventful section in which he applies Revelation 13:4–10 to Antichrist, Olivi arrives at 13:11, the beast from the land. At the time of Antichrist, a bestial group of pseudoprophets will arise not from the sea of infidel nations but from the earth of Christianity, and will join with the (Islamic) beast from the sea in one erroneous sect conflated from both. They are mentioned second because they will follow after the exaltation of the first beast; because they will arise and prevail, not through their own power, but through that of the first beast; and because they will work their false signs and other evils on behalf of the first beast.[38]

Olivi's commentary is stuffed with so much cautious and often noncommital reportage that it is almost disorienting when one happens upon a section in which he seems to be straightforwardly stating his own interpretation of something. Perhaps it stuns him as well, since in this case he immediately lapses back into a discussion of Joachim. He notes that Joachim and other great doctors think the head of this second beast will be a pseudopope. The king of the first beast, the monarch of the whole world, will be deceived by the pseudopope through false miracles, hypocritical *figmenta*, and the fallacious arguments of worldly philosophy. He will cause the pseudopope to be adored as God throughout the whole world. This may also occur because the king will be aided by the pseudopope in acquiring his monarchy, or in tightening his grip on it.[39] Others, however, think that the apostate Antichrist will obtain world monarchy through fraud, then many pseudoprophets will arise from among the false Christians, adulating him and, by working false signs, causing him to be adored by all. They will preach the law given by him and make it seem true. Olivi seems to close the matter with a brief disclaimer: "I myself do not worry much about whether he who will properly be Antichrist, be adored as God, and call himself king of the Jews will be a king, pseudopope, or both. It is sufficient for me to know that he will be deceitful and contrary to Christ."[40]

The matter is not quite so closed as it might appear, however. Olivi cites the opinion of some that the Antichrist will be nurtured, educated, and inhabited by the devil from the womb. Others find this improbable, Olivi says, since it would tend to excuse his sins, whereas the *sancti* consider him the most culpable of all people. Moreover, Antichrist's fault should be similar to Lucifer's, who voluntarily apostatized from the highest and most righteous state. "Thus the doctors believe, not improbably, that he will be an apostate from the state of Christianity and the highest *religio*." For that reason he will be all the more able to simulate many things belonging to religion and more subtly work out the fraudulent errors of his doctrine and law. The implication seems clear: the Antichrist will be an apostate Franciscan. Olivi normally has no trouble deciding where the highest *religio* is to be found.

Olivi's comments on the mark of the beast represent little more than a series of citations from Joachim and Richard, offered without any attempt to judge their truth or falsity. It is in this spirit that he approaches the number of the beast, 666. First he reports on Richard's reading of the numbers as letters, acknowledging that he himself has utilized it in another work.[41] Next he presents Joachim's argument that the six hundred repre-

sents the six ages of the world, the sixty represents the six periods of this
sixth world age, and the six represents the sixth period. Olivi neither affirms nor denies this opinion, but notes that he himself has offered still
other interpretations elsewhere.[42]

Then he turns to yet another view—this one attributed to an anonymous *quidam*—according to which 666 represents the number of years the
Saracens will reign. There are, he says, 666 years from the year A.D. 635,
when the Saracens defeated the Persians, until A.D. 1300. There are also
666 years from the year A.D. 648, when they took Africa, to the year A.D.
1323, which is 1,290 years from the death of Christ. If the number 1,290
(culled from Daniel 12:11) represents the number of years between the
time the yoke of sacrifice was lifted from the Jews and the appearance of
Antichrist, then there should be 666 years between the time the Saracen
kingdom was spread out over Asia and Africa and the arrival of Antichrist.
There are, then, twenty-three years left to go. If the 1,290 years include the
entire reign of Antichrist, then we have only twenty years before the persecution begins. Olivi observes, "I don't know what will happen next. God
knows."[43] The mathematics of this passage are puzzling,[44] but the range
of options is relatively limited. By this logic, the Antichrist should begin
his reign by 1323.

Which Antichrist? In the following passage that question is answered.
"It should be known, however, that wherever in this book the great Antichrist is discussed, the time of the mystical Antichrist preceding the great
is implied *more prophetico*." Olivi goes on to say that

according to this reasoning, through the beast ascending from the sea is signified the bestial life and people of the carnal and secular Christians which,
since the end of the fourth period, has had many heads in the form of carnal
princes and prelates, and this has been going on for six hundred years now.
In this sixth centenary, one head has been almost killed through Francis's
evangelical state; for the higher, more widely, and more perfectly evangelical
poverty and perfection are impressed upon and magnified within the church,
the more powerfully the head of earthly cupidity and vile carnality is killed in
it. But now this head, almost destroyed, is reviving so much that carnal Christians admire and follow its carnal glory. When, however, the apostate beast
from the earth of the religious ascends on high with its two horns of pseudoreligious and pseudoprophets falsely resembling the true horns of the lamb,
the most powerful temptation of the mystical Antichrist will occur. . . . The
pseudo-Christians and pseudoprophets will cause the cupidity and carnality
or earthly glory of the secular beast to be adored by all, and will offer great
signs to this end: first, of its ecclesiastical authority, contradiction of which

will seem to be disobedience, contumacy, and schismatic rebellion; second, of the universal opinion of all its masters and doctors and of the whole multitude or common opinion of all, contradiction of which will seem foolish, insane, and even heretical; third, of arguments and falsely twisted scriptures, as well as of some superficial, ancient, and multiform religion confirmed and solemnized through long succession from antiquity. Thus with these signs they will seem to make the fire of divine wrath descend on those who contradict them . . . and will decree that whoever does not obey should be anathematized, ejected from the synagogue, and, if necessary, turned over to the secular arm of the former beast. They will make the image of the beast—that is, the pseudopope raised up by the king of the first beast— adored in such a way that he is believed in more than Christ and his gospel and honored as if he were the god of this world.[45]

Thus the earlier passages dealt with the great Antichrist, while this last one is concerned with the mystical Antichrist.

The number 666 may also represent the period from the end of the fourth state until this temptation. If we begin the fifth period with Pepin, it has lasted 560 years so far. If we start it from the devastation of the eastern church by Islam, the 666 years will soon be completed, for the Saracens defeated the Persians in 635, captured Damascus two years after that, and took Jerusalem two years after taking Damascus.[46] These calculations make sense if we remember that, for Olivi, periods do not begin and end precisely but rather fade in and out, overlapping contiguous ones. Thus the figure of 666 years is comprehensible if we see the Muslim conquests from 635 on as one signpost of the declining fourth period, and the 560 years make sense if we see the death of Charles Martel in 741 as another signpost of the rising fifth period.[47] In any case, Olivi goes on to report that

Some people, working from many things that Joachim wrote about Frederick II and his seed and from certain things that the blessed Francis is said to have revealed secretly to Brother Leo and certain others among his associates, opine that the aforesaid Frederick and his seed will be, as it were, the slain head in regard to this time, and that in the time of the mystical Antichrist it will be so revived in one of his descendents that he will gain, not only the Roman Empire, but the kingdom of the Franks as well, having conquered the Franks. Five other Christian kings will adhere to him, and he will establish as pseudopope a certain false religious who will plot against the evangelical rule and make deceitful dispensation, promoting to bishoprics professors of the aforesaid rule who obey him, accordingly expelling clerics and previous bishops who were opposed to the seed of Frederick, to him in particular, and to his state, and consequently all who wish to observe and defend the aforesaid rule purely and fully. They say that the fall of these clerics and of the kingdom of France, as well as some other related things, are designated through the earthquake at the beginning of the opening of the sixth seal, although the latter also designates, beyond that, the subversion and blinding of nearly the entire church that will occur at that time. How much of this will or will not happen should, I think, be left up to God.

Once more Olivi has apparently dismissed such baseless speculation, yet once more he immediately returns to it.

The aforesaid people add, however, that at that time . . . almost everyone will fall away from obedience to the true pope and follow the pseudopope, who will indeed be "pseudo" because he errs in a heretical way against the truth of evangelical poverty and perfection, and perhaps also because he will not be canonically elected but schismatically introduced.[48]

This is one of the passages on which Lewis relies most heavily. He remarks that "one can see through this portrait of the pseudopope to the historical figure who stands behind it: Boniface VIII." Boniface qualified as a false religious because he had been a canon; he was "famous for creating pliant bishops out of cooperative Franciscans"; in doing so, he was "dispensing friars from their vows of poverty"; he persecuted those who wanted to observe the rule properly; and the validity of his election was widely questioned.[49]

The Euphrates

The other key passage in Lewis's interpretation occurs in the context of Olivi's thoughts on the Euphrates River. It is in Revelation 16:12f. that the sixth angel pours his vial into the Euphrates and dries it up. Some say, Olivi reports, that because of the constant battles among kingdoms of the Roman church, the size and strength of their armies will be weakened (i.e., dried up), and this will prepare the way for a destruction of the carnal church to be carried out by the ten kings and the eleventh presiding over them. Olivi then briefly alludes to Richard of St. Victor's view and summarizes at greater length another interpretation according to which "Babylonian science" will open the church to every error and prepare the way for the great Antichrist and eastern kings. This process, Olivi says, is seen in Revelation 16:13, where unclean spirits issue from the mouths of the dragon, beast, and pseudoprophet. By subtle suggestion, certain deceitful men, messengers of Antichrist, will induce all the kings of the world to join in battle against the carnal church. These messengers will be sent by the king of a pagan or Saracen people and by the pseudopope or the pseudoprophet, leader of the other pseudoprophets. Knights will be sent by the king, false masters or doctors by the pseudoprophet. Among the latter will be certain pseudoreligious full of the fraud and hypocrisy of the dragon.

Olivi then considers the interpretation offered by Joachim, who links this passage with the temptation of Antichrist, by which he means, in Olivi's terms, the great Antichrist. Olivi affirms, however, that in his own opinion the passage can be applied to both. "Thus some believe that both the mystical Antichrist and the proper or great Antichrist will be a pseudopope, head of pseudoprophets, and that, through the counsel and cooperation of him and his pseudoprophets, empire will be attained by that king through whom he is established in his bogus papacy, but that the king who establishes the great one will, in addition, have him worshipped as a god."[50]

In fact, Olivi already has encountered the Euphrates in dealing with Revelation 9:14 and said something there about its impending dessication. It is this passage that comprises Lewis's other major bit of evidence. There too Olivi identifies the river with the Christian armies that held the infidels at bay and with the Christian wisdom that hitherto resisted the errors of heretics, Saracens and the like; yet he also offers an entirely different possibility. Insofar as this event refers to the third beginning of the sixth period, he says, it stands either for the withdrawal of almost everyone from loyalty to the pope or for "the cessation of [papal] favor toward the evangelical state, through which favor its enemies have been impeded up to now from rushing in upon it as they would wish (*per quem eius emuli sunt usque nunc impediti in ipsum irruere iuxta votum*)."[51]

Lewis reads this passage in a strikingly different way. He takes it to mean that "the pope's own envious rivalry with the Franciscan way is proving a hindrance to his embracing the vow of evangelical poverty 'even until now.' The pope has too much power for his own good and is surrounded by too many worldly-wise philosophers and theologians who only add to the already fatal jealousy that the pope feels for the Franciscan order." Nevertheless, the very lack of finality in that *usque nunc* prevents Olivi from explicitly identifying Boniface as the awaited pseudopope. "The question as to how Boniface will choose is still open, for the man is still alive."[52] Here again we will defer comment until we have examined a final passage.

The Eschatological Fire

Olivi's last significant comment concerning the Antichrist does not even mention the name. It comes in his interpretation of Revelation 19:20, where the beast and pseudoprophet are thrown into the fire. Olivi remarks that

> these two clearly refer to two individuals, one of whom is king and head of the beast—that is, a bestial nation—while the other is the head of the pseudoprophets who produce signs. It is not clear whether the latter is a pseudopope pretending to be God or only a pseudoprophet preaching that the former is God, although the doctors believe that the second claims to be God.[53]

Analysis: The King/Pope Combination

The passages described so far are hardly the only ones in which Olivi speaks of the Antichrist, but they are the most significant. Certainly they demonstrate the difficulties involved in determining precisely what Olivi thought. One might consider ranking his statements according to whether he (1) cites and refutes other people's views; (2) cites others, then announces that he himself does not know or care; (3) cites others without comment; (4) tentatively offers an opinion without citing authority; (5) cites others with approval; or (6) simply affirms a view without citing authority. One cannot place too much weight on such categories, however. The first seems to suggest that Olivi is eliminating interpretations without telling us what he himself believes; yet it often gives a strong hint in that direction, as when he cites Joachim without comment, then cites and refutes Richard of St. Victor's contrasting opinion. The second category is also problematic. The passages considered here contain several such disclaimer statements, and there are many others in the Apocalypse commentary. There is little reason to assume that they signify genuine lack of interest on Olivi's part, since he often pursues with obvious zest precisely the same matters on which he eventually offers a disclaimer. Moreover, the disclaimers often punctuate his discussions rather than terminating them. He examines the matter, commits it to the divine will, then returns to his examination.

Olivi's disclaimers are obviously at least in part an effort at self-protection;[54] yet they are not simply that. They make an exegetical point. Olivi feels that prediction on the basis of prophetic writings is increasingly possible, because the sheer passage of time, coupled with divine revelation of basic exegetical principles like that of concordance, allows us to clarify the future. Prediction is also increasingly desirable, because the days of tribulation are just around the corner. We must still rely on our own fallible reason, however. Thus Olivi's disclaimers often distinguish between some future generality of which he is certain and a particular scenario that cannot be proved.

Nevertheless, some of Olivi's convictions do not seem all that general. In the passages just examined, he routinely accepts an order of events that includes decay in the church leading to rule by a pseudopope who, supported by secular authority, will attack Franciscan poverty and persecute its adherents. It also includes destruction of these carnal leaders by a pagan army, then persecution of the church by a pagan leader who will be supported by renegade Christian leaders. During this latter persecution, the attack will be on Christian dogma itself, and the general path of this attack is already being cleared by heterodox Aristotelianism. This notion of quisling Christian leaders allied with a pagan king may seem an odd thing to be sure of, but it grows easily out of the assumption (hardly unique to Olivi)[55] that "the sea" denotes those outside the faith while "the land" refers to those within it. The scenario is also closely related to Olivi's confidence that what he sees as the Islamicized Aristotelianism currently threatening Parisian philosophy is a preparation for the great tribulation, and his tendency to think of Muslims whenever he mentions pagans. The role of Islam in Olivi's projections is a major one. While he never asserts that the pagan army that crushes Babylon will be Muslim, he is obviously very hospitable to that idea. The king in the second king/pope combination also seems likely to be Islamic, although that, too, is left open. Olivi seems sure that these events will occur soon. His various dating aids yield no single conclusion, but suggest that the mystical Antichrist may be just outside the door.

Olivi is less confident about the identity of either Antichrist. In each case he has two figures, a king and a pseudopope, to choose from. His assumption that the key passages have a double reference—the same words refer both to the mystical and to the great Antichrist—locks him into this parallelism. In both cases he recognizes that there is no way of proving one option or the other, but in both cases he seems to lean toward the pseudopope as Antichrist. His inclination is more understandable in the case of the mystical Antichrist, since the primary tribulation in that case is a battle within the church over evangelical perfection. In the case of the great Antichrist the dynamics are quite different and Olivi anguishes more over the question, never really deciding in favor of either king or pseudopope. That too is understandable. Judgment is rendered more difficult by the nature of the attack—the assault seems directed more toward Christianity itself, and the king in question is a pagan—and by the fact that it is almost by definition impossible for us to imagine the situation at that time. Olivi himself recognizes the mystery surrounding these events and is unwilling to be very concrete in their depiction. Nevertheless, it is significant that he tells us first of "some people" and later of "the doctors," all of whom vote for the pseudopope as great Antichrist, and that he makes the great Antichrist an apostate from the highest religion, presumably the Franciscans. Thus the parallelism between the two Antichrists seems to extend in this direction as well.

In the final analysis, however, one gets the impression that the question is not an major one for Olivi, because the king-pseudopope combination is more important to him than the idea of a single malign leader called "Antichrist." Here Lewis is quite correct. Olivi follows his basic inclination when he comments that the mystical Antichrist is assimilated to "Caiaphas the priest condemning Christ and Herod mocking him," while the great Antichrist is assimilated to "the pagan Nero governing the whole world and Simon Magus calling himself God and the son of God."[56] Thus it is understandable that, in the case of the great Antichrist, he really asks not which of the two will be Antichrist, but which will perform miracles and claim to be God. Nevertheless, in terms of the well-developed Antichrist tradition Olivi inherited, performing miracles and claiming to be God was part of the Antichrist's job-description.

Beyond the elements about which one can speak with confidence, Olivi discerns a number of items about which the exegete can only speculate. Thus he remarks that he does not know whether the same king who destroys the carnal church will then collaborate in the persecution of the great Antichrist. Nor can he do anything with the Frederick legend except present it. He does not discourage speculation on such matters, only unfounded affirmations about them.

The Mystical Antichrist as Individual

If Lewis is completely correct on the importance of the king-pseudopope combination, he is partly so in suggesting that only the great Antichrist is an individual. Olivi does sometimes speak of the mystical Antichrist in collective terms, but he also refers to him as a single person. The explanation for this duality lies not in inconsistency but in Olivi's exegetical principles. He tells us on several occasions that multiple reference is a common characteristic of prophetic scripture. It can refer simultaneously to several specific events, as when it speaks of both Antichrists at the same time; but it can also combine the general with the particular in the sense that it refers to a specific case and yet "ascends and expands" to a wider reference.[57]

Extrascriptural Borrowings

Manselli, in turn, is only partly correct when he asserts that the medieval Antichrist legend does not appeal much to Olivi, that he "cleanly and bluntly eliminates all the pretended revelations that have come down to him from the past," and that he "also excludes without hesitation anything that cannot be extracted directly from the sacred texts."[58] Olivi is willing to take Richard of St. Victor to task for saying without proper scriptural warrant that Antichrist will be from the tribe of Dan.[59] It costs him nothing to be scrupulous on this score, since the Dan connection, traditional though it might be, does not fit into his general view anyway. As Heiko Oberman has observed,[60] Olivi's apocalyptic expectations placed him at variance with the notably anti-Semitic tenor of much medieval speculation on the Antichrist. His frequent references to the Jews are almost inevitably allusions to their impending apocalyptic conversion. He emphasizes the Muslims rather than the Jews as the great adversaries of Christendom.

Nevertheless, Olivi willingly embraces Joachim's concordances—which he (along with Joachim himself)[61] sees as divinely revealed—and accepts the basic pattern they provide. This is no minor decision on his part. One is apt to overlook the impact of the Joachite concordances on Olivi's speculation because in the Apocalypse commentary he inevitably concentrates on church history and, when he quotes Joachim, he normally cites Joachim's Apocalypse commentary rather than the *Liber de concordia*. Nevertheless, the concordances form an unspoken assumption from which much of his thought proceeds. It is thanks partly to the double Old Testament tribulation posited by Joachim to solve the problem of fitting the books of Esther and Judith into Old Testament chronology that Olivi anticipates an impending double tribulation in church history and thus finds it convenient to posit a double Antichrist. Olivi solves the problem in his own way, but it is very much Joachim's problem that he is solving.[62]

Olivi also depends on another set of ideas not easily reducible to sacred scripture. He combines the Apocalypse and the concordances with a Franciscan theology of history in which the order, its tribulations, and its destiny are promoted to apocalyptic status. Here as in the case of the concordances, we have a body of thought that Olivi would have insisted was not only consistent with scripture but implied in it; yet here as with the concordances, Olivi thinks he is dealing with a body of material at least partly validated by more recent revelation. Certainly he has no doubt that the Franciscan rule was divinely revealed, and he is cautiously interested in the very "revelations" that Manselli feels he rejected. When he presents the theory that Frederick and his seed are the killed and revived head, describing it as a view held by "certain people" and based on "many things written by Joachim concerning Frederick and his seed and certain things that the blessed Francis is reported to have revealed secretly to Brother Leo and certain others,"[63] he is not explicitly accepting the view, but he can hardly be described as dismissing it either. We have had occasion to note that when Olivi speaks of "certain people," he is occasionally offering a view that he himself finds attractive. It would be presumptuous to say that he is one of the *quidam* in this particular case, but he is certainly leaving the matter open. On the other hand, when he says, "I have heard from many who are worthy of belief that our father Francis predicted this temptation [of the mystical Antichrist] many times and also said that professors of his state would be principally and more maliciously attacked in it,"[64] it seems obvious that he finds the report, like the sources, worthy of belief, even though he does not explicitly assert its truth.

To say this much is not equivalent to claiming that Olivi's double Antichrist was an inevitable result of combining Joachite concordances with Franciscan apocalyptic. Even when one has explored the embarassing problem of where to put Esther and Judith or the disquieting predictions purportedly offered by Francis to Brother Leo, one is still left with the feeling that Olivi's scenario has not been adequately accounted for. Obviously there was something more at stake, but what? Part of the answer seems to lie in his reading of contemporary history and his relative pessimism about the immediate future of ecclesiastical leadership, particularly at the highest level. The thing that strikes one most about Olivi's prediction is his willingness to accept a scenario in which the papacy is captured by the forces of evil not once but twice, not only during the reign of the great Antichrist but substantially earlier. To be sure, Olivi refers to the evil leader as a pseudopope and raises the possibility that he may be schismatically elected. Such comments offer momentary reassurance because they seem to present the great tradition of imperial-papal struggle from Henry IV on as a model for the coming tribulation; yet on sober reflection these suggestions are less comforting than they seem. Olivi shows no interest whatsoever in following the familiar pattern. He expends no energy wondering where the *real* pope will be. The man sitting on the papal throne may be nothing but a pseudopope, but he will have all the administrative authority a real one normally has. He will rule over the ecclesiastical hierarchy. Such a dire prediction—and this seems one of the things concerning which Olivi is relatively confident—does not follow inevitably from the concordances, for Joachim accepted no such conclusion. It might follow from some of the prognostications circulating among Franciscan zealots, but Olivi did not accept all such prophecies uncritically. He found this one interesting because it tallied with his reading of the church in his time. In the final analysis, Olivi's remarkable willingness to accept a central papal role in the coming persecution is based on more than exegetical logic or credulous acceptance of prophecy. It also rests on a very negative appraisal of current ecclesiastical leadership.

Boniface VIII as Antichrist

Is Lewis then correct in suggesting that Olivi's comments on the great Antichrist are aimed at Boniface VIII? One would like to think this, but there is little reason to do so. As for the key passage regarding the Euphrates (which Lewis takes as a criticism of Boniface), a comparison between Lewis's reading and mine will suffice to show that I interpret the key phrase in a wildly different manner. Here I can only appeal to the Latin text in the appropriate footnote and ask the reader to judge. The other passage on which Lewis depends heavily is the one in which Olivi predicts that the pseudopope will be a false religious; will promote Franciscans to bishoprics; will persecute those who wish to observe the Franciscan rule fully; and perhaps will not be canonically elected. This passage offers more food for thought, yet in the final analysis much of Lewis's argument seems at odds with Olivi's own words. For example, even if we ignore the question of whether Olivi would have considered Boniface a false religious simply because he had been a canon at Todi and Anagni, we must still acknowledge that elsewhere Olivi favors the notion that the great Antichrist will be apostate from the highest *religio*, that is, the Franciscan order. Moreover, we have seen that the passage in question addresses the time of the mystical Antichrist, not the great one.

Even if we alter Lewis's argument and apply it to Boniface as the mystical Antichrist, it remains unconvincing. If Boniface is the pseudopope, then where is his partner, the evil ruler? Descendents of Frederick were not prospering in 1297 or 1298, nor was Boniface getting along all that well with any existing ruler. Of course lack of a secular accomplice could not be taken as a definitive argument *against* his candidacy, since Olivi remains nonassertive as to whether the pseudopope is installed by a wicked ruler or, conversely, the wicked ruler is aided in his quest for dominance by a pseudopope. Thus it is theoretically possible that the wicked ruler is yet to come. Here again, however, the best one could say is that Boniface's situation is not absolutely inconsistent with Olivi's view of the mystical Antichrist, not that it matches it.

The reference to appointment of cooperative Franciscans as bishops seems more promising, but it too ultimately founders. Olivi would not have seen Boniface as dispensing friars from their vows of poverty through the very act of nominating them bishops, since he did not oppose the idea of Franciscan bishops. He simply insisted that they could not be dispensed from the vow of poverty. He had been fighting that battle since at least 1279 and his position had been rejected within his own order by 1283.[65] It is hard to imagine what novel twists to the plot Boniface might have been adding. Nor can we assume that Olivi would have been enraged by the number or nature of Boniface's appointments. Lewis notes that Boniface nominated forty-two Franciscan bishops in nine years. He gets that figure from John Moorman's *History of the Franciscan Order*, and Moorman in turn gets it from the *Bullarium Franciscanum*.[66] Whatever sort of library Olivi had at his disposal in Narbonne, it would not have included either of these works. Thus he would have known only about those appointments already made at the time he wrote, and Boniface had appointed only ten Franciscan bishops by the beginning of 1297, with another ten to come that year. Moreover, of those appointed by that date, Olivi probably would not have known about all of them and would have cared about even less. It is hard to imagine him getting too exercised about the episcopacy in Scandinavia or North Africa, for example. One suspects that he would have been concerned about only those appointments made in his area or those involving people with whom he had had significant contact.

Four names come to mind. The first is Iterius, appointed bishop of Lodève in 1296. He is of interest simply because a letter to King Philip IV suggests that in 1299 Iterius was present at a provincial synod that censured the Beguins for their apocalyptic enthusiasm. The Beguins were a major source of lay support for Franciscan zealots. This sort of guilt by association does not carry one far, however. We know little about what these particular Beguins were saying. Moreover, Iterius was not the principal ecclesiastic at the synod. In fact, the censure itself lists those present and does not mention Iterius, so he may not even have been there when it occurred.[67] The second name is Guillaume de Falgar, bishop of Viviers from 1296 until his death in 1297 or 1298. His significance lies in the fact that he served as vicar of the order during part of the time Olivi was under censure in the 1280s. According to Salimbene, he nearly became minister general in 1285.[68] It is at least possible that Olivi saw him as an opponent, but we do not know that.

Obviously we are not doing very well so far, but with the next two names we can do substantially better. One of them is Saint Louis of Anjou, one of the royal captives to whom Olivi wrote in 1295. He was appointed bishop of Toulouse in 1296. Louis apparently took his poverty seriously. The fourth name on our list is that of a man who was appointed to one bishopric and one archbishopric in 1295 and refused both. That man was Raymond Geoffroi. Thus the only two appointees whose connections with Olivi we can document are people who supported strict observance of the rule. Perhaps Olivi thought these appointments sinister, but if he did, one is hard put to imagine what would have pleased him.

Such an observation might strike the reader as incredibly naive, since Raymond's first episcopal appointment probably represented an effort on Boniface's part to end his tenure as minister general of the order. According to the *Chronicle of the Twenty-four Generals*, when Raymond refused the see of Padua on the ground that he was not worthy to be a bishop, Boniface replied that he should then consider himself even less worthy to rule the entire Franciscan order and removed him from that position.[69] Then he apparently exercised considerable influence in John of Murrovalle's subsequent election. This was undoubtedly a reversal for Olivi's cause.

Of course, however damaging these events may appear in retrospect, it is less clear what Olivi would have thought of them in 1297. John would eventually launch a vicious attack on Olivi's memory and followers, but there is no evidence that the attack began before Olivi's death in 1298. Olivi would have recognized John as a member of the Parisian commission that censured him in 1283 and as a man who did not share his position on Franciscan poverty; yet if John's subsequent behavior as minister general is any indication of his views in 1297, Olivi had no reason to think of him as an advocate of extreme laxity either.[70] Nor had Franciscan zealots in southern France been doing all that well under Raymond Geoffroi. One group had been severely punished in the early 1290s. Olivi had escaped that particular purge, but it is hard to say by how much. Certainly he was forced to clarify his position at the 1292 general chapter meeting. If we take his letter to the captive princes as evidence that things were getting worse for him in Narbonne, then they were worsening five months before Raymond's dismissal. Thus the transition from Raymond to John may not have been as fraught with significance for Olivi as it is for modern historians.

Even if one grants that Olivi should have recognized the evil drift of things by 1297—in fact, even if one grants that he *did* see it—there is still the question of whether he saw Boniface as a central figure in the drama. There is no way of denying that he did so, but there is also no evidence that he did. He may have been thinking of Boniface and Raymond Geoffroi as he wrote, but the thought was not translated into any recognizable allusion.

Why else might Olivi have seen Boniface as auditioning for the role of Antichrist? Boniface was proceeding against some groups of Italian zealots by the time Olivi wrote, but anyone who examines the description of these groups in Boniface's letters will see an odd resemblance to the views Olivi criticized so harshly in his 1295 letter to Conrad of Offida, the same letter in which he defended the legitimacy of Boniface's election. Nor would Olivi have had any reason to condemn Boniface for the decision that most offended Italian zealots, his abrogation of Celestine's decree granting independence from the order to Angelo Clareno's dissident group. In fact, everything we know about Olivi suggests that it would have been the decree, not its abrogation, that disturbed him.

In fact, there is no evidence that Olivi had any more reason to see Boniface as a betrayer of the Franciscan cause than he did to see either of the two preceding popes as such. When he mentions "the novelty of the elections of Pope Celestine and his successor, and other worsening matters," his general point is not that the Celestine-Boniface succession was an unfortunate one, but that it is one more example of the increasing strife that heralds the approaching temptation of Antichrist. It may be significant that he leaves Boniface unnamed; yet it seems equally worth noting that he cites not Celestine's resignation, but his election. Nor should he have been any more pleased with Nicholas IV, the first Franciscan pope, Celestine's predecessor. As minister general, Nicholas (or Jerome of Ascoli, as he was then called) had subjected Olivi to disciplinary action. As pope, he had pressed for an investigation of the spirituals in southern France, and it was this investigation that forced Olivi to clarify his stand at the 1292 chapter meeting. Nicholas's actions as pope suggest that his notion of helping the order did not go beyond showering it with privileges and defending it against all comers.[71] Boniface may not have done the Franciscans any more good than that, but it is hard to see how, from Olivi's viewpoint, he could have done them any more harm.

Certainly Olivi saw Boniface as part of the great apocalyptic countdown. Perhaps the circumstances of his election and early pontificate influenced Olivi's portrayal of the Antichrist as pseudopope, although the earlier papal-imperial battles offer a closer parallel and thus were probably more influential. In some ways Nicholas IV also presents a closer parallel. In any case, Olivi's portrayal of the Antichrist as pseudopope is not close enough to Boniface's actual situation to give us any confidence that we are dealing with a *roman à clef.*

Notes

1. For a general study see Richard Emmerson, *Antichrist in the Middle Ages* (Seattle, 1981).
2. See Robert Lerner, "Antichrists and Antichrist in Joachim of Fiore," *Speculum* 60 (1985): 553–70. Olivi briefly pays his respects to this view, however. See *Lectura*, 927. For the double Antichrist tradition before Joachim see McGinn, *Calabrian Abbot*, 111 and 121n.63.
3. Manselli, *La "Lectura super Apocalypsim" di Pietro di Giovanni Olivi* (Rome, 1955), 225–30.
4. "La terza età, Babylon e l'Anticristo Mistico," *Bulletino dell'Istituto Storico Italiano per il Medio Evo e Archivio Muratoriano* 70 (1970): 76. See also Manselli, *Lectura super apocalypsim*, 223–32.
5. Lewis, "Peter John Olivi," introduction, 225.
6. Manselli, *Lectura super apocalypsim*, 225, identifies Olivi's comments on the Frederick legend as an aspect of his thought on the mystical Antichrist, whereas Lewis, "Peter John Olivi," introduction, 227, considers it in connection with the great Antichrist. On the Frederick legend see Robert Lerner, "Frederick II, Alive, Aloft, and Allayed, in Franciscan-Joachite Eschatology," in *The Use and Abuse of Eschatology in the Middle Ages* (Leuven, 1988), 359–84.

7. Lewis, "Peter John Olivi," introduction, 227.

8. See, for example, Harold Lee, Marjorie Reeves, and Giulio Silano, eds., *Western Mediterranean Prophecy* (Toronto, 1989), 24f., 63, 77, which ignores Lewis but quietly revises Manselli, agreeing that Olivi favors the idea of a pseudopope as mystical Antichrist yet concluding that the great Antichrist will be "a political scourge" and that the two will reign concurrently. They also assume that Olivi accepted the Frederick prophecy, applying it to the time of the mystical Antichrist.

9. "Peter John Olivi," introduction, 231f.

10. *Lectura*, 394–96.

11. *Lectura*, 396, 408.

12. *Lectura*, 628–33.

13. Joachim's interpretation of the seven heads in 12:3, 13:1, and 17:9 was perhaps the most widely appropriated aspect of his apocalyptic thought among thirteenth-century mendicant commentators. None looked quite so deeply into the matter as Olivi, however. I can recall no other discussion of Gog's role as tail.

14. There is some confusion in the manuscripts at this point. Some omit the fourth head entirely, and the text regarding the fifth has some notable variations.

15. *Lectura*, 836–40, citing Joachim, *Expositio*, 196ra–vb and *Liber de concordia*, 379, 388. Olivi considers Richard of St. Victor's idea (*In Apocalypsim Ioannis*, 835) that the beast is the devil and the seven kings represent all evil people throughout history, but rejects both notions, calling the second *valde absurdum*. See also *Lectura*, 847–53, in which Olivi notes Joachim's uncertainty as to whether the great king who crushes Babylon will be the one who later makes war on the saints.

16. Ibid., 643.

17. Ibid., 646–53. One thousand and two hundred and sixty years equals forty-two generations of thirty years each.

18. Ibid., 653–55.

19. Ibid., 655–57: "Quidam tamen satis probabiliter opinantur ipsas sub diversis rationibus ab omnibus prescriptis terminis inchoari et secundum hoc diversos finales terminos eis dari. Nam et inchoatio earum a Christi incarnatione, quas ab illo initio clare et cum mira concordia ipsarum ad generationes veteris testamenti prosequitur Ioachim usque ad tempus suum, habet magnam rationem et notabilem veritatem. Nam in sexto anno XLI generationis initiatus est fundamentaliter tertius status, concurrendo tamen adhuc cum secundo; initiata etiam est apertio sexti sigilli concurrendo tamen usque adhuc cum quinta. Franciscus enim tanquam angelus apertionis sexti sigilli est illo sexto anno conversus, qui est et sextus annus XIII centenarii incarnationis Christi. Ex tunc autem omnis persecutio sui evangelici status spectat ad persecutiones antichristi et secundum hoc in sequenti XLII generatione cepit Parisius persecutio quorundam magistrorum condemnantium evangelicam mendicitatem. In ipsa etiam fuit Fredericus II cum suis complicibus persequens ecclesiam; propter quod et in ipsa ab imperio depositus fuit in concilio generali per Innocentium IIII facto Lugduni.

"Prout autem inchoantur a Christi baptismo, id est post XXX annos a primo initio, sic in XLI generatione cepit ordo evangelicus per totam latinam ecclesiam esse in doctrina famosus; et in XLII cepit persecutio seu error dicentium statum religionis esse inferiorem statu seculari clericorum curam animarum habentium,

et iterum error dicentium quod habere aliqua in communi est de evangelica perfectione Christi et apostolorum ac per consequens quod nichil tale in communi
habere non est de evangelica perfectione. Insurrexerunt etiam alii non modici contra evangelicam paupertatem errores, contra quos est declaratio seu decretalis domini Nicholai III in eadem generatione edita. In eadem etiam Parisius prodierunt
errores philosophici seu potius paganici, qui a doctoribus estimantur magna seminaria secte magni antichristi, sicut et precedentes sunt seminaria et etiam plante
errorum mistici antichristi.

"Prout vero inchoantur a Christi morte vel ascensione, sic in initio XLI apparuit circiter per tres menses stella comata valde grandis et stupenda. Tuncque
Manfredus, Frederici filius, usurpatorie regnum Sicilie contra ecclesiam tenens, est
per Carolum devictus et occisus et paulo post Colradus filius Colradi filii Frederici.
Et in XLII generatione Petrus rex Aragonum invasit Sicilie regnum et ex tunc
secuta sunt multa discidia inter reges et regna, que quibusdam non indoctis videntur esse preparatoria magni mali. In fine autem huius XLII generationis contigit
novitas electionis Celestini pape et successoris eius et quorundam aliorum nunc
ingravescentium. Si vero inchoetur a septimo anno passionis Christi, in quo Petrus
post cathedram Ierusaleme fertur secundam cathedram in gentibus et in urbe gen-
tilium accepisse, sicut postmodum accepit tertiam Rome, sic fine huius XIII centenarii incarnatinis Christi terminabuntur XLII generationes seu MCCLX anni, de
quo numero non restant nunc nisi tres anni."

20. There are places in the *Lectura* where Olivi, in stating the number of years
between one date and another, obviously counts the starting date. If that were the
case here, then he would be writing in 1298; yet he died in March 1298 (see Burr,
Persecution, 5), and in southern France it was customary to begin the new year at
Easter, not January 1. Thus, if he himself used the southern French method of
dating, by his reckoning he would never have seen the year 1298.

21. *Lectura*, 657–64.

22. Jerome, *Commentariorum in Hiezechielem libri XIV*, book 1, in CCSL
75:46–48.

23. *Historia Scholastica*, "Historia libri Judith," chapter 1, in *PL* 198:1475.
Olivi returns to this problem in *Lectura*, 849f.

24. *Lectura*, 664f.

25. At ibid., 681f., he again sees the 1,260 years as running from the migration
to the conversion of the Jews.

26. Ibid., 667–69. In fact, these dates are roughly supported by most of
Olivi's comments about chronology in the Apocalypse commentary. See the next
chapter.

27. Ibid., 694.

28. Ibid., 697f.

29. Ibid., 698f.

30. Note that in the process, at ibid., 702, he again demonstrates the problems caused by fitting the book of Judith into a chronology.

31. Ibid., 701.

32. Ibid., 706: "Possunt specialiter intorqueri ad bestiam a quarto tempore
usque ad finem ecclesie consurgentem." Since he means the Saracens and feels they

will last only until Antichrist, he seems to limit the church to the second age. This is hardly the only place where he speaks of the end of the second age as the end of the church; yet he cannot mean it in any strong sense, since the third age is equivalent to the seventh period of church history.

33. Olivi makes Saladin the fifth and assigns the last two to the time of Antichrist, but accepts the possibility that the sixth refers jointly to those kings under whom the Saracens have been triumphing in the thirteenth century.

34. Joachim, *Expositio in apocalypsim*, 164rb–165ra; *Lectura*, 708f. Joachim actually gives both possibilities but eventually states a preference for the latter.

35. Richard, *In apocalypsim Ioannis*, 803.

36. Joachim, *Liber de concordia* (Venice, 1519), 130vb (expositing Dan. 11: 13–24).

37. *Lectura*, 711–14.

38. Ibid., 718.

39. Ibid., 719. See Joachim, *Expositio*, 168ra.

40. *Lectura*, 720: "Mihi autem non est magne cure an ille qui proprie erit antichristus et qui adorabitur ut deus et qui dicet se messiam Iudeorum sit rex vel pseudopapa vel simul utrumque. Sufficit enim mihi scire quod erit fallax et Christo contrarius."

41. Ibid., 731. See Richard, *In apocalypsim Ioannis*, 808. For the Olivi text question cited by him at this point (*Quaestiones de perfectione evangelica*, q. 16), see David Burr and David Flood, "Peter Olivi: On Poverty and Revenue," 37f. Most thirteenth-century mendicant scholars interpreted the number as letters rather than years. Alexander Minorita was an exception.

42. *Lectura*, 732f. See Joachim, *Expositio*, 169ra. In question 16 of the *Quaestiones de perfectione evangelica*, published in Burr and Flood, "Peter Olivi: On Poverty and Revenue," 47f., Olivi recites a view borrowed from Bonaventure's *Collationes de septem donis spiritus sancti*, one Olivi also states in *Quaestiones in secundum librum sententiarum*, 1:98., in which the accent is on the circularity implied by the number. Both Olivian sources also link the number with heterodox Aristotelianism, as does Bonaventure. In question 16, Olivi also links it with the attack on Franciscan poverty. See Burr, "Apocalyptic Element."

43. *Lectura*, 733f.: "Quidam vero ultra hoc opinative dicunt hic significari numerum annorum regni secte sarracenice, nam ab anno domini DCXXXV, in quo secundum chronicas Sarraceni vicerunt Persas et obtinuerunt regnum eorum, usque ad completos MCCC annos domini, sunt DCLXVI. Ab anno autem domini DCXLVIII, in quo Sarraceni ceperunt Africam, capta prius Damasco et Phenice et Egypto et Ierusalem, usque ad MCCXC annos a morte Christi, id est usque ad MCCCXXIII a Christi nativitate, sunt DCLXVI anni. Si ergo numerus Dan. XII, prefixus a tempore quo a Iudeis fuit ablatum iuge sacrificium, currit usque ad antichristum, tunc a tempore quo regnum Sarracenorum fuit solemniter per Asiam et Africam dilatatum, erunt DCLXVI anni usque ad antichristum, de quo quidem numero restant adhuc XXIII anni; et si triennium tribulationis antichristi in numero prescripto includitur, tunc usque ad initium illius trienii restarent viginti anni. Quid autem inde erit, nescio. Deus scit."

44. Burr, "Olivi's Apocalyptic Timetable," *Journal of Medieval and Renais-*

sance Studies 11 (1981): 253, examines the passage without making sense of it. Textual variants in the manuscripts suggest that a few scribes were equally confused. Reference to A.D. 1300 as 666 years after A.D. 635 suggests that he includes the starting year within the number of years to go. This insight helps in dealing with the first set of numbers, but the rest is chaos: 666 plus 648 is 1313, not 1323. Moroever, if he is writing in 1297 or 1298 and thinks only twenty-three years remain, he is speaking of 1319 or 1320 as the target date. Thus we have possible target dates of 1313, 1319/20, and 1323.

45. *Lectura*, 734: "Et secundum hoc per bestiam ascendentem de mari significatur hic bestialis vita et plebs carnalium et secularium christianorum, que a fine quarti temporis et citra multa habuit capita carnalium principum et prelatorum quasi iam per DC annos. Et in hoc sexto centenario per evangelicum statum Francisci fuit unum caput eius quasi occisum. Quanto enim altius et latius evangelica paupertas et perfectio imprimitur et magnificatur in ecclesia Christi, tanto fortius caput terrene cupiditatis et vilis carnalitatis in ipsa occiditur. Sed iam hoc caput fere extinctum nimium reviviscit, ita ut carnales Christiani admirentur et sequantur terrenam et carnalem gloriam eius. Cum autem apostratrix bestia de terra religiosorum ascendet in altum cum duobus cornibus pseudoreligiosorum et pseudoprophetarum falso similibus veri cornibus agni, tunc erit validissima temptatio mistici antichristi. Surgent enim tunc pseudochristi et pseudoprophete, qui facient ab omnibus adorari cupiditatem et carnalitatem seu terrenam gloriam bestie secularis, dabuntque ad hoc signa magna. Primo scilicet sue ecclesiastice auctoritatis, cui contradicere videbitur stultum et insanum et etiam hereticum. Tertio dabunt signa rationum et scripturarum falso intortarum, et etiam signa alicuius superficialis ac vetuste et multiformis religionis per longam successionem ab antique firmate et solemnizate, ita ut cum hiis signis ignem divine ire super contradictores videantur facere descendere et econtra quasi ignem sancti et apostolici zeli videantur ipsi de celo in suos discipulos facere descendere. Statuent etiam ut qui non obedierit, anathematizetur et de synagoga eiciatur et, si oportuerit, bracchio seculari bestie prioris tradatur. Facient etiam quod imago bestie, id est pseudopapa, a rege bestie prime sublimatus, adoretur, id est ut sibi plusquam Christo et eius evangelio credatur et ut adulatorie quasi deus huius seculi honoretur."

46. Ibid., 736f.: "Et forte a tempore remissionis quarti status usque ad tempus istius erunt anni DCLXVI. Nam quintus a Pipino usque nunc habet iam DLX annos, et a vastatione anachoritarum et ceterorum fidelium commorantium in Perside et Syria et Egypto est numerus predictus cito complendus. Nam prout superius dixi, anno domini DCXXXV ceperunt Sarraceni regnum Persarum et post biennium capta Damasco, ceperunt Phenicem et Egyptum et post aliud biennium ceperunt Ierusalem."

47. That does not explain why Olivi says that the period from Pepin to the present has already lasted 560 years, unless he is counting from the death of Theodoric IV in 737.

48. *Lectura*, 738: "Quidam, ex pluribus que Ioachim de Frederico II et eius semine scribit et ex quibusdam que beatus Franciscus secrete fratri Leoni et quibusdam aliis sociis suis revelasse fertur, opinantur quod Fredericus prefatus cum suo semine sit respectu huius temporis quasi caput occisum et quod tempore mis-

tici antichristi ita reviviscat in aliquo de semine eius, ut non solum romanum imperium, sed etiam Francis ab ipso devictis obtineat regnum Francorum, quinque
ceteris regibus Christianorum sibi coherentibus statuet in pseudopapam quemdam
falsum religiosum, qui contra regulam evangelicam excogitabit et faciet dispensa-
tionem dolosam promovens in episcopos professores regule prefate sibi consen-
tientes et exinde expellens clericos et priores episcopos, qui semini Frederici et
specialiter illi imperatori et sibi et suo statui fuerant adversati, ac per consequens
omnes qui regulam predictam ad purum et plene voluerint observare et defensare.
Prefatum autem cleri et regni Francie casum et aliquem alium, illi annexum vel
previum dicunt designari per terremotum in initio apertionis sexti sigilli tactum,
quamvis et preter hoc designet spiritualem subversionem et excecationem fere totius ecclesie tunc fiendam. Quid autem horum erit vel non erit, dispositioni divine
censeo relinguendum. Addunt etiam predicti quod tunc in parte implebitur illud
apostoli secunda ad Thessalonicenses II scilicet: 'Nisi venerit discessio primum.'
Dicunt enim quod tunc omnes fere discedent ab obedientia veri pape et sequentur
illum pseudopapam, qui quidem erit pseudo, quia heretico modo errabit contra
veritatem evangelice paupertatis et perfectionis, et quia forte ultra hoc non erit
canonice electus sed scismatice introductus."

49. Ibid., 73f.

50. Ibid., 809: "Puto autem quod respectu diversorum temporum utrumque
sit verum. Unde et quidam putant quod tam antichristus misticus quam proprius
et magnus erit pseudopapa caput pseudoprophetarum et quod per eius et suorum
pseudoprophetarum consilia et cooperationes acquiretur imperium illi regi, per
quem statuetur in suo falso papatu. Sed ille rex, qui statuet magnum faciet ipsum
ultra hoc adorari ut deum."

51. Ibid., 537f.: "Designatur per hoc aut discessio fere omnium ab obedientia
summi pontificis, de qua dicit apostolus secunda ad Thessalonicenses II: Nisi venerit discessio primum, et cetera; aut cessatio favoris eius ad statum evangelicum,
per quem eius emuli sunt usque nunc impediti in ipsum irruere iuxta votum. Po-
testas enim pape et multitudo plebium sibi obediens et favor ipsius est quasi magnus fluvius Euphrates impediens transitum et insultum emulorum evangelici status
in ipsum."

52. Lewis, "Peter John Olivi," introduction, 228f.

53. *Lectura*, 906: "Patet quod bestia et pseudopropheta designant hic per-
sonaliter duos viros, quorum unus est rex et caput bestie, id est bestialium nationum, alius vero est caput pseudoprophetarum facientium signa. Sed an iste sit
pseudopapa et fingens se deum vel solum pseudopropheta predicans primum ut
deum, non constat, quamvis a doctoribus credatur quod hic secundus dicat se
deum."

54. In his letter to R. in *Quodlibeta*, 53(65)r, written just before his 1283 censure and discussed earlier, Olivi uses a similar disclaimer for just that purpose. He
notes that he has been criticized for discussing "dreams and certain fantastic visions" and temerariously making predictions about future events; yet he has never
asserted particular things would occur, "that is, that this thing would happen that
particular day or year, or this or that person would do this or that thing, etc."
Nevertheless, he does hold as certain that the Franciscan order, having been purged

through punishments and temptations, will restore divine worship throughout the world and bring all to Christ. Since one cannot think of such general matters without clothing them in particular images, even though one recognizes that these images are not the truth, he examines "conjectures concerning future particulars through the mirror of holy scripture," but makes it clear that he is not certain about such particulars and displays "more moderation in these matters than many people think." See my discussion in "Olivi, Apocalyptic Expectation, and Visionary Experience," 277f. In the roughly contemporaneous *Tractatus de usu paupere*, in *De usu paupere: The Quastio and the Tractatus*, 135, Olivi also states his faith that the order will be purged.

55. Richard of St. Victor, *In apocalypsim Ioannis*, 804 interprets the two in this way. Franciscans in Olivi's time could find three possibilities in earlier exegesis. One was that the sea stood for Judaism; a second approach translated the sea/land opposition into a secular/ecclesiastical distinction, with the beast from the sea representing evil secular princes while the beast from the land stood for corrupt ecclesiastics; and a third approach saw the sea/land opposition as one between non-Christians and bad Christians, with the sea as *gentilitas* and the land as *christianitas*. Obviously the three were not mutually exclusive.

56. *Lectura*, 525.

57. Ibid., 698f.: "Mos est scripture prophetice . . . a specialibus ad generalia ascendere et expandi."

58. Manselli, *Lectura super apocalypsim*, 231.

59. *Lectura*, 434f.

60. Oberman, "The Stubborn Jews: Timing the Escalation of Antisemitism in Late Medieval Europe," *Leo Baeck Institute Yearbook* 34 (1989): XI–XXV.

61. Joachim, *Expositio*, 39r–v.

62. This connection was first remarked upon by E. R. Daniel in a paper at Kalamazoo some years ago. The idea of a double persecution is not confined to Joachim and Olivi. See my remarks on Gerard of Borgo San Donnino in Chapter 1 above.

63. *Lectura*, 737.

64. Ibid., 423f.

65. See my *OFP*.

66. John Moorman, *History of the Franciscan Order* (Oxford, 1968), 296; *BF* 5:605–18.

67. Johannes Mansi, *Sacrorum conciliorum nova et amplissima collectio* (Florence, 1759–98), 24:1213–1216.

68. *Chronica*, 578, 643.

69. *Chronica XXIV generalium*, 431.

70. See my *OFP*, 127f.

71. See ibid., 108, 127.

7. The Apocalyptic Timetable

In the process of dealing with Olivi's double Antichrist, the preceding chapter unavoidably investigated the problem of how soon he expected these events to arrive. In this one we will review the passages considered there, adding a few more.

The Prologue

In his prologue to the Apocalypse commentary, Olivi raises the question of why the fifth period has lasted so much longer than any preceding one. It has been going on for 500 years if one dates it from the coronation of Charlemagne and for nearly 560 years if one starts with Pepin's campaign against the Lombards.[1] In the process of answering this question, Olivi cites a passage from the *Liber de concordia* in which Joachim links the four animals and the throne of Revelation 4:2–8 to the first five periods.[2] The four animals have a total of twenty-four wings representing twenty-four generations of thirty years each, a total of 720 years. The seat itself, standing for the fifth period, "has sixteen generations, that is, 450 years."[3] There is, of course, a minor mathematical problem here, but the figure will do for our purposes.

Nevertheless, Olivi says, according to some people the fifth period should last 500 years from the beginning of the Carolingian empire, "that is, from the year 801," for those within it need to regulate their five bodily senses. Beginning the period from the reign of Pepin, one would then have eighteen generations, three units of six representing the threefold perfection of Christ's works and councils as well as the total immersion of carnal people in worldly pursuits. Olivi says no more, but the logical conclusion is easy to draw. The anonymous *quidam* expect the end of the fifth period around the year 1301. If, like Olivi, those *quidam* expect the period to end with the destruction of Babylon, then one would have to fit the temptation of the mystical Antichrist in before that time.

Olivi turns at this point to the sixth period, noting that Joachim occasionally seems to say it will last only three-and-a-half years. After analyzing a series of relevant passages from Joachim, Olivi concludes that the period from the fall of Babylon to the last judgment must contain enough time for the whole world to be converted to Christ and for the period to follow a pattern of growth, zenith, and decay, ending with a decadence so profound as to justify Christ's third advent in judgment.[4]

The Four Openings of the Sixth Period

Another approach to the length of the sixth period is found in a passage cited earlier, in which Olivi lists the various opening dates for the period offered by a mass of anonymous *quidam*, then suggests that, properly interpreted, all are correct.[5] We have seen how he takes this occasion to suggest four different beginnings for the period: the revelation to Joachim; the renewal of the evangelical rule in Francis; the preaching of spiritual men at the time when the rule is opposed by the carnal church; and the destruction of Babylon. "In the same way," Olivi says, "the law was killed as far as obligation is concerned in the passion and resurrection of Christ, yet was buried and made deadly in the full promulgation of the gospel and in the destruction of the temple of the law by Titus and Vespasion."[6] Here as elsewhere the first opening with Joachim seems less important and does not rate a first-century parallel.

The comparison has chronological implications. Olivi recognizes that the parallel between first- and thirteenth-century events is not complete, and soon finds himself asking why Francis and his original followers are not personally involved in the third and fourth beginnings, even though Peter and Paul suffered under Simon Magus and Nero, who sent Vespasian to begin the destruction of Jerusalem.[7] He offers no less than eight reasons for the discrepancy, one of them being the observation that "in the sixth [period] an order of many persons corresponds to the person of Christ."[8] Thus it is not simply Francis but his entire order that conforms to the life, death, and resurrection of Christ, an idea which has already surfaced in our investigation. Other reasons display the full spectrum of standard Olivian concerns and each has its own fascination, but only one is relevant to our present investigation. Olivi remarks that "according to some people the three years and three months from Christ's baptism to his death are applicable to it, taking a year for thirty years." Unfortunately the "it" in this case seems to be identified as the fifth rather than the sixth period, but closer inspection reveals that what Olivi apparently intended to say is that the three years and three months correspond with that part of the late fifth period overlapping the early sixth. He adds that "some people add to this the three months of John the Baptist's preaching, so that there will thus be 105 years." Obviously the total without those extra three months would be 97.5 years. Olivi does not mention when the counting should begin and we have no way of knowing when he thought Joachim's revelation took place, but neither of these uncertainties is fatal, since Olivi shows little interest in counting from Joachim's revelation anyway. If we start with Francis's first rule, the 105 years elapse midway through the second decade of the fourteenth century, and if we begin with the definitive rule of 1223 it will still bring us only to 1328. Using 97.5 years would bring the end point even closer.

Having offered this theory, Olivi proceeds to distance himself from it. He notes that "coaptations of this sort have no certainty unless they are supported by actual events or indubitable revelation, or unless they are necessarily proved by another part of sacred scripture; for we could form such coaptations in many (in fact, almost innumerable) ways, taking one year for one hundred, one thousand, forty, ten, or whatever."[9]

The Plague of Locusts

Another chronological signpost is erected by the locusts of Revelation 9:3–11. When the fifth trumpet sounds, they rise from the pit and torment mankind for five months. Olivi reports that "according to some people these months stand for five units of thirty days (taking each day for a year), that is, 150 years."[10] Thus these people think that the plague of locusts at the end of the fifth period will last for around 150 years. Olivi mentions twice in the course of this passage that Joachim says this without assertion concerning the plague of the Cathari. That unfortunate suggestion encourages Olivi to explore Joachim's obsession with the Cathari and his assumption that the fifth period will end substantially earlier than Olivi and his contemporaries, in their wisdom, know will be the case. It is in the course of these meditations that Olivi makes the comment cited earlier about the difference between Joachim's divinely revealed first principles and his all too errant conclusions.[11]

By this point Olivi already has offered an alternative interpretation of the passage which seems to please him. The five months might stand for the entire fifth period, while the locusts could be taken in general for all evil Christians and in particular for the "wicked multitude of clerics, monks, judges and other *curiales*" who plague Christendom. Olivi seems to be spreading the plague of locusts across the entire expanse of church history, but his intention is more complex. He still wants to identify the five months and the locusts with something that will occur at the end of the fifth period, and at this point he mentions the three special threats already examined by us in Chapter 4. He also tentatively suggests that the five months represent the final five months of the three-and-a-half year persecution at the end of the fifth period, parallel to the last five months of Christ's ministry when he was most grievously persecuted; or perhaps they represent five years encompassing the three-and-a-half-year perse-cution and another one-and-a-half years of preparatory strife.[12] The perse-cution he has in mind is, of course, that of the mystical Antichrist. This is hardly the limit of his speculation concerning the five months, but it must be the limit of ours.

The Woman in the Desert

Nevertheless, a great deal more should be said about the three-and-a-half years. Olivi returns to them on several occasions, and his discussion sug-gests that he is at least open to the notion that both the temptation of the mystical Antichrist and that of the great Antichrist will last that long;[13] yet the number can be given a different significance by identifying it with the 1,260 days of Revelation 11:3 and 12:6. In dealing with the first of these passages, Olivi confines his attention to the temptation of Antichrist, but when he faces the second, the woman fleeing into the desert, he identifies the number with the period between "the full flight of recession of the church from the synagogue" and the promised conversion of the Jews. Since Christ and John the Baptist preached in vain among the Jews for three-and-a-half years, the Jews are being punished by exclusion from the church for three-and-a-half years of days, or 1,260 years. We offered this passage a very close inspection in the last chapter and hardly need to go through that process again. The conclusion suggested there, augmented by Olivi's thoughts on Daniel 12:11f., was that the destruction of the carnal church can be expected by 1332 and the great Antichrist should be along by 1362 at the latest, but both events could occur substantially earlier. Unfortunately, as we have seen, Olivi closes his analysis with the observation that the numbers he has been considering may tell us only how long the persecution of Antichrist will last, not when it will begin.

The Two Beasts

We have examined Olivi's comments on the beast from the sea.[14] Here we need only recall that Olivi speaks there of seven centuries between the rise of Islam and the coming of the great Antichrist. Since he dates the former event around A.D. 635, that would place the rule of the great Antichrist around A.D. 1335. Revelation 13:18, the number of the beast, gives him another chance to indulge in higher mathematics. Here we found that Olivi's calculations are at best bewildering but suggest that the great Antichrist should reign by circa A.D. 1323. We also saw that he applies the number to the mystical Antichrist as well, suggesting that it may represent the period from the end of the fourth period until that temptation. Since in this passage he seems to take the rise of Islam as an indicator of the declining fourth period, he is apparently contemplating a date 666 years after circa A.D. 635, which would place the mystical Antichrist around 1301.

The Millennium

Another choice passage occurs in Olivi's treatment of Revelation 20:2, the binding of Satan. His comments are important not only for our understanding of his apocalyptic timetable, but also for the light they shed on his handling of tradition. The thousand-year binding of Satan arrived at Olivi's door encased in a long interpretive history, one largely dictated by Augustine. Late in the *City of God* Augustine turns to the vexing problem of what should be done with Revelation 20:1–10. Some people, he notes, read the passage as a promise that after six thousand years of world history there will be a bodily resurrection for the saints followed by a thousand-year rest period.[15] Their view would be at least tolerable if they were speaking of spiritual delights. Augustine admits that he himself once thought along these lines. Unfortunately, the people he has in mind anticipate real banquets with plentiful food and drink. Only the carnally minded can believe in such things.[16]

Now, however, Augustine sees that the millennium of Revelation 20 can be understood in two ways. Either it is a synecdoche, the whole being taken for one of its parts, and "millennium" stands for the remaining part of the sixth and final millennium of world history; or it is simply a perfect number used to signify the entire Christian era.[17] Augustine himself interprets the passage to mean that, from the beginning of the Christian era, the devil has been "bound" in the sense that he is limited in his ability to delude those within Christian nations. The binding is thus, in effect, a progressive affair which will continue throughout history as people are converted and enter the church.[18] The thousand-year reign of the saints and the first resurrection mentioned in the text both refer to the same period. The reign of the saints has a double focus, referring both to the church militant and to the church triumphant. The first resurrection is a spiritual one, the revivification of the world through grace.[19] Toward the end of history, Elijah will return from heaven and preach to the Jews, who will be converted. The devil will be loosed and will run wild for three-and-a-half years, aided by Gog and Magog, who signify the wicked throughout the world.[20] The persecution of Antichrist will occur at this time. Satan and his minions will eventually be defeated by the constancy of the saints, thus clearing the way for the second resurrection, a physical rising of the dead, and for the final judgment.

Augustine's interpretation does not completely spiritualize Revelation 20. A chain of events is projected, but until the final days it is a remarkably simple one. Augustine's is an *histoire de la longue durée*. The church will keep doing what it is currently doing until some time in the indefinite future just before the end of the world, when things will go badly for it. This final, brief period is more complex, involving Elijah, Antichrist, Gog, and Magog, but Augustine feels these are not events we should worry about anyway, since we cannot predict their time, nature, or sequence.[21]

Augustine's interpretation was not entirely original,[22] but it was determinative inasmuch as it was the one cited and accepted for several centuries. From Bede on, there was a growing tendency to open up a brief period of peace between the fall of Antichrist and the final judgment, but it was based on Daniel 12 as interpreted by Jerome, not on Revelation 20.[23] The real break with Augustine regarding the latter passage did not begin until the late twelfth century with Joachim of Fiore. In his Apocalypse commentary, Joachim agrees with Augustine on some important issues. He acknowledges that it is impossible for us to project a timetable for the apocalyptic countdown.[24] Thus we cannot speak of a literal thousand years. He also agrees that there is a sense in which the millennium applies to the entire history of the church. Nevertheless, Joachim anticipates a more complex scenario than did Augustine, since he sees the church as progressing through seven periods, each of which entails change. He sees himself as living on the edge of the sixth period. In the fifth, there is conflict between the church and the beast, the latter being conceived as the Muslims, heretics, Holy Roman Empire, and various sinister elements within the church itself. In the sixth, the warfare will escalate as spiritual men within the church are subjected to the persecution of Antichrist. Then a great sabbath of peace and contemplation will begin. At its end, Antichrist will return with Gog for a final offensive.[25] The last judgment will follow.

Thus stated, Joachim's position does not seem strikingly different from the one held by other commentators who, as we have seen, projected a brief seventh period but also acknowledged Augustine's interpretation of Revelation 20. The difference lies in Joachim's seventh period. His sevenfold pattern is developed in concert with his threefold one. The transition to the seventh period also signals the final disappearance of the second *status* and the complete emergence of the third.

Thus Joachim has more use for Revelation 20 than Augustine had, since he projects, between the temptation of Antichrist and the end of history, a period of indeterminate length in which Satan will be bound and the saints will reign in a much different sense than before. For that reason, despite his willingness to accept the general correctness of Augustine's view, he defends the opposing position as well. He argues that identification of the thousand years with the seventh period is a "rational opinion" consistent with the faith. Augustine was correct in attacking the notion of a physical resurrection of the saints followed by a thousand years of *haute cuisine*, but the idea of an earthly sabbath of peace and contemplation in a seventh period of church history is not merely an acceptable opinion but a *serenissimus intellectus*.[26]

Joachim's rejection of Augustine was therefore significant but incomplete. It could be extended, and Olivi did just that. He too had use for Revelation 20, since he too identified the seventh period with the full blossoming of a more or less Joachite third age. Thus when he arrives at Revelation 20 in his commentary, Olivi turns almost immediately to the binding of Satan.[27] It refers, he says, to three different episodes in history. It refers to Christ's death and resurrection; to Constantine's Christianization of the Roman Empire; and to the seventh period following Antichrist's death. Thus, where Joachim had accepted Augustine's interpretation and added another, Olivi accepts Augustine's and Joachim's, then adds a third, though without mentioning either of the other two authors (at least at that point). The passages immediately following examine questions like whether Satan is bound in relation to all or only in relation to the elect, and what is meant by the abyss in which he is enclosed. These are relatively safe ways of letting Augustine into the discussion, and Olivi quotes him at length.

Eventually, though, he must face those thousand years. When he finally does so,[28] he asks whether the figure should be taken as literally true, gives Augustine's answer, then dutifully notes that it is seconded by Joachim and Richard of St. Victor. Nevertheless, Olivi desperately wants a real millennium. He observes that in the opinion of "some people," if we begin the binding of Satan with Constantine, then the millennium will match the 1,260 years spent in the desert by the woman in Revelation 12:6, a passage that Olivi takes as referring to the church among the Gentiles. The figure also matches the 1,290 years after Christ's crucifixion predicted by Daniel 13:11. Pope Sylvester died in A.D. 334, and by the time of his death Christianity was well established in the empire. If we add 334 to 1,000, then subtract the 34 years of Christ's life, we have 1,300. In other words, the 1,260 years of Revelation 12:6, the 1,290 of Daniel 13:11, and the 1,000 of Revelation 20:2 all lead to the end of the thirteenth century. Taken in this sense, the millennium terminates not with the future Gog who will appear around the time of the last judgment, but with a symbolic Gog, the mystical and great Antichrists. We now see why Olivi added his third sense of Satan's binding. Beginning with the rise of Christian empire there is, in effect, a millennium of the second age, the age of the Son.

What about the age of the Holy Spirit? Olivi announces that his unnamed informants know much less about that subject, yet following "the Hebraic truth" that there were four thousand years between Adam and Christ,

they suggest—not boldly, in fact very mildly—that around the end of the sixth millennium, at the close of the sixth day as it were, God will perfect the whole universe and there will follow a sabbath of eternal glory in which God and his saints rest from the works of this life. And this is in harmony with the opinion of certain ancient masters of the synagogue who said that two thousand years before the law (that is, to Abraham), two thousand under the law, and two thousand under the Messiah would form three pairs of millennia according to a threefold pattern of nature, scripture, and grace. According to

these people, about seven hundred years of the sixth millennium remain, and
this fits well with the third general age of the world appropriated to the Holy
Spirit. . . . Insofar as the beginning of the third age is in some sense found
seminally in the period when Christ's spirit caused a great army of Christians
to sail to the Holy Land and, having killed innumerable Saracens, restore
Jerusalem to Christian worship, a period in which the Cistercians, Grand-
montensians, Carthusians, Templars, and Hospitalers began, then instead of
the aforementioned seven hundred years there are about one thousand years
[in the third age], or at least nine hundred. Moreover, if you begin the un-
loosing of Satan in connection with the time of the great Antichrist from the
time when, under the fifth trumpet, the star falling from heaven took the key
to the bottomless pit and opened it, then from Christ's resurrection to that
time there are around one thousand years during which the saints reign with
Christ.[29]

The final sentence of the passage presupposes what Olivi has said earlier
about Revelation 9:1f. There he identifies the opening of the abyss with
the evils flowering at the end of the fifth period.[30]

Olivi's "ancient masters of the synagogue" thus afford him a pattern
that is in some ways similar to Augustine's, but in other ways very different. Augustine had posited a world week of seven ages with six "days"
from creation to final judgment and a seventh more or less in eternity. The
period from Christ to final judgment comprised the sixth "day." He was
also willing to entertain as possible the widespread notion that each of the
first six "days" might be one thousand years long. Olivi accepts the Augustinian world week and, as we have seen, derives great satisfaction from
correlating it with the seven periods of church history, since it allows him
to draw a parallel between Christ's function in the sixth age and Francis's
in the sixth period. Like Augustine, he sees the sixth "day" as extending
to final judgment. Nevertheless, he differs sharply from Augustine in making the first five "days" total only four thousand years and in placing the
other two thousand years within the sixth. Olivi therefore can view the
time from Christ to final judgment as divided into two periods of roughly
one thousand years each. The boundaries are hardly clear. At one point he
seems content with a period of 1,300 years running from Christ to circa
A.D. 1300, followed by another 700 years to the end.

It follows that the third age is almost twice as long as the second age.
If one identifies the second age only with the seventh period (when it has
separated completely from the age of the Son), then it is almost exactly
half as long as the second. Such an unequal division is by no means unacceptable to Olivi, and somewhat later he justifies it by citing "certain

people" who interpret the half hour of silence in Revelation 8:1 as an indication that the third age will be around half as long as the second.[31] Nevertheless, in the passage just quoted he obviously thinks he can do better. By shifting the opening of the sixth period (and therefore of the third age) back beyond Francis to a "seminal" beginning in the late eleventh century, he moves closer to parity, allowing somewhat less than 1,100 years for the age of the Son and slightly over 900 for the age of the Holy Spirit.

Thus we have two quasi-literal millennia corresponding to two of the three events associated with the binding of Satan. The age of Constantine is followed by a period of almost precisely one thousand years leading to the Antichrists, while the seventh period, if dated from its "seminal" beginning, will run for slightly over 900 years. The third event, Christ's resurrection, seems to have the least tidy millennium of all (1,300 years) if we see it as continuing until the arrival of the two Antichrists; yet if we allow the third age to be dated from its "seminal" beginning, then the second age will run for around 1,100 years after Christ. There are still other ways of looking at the matter. In the final sentence of the passage just quoted, Olivi suggests yet another way of counting. He observes that approximately one thousand years passed between the resurrection and the period after Charlemagne, when the church began to descend the long, slippery slope toward Antichrist.

Thus Olivi manages to refute Augustine very directly and unambiguously. Having done so, he proceeds to pay his respects, noting that Augustine correctly castigated the carnal aspirations of those millenarians who thought the saints would be resurrected for a thousand years of banqueting. Shortly thereafter, he grants that Augustine was right in identifying the seats of judgment in Revelation 20:4 with church offices.[32] Immediately after that, however, he observes that, in contrast with Jerome and Joachim, Augustine refuses to see Gog and Magog as referring to a particular people. Apparently feeling that he has humored Augustine enough, Olivi cites Ezechiel 38 against him.[33]

Lessons of the Alphabet

By this point, however, Olivi has struck out on an entirely new path in pursuit of the same chronological conclusion. Having put the "ancient masters of the synagogue" to use, he now enlists another ally, the pseudo-

Joachite *Liber de seminibus scripturarum*.[34] Olivi announces that, "just as in accordance with the twenty-two letters of the Hebrew alphabet there were twenty-two centuries from Heber . . . to Christ, so in accordance with the twenty-three letters of the Latin language there were twenty-three centuries beginning with the construction of the city of Rome, the locus of the principal seat of the Latins and of the church of Christ." Daniel 8:14 says, "Two thousand and three hundred evenings and mornings, then the sanctuary will be cleansed." Since in this passage a day stands for a year, we have a period of twenty-three centuries. In Daniel's time, Rome was in its second century, its first having been concurrent with the captivity of the ten tribes of Israel. It was through this captivity that the sanctuary of God began to be "trampled under foot," as Daniel 8:13 says, although that passage refers literally to the six years, three months, and twenty days from Antiochus's entry into Jerusalem until his death in the 149th year of the kingdom of the Greeks.

Olivi has plugged history into Daniel 8 and the Latin alphabet, but where will it lead him? The answer begins to appear when he observes that Christ came in the eighth century of Rome, and *H*, the eighth letter of the Roman alphabet, is not properly a letter but a mark of aspiration, just as Christ was born not through human activity but through the breath (*aspiratio*) of the Holy Spirit. Olivi's own century is equivalent to the twentieth century of Rome, and the twentieth letter of the Roman alphabet is *V*, pronounced on the end of the lips as if one were breathing out (*quasi aspirando*). Thus the carnal church will expire (*expirabit*) at the end of this century. In the following century (designated by the letter *X*, which has the shape of a cross), the cross of Christ will be renewed and exalted. Olivi notes that on the order of 1,260 years will elapse between the flight of the church into the wilderness of the Gentiles and the century designated by the letter *X*. He has now covered twenty-one centuries of Roman history symbolized by twenty-one letters of the Latin alphabet. In the process, he has brought his history into the fourteenth century and into the third age. He still has two letters to go and presumably some history to which he can apply them, but he is uninterested in doing so. He announces that, according to the *quidam* who offer this interpretation, the last two letters were carried over into the Latin alphabet from the Greek and do not signify years at all, but rather "the extension of the church to the Greeks and to all peoples," an obvious allusion to global conversion in the third age.

Having presented this view in some detail and with unquestionable enthusiasm, he offers his standard word of caution: "I have recited these things briefly, being able to offer nothing certain here or even any argument worthy of the name except that scripture, in its own way, helpfully tells us that from the time of the sixth and seventh periods the last judgment is close and, as it were, stands at the door." Here again, however, having apparently ended the discussion, he returns to it. The people in question, he adds, adapt the half hour of silence in Revelation 8:1 to their argument, suggesting that the period after Antichrist will be approximately half as long as the one from Christ's crucifixion to the crucifixion of the church carried out under Antichrist. The latter period will be 1,300 years long, the former "at least six or seven hundred."[35] These people also say that, if one counts 2,300 years from the trampling of the sanctuary in the time of Antiochus (which, we recall, is offered as the literal significance of Daniel 8:13), then there were around two hundred years to Christ's birth and 1,500 to the end of the thirteenth century, "and thus beyond the century of crucifixion designated by X there remain seven hundred years for the seventh period of the church."[36]

Olivi has wrung two different interpretations from the same data, but both point in the same general direction. If we take the first to mean that we should begin counting from 753 B.C., the legendary date for the founding of Rome, then Olivi would be correct in saying that Christ came during the eighth century. It might seem to follow that the twentieth century would then run from A.D. 1153 to 1253, placing Olivi in the twenty-first century, not the twentieth as he imagines; but when he speaks of the thirteenth century he is probably thinking of the centuries in standard Christian terms. If so, the twentieth century would extend to A.D. 1300 and the destruction of the carnal church would occur around then, a date roughly consistent with his remark that 1,260 years will elapse between the flight of the church to the Gentiles and the century designated by the letter X.

The message of the second interpretation meshes well with this scheme if one assumes that Olivi is not treating the letters of the alphabet as centuries this time around. If that much is granted, then he is again projecting thirteen centuries from Christ to Antichrist and another seven centuries in the seventh period. If he still assuming that the letters represent centuries, then the passage is absolutely incoherent. In order to get the requisite twenty-three centuries, he must count the "century of crucifixion designated by the letter X" as a separate century distinct from both the preceding fifteen and the following seven or he will have one century too few. If he invokes the previous explanation that only twenty-one of the twenty-three letters really count as centuries, then he need not consider the "century of crucifixion" as a separate unit but he will still have one century too many, since 1,500 plus 700 is 2,200. In either case the logic of identifying the centuries with letters will be destroyed, since he will be only fifteen or sixteen centuries into the pattern when the "century of crucifixion designated by X" arrives, and X is the twenty-first letter.

Conclusion

None of this strikes one as excessively precise. Olivi seems to be suggesting that the Holy Spirit speaks in very round figures, accurate to the nearest three centuries or so. This is not entirely fair to Olivi, however, since he offers a series of very good reasons why predictions cannot be accurate to the day and hour. There is, in the first place, the stubborn fact that human beings function with finite intellects and often miss the point, even when the point is there to grasp. Second, one must recognize that the relevant biblical evidence is not limited to a single meaning. It does not simply function as a series of chronological signposts, but does a whole series of other things simultaneously. Remember that Olivi acknowledges a mystical as well as a literal meaning in scripture and, even in the area of historical reference, assumes that the same passage may have both a particular and a general reference. It may even refer to a series of particular events. As Olivi chooses to put it, the numbers he is manipulating "are diversified because of the exigencies of various mysteries."[37] The resultant text is rich in signification but, as a result, necessarily vague in the particular area of apocalyptic prediction.

   Third, there is the matter of historical progression itelf. Olivi is consistently aware that the birth of a new period is not the sort of thing one can record on an appointments calendar. There is inevitably a transitional time when the old is dying and the new is growing up. A period can be seen as beginning at some point in one sense, but at a different point in another sense. Thus various bits of evidence may seem to yield slightly different timetables, but they all make sense when viewed in the proper context.

   In short, an apocalyptic timetable can never be employed as a precision tool. Nevertheless, impossible though it may be to predict the day of Antichrist's arrival, it is worth one's while to know as much as possible about when and how he will arrive, because his impact will be rather difficult to avoid. Moreover, as we have seen, Olivi feels that his era, however limited it may be, is still better equipped than any previous period for such speculation. Time and the Holy Spirit have combined to offer his generation more insight into the shape of history than has been enjoyed by any former age. It is no wonder that he feels free to contradict Augustine, who lived a mere four centuries after Christ and thus could not foresee how the historical pattern offered by the Apocalypse would match the actual course of church history. Nor is it surprising that he is heavily indebted to and yet in some ways quite independent of Joachim, who wrote a century earlier when the early dawn was still concealed by lingering shadows.

Having said so much, we find that in the final analysis Olivi's discussions all seem to tend in the same direction. However general the numbers may be, they regularly place the destruction of Babylon and temptation of the great Antichrist somewhere in the first four decades of the fourteenth century. The temptation of the mystical Antichrist is both present and future for Olivi. He describes the temptation itself as already underway, but seems to expect an individual under whom the perscution will escalate in the near future.

The third age, that of the Holy Spirit, will separate definitively from the second at some point before the middle of the fourteenth century. According to a view which Olivi discusses enthusiastically if noncommittally, it will end somewhere around the year 2000. For a denizen of the late twentieth century, these are hardly glad tidings. We are coming into the home stretch and can look forward to little except our encounter with Gog. For Olivi, however, the best is yet to come. What, then, does he expect to happen in the dawning new age of the Holy Spirit? We must turn to that question in the next chapter.

Notes

1. *Lectura*, 79.
2. *Liber de concordia*, 209–11.
3. *Lectura*, 84.
4. Ibid., 85–88.
5. Ibid., 394–96. See Chapter 5 above.
6. *Lectura*, 395f.
7. Ibid., 401f. See ibid., 525, for Nero and Simon Magus as assimilated to the great Antichrist.
8. Ibid., 402: "Secunda est quia persone Christi correspondet in sexta apertione unus ordo plurium personarum."

9. Ibid., 405f.: "Septima est ut prima pars conformaretur principio et medio et termino quinti status, cum quo concurrit; et etiam totius ecclesie cuius initium humile et plenum egestate, medium vero preclarum et expansum in orbem, finis vero vespertinus et tepidus; et secundum quosdam coaptantur ei tres anni et tres menses a Christi baptismo usque ad eius mortem elapsi sumendo annum pro triginta annis, quidam vero hiis addunt tres menses predicationis Iohannis baptiste ut sic sint CV anni. Sciendum tamen quod huiusmodi coaptationes nichil habent certitudinis nisi aut per facti evidentiam inclarescant aut per revelationem indubitabilem aut nisi per aliam auctoritatem scripture sacre necessario probentur. Multis enim modis et quasi innumeris possunt tales coaptationes formari. Iuxta quod possemus dicere, quod per unum annum intelligantur centum anni vel mille vel quadraginta vel decem et sic de aliis." Note that here as elsewhere (e.g., earlier on p. 405) the morning/noon/evening image is applied to the Franciscan order in the thirteenth century, just as it is applied to each of the three world ages.

10. Ibid., 500: "Per menses quinque designantur secundum quosdam quinque tricenarii dierum sumendo diem pro anno, id est CL anni."

11. Ibid., 512. See Chapter 4 above.

12. *Lectura*, 519.

13. See, for example, the passage just analyzed; ibid., 527–32, a melange of Joachim citations which, Olivi concludes, show that Joachim offered a number of ideas as opinions rather than as assertions; and ibid., 586f., which establishes in opposition to Richard of St. Victor that the period designates the persecution, not the entire reign of Antichrist.

14. See Chapter 6.

15. *De civitate dei contra paganos*, 20:7 (*CCSL* 48).

16. For materialistic views of the millennium see the account of Papias's opinion in Eusebius, *Ecclesiastical History*, 3:28 and 39, in *Loeb Classical Library* (Cambridge, MA, 1942–49), vol. 53; Lactantius, *Divinae institutiones*, 7 (*CSEL* 19).

17. Augustine's actual words are "aut certe mille annos pro annis omnibus huius saeculi posuit, ut perfecto numero notaretur ipsa temporis plenitudo." Translators normally render *huius saeculi* as "of this world," in which case Augustine rejects this second possibility and chooses the first; yet he does not explicitly do so, but simply proceeds on the assumption that the binding represents the Christian era, as if that much were assumed in either alternative. Thus I suspect that he was actually thinking of the Christian era when he said *huius saeculi*, and the difference between the two options is really whether one thinks the sixth period is destined to last one thousand years.

18. *De civitate*, 20:8.

19. Ibid., 20:9.

20. Ibid., 20:29. Augustine explicitly rejects the view of Gog and Magog as specific barbarian peoples. For this opinion see Jerome, *In Ezechielem* (*CCSL* 75), 525f.

21. *De civitate*, 20:11, 20:30. Augustine does suggest a sequence that seems right to him, but says in the same breath that we cannot know if it is the correct one.

22. The most important influence on him was probably Tyconius. See the discussion and bibliography in Bernard McGinn, *The Calabrian Abbot*, 80–84.

23. See Lerner, "Refreshment of the Saints," 97–144.

24. *Expositio in apocalypsim*, 123rb, 210ra, 210va–215va. A brief, succinct discussion of Joachim on Rev. 20 is offered by McGinn, *Calabrian Abbot*, 154f.

25. Antichrist will spend his exile among the Scythians. *Expositio in apocalypsim*, 210vb. On the possible identities of Gog see 10vb–11ra, 215ra.

26. *Expositio in apocalypsim*, 211ra. Ibid., 123rb, seems to accept as one of several possibilities that the half-hour of Rev. 8:1 signifies a mere six-month duration of the seventh period; yet in 210va–vb he leaves its length up to God.

27. *Lectura*, 908.

28. Ibid., 916.

29. Ibid., 919f.: "An autem septimus status a morte huius antichristi usque ad Gog novissimum habeat ad litteram mille annos, multo minus sciunt. Quidam tamen sequendo hebraicam veritatem, que ab Adam usque ad Christum ponit circiter quattuor milia annos, non fortiter sed valde exiliter opinantur quod circa finem sexti millenarii quasi in fine sexte diei perficiat deus totum opus universi et sequatur sabbatum eterne glorie, in quo deus cum suis sanctis requiescat ab operibus huius vite. Concordatque hoc opinioni quorumdam antiquorum magistrorum synagoge, qui dixerunt quod duo milia anni ante legem, scilicet usque ad Abraham, et duo milia sub lege et duo milia sub Messia, ut sic secundum trinam legem nature, scripture et gratie sint tria paria millenariorum. Secundum hos autem de sexto millenario restant circiter DCC anni, qui satis congruunt tertio generali statui mundi, qui appropriatur spiritu sancto, qui in suis donis et hoc libro multum describitur septiformis. Prout autem initiatio tertii status aliqualiter et seminaliter sumitur a tempore, quo spiritus Christi magnos exercitus Christianorum fecit transfretare in terram sanctam et innumerabilibus Sarracenis occisis restituere Ierusalem cultui christiano, a quo etiam tempore ordo cisterciensium et grandimontensium cepit et etiam cartusiensium et templariorum et hospitalariorum, tunc cum predictis DCC annis sunt circiter mille anni aut saltem DCCCC. Si etiam solutionem Satane respectu temporum antichristi magni inchoes a tempore, in quo sub quinta tuba stella de celo cadens accepit clavem putei abissi et aperuit illum, tunc a Christi resurrectione usque ad tempus illud sunt circiter mille anni, quibus sancti regnant cum Christo."

30. Ibid., 494f.

31. Ibid., 922. When expositing 8:1 at ibid., 458f., he remarks that we do not know how long a period the half hour signifies, but offers two possible interpretations: first, the third age will be shorter than the entire period of church history (a self-evident proposition); second, that it will be much shorter than the second age (a view he assigns to "some people").

32. Ibid., 923–25.

33. Ibid., 926–29.

34. Ibid., 919–23.

35. Ibid., 922.

36. Ibid., 923.

37. Ibid.

8. Life after Antichrist

Medieval exegetes who treated the Apocalypse as prophecy had to face the problem of what would happen after Antichrist. In the first place, they had to face the problem of whether Antichrist would come right at the end of history as Augustine believed or would be followed by a discernable period with its own characteristics. We have seen that most mendicant exegetes in the thirteenth century concurred with what had become by then an accepted tradition when they looked forward to a seventh period of history between Antichrist and final judgment. Nevertheless, they differed somewhat in describing its length and character.

The Great Tradition

A brief review is in order. We noted in the second chapter that most extant mendicant Apocalypse commentaries see the Apocalypse as divided into seven visions, the first four dealing with all of church history (or, as they often say, the *status generalis* of the church) and the last three dealing with the final times (the *status finalis*). They also see church history itself as divided into seven periods.

What do these commentators say about the seventh period? In one sense they are quite consistent. They always see it as a genuine interval of indeterminate length lasting from the death of Antichrist until the final judgment. This interval is based not on the thousand years of Revelation 20, but on Daniel 12. Here too they are consistent not only with one another but with the whole exegetical tradition in which they lie. While there is no reason to trace this tradition in detail—that task already has been performed admirably by Robert Lerner[1]—there is something to be gained by describing it briefly here.

The story begins with Augustine. As we saw in the last chapter, most commentators accepted his argument that the millennium in Revelation 20 referred to the Christian era as a whole, not to the period after Antichrist.

Nevertheless, as Lerner shows, even while Augustine was ruling out Revelation 20 as an entrée to millennial fantasies, Jerome was allowing at least a narrow entrance through Daniel 12. Jerome explicitly rejected the notion that Revelation 20 predicted an earthly kingdom;[2] yet in Daniel 12 he found a reference to 1,290 days, which he identified with the reign of Antichrist (partly by way of the forty-two months of Revelation 13:5), and an announcement that he who waits and arrives at the 1,335th day will be blessed. He took this latter figure as the time from the beginning of Antichrist's reign until the last judgment. The result was a period of forty-five days between the death of Antichrist and final judgment, which he explained provisionally as a period designed to test the faith of believers. For Jerome, this time of testing dovetailed with the prediction in Matthew 24: 37–39 of eating and drinking, as well as the prediction in 1 Thessalonians 5: 3 that destruction would come even as the damned spoke of peace and safety. In short, the forty-five days would be misinterpreted and misused by all except the elect.

Bede accepted both Augustine and Jerome in that he used Augustine's explanation of Revelation 20 but interpreted the half-hour of silence in Revelation 8:1 as another reference to Jerome's forty-five days after Antichrist. His interpretation fit handily into his portrayal of the seven seals as seven periods of church history. Elsewhere, anxious to reconcile Jerome's prediction with the general New Testament insistence that the end cannot be predicted (e.g., Acts 1:7), Bede suggested that the forty-five days should not be taken literally. He offered no explanation of what this period was supposed to accomplish beyond testing patience, although immediately thereafter he spoke vaguely of rest for the church.

These ideas continued to reverberate through succeeding exegesis. Haymo of Auxerre suggested that the delay would offer a chance for penance to those who had wavered during the persecution of Antichrist. Elaborating on Jerome's appeal to Matthew 24 and 1 Thessalonians 5, he predicted that those who had served Antichrist would take heart, marry, and banquet, boasting that even though their leader was dead they themselves were secure. Moreover, he presented the forty-five days as, in effect, a minimum number. How much more time there would be, God only knew.

Later authors made their own additions or corrections. Adso of Montier-en-Der referred to forty instead of forty-five days,[3] and the *Glossa ordinaria* saw in the delay a "refreshment of the saints."[4] Honorius Augustodunensis placed conversion of the heathens in this period. Otto of Freising and Hildegard of Bingen predicted the same for the Jews, and

Gerhoch of Regensburg anticipated a period of "great tranquility" in which "the church of God will be cleansed of filth and simony and adorned with crowns of gold so that great joy may be had by the people of God."[5]

Nor did one have to envision the seventh period only in connection with the seven seals, although Bede did so. He provided a ghostly reflection of his seven periods in the process of explaining the seven trumpets, although he portrayed the seventh as announcing eternal bliss.[6] Richard of St. Victor read the seven periods into the seven seals, trumpets, and vials, in each case identifying the seventh with a period after the death of Antichrist.[7]

Joachim, of course, was also a twelfth-century commentator, and in some ways he followed the same tradition as Richard. He too divided the Apocalypse into seven visions, saw the church as progressing through seven periods, and portrayed the seventh as a space of time between Antichrist and judgment.[8] Nevertheless, he departed from—or expanded—the tradition in significant ways. It is hardly unimportant that he saw himself as living on the edge of the sixth period and developed his sevenfold pattern in concert with his threefold one. This may not seem a radical break with tradition, since it is possible to see Joachim's seventh period/third age as a further extension of preceding speculation on the time after Antichrist; yet there were significant differences. One of them is that Joachim's historical schema suggested a pattern not so much of decline and reform as of genuine progression. That was at least partly what made it both exciting and dangerous. Another difference is that Joachim, unlike his predecessors, attempted to incorporate Revelation 20 into his picture of the seventh period and in the process challenged Augustine's reading of the millennium. More precisely, he both challenged and defended it, as we have seen. He was hardly precise in dealing with the length of the seventh period. In treating the seventh seal, he seemed to accept as one of several possibilities that the half-hour of Revelation 8:1 signified a mere six-month duration of the seventh period;[9] yet in his discussion of Revelation 20 he more characteristically left its length up to God. In any case, he hardly expected it to last a mere forty-five days.

The Main Line of Mendicant Exegesis

By the thirteenth century any exegete who approached the Apocalypse with Bede, Haymo, the *Glossa ordinaria,* and Richard of St. Victor available could expect to encounter variation, but within a relatively consistent general structure. If the exegete also wished to incorporate Joachim, he would have a few more decisions to make. It is hardly surprising then that our mendicant commentators should vary somewhat in their attention to the seventh period. This variation—and the underlying agreement—is apparent even if we limit our investigation to five commentaries, those by John of Wales, John Russel, William of Middleton, "Alexander," and Vital du Four.

John of Wales, in dealing with the seventh seal, predicts a brief period of tranquility after Antichrist's death. John, who meticulously piles up authorities in a way calculated to give modern scholars an uncomfortable sense of *déjà vu*, here mentions the *Glossa*, Bede, and Jerome, but speaks of forty days instead of forty-five.[10] He returns to the matter in commenting on the seventh trumpet, again anticipating forty days but citing Bede, Berengar, Haymo, and Jerome. This time, he makes it clear that forty days is a minimum figure. After that, God alone knows how long it will be before judgment.[11]

John Russel proceeds through the seven periods of church history only in the context of the seven trumpets. The seven seals are seen as a history of God's people up to Christ, while the seven vials are connected with the seven deadly sins. His view of the seven trumpets is heavily dependent upon the twelfth-century exegete Robert of Bridlington, whom he quotes as saying that, according to what we can deduce from Daniel, a period of forty-five days will be conceded to the elect for the purpose of repentence. He also quotes Robert as saying that, during the seventh period, all of the Gentiles having entered, Israel will be saved.[12]

William of Middleton mentions the seventh period in the context of the second and third visions. In the seventh seal is shown, he says, a future period after the death of Antichrist when peace will be given to the church, allowing holy men to preach without impediment. The silence (that is, the peace) will be brief, to be completed *in patria*, but while it lasts it will be enjoyed by good and evil alike. Those who participated in the persecution of Antichrist will be given forty days to repent, just as the Jews had forty-two years to repent after the crucifixion. Rather than using the time in this way, though, many of them will gain hope and anticipate ultimate victory. They will take wives and hold banquets, saying, "Although our prince is dead, we have peace and security." Then, as 1 Thessalonians 5 tells us, the day of the Lord will come upon them like a thief in the night. As for how it can be such a surprise if the number of days is already established, William notes that, as Matthew 24 tells us, no one knows how much time will elapse between the promised forty-two days and Christ's arrival.[13] William touches upon the matter again in commenting on the seventh trumpet. He explains that it is described as only beginning to sound because the world will not last long after the death of Antichrist.[14] During that time, the elect will preach freely and Israel will be saved. The church in these last days will revert to the humility of the first period.[15] William offers these suggestions in the process of discussing Enoch and Elijah. He mentions as one possible interpretation that they stand for two orders of preachers who will be commendable for their external humility, unction, and manifest truth. Later he returns to the notion of Enoch and Elijah as two orders and speaks of their *vilitas habitus*.[16] This *Gestalt* is intriguing in light of what we will soon see in Olivi's commentary.

Of these five commentaries, it is the one published under the name of Alexander of Hales—we have been referring to it simply as "Alexander," but without illusions concerning the accuracy of this designation—that makes the strongest statement on the seventh period. "Alexander," who treats the second, third, and fifth visions as reflecting seven periods of church history, asserts that Antichrist's downfall will be followed by a period of peace, "exultation, and praise in the church, which will then be most heavenly, having put aside earthly cares." Followers of Antichrist will have a chance to repent. A seventh order of preachers "will sweetly preach to the church." The Jews and the rest of the Gentiles will be converted. The Devil's power will be destroyed "and we will be like sons of God, for there will be no dominations or powers then, but all things will be subject to God alone, and God alone will reign in heaven, on earth, and in hell."[17] Elsewhere he qualifies his optimism, but just a bit. In the seventh period, "only the demons will persecute the faithful," continuing to buzz around us like flies until the judgment.[18] The period will provide only a brief rest, for it is described as lasting only around "a half-hour." "Alexander" speculates, however, that it is called such either because judgment will follow swiftly or because "the peace from Antichrist's death to judgment day will seem to last only about a half-hour," presumably because time flies when one is having a good time. Some say it will last forty days, thus paralleling the interval given the Jews to repent after Christ's death.[19] The choice he seems to give us here is intriguing, and raises the question of what else besides Bede, Haymo, et al. he has at his disposal. We will return to this point in a moment.

Vital du Four, whose commentary echoes "Alexander's" at so many points, seems less comfortable with this matter and tends to deal more cursorily with it. Still, he too accepts the notion that there will be a distinguishable period after Antichrist's demise in which peace will reign and a final order of preachers will call for penance.[20] Thus all five commentaries seem, in various ways, to represent a continuation of the developing exegetical tradition from Bede through Richard of St. Victor. They are hardly unaware of Joachim. John of Wales cites him occasionally and John Russel does so often, but in contexts that allow them to avoid his reflections on the third age. I know of only one reference to Joachim in Vital's commentary and none at all in "Alexander's," yet in some ways they are more influenced by him, although only "Alexander" shows Joachim's influence in dealing with the seventh period.

Alexander Minorita

As we have seen, Alexander Minorita approaches the Apocalypse with a completely different set of assumptions. He sees it as a continuous reading of church history proceeding from the primitive church in chapter 1 to the eschaton in chapter 22. We also saw that Alexander moves slowly. Dominic and Francis do not appear until 20:6. Thus the thousand-year binding of Satan at 20:3 cannot refer to the time after Antichrist. Alexander violates his orderly chronological development by identifying this binding with the end of persecution under Constantine. From the time of Pope Sylvester, he explains, the Devil has been prohibited from afflicting the church through external persecutors.[21] He also suggests, though obliquely, that the number of years cannot be taken literally and seems at one point to grant some validity to the Augustinian notion that it began with Christ; yet he takes the notion of a thousand-year reign of Christ after Sylvester seriously enough to note that there are at least seventy years of it left in his own day. Thereafter, we can expect the reign of Antichrist at any time, although God can add a space for conversion if he wishes.

The millennium expires at Revelation 20:7 and the world is left vulnerable to the incursions of Gog, Magog, and Antichrist.[22] Alexander's discussion of these matters is an odd and not particularly consistent mixture of Augustine, the Tiburtine Sybil, and Hildegard of Bingen. In any case, by 20:15 Gog, Magog, Antichrist, and those not included in the book of life have been deposited in the lake of fire. The world is ready for a new heaven and earth.

Since Alexander interprets the descent of the heavenly Jerusalem as souls returning from heaven to reanimate their bodies for final judgment,[23] he should logically have run though all of history at this point; but when he reaches 21:9 and the angelic tour of the holy city, he makes an important remark that leads him right back to his own period. Alexander observes that, while this section of the Apocalypse speaks of the holy city after the last day, Jerusalem must be built by the elect with good works before the last day.[24] This is an important idea for him, and he repeats it no less than three times in sixteen lines. It leads him to an extended interpretation of the new Jerusalem as a prediction of the mendicant orders, with Innocent III in the role of the angelic tour guide.[25] This is hardly a passing thought. He develops it at remarkable length, noting that "rarely in the entire book does the text harmonize with history so manifestly as in this case."[26] For example, the mendicants "descend from heaven" through humility; they "have the clarity of God" because he is clarified through them; they are "like a diamond" in their purity and firm faith; and they "have a great, high wall" because they are defenders of others. The twelve angels at the gates are the ministers and priors. Thus he proceeds line by line through the entire chapter, applying all to the mendicants. The foundations of the wall decorated with precious stones are Francis, Dominic, and other founders, decorated with virtues. People will not need the sun and moon of good example from others because they will have the mendicants, men of great perfection, for "no one stained with uncleanness, . . . no liars will enter."

The passage runs from 21:10 to 22:5,[27] leaving no room in Alexander's exegesis of the final chapters to develop a theory of life after Antichrist. On the whole, he seems to assume with Augustine that Antichrist will come at the end. After his demise, the world will move straight on to the final judgment.[28]

Olivi's Departure from Tradition

How does Olivi compare with his fellow Franciscans? He was a Paris-trained scholar exposed to the tradition that shaped all the others except Alexander Minorita, and he shows it. He too sees the Apocalypse as a prophecy of church history in seven visions, and sees church history as divided into seven periods. Even the periods are similar, though there are some differences. One of the most important is that Olivi places himself in the early sixth period and sees the sixth and seventh as bound together in a Joachite third age of the Holy Spirit. Thus his seventh period is future, but it nonetheless represents the fulfillment of what Olivi sees already occurring around him. This perspective is hardly unique. Bonaventure too places himself in the sixth period, describes it as a period of "clear doctrine" in which remarkable advances are balanced by persecution and temptation, and looks forward to a seventh period of peace and enlightenment mirroring to some extent the original state of the church, a period in which the church militant "will be conformed with the triumphant as far as is possible on the pilgrim way." This shared perspective enables both Bonaventure and Olivi to read Francis into the new age and make him a model for it.

Olivi is not simply echoing Bonaventure. We have seen that his appropriation of the Joachite three ages is more explicit. He is not simply echoing Joachim either, however. There is, for example, the matter of how long the seventh period will last. We have seen that in dealing with the millennium of Revelation 20 Olivi carries Joachim's correction of Augustine well beyond the point where Joachim left it, arguing not only for application of Revelation 20 to the period after Antichrist (which Joachim already had done), but for a quasi-literal interpretation that would allow a seventh period of at least seven hundred years. He also goes beyond Joachim in describing the nature of the third age. Here the most important source of his difference with Joachim is precisely the thing Olivi shares with Bonaventure, the absolute centrality of Francis and his rule. The third age is patterned after them.

Progress and Return

Olivi does not even come close to saying that Francis and the rule will replace Christ and the New Testament, but no thirteenth-century author goes further than Olivi in portraying Francis as *alter Christus*, a model of Christ. None is more insistent upon identifying the Franciscan rule with the gospel. One might conclude from this that the third age is essentially one of rebirth, a return to the apostolic pattern. In some ways it is just that. It is certainly a return to apostolic poverty.[29] In this return, the Franciscan rule is central. Identification of that rule with the gospel had become a commonplace in not only Franciscan but papal writings of the thirteenth century, but by Olivi's time both papacy and order were beginning to appreciate the problems lurking in such a notion. From the late 1270s on, the order itself explored them in the *usus pauper* controversy. The papal bull *Exiit qui seminat*, issued by Nicholas III in 1279, was also partially aimed at clarifying this matter.

Like the rest of his order, Olivi portrays the apostles as having rejected both individual and common possessions. He feels that the shocking state of the church in his own time is closely related to its departure from the apostolic model in favor of ecclesiastical possessions. He dates that change from the reign of Constantine, but he is remarkably uninterested in blaming Constantine for it. The change to a possessing church, far from being evil, was instituted for tactical reasons by God himself. It was useful for the popes to be given temporal possessions during the age of the Son. Nevertheless, in the third age they will be called upon to surrender those possessions and return to the apostolic state.[30]

The third age is not simply a renewal, however. Olivi stresses its novelty. He compares the transition to it with that between synagogue and church, and occasionally speaks of the "new church" or even the "new world" of the third age.[31] In some ways it will surpass previous ages. Olivi sees the danger in this view and is careful to emphasize not only Christ but the apostles as early models of that evangelical perfection that will characterize the third age.[32] There is nevertheless a strongly progressive element in his thought that pulls him in a different direction. This element is strengthened by his penchant for developing a *concordia* between the seven ages of world history and the seven periods of church history, with the transition from synagogue to church paralleling the one from fifth to sixth period.

> In the first five periods of the church it was not conceded to the saints, however illuminated they might be, to open the secrets of this book, which were to be opened more fully only in the sixth and seventh periods, just as in the first five periods of the Old Testament the prophets were not given the ability to open clearly those secrets of Christ and of the New Testament which were to be opened and actually were opened in the sixth age of the world.[33]

The suggestion of progression beyond the apostles is also inherent in Olivi's esteem for historical perspective. After all, those in his century have climbed another of the three mountains[34] and thus have additional insight into biblical prophecy. The idea of progression is inherent as well in his tendency to draw a parallel between church history and progress through the various grades of perfection or contemplation. This progressive element might be said to underline Olivi's link with Joachim, but he surpasses even Joachim in this respect. Joachim's progressive tendencies are counterbalanced by the very complexity of his symbolism. Note, for example, the ongoing discussion among scholars as to whether his *status* are periods at all. It would be absurd to ask the same question concerning Olivi, whose approach is more linear.

If Olivi is able to balance his progressive and recapitulative tendencies, it is ultimately by making Christ and the apostles charter members of the sixth period. In Christ's case, this task is simplified by Olivi's notion of the three advents. Christ's second coming in the spirit in the sixth period makes possible a "singular participation and solemnization of his holy life and love."[35] The result will be so striking that "a certain new world or new church will then seem to have been formed, the old having been rejected, just as in Christ's first advent a new church was formed, the synagogue having been rejected."[36] The word "seem" is important here. Christ's church will remain, but it will be radically renewed.

Nevertheless, even if Christ is allowed a second and third advent, the apostles are not. Their position is more tenuous. In the area of poverty, they are quite safe. Olivi's notion of the Franciscan life allows him to see *viri spirituales* of the final age as emulating apostolic poverty without surpassing it. The problem lies in the area of knowledge. After all, the light of knowledge will be turned up sevenfold in the new age, just as it increased sevenfold at the time of Christ's first advent.[37] We can train 700 percent more candlepower on the scriptures than the apostles could, and 4,900 percent more than the prophets. Again, there is the matter of that second mountain with its better view of past and future.

Olivi does his best to avoid this conclusion. Even two decades earlier, in the eighth of his *Questions on Evangelical Perfection*, he saw the problem and attempted to counter it with an argument similar to the one he would use in the Apocalypse commentary. The sixth period is, he says, preeminent over the first five.

> Nevertheless, if someone should argue against this view that according to it the status of Christ and the apostles, who lived in the first period of the church, would be inferior to the status of the sixth and seventh periods, whoever says this should know that Christ is part of the first period in one sense and part of the final period in another, but absolutely speaking he is head of the whole church in all periods.[38]

Olivi goes on to develop Christ's role at some length, suggesting that he belongs more to the first century as far as the original foundation of the church is concerned, but more to the sixth and seventh as far as the fullness of his spiritual inhabitation and presence is concerned. Then he offers a final, terse comment on the apostles: "And it is thus with Christ's apostles and disciples, who were certain universal vessels of him."

In the Apocalypse commentary Olivi expands the circle, offering a similar observation about the *sancti* in all ages.

> Again, [perfect contemplation] will not be entered into until after the seventh angel pours out [his vial], just as the book will not be perfectly open nor the mysteries of God entirely consummated until the seventh angel begins to blow his trumpet. It should be known, however, that these seven grades of purgation may be perfected (and may have been perfected) in any saints of any period, allowing them to enter into the temple without waiting for the seventh period of the church, for in them [the seventh period] was virtually or spiritually attained, so that it is just as if they temporally belonged to the time and activity of the seventh period.[39]

This passage, like others stressing the continuity of church history, acts as a counterweight to the emphasis on novelty. In the areas of poverty and perhaps of general spiritual gifts the balance is struck nicely. Whether the scales hang so evenly in the area of knowledge is another matter. In order to answer this question we must look closely at the sort of novelty expected.

Peace

The world after Antichrist will witness a more profound peace than it has ever known. Olivi is, as we have seen, hardly the first person to speak of peace in describing the seventh period, but he develops the theme in his own way and at much greater length, describing this peace as internal and external. It will mean the end not merely of physical warfare but of heresy, schism, and religious difference of every kind, as well as of the interior warfare that devastates the human soul. People will be free to explore new psychic as well as social possibilities.[40] We will see more of these possibilities in a moment, but first it is worth noting that in Olivi's hands this traditional picture of peace in the seventh age takes on a profoundly Franciscan coloration. The connection with Francis rests on more than the fact that in the rule he instructed his followers to say "Peace to this house" whenever they entered one.[41] It is also based on Francis's life as any friar understood it, a life devoted to ending political strife, seeking religious unification by pacific means, and achieving an inner tranquility that led to profound contemplative experience.

Conversion

This internal and external peace is closely related to (and partially dependent upon) another novelty of the third age, universal conversion. The internal and external peace of the third age will not be perfect until the whole world is converted.[42] Here again we are dealing with a theme already explored by Olivi's Franciscan predecessors, but here again Olivi is unique, not only in the heavy emphasis he places upon it, but in the peculiar coloration he imparts to it.[43] In this case too the plot has a decidedly Franciscan twist. Francis himself tried to convert the Saracens and devoted the final chapter of the rule to missionary activity. The fact that Francis's third attempt to convert them took place in the thirteenth year of his conversion was a sign that in the thirteenth century the Saracens and other infidels would begin to be converted by the Franciscan order.[44] This missionary activity is closely connected in Olivi's mind with opposition to evangelical renewal. Just as the apostles, seeing the lack of acceptance within Judaism, directed their missionary efforts primarily at the Gentiles and only secondarily at the Jews, so the spiritual men of the sixth period, seeing the same sort of hostility within the Latin church, will turn to the Greeks, Saracens, and Tartars, who will prove more receptive. At one point Olivi very tentatively suggests a general order of conversion: the Latins, then the Greeks, then the Saracens and Tartars, and finally the Jews.[45] Olivi remarks that, among the Latins, the fishing has been better among laymen than among the secular or regular clergy from Francis's day to the present. Simple, unlettered men are more easily brought to penance than scholars and monks. Here too Olivi sees a parallel between the thirteenth-century crisis and the transition from synagogue to church in the first century.

Knowledge

The themes of peace and conversion are closely related to a third theme, that of increased knowledge in the third age. Here we return to Olivi's notion of *intellectus spiritualis* and his tendency to see the third age not only as a progressive development beyond the first and second but also as a progressive development in itself. The third age begins in the sixth period but reaches its earthly fruition in the seventh, then its heavenly fruition in eternity. We have seen that, when Olivi talks about *intellectus spiritualis* in the sixth period, it is usually in the context of biblical exegesis. It involves fuller knowledge of scripture, and this knowledge involves better understanding of both the spiritual and literal senses. Greater insight into the shape of church history is obviously one central aspect of the new knowledge. Olivi feels that wringing a schedule from biblical prophecy is a task which, however difficult, can be performed more effectively in his own day than it could have been in Augustine's or even Joachim's. The improvement will continue in the seventh period, although ultimate clarification will be possible only at the end.[46]

Nevertheless, in Olivi's description of the seventh period emphasis shifts from biblical exegesis to mystical vision. Commenting on John's announcement in Revelation 21:22 that he saw no temple in the new Jerusalem, Olivi remarks that this has been fulfilled to some extent throughout church history, since the church has been bound neither to a physical location like the Jerusalem temple nor to a ceremonial law like that of Judaism. "In the church of the seventh period, however, this will be fulfilled even more fully inasmuch as it will not need many earlier doctrines, since Christ's spirit will teach it all truth without mystery of external voice and book." He hastens to add that he does not expect the church to abandon use of scripture and doctrine before the eschaton, for this prediction "is being fulfilled and will be fulfilled *secundum quid* in the church militant, but *simpliciter* in the church triumphant."[47]

Notice that Olivi thinks this prophecy "is being fulfilled." The phenomenon can be witnessed even in the sixth period, for it is a characteristic of the third age. Like Joachim he distinguishes the second and third ages partly by describing two different types of knowledge. The second age is characterized by the sort of scholarship practiced by clerics, the third by "that chaste and sweet contemplation typical of monks or religious." The Holy Spirit "will reveal itself as a flame and furnace of divine love," and divine truth will be revealed "not only by simple conceptual understanding but also by gustatory and tactile experience."[48] Here again, once we recover from our initial shock and examine what Olivi is really saying, we are struck by the Franciscan overtones of his scenario. As we have seen, his continuous use of words like *gustus* to characterize the contemplative knowledge of the third age is closely related to his characteristically Franciscan view that contemplative experience is principally an activity of the will rather than of the intellect. In offering Francis as a model of this new, improved knowledge of the third age, he is simply developing the tradition already available to him, not only in the works of immediate predecessors like Bonaventure, but even in earlier writers like Thomas of Celano.[49]

Church Government

There is another area in which Olivi apparently foresees novelty in the third age. He seems to expect a change in church government. Viewed from one perspective, there will be no change whatsoever. There will still be hierarchy, and we have every reason to assume that it will contain pope, bishops, and so forth, although Olivi is vague on the matter. From another perspective the institution will be radically altered. After centuries of possessing temporal wealth, leaders will return to the apostolic model.[50] They will be not only poor but humble. Prelates will refuse to be honored in servile fashion because they will see themselves not as lords but as ministers and servants of their subordinates. Such behavior will make the subordinates honor them all the more, "and thus there is a blessed contention of evangelical humility in which the superiors prohibit such honors and the inferiors never cease to honor them and subject themselves to them."[51] The evangelical poverty and humility characterizing leadership in the third age will stem from the increased contemplative gifts of that age. Leaders will display the sort of *intellectus spiritualis* discussed earlier. The higher the level of contemplation, the greater the level of humility in leaders and subordinates alike.[52] Thus in the third age the hierarchy will remain intact, but its basis will be charismatic rather than juridical. The church will be led by those who deserve to lead. Subordinates will obey because they want to do so.

Here again we are struck by the Franciscan roots of Olivi's vision. The leadership he foresees in the seventh age is modeled on Francis himself as portrayed by Franciscan tradition, and on Francis's guidelines for leadership within the order. The rules of 1221 and 1223 stress that leadership is to be seen as a form of service. Whenever the word "minister" is used, its literal meaning is recalled by linking it with the word "servant." The very titles chosen—"minister," "custodian," "guardian," but not "prior"— make the same point.[53]

The qualities that will characterize leaders of the seventh period will be developing in the sixth, but not necessarily in the leaders of that era. We have seen that the forces of Antichrist will gain control of the church and persecute harbingers of the third age. The leadership pattern characteristic of that persecuted minority will be legitimized in the seventh period and applied to the church as a whole.

Or so it would seem. Olivi actually says remarkably little about church government in the seventh period. We can do little more than explore the implications of a few scattered comments.

The Capital City

This brings us to another aspect of leadership in the third age. Olivi is open to the possibility that the capital of Christendom will be moved away from Rome in the seventh period. A complex tangle of considerations lie at the heart of this suggestion. One is the common medieval notion of *translatio*. Olivi prepares the ground for this one early in his commentary while dealing with the warnings of Revelation 2:5 and 3:11.[54] In the first case, he speaks of the *translatio* in the first period from Jerusalem to Rome, then compares it with that from Babylon to the New Jerusalem at the end of the fifth period. In the second case, he describes the first and sixth periods as each enjoying its own sort of primacy, then takes the passage as a warning to each lest pride should cause it to lose that primacy through *translatio*.

In neither case does he explicitly apply the idea of *translatio* to the city of Rome, nor does he ever do so. In dealing with Revelation 17:18, "the woman whom you see is a great city who rules the kings of the earth," Olivi notes that Rome and the Roman people ruled the world in John's time. Then, "for the whole time of the fullness of the Gentiles, right down to the time of Antichrist or to that of the ten kings, Christ established in it the principal and universal seat and power of his rule over all churches and over the whole world." Nevertheless, Olivi's apocalyptic timetable predicts that Rome and many other cities will be destroyed by a pagan army just before the reign of the great Antichrist. The blow will be aimed at Christianity, but its effect will be to crush the carnal church. Then the great Antichrist will reign.

Once Antichrist is dead and the seventh period blossoms, will Rome be repaired and serve again as the principal seat of Christ, or will Christ move his seat to some other city like Jerusalem? Neither, Olivi says, can be proved from scripture or sacred doctrine.[55] One naturally assumes that he has returned to the notion of *translatio* as the price of failing to measure up, and there is probably some virtue in that assumption, even though he does not use the word. There is a good deal more at stake here, however. We have seen that Olivi describes church history as a complex ebb and flow. The apostles turned primarily to the Gentiles after being rejected by the Jews. Spiritual preachers of the third age will swing back to Greeks, Muslims, and Tartars, then finally to the Jews. The swing will occur partly because of rejection within the carnal western church, but only partly so. In the final analysis, this rejection provides little more than an encouragement to do what the spiritual preachers would eventually have done anyway. Universal conversion is on the divine agenda. Olivi's attitude toward the possibility of a new capital probably emerges from this expectation. A shift from Jerusalem to Rome in the first period, then from Rome back to Jerusalem in the seventh, would reflect the rhythm of conversion in church history.

It would also reflect the realities of Christian geography. In commenting on Revelation 14:5 Olivi raises the possibility that the seventh age will see a *sublimissimus cultus Christi* on Mount Zion. "Nor would it be surprising if the place of our redemption should be exalted over all other places at that time, especially in view of the fact that the highest rulers of the world will find that place more suitable for the conversion and later the governance of the whole world, since it is the geographical center of the habitable world."[56] In other words, Rome made sense as capital of Christianity as it existed in the second age. The Christian faith was then essentially a Mediterranean phenomenon radiating out from its center at Rome. Nevertheless, as any decent *mappa mundi* will show, Jerusalem is the center of the entire world. In the third age of universal conversion, as the geographical center of Christianity shifts east, it would be sensible for the capital to follow it, settling in Jerusalem. Our end is our beginning.

Decline

One final aspect of the seventh period should be mentioned. Olivi regularly views it as a progress, a transition from the church as we know it to the state of eternal glory.[57] Nevertheless, he also predicts that, like the second age, the third age will eventually suffer such a decline "that there will scarcely be found faith upon the earth, and Christ will be, as it were, compelled to come in judgment on account of the abundance of evil."[58] Here again he accepts and develops an insight derived from Joachim.[59]

Notes

1. Lerner, "Refreshment of the Saints."
2. The following is based on Lerner, "Refreshment."
3. Ibid., 108, suggests that the number "was probably chosen as an analogy to Lent or to the time between Easter and Ascension."
4. *Biblia sancta cum glossa ordinaria*, (Nürnberg, 1481), III, referring to Dan. 12:12.
5. For bibliographical citations see Lerner, "Refreshment," 110–14. I use Lerner's translation of the passage from Gerhoch, who also predicted that the church would be reformed by "spiritual men."
6. *Explanatio Apocalypsis*, 166.
7. *In apocalypsim Ioannis*, PL 196, 775f., 794, 830. Richard emphasizes that it will be a short interval but speaks of it as one of peace and tranquility. Thus, he suggests, our heavenly reward will actually begin on earth. It will also be a time in which some are converted.
8. *Expositio in apocalypsim*, 123rb, 210ra, 210vb. Lerner, "Refreshment," 117 notes that Joachim's debt to the tradition is shown by his appeal to Haymo in *Expositio*, 210ra (under the name of "Remigius").
9. *Expositio*, 123rb.
10. Johannes Gallensis, *Expositio*, 48vb.
11. Ibid., 57va.
12. Johannes Russel, *Expositio*, 122ra, 122va. On Robert of Bridlington see Smalley, "John Russel," 227. Russel thinks highly of Robert and cites him on several occasions.
13. Guilelmus de Militona, *Expositio*, 52vb–53ra. I repeat the numbers exactly as MS Assisi 321 gives them. I do not know if Assisi 82 contains the same inconsistency.
14. Ibid., 67rb.
15. Ibid., 68ra, 69vb.
16. Ibid., 70vb. At ibid., 98rb, William also treats the seven vials as a progression through church history, but says nothing to the point in speaking of the seventh vial. He simply asserts that it represents the damnation of the demons.
17. Alexander Halensis, *Commentarii*, 204–6, regarding Rev. 11:15–18. See also ibid., 137, regarding Rev. 8:1.
18. Ibid., 304, regarding Rev. 16:17–21.
19. Ibid., 137.
20. Vitalis de Furno, *Expositio*, 71ra–rb and 89ra. Ibid., 119va, echoes the point about demons buzzing around like flies.
21. Alexander Minorita, *Expositio*, 412ff.

22. Ibid., 450–58.

23. Ibid., 462.

24. Ibid., 467f.

25. Ibid., 469.

26. Ibid., 470.

27. Ibid., 469–501.

28. Ibid., 450–67 and 509, suggest as much, although ambiguously.

29. *Lectura*, 51, 97.

30. Ibid., 51: "Consimiliter autem pontificatus Christi fuit primo stirpe vite evangelice et apostolice in Petro et apostolis datus, ac deinde utiliter et rationabiliter fuit ad statum habentem temporalia commutatus, saltem a tempore Constantini usque ad finem quinti status. Pro quanto autem multi sanctorum pontificum fuerunt regulares et in suis scriptis et in habitu sui cordis preferentes paupertatem Christi et apostolorum, omnibus temporalibus ecclesie datis, pro tanto quasi usque ad duplum preeminuit primus ordo sacerdotii apostolici. Congruum est ergo quod in fine omnino redeat et assurgat ad ordinem primum, ad quem spectat iure primogeniture et perfectionis maioris et Christo conformioris."

31. E.g., see ibid., 48, 55, 57, 102, 882.

32. E.g., in the passage cited in the previous note. His view of the Franciscan rule (as embodying the life observed by Christ and the disciples) fits with this emphasis.

33. *Lectura*, 564: "Nam in prioribus quinque ecclesie statibus non fuit concessum sanctis, quantumcumque illuminatis, aperire illa secreta huius libri, que in solo sexto et septimo statu erant apertius reseranda, sicut nec in primis quinque etatibus veteris testamenti fuit prophetis concessum clare aperire secreta Christi et novi testamenti in sexta etate seculi reserandis et reseratis." The passage is confusing but makes sense if the phrase "in primis quinque etatibus veteris testamenti" is taken to mean "those five ages of world history that constitute the Old Testament period," although the grammar still seems odd.

34. See Chapter 5.

35. *Lectura*, 47: "Sancta vero et singularis participatio et solemnizatio sue sanctissime vite et caritatis"; and ibid., 57: "In sexto tempore ecclesie est revelanda singularis perfectio vite et sapientie."

36. Ibid., 57: "Vetustas prioris temporis est sic universaliter repellenda, ut videatur quoddam novum seculum seu nova ecclesia tunc formari veteribus iam reiectis, sicut in primo Christi adventu formata est nova ecclesia veteri synagoga reiecta."

37. *Lectura*, 1 and 46, developing Isa. 30:26.

38. *Das Heil der Armen*, 151: "Si tamen quis contra hoc dicat quod secundum hoc status Christi et Apostolorum qui fuerunt in primo tempore ecclesiae, esset inferior statu sexti et septimi temporis: scire debet qui hoc dicit, quod Christus secundum aliquid est quasi pars, si tamen pars prioris temporis, secundum aliquid vero finalis temporis, simpliciter tamen ipse est caput universale omnis temporis. Sicut non est dubium quod ipse secundum aliquid et prius fuit sub Lege, antequam evidenter in se inchoaret statum ecclesie, quando scilicet baptizatus est. Christus igitur quantum ad fundamentalem plantationem fidei seu Novi Testa-

menti et ecclesiae stat convenienter in primo eius tempore, quantum vero ad pleni-
tudinem spiritualis suae inhabitationis et praesentiae quae est per vitam perfecte
christiformem, magis aspicit sextum tempus et septimum quam primum. Omnes
tamen status ecclesiae aspicit secundum varias influentias et aspectus. Et sic etiam
est de Apostolis Christi et discipulis qui fuerunt quaedam universalia vasa eius."

39. *Lectura*, 791: "Item communiter non intrabitur plene nisi post effusionem
septimi angeli, sicut nec liber erit perfecte apertus nec misteria dei omnino consummata, usquequo septimus angelus ceperit tuba canere. Sciendum tamen quod
in quibusdam sanctis cuiuslibet status possunt hii septem gradus purgationum per-
fici vel fuisse perfecti et sic in hoc templum intrasse, non expectando septimum
tempus ecclesie, quia in ipsis fuit virtualiter seu spiritualiter completum, ita quod
perinde est ac si temporaliter pertigissent ad tempus et opus septimi status."

40. See especially ibid., 457–60, where he provides an essentially moral interpretation of Isa. 2:4.

41. *Regula*, chapter 3.

42. *Lectura*, 458.

43. For the following see ibid., 52–54, 61, 458, 560–66, 577f., 612f., 883, 956,
974, 982.

44. Ibid., 562. See also 578, where he applies Rev. 10:11 to his order.

45. Ibid., 974.

46. Ibid., 341, 791. The latter passage acknowledges that some *sancti* have
been allowed to anticipate the end condition.

47. Ibid., 979. The passage actually draws a parallel between knowledge and
use of material things. For further discussion and citations of this point and the
next, see my "Olivi, Apocalyptic Expectation, and Visionary Experience."

48. *Lectura*, 230.

49. See Chapter 5 above and my "Olivi, Apocalyptic Expectation, and Visionary Experience," 282–84. There is a curious parallel with Bonaventure's *Collationes
in hexaemeron* as I describe that work in "Bonaventure, Olivi and Franciscan Eschatology," 29–32.

50. *Lectura*, 51.

51. Ibid., 892, 994.

52. Ibid., 164, 993.

53. *Regula non bullata*, cc. 4–6; *Regula*, cc. 8–10.

54. *Lectura*, 184–89, 245f.

55. Ibid., 858.

56. Ibid., 751: "Nec mirum si locus nostre redemptionis super omnia loca
terre tunc temporis exaltetur et maxime quia ad conversionem totius orbis et ad
gubernationem totius iam conversi ille locus erit congruentior summis rectoribus
orbis tanquam centrale medium terre habitabilis."

57. E.g., ibid., 10f., 12, 613f.

58. Ibid., 88. See also 18, 66–68.

59. See Lerner, "Refreshment of the Saints," 119.

9. The Condemnation Process, 1318–19

Having examined Olivi's commentary, we turn to its reception, particularly by the authorities. It is a long story, but circumstances allow us to divide it into two episodes, 1318–19 and 1322–26. The three-year hiatus may stem more from the paucity of our sources than from the actual rhythm of the condemnation process, but those sources that have survived are very good indeed. Before examining them, we will get a running start at our topic by summarizing some data relevant to the period before 1318.

The Council of Vienne, Its Prehistory and Its Result

The condemnation of Olivi's Apocalypse commentary has a long prehistory, but it is difficult to say how long. Even before the 1283 censure he thought it necessary to defend his taste for apocalyptic speculation, although such speculation was not a target of the Paris commission. There is no evidence that it was attacked before his death, but we might suspect that the 1290s were nonetheless a watershed period. The antagonism between spirituals (as the rigorists were now termed) and their superiors escalated seriously during that period and led to trouble in southern France as well as Italy. We cannot say whether the French spirituals punished in the 1290–92 investigation were motivated by apocalyptic expectation, but we do know that the Italian spirituals who opposed Boniface VIII from 1295 on were citing the line from Revelation, "Come out of her, my people," as a call to separate from the carnal leadership of church and order.[1] Of course there is no evidence that even the latter group saw Olivi as an influence. The important thing is that from 1295 on we see fractious elements within the order offering an apocalyptic justification for resistence to authority.

The first decade of the fourteenth century was a bad time for Franciscan zealots in southern France. It was an equally bad time for Olivi's reputation. At the general chapter of 1299 his teachings were condemned and those who used his books were excommunicated. The general minister,

John of Murrovalle, launched a determined effort to break up "the sect of Brother Peter John" and to collect his writings so that they could be burned.[2] The effort was aided by Boniface VIII, and so many brothers were disciplined that "a great book was made of the punishments and errors involved."[3] All brothers in the province were required to abjure three things: the assertion that *usus pauper* was part of the vow; the idea that the wound in Christ's side occurred before his death; and veneration of those who had not been officially canonized.[4] That list is very much about Olivi. The first two items represent his views (we will hear more of Christ's side wound in 1312 at the Council of Vienne) and the third is a veiled reference to the Olivi cult centered around his grave at Narbonne, which was already the target of pilgrimages by 1305.[5] Stories about Matthew of Bouzigues and Jerome of Catalonia, traveling circa 1299–1301 with laypersons and Olivi's books, suggest that the encounter between Olivi's ideas and a potentially unruly laity occurred even earlier.[6]

The list of things to be abjured omits any mention of Olivi's Apocalyptic views, but there are other indications of their growing importance. In 1299 a provincial council at Béziers—presided over by the archbishop of Narbonne—complained of certain educated men from approved orders who were stirring up *beguini seu beguinae*, telling them, among other things, that the end of the world was near and the time of Antichrist had begun, "or just about."[7] Here we have mention of apocalyptic expectation but none of Olivi, who was already dead by then; yet mention of a fervent, apocalyptically oriented laity guided by religious, combined with our awareness of a burgeoning Olivi cult, suggests that the pattern that concerned inquisitors two decades later was already taking shape within a year after Olivi's death. Moreover—and this is the most tantalizing yet enigmatic bit of evidence—we know that on orders from Boniface VIII, Giles of Rome undertook a refutation of Olivi's Revelation commentary.[8] We know neither the date nor the result, but it obviously occurred before Boniface's death in 1303. Olivi's commentary must have been put to questionable use somewhere, although not necessarily in southern France. In 1305 Ubertino da Casale put it to very questionable use indeed in his *Arbor vitae*, written during his stay on Mount Alverna.[9]

The persecution continued long after John and Boniface were out of office, ending only when Pope Clement V intervened in 1309. Clement summoned spokesmen for both factions to a protracted hearing that culminated at the Council of Vienne in 1312. Both sides were to address four issues: whether the spirituals had been infected by the heretical sect of the *spiritus libertatis*; whether the rule and the papal bull *Exiit qui seminat* were being observed properly within the order; Olivi's orthodoxy; and the persecution in southern France.

Obviously our major concern is with the third item on the agenda. The community, determined to weaken the spirituals by besmirching Olivi's reputation, revisited the censure of 1283 and added two new charges. One was that Olivi had contradicted the text of John 19 by asserting that Christ was alive when he received the lance wound in his side, an accusation that would impress the pope enough to encourage comment on it in *Fidei catholicae fundamento*.[10] The other was that Olivi disseminated "false and fantastic prophecies concerning the church" in his writings and especially in the Apocalypse commentary, "calling the church a great whore and dogmatizing many other things in disparagement of the church." The apocalyptic enormities of Olivi's *sectatores* were also explored. This group revered him as a saint. Some were portrayed as saying that his views, revealed to him by the Holy Spirit, should be accepted as gospel truth. They were also said to have asserted that Olivi himself is predicted when the Apocalypse speaks of another angel who comes after the angel with the sign of the living God (presumably a reference to Rev. 10:1). Some were reported to have termed marriage nothing more than a disguised brothel. Some were said to believe that an angel withdrew pontifical authority from Nicholas III because of his iniquities, giving it to certain brothers and their followers who observed the spirit of evangelical perfection, after which no valid pope had been elected and only those who had the spirit of poverty were true priests. Some had carried this view to its logical conclusion and elected their own pope. Some expected a reformation of the church to occur in Constantinople.[11]

It is impossible to say how many of these charges were true, but we can assume that they accurately described at least some of those who admired Olivi, since some had long considered him a saint and we can find, a decade later, people who believed most of the other things said here about him. The notion of a *translatio* disempowering the papacy was held by some of the dissident Franciscans as early as the 1290s, and by 1309 it may well have been adopted by some of Olivi's followers.[12] As to whether Olivi himself called the church a great whore, that matter will be considered anon. For the moment it is sufficient to note that the accusation was explicitly rejected as *mendacissimum* by Ubertino da Casale, who went on to offer a selection of quotations intended to demonstrate Olivi's veneration for papal authority.[13]

However much interest these charges might have been expected to excite in papal circles, Clement V seems to have been unimpressed by them. The hearing culminated in two bulls, *Fidei catholicae fundamento* and *Exivi de paradiso*, issued in 1312 at the Council of Vienne. Neither the former, which addresses three doctrinal irregularities the pope apparently thought to be Olivi's, nor the latter, aimed at the poverty question, refers even obliquely to Olivi's apocalyptic expectations. Nevertheless, *Exivi de paradiso* moved those expectations one step closer to fulfillment and eventual condemnation when it attempted to settle the split within the order with a compromise that soon proved unworkable. Clement encountered an order in which a substantial body of spirituals were being punished for disobedience, but that disobedience was defended as an act of conscience stemming from the fact that their superiors were demanding a standard of life that violated the level of poverty required by the vow. The pope attempted to solve this problem by stressing the superior's responsibility for determining the proper level of poverty and the subordinate's duty to obey the superior's commands, while easing the conscience problem by eliminating abuses and allowing the spirituals a degree of autonomy.

The difficulty with this solution was that the pope tried to carry it out while disturbing as little as possible. He was against splitting the order as Ubertino da Casale and Angelo Clareno would have wished. The farthest he would go in that direction was to assign the houses at Narbonne, Béziers, and Carcassonne to the spirituals and remove those provincial leaders who had proved most hostile. That solution lasted no longer than Clement himself did. After his death in 1314, the old leaders recovered power and the French spirituals were again desperate.[14] Since they could appeal to neither pope nor minister general—death had rendered both positions vacant—the beleaguered spirituals decided to settle their own problems. With lay support, they seized control of the convents at Narbonne and Béziers, which then became havens for escapees from other houses in the provinces of Provence and Aquitaine. Eventually about 120 spirituals had congregated there.[15]

In Italy, where the pope's restraining hand on persecuting superiors had never been felt as it had in southern France,[16] the same thing happened even earlier. Early in 1312 a group of Tuscan spirituals took over convents in Arezzo, Asciano, and Carmignano. Here too the liberated convents became havens for fugitives.[17] In May 1314 a sentence of excommunication was promulgated against thirty-seven of them, but by that time about forty already had escaped to Sicily.[18]

John XXII's Early Activity

For a while, both the French and Italian rebels enjoyed a degree of protection. Those in France were supported by local laymen and by several influential prelates, while those in Sicily were shielded by King Frederick III. In 1316, however, Michael of Cesena was elected minister general and John XXII was elected pope. Both saw the spirituals as a subversive element that had to be suppressed. John applied pressure on the kingdom of Sicily until the citizens of Messina informed their ruler that they would suffer death for him, but not excommunication as supporters of heresy. Frederick then officially acceded to the pope's demands, although he seems to have put little effort into the project. A number of the rebellious spirituals either lived on in the more remote areas of Sicily or filtered back into southern Italy.[19]

John moved more slowly against the French spirituals, but with equally mixed results. In April 1317 he summoned sixty-two spirituals from Narbonne and Béziers to appear before him.[20] Over the next few months, he clarified his position in a series of bulls. *Quorumdam exigit* (October 1317) settled the *usus pauper* controversy in short order by asserting that it was the superior's task to define proper usage and the subordinate's duty to obey.[21] From that point on, the spirituals could be sorted out simply by asking them whether they accepted *Quorumdam exigit*. Those who replied in the negative could be considered ripe for inquisitorial action. Two other bulls, *Sancta romana* (December 1317) and *Gloriosam ecclesiam* (January 1318), presented John's revisionist history of the *usus pauper* controversy, according to which his predecessors' attempts to deal gently with the obstinate zealots had been rewarded only with further intransigence, leaving John with little choice except disciplinary action.[22]

Gloriosam ecclesiam is the most interesting bull from our perspective, since in it John lists some of the errors that, he says, the group is reported on good authority to hold. First, they say that there are two churches. The carnal church, rich and worldly, is led by the pope and other lesser prelates. The spiritual church, poor and virtuous, is composed of themselves and their supporters. This view—of oneself as spiritual and of everyone else as carnal—is, John observes, hardly an unusual one among heretics. His refutation of the first error naturally leads him to assert the unity of the church expressed in the Petrine succession, and to emphasize the mixed nature of the church in history, with good and bad growing up cheek by jowl until judgment day. He also underscores the legitimacy and usefulness of ecclesiastical wealth.

The second error held by these rebels is to assert that the priests and other ministers of the church, having been deprived of jurisdiction, can no longer validly confer the sacraments or instruct the faithful. Here they follow the error of the Donatists. In opposition, John asserts that, by God's immutable will, ecclesiastical authority will remain with the Roman church until the end of time. Their third error is that, like the Waldensians, they denounce all oaths as sinful. Their fourth is that, also like the Waldensians, they believe a sinful priest is devoid of power to confer the sacraments. Their fifth is that, somewhat in the style of the Manicheans and Montanists, they see the gospel as fulfilled for the first time in them. They assert that the promise of the Holy Spirit has been fulfilled in them rather than in the apostles at Pentecost, and thus the gospel has been opened to them alone. These presumptuous people also attack the sacrament of marriage, spin out dreams about "the course of time and the end of the world," and assert that the time of Antichrist has just begun. John comments that such assertions, which he considers "partly heretical, partly insane, and partly fabulous," should simply be condemned rather than seriously refuted. Devoid of any reason, authority, or likelihood, they stand as their own refutation. John notes that he has admonished King Frederick of Sicily to aid in capturing these pseudofriars. His majesty, an obedient son, has done so, although a number remain at large.[23]

If *Gloriosam ecclesiam* offers an accurate picture of any group, it is of the Italian rebels, since those in Narbonne and Béziers were still fruitlessly seeking John's support. We again face the question of Olivi's influence in Italy. This time an answer is provided by Angelo Clareno, who says the Italian rebels, ignorant of Olivi's actual opinions, claimed him as an authority.[24]

The Olivi Process: An Overview

The connection between Olivian apocalyptic and Franciscan dissidence was not lost on the pope, either. He soon extended his inquiry in Olivi's direction. Evidence of his activity is seen in the sentence handed down by the inquisitor Michel Le Moine on May 7, 1318, when four spirituals were burned at the stake in Marseilles.[25] After outlining the spirituals' heresy, Michel identifies its source. It flows from a "poisoned fountain of doctrine," Petrus Iohannis Olivi. In his Apocalypse commentary and elsewhere, Olivi temerariously attacked the honor and authority of the Roman church. His writings were condemned and burned by his own order. Nevertheless, since John XXII has submitted them to certain cardinals and masters for still another decision, Michel simply warns all and sundry that in the meantime they are not to read these works, nor are they to revere Olivi as a saint—another reference to the thriving Olivi cult—or even as a "catholic and approved man."

The basic outlines of the ensuing process are clear enough.[26] John entrusted Niccolo da Prato, cardinal bishop of Ostia, with the task of examining Olivi's Apocalypse commentary. The cardinal extracted certain passages and gave them to a single theologian, who reported his findings in 1318. The problem was then entrusted to a commission of eight, which included two Franciscans.[27] It reported in 1319. Meanwhile, in the spring of 1319, the order carried out its own condemnation of Olivi's works at the general chapter of Marseilles. This condemnation was approved by a commission of twelve Franciscan masters.[28] Moreover, during roughly the same period two other theologians, the Carmelite Guido Terreni and the Dominican Pierre de Palu, passed negative judgment on a Catalan work based heavily on Olivi's Apocalypse commentary.[29]

By this time there seemed little doubt that the Apocalypse commentary was headed for papal condemnation, but none occurred for another seven years. There is no evidence of further activity before 1322, when John announced that he was reserving final judgment on the matter for himself. Even then he moved slowly. At some point he extracted at least four passages from the commentary and sent them, with a specific query on each passage, to individual theologians.[30] It is impossible to say precisely when he did so, but one of the replies can be dated after November 24, 1324, since it cites the papal bull *Quia quorumdam*. Finally, on February 8, 1326, he issued his condemnation.

Much of this process can be reconstructed from primary sources. The opinion of the first theologian (identified by Koch as probably Guillelmus de Lauduno)[31] is available in its entirety in a Paris manuscript and in fragments in a Vatican manuscript.[32] The judgment of the eight-man commission was published in the seventeenth century.[33] The articles extracted from the Catalan work and the judgments passed on them by the two investigators are available in a modern edition.[34] Koch tentatively suggests that a list of impugned articles contained in a Florentine manuscript represent the first five articles condemned at the Marseilles general chapter.[35] The additional articles sent to various theologians are found in one Roman and one Parisian manuscript, although it is unclear whether they represent the replies of two or three theologians.[36] Ironically, the only stage of the process about which we know almost nothing is the final one, John's 1326 condemnation. We hear of it only from the inquisitor Bernard Gui, who does not disclose its contents.[37]

How we regard these documents and the relative attention we give to each will depend on how we view the developing investigation. The preliminary opinion of the lone theologian has been granted little attention, and with good reason. It examines eighty-four articles in a staggering 552 pages. Even Niccolo da Prato must have had trouble deciding what to do with it. The author sees Olivi's commentary as a revised edition of the errors promulgated nearly a half century earlier by Gerard of Borgo San Donnino. He considers it to be not merely wrong but heretical, yet he goes well beyond merely censuring suspect passages. He attempts a genuine refutation of them that proceeds on several levels. On the one hand, he attacks Olivi on the basis of a theology of the church supported at inordinate length by appeals to scripture and tradition. Thus he incessantly refutes Olivi's comments on the fall of Babylon (which he takes as a code name for the Roman church) by arguing that Christ has promised the see of Peter his aid and will never abandon it. At the same time, he engages in the trench warfare of biblical hermeneutics. He argues that Olivi's reading of the Apocalypse is wrong both because it attacks established ecclesiastical power and because it is bad scholarship at odds with the exegetical tradition incarnated in the *Glossa* and Richard of St. Victor.

The resultant work is hardly devoid of interest. It says a great deal about the state of biblical scholarship in the early fourteenth century and is particularly illuminating at those points where the writer makes an effort at fairness, suggesting how far he might go toward accepting one of Olivi's dubious opinions; yet in the long run the very length and complexity of his offering makes it hard to include here, and we will turn to more succinct, less inclusive documents. Little will be lost in the exchange, since we are primarily interested in discovering what various critics found wrong with Olivi's commentary, and what this theologian discovered is not strikingly different from what others saw. He simply noted the same problems in more passages. Thus his work is (like most of the other documents) quite repetitive, but on a grander scale.

The work of the Marseilles general chapter is a subject about which little can be said, since it is impossible to decide whether the Florentine manuscript is related to it, and that manuscript gives us little to work with anyway. The articles extracted from a Catalan work and the accompanying judgments might seem irrelevant to our quest, since the work under examination was not by Olivi, but even a casual inspection indicates that it was heavily dependent upon Olivi's Apocalypse commentary. Thus the source provides an important supplement to the 1319 condemnation by the commission of eight, and as such it has received some recent attention.[38]

The 1319 condemnation is obviously an important document, but whether one considers it the central document depends to some extent on how one views the four passages later sent to individual theologians. If one chooses to see these passages and the accompanying questions as a further refinement of the process, in which the major enormities contained in the commentary are succinctly summarized in four basic theses, then they are absolutely central and the 1319 commission report should be seen as a preliminary stage beyond which the investigation eventually moved.[39] One might then believe that the final condemnation was based on these four articles.

The following discussion will proceed from a slightly different assumption, namely that these later opinions were essentially supplemental. After John had received the report of the eight-man panel, he felt that a few things still ought to be clarified. John felt the commission had ignored the dangers of three passages in Olivi's commentary and had passed too gentle a verdict on still another. Thus he sent those four passages to other theologians requesting their opinions. Perhaps he sent other passages to other theologians. We know only what the extant evidence allows us to know. In any case, on this basis one can imagine that the 1326 condemnation may have included a great deal of material found in the 1319 commission report but not included in the four passages.

The Commission Report and the Catalan Process

The Catalan process and report of the eight-man commission are strikingly similar in some ways. Both concentrate their fire on Olivi's comments concerning the carnal church, Babylon and (less often) the harlot, beast from the land, and Antichrist. They continually emphasize that Olivi's statements on these matters are dangerous in view of the fact that, when he employs such terms, he means by them the Roman church, the catholic church, or the pope. Of the sixty articles censured by the commission, thirty-three deal directly and another five obliquely with Olivi's misuse of these terms. In the Catalan process, there are sixteen direct references in forty-one articles. Given the identification of such terms with the pope and catholic church, the complaints registered are fairly predictable. Both the commission and the Catalan process recoil from the suggestion that the church will turn from Christ, attempt to suppress Christ's gospel, and persecute spiritual men.

The Catalan process acknowledges that the identification itself is not beyond question. Olivi could be using the term "carnal church" in either of two ways: as the Catholic church having possessions, or merely as the congregation of the unfaithful adhering to Antichrist. Nevertheless, the total work seems to suggest that he means the former. Of course the specific target of the Catalan process is not Olivi's commentary but a later document based on it, and the authors seem justified in assuming that this document does use the term in the former sense, since the process cites a series of passages in which the work refers to persecution of the spirituals by the church. Nevertheless, in a passage that attacks Olivi as much as it castigates his later followers, the process notes that his statements contradict the Bible even if they are taken in the second sense, since they suggest that the carnal church will be destroyed before Antichrist comes.[40]

The other major target is Olivi's claim that the sixth and seventh periods of church history have a preeminence over previous periods and, as a natural corollary, the third age of world history has a preeminence over the first and second. The commission devotes fifteen articles to this problem insofar as it concerns the sixth and seventh periods, and three more articles to it insofar as it involves the third age. The Catalan process distributes its concern more equally, spending three articles on the preeminence of the sixth and seventh periods and another four on that of the third age. In both documents there is some concern with Olivi's views on the length of the third period,[41] but the main focus is on the progressive element in his interpretation. Fifteen articles in the commission report and three in the Catalan process attack the implication that the sixth and seventh periods will witness knowledge and virtue superior to that of the apostles, while eight in the commission report and one in the Catalan process criticize the notion that these periods are related to preceeding periods as the church was related to the synagogue. Both sources emphasize that Christ's promise of the Holy Spirit was fulfilled at Pentecost and thus does not point toward a new, final age.

It follows from the general rejection of a progressive pattern in church history that neither the commission report nor the Catalan process is enthusiastic about the idea that a new evangelical order will arise in the third age and offer the pattern for a different sort of church leadership. Both documents are particularly unenthusiastic in view of the scenario offered: the pope and his minions will oppose the new order and must be disobeyed in the name of the gospel. The new leadership will not be the old one in modified form but will represent an entirely different group in opposition to and opposed by the old. Even without this element, however, the idea of a new order and leadership is repugnant to the commission report and to the Catalan process. The latter spells out its objections more explicitly. It takes issue with Olivi's image of evangelical humility among future leaders, arguing that it implies an absence of such among present ecclesiastics. More important, the process consistently opposes the idea that future leaders will lack common possessions, since it sees this prediction as implying that such possessions are wrong. In both cases, the example of the apostles is cited.[42] The report and process also take issue with Olivi's prediction of massive conversions among the infidel by the new order.[43]

Concommitant with the greater specificity of the Catalan process in rejecting Olivi's vision of the new order is its willingness to condemn the assumption underlying that vision, his identification of the new order with the Franciscans. The process devotes no less than nine articles to this matter, arguing that the Olivian view damns all of the church except the Franciscans. The authors, clearly irked by Olivi's minorite chauvinism, refer to his statements as presumptuous and remark twice that it is a great perversion to interpret the Apocalypse, which is written for the church in general, in such a way that it applies to a single order.[44] The commission report is more circumspect. It explicitly refers to this element in censuring the idea that the brunt of missionary preaching in the new age will be born by the Franciscans,[45] but manages to dodge it elsewhere by presenting Olivi's statements as references not to the Franciscan order but to "his sect."[46]

Nevertheless, there is one point at which neither the commission report nor the Catalan process can avoid the problems lurking in this area, and that is in dealing with Olivi's apocalyptic interpretation of Saint Francis himself. Each rejects some part of his comments on Francis as angel of the sixth seal. The commission cites two different passages in which Olivi asserts that Francis is the angel of Revelation 7:2, but in both cases it ignores the assertion itself. In dealing with the first passage, it concentrates on Olivi's insistence that the Franciscan rule is identical with the gospel observed by Christ and imposed by him on the apostles.[47] The commission sees the perils of denying this claim, since it is affirmed by *Exiit qui seminat*, but resolves the dilemma by suggesting that the claim can be taken in a good (papal) or bad (Olivian) sense. The difference between these two senses is not clearly delineated. The papal interpretation is not explained at all, and the Olivian view is simply identified as involving the ideas that "the rule of blessed Francis is truly and properly one and the same as the gospel of Christ," that "the pope does not have any more authority over it than he has over the gospel," and that "whatever is in the rule of blessed Francis was observed to the letter by Christ and imposed by him on the apostles." The second element is an important one. The power of the church to approve orders is seen as so central to the discussion that the commission asserts it in three different articles.[48]

In considering the second passage, the commission brands Olivi's comments as "false, fatuous, and temerarious" in two respects. First, in describing Francis as the highest observer of evangelical perfection after Christ and his mother, Olivi slights the apostles and other New Testament saints. The commission says such a view "is temerarious, and we believe it to be false." Second, Olivi's prediction of a bodily resurrection on Francis's part to aid his followers in their moment of need strikes the commission as a "fantastic fiction unworthy of being recited or written."[49]

Two other articles consider Olivi's identification of Francis with the angel of Revelation 10 : 1–3. In the first, the commission labels as heretical the assertion that Francis is, after Christ, the first and principal founder of the sixth period. This statment is considered heretical insofar as it allows Francis preeminence over the apostles, and it is temerarious insofar as it accords him preeminence over other saints in his own time. As for Olivi's suggestion that, in the thirteenth century, the Franciscan order will convert the Saracens and other infidels and be assimilated with Christ's passion and exaltation, the commission brands these ideas "temerarious, fictive, and based on no sound reasoning or authentic scripture."[50]

In the second article dealing with Olivi's exegesis of 10 : 1–3, the commission confronts Olivi's expectation that Christ and Francis will spiritually descend in order to aid their servants during the temptation of the mystical Antichrist.[51] This belief is seen as heretical in its assumption that the evangelical life will be condemned by the church. What Olivi says about the descent itself is less serious, merely a temerarious, invented fiction.

The Catalan process treats the identification of Francis as angel of the sixth seal at length in two articles and briefly in still another.[52] Its criticism is more exegetical in nature and is aimed directly at the idea of Francis as the angel of Revelation 7:2. In one article, the process observes that Olivi's interpretation, if taken literally, contradicts the Bible, for according to the letter the angel is Christ. Even if it is not taken literally, it is still problematic. If one applies the passage to Francis by virtue of his sanctity, stigmata, or wisdom, just as one would apply it to any saintly man, then there is no more reason to apply it to him than to Paul or John.

Nor is the report impressed by Olivi's appeal to a vision attested to by Bonaventure. The vision does not seem authentic and, even if it is, it should be understood not literally but through a certain appropriation, just as Francis, though not literally the angel who appeared to Isaiah in Isaiah 6, is nonetheless often described and visually represented as such. In another article, the identification of Francis as angel of the sixth seal is described as temerarious if taken literally, since Haymo, Richard of St. Victor, and others apply the passage to Christ. It can be identified with Francis "through a certain participation and appropriation," but no more than to Peter, Andrew, or Paul. The third article addresses Olivi's claim of greater knowledge for Francis, disputing it on behalf of the apostles.

Two more articles in the Catalan process dispense with Francis's reputed resurrection and descent.[53] His resurrection is given short shrift as "a fable lacking any authority." As for the descent, there is no more reason for Francis to descend than there is for Paul or others to appear, since they were more principally founders and observers of the evangelical life. None of these articles in the Catalan process explicitly comes to terms with Olivi's willingness to identify the Franciscan rule with the evangelical life observed by Christ and his disciples, but the process is perfectly willing to face that issue elsewhere.[54] It bluntly rejects the assertion as heretical, since it would mean that the entire rule was as firm as the gospel and thus could not be altered by the pope, nor would it need to be confirmed by him. That is, of course, precisely what the commission finds disturbing about the identification.

The Catalan process has to deal with still another apocalyptic identification. The document it is examining sees the angel of Revelation 10:1 not as Francis, but as Olivi. The process dismisses this interpretation as "temerarious and false," remarking that far from being a divinely designated bearer of truth, Olivi deviated from it in his Apocalypse commentary.[55]

Obviously these two documents take issue with Olivi in some very basic ways. On one level, the difference can be decribed as ecclesiological. Olivi's critics are combatting an implied challenge to papal authority. They read Olivi as predicting a time in the near future when the elect will find it necessary to disobey the pope. They read him as justifying the Franciscan rule in such a way as to make it independent of papal authority, and they are appalled. The commission states the matter clearly and concisely: "In the entire church there is a single primacy residing within the Roman church. Beginning with Peter it has continued without interruption or transference until now and will always continue in his legitimate successors until the consummation of this world."[56]

To put it this way, however, is to suggest another, perhaps more basic issue: Olivi and his critics proceed from radically diverse views of history. One view is essentially dynamic, the other static. For Olivi's critics, the church bloomed at an early age, having received almost from the beginning both the organization it would retain for all time and the spiritual direction it would need to function as well as possible in a fallen world. The papal seat has been promised not only power but divine guidance as well. It is unthinkable that at this late date God should so abandon it as to allow it to persecute the elect. It is equally unthinkable that, after 1,300 years, He should allow His chosen institution to be destroyed and replace it with a new sort of church in a new age. Olivi's emphasis on a pre-eminence of the sixth and seventh periods defies their most cherished assumptions.

There is a certain irony here. We have seen that Olivi himself is perhaps a bit uneasy on this score. He attempts to balance his emphasis on progress and innovation with frequent reference to reform and renovation. Francis moves the church forward by inaugurating a new age, but he also moves it backward by reviving the life observed by Christ and the apostles. Olivi is somewhat inconsistent as to whether the apostles, having been presented with this life, actually practiced it as fully as Francis would, but on the whole one suspects that he would have assented to that proposition if forced to face it seriously. Even when Olivi underscores the element of renovation, however, he does so in a way that is equally unacceptable to his critics. He suggests that the present reform will move the church from the thirteenth century straight back to the first in such a way as to pass implicit judgment on the intervening millennium. Olivi cheerfully acknowledges that God must have had his own reasons for introducing wealth into the church after founding it on the basis of apostolic poverty, but he is equally sure that these reasons no longer hold and God is now ready to change it back to its original state. In other words, his notion of reform is, absolutely speaking, renovation, since it restores the original pattern, but relatively speaking it is innovation, for it implies radical alteration of the church as it has existed for the last few centuries.

The Catalan process and the commission report are both quite aware of what is involved here. Their preoccupation with Olivi's implied judgment on the present establishment is evident in the former's response to the notion that Francis is, after Christ and Mary, the principal observer of evangelical perfection.[57] The Catalan process presents the apostles' case, then—as is often the case in this document—it presents an alternate refutation based on another possible reading of Olivi's statement. If his main point is simply that the sixth period restores the original situation, they say, then the apostles are allowed into the charmed circle, but everyone between the first and sixth periods is still excluded. There were, however, equally holy men in the intervening centuries, men equally zealous in their observance of the evangelical life.

Olivi's critics feel that his misreading of church history is closely related to his misinterpretion of the evangelical life. His willingness to relegate religious leaders like Benedict and Augustine to a lower order of sanctity is predicated upon his assumption that Christ and the apostles renounced both individual and common possessions. This same assumption allows him to believe that the Franciscans observe Christ's precepts and counsels in a way that the Benedictines and Augustinians do not. It also encourages him to imagine that the pope has no authority to alter the Franciscan rule, since he has no authority to alter the gospel.

If the difference between Olivi and his critics can be examined from the perspectives of ecclesiology and theology of history, it can also be viewed from that of exegetical theory. The contrast here is less obvious in the commission report than in the Catalan process. In the former, Olivi is constantly castigated for offering, not solid exegesis, but *divinatio temeraria et fatua*.[58] His use of the Greek and Latin alphabets for historical prognostication is described as *ridiculosum et fictitium*.[59] It is hard to carry the matter much further, however. The commission chastises Olivi on one occasion for rejecting Richard of St. Victor's interpretation on the basis of what it considers "frivolous arguments,"[60] but the hermeneutical roots of its criticism remain otherwise hidden.

The Catalan process is more instructive in this respect. It is more willing to treat the document before it as a work of exegesis and to respond on that level. We see as much in the case of Olivi as the angel of Revelation 10:1, where the process offers this interpretation more respect than the modern reader might think it deserves by citing Richard and Haymo against it. We also see it in the case of Francis as the angel of Revelation 7:2. Here the process refutes this identification as the literal meaning by appealing to Richard and Haymo, then explores its possibilities and limitations if taken in a nonliteral sense. This tendency is equally evident in its comments on the length of the third age. If the process rejects as unbiblical the idea that the world must last long enough after the death of Antichrist to accomodate first universal conversion, then moral decline to the point where Christ is forced to come and destroy the world, it does so because it follows the interpretive tradition according to which Antichrist's death will be followed by forty days in which those who stood by Christ will be given respite and those who did not will have time to repent.[61]

Other passages could be cited in which the Catalan process displays its hermeneutical pedigree. In response to the notion that the carnal church will be destroyed in the sixth period and the elect separated from it as the apostles were from the synagogue, the process observes that, according to the Bible, evil and good will be mixed in the church until the final judgment.[62] It rejects as unbiblical the notion of a great change in the sixth period, for such a view, it says, shifts to the sixth period the renewal that will occur in the seventh period after the death of Antichrist.[63] The authors of the document can be placed rather neatly within the exegetical tradition outlined earlier. They are rejecting a Joachite interpretation of the Apocalypse in favor of the one taught them by their masters at Paris.

This hermeneutical aspect of the Olivi process deserves emphasis, not because it is somehow the key to all else, but because it is the dimension most easily ignored. Thus it is worth remarking that in this respect the commission report and the Catalan process are at one with that verbose, anonymous consultant reporting his reactions in 1318. The latter launches no less than two attacks on the notion of Francis as angel of the sixth seal. In the first he underlines that the passage applies literally to Christ alone. Directly responding to Olivi's invocation of Bonaventure as his authority, he remarks that Bonaventure is hardly a canonical text and thus "one can deny that he said it or even that he was right in saying it, or one can argue that he meant Francis was the angel metaphorically and *secundum quid*, not literally and *simpliciter*." Later this consultant remarks that Revelation 7:2 refers literally to Christ alone, although it can be taken as referring to one of his members *in mistico*.[64] His reaction to this particular interpretation is merely one of many points at which he attacks Olivi's exegesis. In another passage, he lays down a seemingly endless barrage of biblical and patristic citations in the course of refuting the idea that the third age will see a general conversion of the world and will last significantly longer than the forty-plus days traditionally projected after the death of Antichrist.[65]

The Question of Accuracy

Thus one should perhaps think twice before accepting the widely accepted theory that the commission rejected Olivi because it misunderstood him, and that it misunderstood him because it read not the Apocalypse commentary but a series of *articuli* wrenched from context. This theory has at least the virtue of antiquity. It was advanced in nuclear form by Ubertino da Casale, probably even before the commission issued its report. Ubertino told papal auditors grilling him at Avignon that Olivi "asserted in substance the very propositions [cited against him] and all the articles contained in them, . . . but with many other things before, after, and in between, through which his intention is more fully manifested than by bare articles (*nudos articulos*)."[66]

The commission did, of course, censure a series of "bare articles," but it was not doomed to see only these. The preface to their report explains that Bishop Niccolo sent them both the articles and the entire Apocalypse commentary. Their charge was twofold: to see if the articles actually were contained in the commentary and to decide whether they were erroneous. They could have read the articles in context had they wished to do so. The question is whether they so wished.

The answer to that question depends on what one means by reading the articles in context. If the question is whether the commission report addressed the problem of how the individual articles fit into the total context of the commentary, the answer is that it did not. A modern scholar would feel obliged to do so, but the commission members were not modern scholars. If, on the other hand, the question is simply whether the meaning given individual articles by the commission is the one derived by reading them in context, then the answer is a more ambiguous one. The commission misread Olivi in certain respects, and they are by no means unimportant ones. Their report consistently interprets Olivi's references to "the carnal church" as if that term were synonymous with "the Catholic church" or "the Roman church." Thus they view these references as frontal assaults on the institution they love and serve. Olivi's conception of the carnal church is more complex. In his mind, the carnal church is not primarily an institution at all, but rather the totality of anti-Christian forces operating in the guise of the true church while pursuing radically different ends.

One reason why the commission report tends to institutionalize the notion of the carnal church is that it reads the articles in peculiarly anachronistic fashion. It interprets them in the context of present battles and thus treats Olivi as if he were one of his own later followers. This process is demonstrated in one of the passages dedicated to proving that Olivi's "carnal church" is a code name for the Roman church.[67] Olivi, the commission notes, asserts that the evangelical life will be defended by its professors and condemned by the carnal church. Since those in his sect pertinaciously defend an interpretation of the rule condemned by the church, while the majority of Franciscans accept the ecclesiastically sanctioned interpretation, it follows that when Olivi mentions the carnal church he really means the Catholic church. Such an argument strikes one as stunningly ahistorical. It seems to assume that Olivi not only held substantially the same opinions as the later spirituals but actually wrote with their case in mind.

The commission report could also be criticized for its failure to read Olivi's progressive view of church history in the context of passages tempering that view, passages which offer an equally strong emphasis on renewal, return to the apostolic model. This tendency on the commission's part is seen in its willingness to cite the apostles in refuting the preeminence of the sixth and seventh periods. Olivi himself is concerned about the apostles. He interprets them as a fulfillment of evangelical perfection occurring at the beginning of the first period and rivaled only in the sixth. The commission, concentrating on the articles as discrete entities, simply ignores such evidence if it lies outside the designated target zone.

Having said so much, one must go on to say that in some ways the commission members' reading is quite accurate. Even if Olivi's carnal church cannot be equated with the Roman church, it is related to the latter in a significant way in the fifth period. By the end of that period, elements of the carnal church have infiltrated the leadership structure of the Roman church so completely that the institution is serving their purposes. It has "become, as it were, a new Babylon." The word *quasi* in Olivi's formulation adds a note of ambiguity and thus keeps it from being an absolute identification, but that is small enough comfort. Certainly Olivi does not view the church as *completely* Babylon. Certainly not every leadership position is working toward essentially non-Christian ends. Of course the true church is still somewhere within it. This is simply to grant, however, that Olivi sees a fundamental continuity between the churches of the second and third ages. They are essentially the same church, for Christ is lord of all history, and the ideals of the church in the third age will be those of Christ and the apostles at the beginning of the second. The fact remains, however, that by the end of the second age leaders of the church will be impeding Christ's work by opposing the birth of the third.

The Catalan process points almost at the beginning to the ambiguity of the carnal church as Olivi describes it. The process acknowledges that Olivi could mean two different things. He could mean "the Catholic church having possessions," or he could simply mean "the congregation of the unfaithful adhering to Antichrist." The second meaning is, of course, rather close to the one we have accepted as accurate. The process dismisses the first sense as heretical, then attacks the second as unbiblical, since it suggests that the carnal church will be destroyed before Antichrist actually appears. This argument complicates matters by adding Antichrist to the definition and throwing in the element of biblical hermeneutics, but it points to something worthy of attention. If "the carnal church" is used only in the general sense accepted by us so far, it is nonsense to say that it will be destroyed by a pagan army. It is clear from Olivi's scenario that carnal elements will survive the onslaught and unite with Antichrist in the sixth period. Thus, when he says the carnal church will be destroyed at the end of the fifth period, he must be referring to the institution serving the purposes of carnality at that moment, and that institution seems physically identical with the leadership of the Roman church, however diverse the two might be conceptually.

Moreover, the commission is correct in reading Olivi's vision of the third age as something more than a reform of present institutions. One can assume that he envisions a survival of the existing ecclesiastical structure into the new age—although in fact he never commits himself either way—but it will be transformed radically in any case. Wealth will be replaced by poverty. Authority will be anchored in moral excellence, not juridical power. Subordinates will obey because they want to do so, not because they have to. The transformation of learning will be equally impressive, thanks to the *intelligentia spiritualis* of the third age. The church on earth will have moved one step closer to the situation of the church in heaven.

Consideration of this projected scenario should make one cautious about asserting that the commission overestimates the progressive element in Olivi's thought. Certainly it ignores the passages in which Olivi attempts to give the apostles their due, just as it ignores the ones in which Olivi suggests that *intelligentia spiritualis* was available to a few men in all ages; but it is right in believing that Olivi's vision of the third age places it well beyond earlier periods in the general tenor of church life. What was attained piecemeal by isolated figures in the second age will become characteristic of the third age. Moreover, even if the commission report tends to treat the element of innovation in isolation from the element of renovation, it nonetheless recognizes the latter, reads it more or less correctly, and rejects it. The commission simply will not accept Olivi's identification of the Franciscan rule with the form of life practiced by Christ and imposed by him on his disciples, nor will it credit his assumption that the Franciscan rule and life embody the evangelical perfection that will become the model for church life in general during the third age.

The preceding should discourage us from seeing Olivi's condemnation merely as a failure in communication, or reducing it to a difference in ecclesiology. It was partly both, but it was also a critique of Olivi's exegetical choices. The theologians who judged his commentary were schooled in an approach to the Apocalypse that accorded ill with what they found in Olivi's work. In retrospect, it is clear that on those occasions when Olivi rejected Richard in favor of Joachim or (worse yet) his own brand of Franciscan Joachism, he made himself peculiarly vulnerable to his later judges.

Notes

1. Olivi, *Epistola ad Conradum de Offida*, in Livarius Oliger, "Petrus Iohannis Olivi de renuntiatione papae Coelestini V quaestio et epistola," *AFH* 11 (1918): 273. The various bulls by Boniface mentioned in Chapter 5 also suggest some degree of apocalyptic awareness on the part of his targets, but he says too little for us to be sure. It is tempting to place Jacopone da Todi's apocalyptically oriented Laud 50 in this same period.

2. Amorós, "Series condemnationum," 504; Raymundus de Fronciacho, *Sol ortus*, in *Archiv* 3 : 15f. On the persecution see Lambert *Franciscan Poverty* (London, 1961), chapter 7.

3. Amorós, "Series condemnationum," 505.

4. Raymundus de Fronciacho, *Sol ortus*, in *Archiv*, 3 : 17. Ubertino da Casale, *Sanctitati apostolicae*, in *Archiv*, 2 : 385f., cites a letter from John of Murrovalle presenting *usus pauper* as the basic issue in the persecution.

5. William May, "The Confesson of Prous Boneta, Heretic and Heresiarch," *Essays in Medieval Life and Thought* (New York, 1965), 10f.

6. On Matthew see Paul of Venice in Girolamo Golubovich, *Biblioteca bio-bibliografica della Terra Santa e dell'oriente francescana* (Quaracchi, 1906–48), 2 : 80f., 96f. On Jerome see Angelo Clareno, *Epistole* (Rome, 1980), 247f.

7. Johannes Mansi, *Sacrorum conciliorum nova et amplissima collectio*, 24 : 1216. The decree mentions distinctive clothing and rites, vows of chastity, secret conventicles, and usurpation of the preaching office.

8. Leon Amorós, "Aegidii Romani impugnatio doctrinae Petri Ioannis Olivi an. 1311–12, nunc primum in lucem edita," *AFH* 27 (1934): 403; Pásztor, "Le Polemiche sulla 'Lectura super apocalypsim' di Pietro di Giovanni Olivi fino alla sua condanna," *Bulletino dell'Istituto Storico Italiano per il Medio Evo e Archivio Muratoriano* 70 (1958): 321n.2.

9. Ubertino identifies Boniface VIII and Benedict XI with the mystical Antichrist.

10. See Burr, *Persecution*, 76 and 79f.

11. Raymundus de Fronciacho and Bonagratia de Bergamo, *In nomine domini*, in *Archiv*, 2:370f.

12. See Burr, *OFP*, 112–24.

13. Ubertino, *Sanctitati apostolicae*, in *Archiv*, 2:407f.

14. See the sources in *Archiv*, 2:159–64 and 4:52–57; and in Livarius Oliger, "Fr. Bertrandi de Turre processus contra spirituales Aquitaniae (1315) et Card. Jacobus de Columna littera defensoria spiritualium provinciae (1316)," *AFH* 16 (1923): 323–55.

15. Raymundus de Fronciacho, *Sol ortus*, in *Archiv*, 3:26f.; Angelo, *Historia septem tribulationum*, 142.

16. Angelo, *Historia septem tribulationum*, 138f., says that even while the great debate was in progress, spirituals in southern France, Tuscany, and the Val di Spoleto were persecuted more harshly than ever.

17. See especially the documentation assembled by Anna Maria Ini, "Nuovi documenti sugli spirituali di Toscana," *AFH* 66 (1973): 305–77. They also tried to seize control at Colle Val d'Elsa but failed. Ini's sources suggest that about eighty brothers were involved, one of them from southern France.

18. For the excommunication see Niccola Papini, *Notizie sicure della morte, sepoltura, canonizzazione e traslazione di S. Francesco d'Assisi*, 2d ed. (Foligno, 1824), 253–64. Documents regarding the Sicilian escapees are in Heinrich Finke, *Acta aragonensia* (Berlin, 1908), volumes 2 and 3, as listed by Ini.

19. Some may even have settled in Islamic territory through an arrangement worked out by Frederick. See Finke, *Acta*, 2:671f.

20. *BF*, 5:119f.

21. *BF*, 5:128–30.

22. *BF*, 5:134f. and 137–42.

23. John says that some have escaped to pagan lands, while others are protected by supporters in remote parts of Sicily.

24. *Epistole*, 121–31. It is also partly supported by MS Paris Bibl. Nat. lat. 4190, 45v. This document, which will be discussed at length later, credits the rebels with a theology of history similar to Olivi's. Angelo says they also support their stance with "secret revelations of a certain holy person."

25. In Mansi, *Stephani Baluzii Tutelensis Miscellanea* (Paris, 1761–64), 2: 248–51.

26. For these processes see Pásztor, "Polemiche," and "Giovanni XXII e il Gioachimismo di Pietro di Giovanni Olivi," *Bulletino dell'Istituto Storico Italiano per il Medio Evo e Archivio Muratoriano* 82 (1970): 82–111; Joseph Koch, "Der Prozess gegen die Postille Olivis zur Apokalypse," *Recherches de Théologie Ancienne et Mé-*

diévale 5 (1933): 302–15; Malcolm Lambert, "The Franciscan Crisis under John XXII," *Franciscan Studies* 32 (1972): 123–43.

27. One of the Franciscans, Bertrand de la Tour, was provincial minister of Aquitaine and had recently engaged in a vain attempt to recover spirituals of his province who had escaped to the rebellious houses in Provence. See Oliger, "Fr. Bertrandi de Turre." Thus he was an enemy of the spirituals. The other Franciscan was Arnaldus Royardi.

28. Amorós, "Series condemnationum," 509, places the condemnation at the Pentecost chapter held in Marseilles and before the commission of eight reached a conclusion. The *Allegationes*, MS Paris Nat. lat. 4190 (to be examined shortly), says (f. 40r) that, lest anyone should believe the order approved of statements against the Roman church found in Olivi's commentary, it condemned the commentary and asked the pope to condemn it as well. The *Allegationes* notes that other Olivian works were also condemned at that chapter. For other references to this condemnation see Pásztor, "Polemiche," 378.

29. José Pou y Marti, *Visionarios, Beguinos y Fraticellos Catalanes (Siglos XIII-XV)* (Vich, 1930), 483–512. Manselli, *Spirituali e beghini in Provenza*, 164–69, argues persuasively that the Catalan work was written after May 7, 1318, and the judgment on it in late 1318 or early 1319.

30. See Pásztor, "Polemiche"; idem, "Giovanni XXII": Koch, "Prozess," 310f.

31. "Prozess," 304.

32. Paris Bibl. Nat. lat. 3381A; Rome Vat. lat. 11906, ff. 63r–188v). Incipit: *Ista sunt que in postilla fratris Petri Johannis super apocalipsim videntur esse heretica.* Excerpts purportedly taken from a Florence, Biblioteca Laurentiana MS and compared with the Paris MS are published in Ignaz von Döllinger, *Beiträge zue Sektengeschichte des Mittelalters* (Darmstadt, 1968), 2:527–85, but they are almost entirely the anonymous theologian's citations of the Olivi text rather than his judgments on it.

33. Originally published in *Stephani Baluze Miscellaneorum* (Paris, 1678), 213–77. I shall cite the same text as republished in Mansi, *Miscellanea*, 2:258–70. On the accuracy of this edition see Koch, "Prozess," 306.

34. See note 29 above.

35. MS Florence Biblioteca Laurentiana, Santa Croce Plut. 31 sin. cod. 3, 175rb–va. Incipit: *Articuli abstracti de scripturis suis ab impugnatoribus.*

36. MS Rome Vat. Arm. seg. XXXI, t. 42, 82v–91v, incipit: *In nomine domini*; MS Paris Bibl. Nat. lat. 4190, 40r–49v, incipit: *Allegationes super articulis.* Koch, "Prozess," 310f., assumes that both replies in the Rome MS are by the same person, while Pásztor, "Polemiche," 309–406, argues that they must be by different people.

37. Bernard Gui, *Flores chronicarum*, in Baluze-Mollat, *Vitae paparum Avenionensium* (Paris, 1914), 1:142 and 1:166.

38. Thomas Turley, "John XXII and the Franciscans: A Reappraisal," in *Popes, Teachers and Canon Law in the Middle Ages* (Ithaca, 1989), 74–88.

39. Edith Pásztor seems to see them in this way. See particularly "Giovanni XXII," 83f., where she describes them as "quelle tesi dell'escatologismo gioachimitico francescano che risultavano più pericolose nelle loro implicazioni ecclesias-

tiche" and as "affermazioni . . . adatta a fornire le pezze d'appoggio di una condanna." Thus both her articles concentrate on the responses to these questions and are less interested in the 1319 opinion.

40. Catalan process, article (hereafter "art.") 2. Art. 5, 8, and 20 make the same point.

41. Commission report, art. 7; Catalan process, art. 27.

42. On humility see Catalan process, art. 33. On poverty see especially art. 3, 4, 6, 9, 21, 23, 38, 40. Commission report, art. 34, does argue that the apostles had common possessions, but uses this assertion in a different way.

43. Commission report, art. 8, 38, 40, 47; Catalan process, art. 24.

44. Catalan process, art. 22, 41.

45. Commission report, art. 41.

46. See, for example, art. 30, 36.

47. Commission report, art. 22. See *Lectura*, 393.

48. Commission report, art. 22, 23, 26.

49. Commission report, art. 28. See *Lectura*, 416–18.

50. Commission report, art. 38. See *Lectura*, 560–63.

51. Commission report, art. 39. See *Lectura*, 563.

52. Catalan process, art. 7, 14, 28.

53. Ibid., art. 15, 25.

54. Catalan process, art. 6, which argues that they differ because the Franciscan rule prohibits common possessions while the gospel does not, and the rule prohibits money while the apostles accepted it. The rule simply binds Franciscans to observe the gospel counsels plus some other things.

55. Catalan process, art. 22.

56. Commission report, art. 18.

57. Catalan process, art. 23.

58. E.g. commission report, art. 44, where he uses the expression twice.

59. Ibid., art. 58.

60. Commission report, art. 32.

61. Catalan process, art. 27

62. Catalan process, art. 29.

63. Ibid., art. 32.

64. MS Paris Bibl. Nat. lat. 3381A, 69r–v, 113r.

65. Ibid., 13r–15r. The number given at 15r seems to be 45.

66. Mansi, *Miscellenea*, 2:276. The document, representing a process in 1325, is citing a statement made by Ubertino before papal auditors, probably during a process against the spirituals begun by John XXII at Avignon in 1317. See Frédégand Callaey, *L'Idéalisme franciscaine spirituel au XIVe siècle* (Louvain, 1911), 236–38; Pásztor, "Polemiche," 374–77.

67. Commission report, art. 29. See art. 30, 34, 35 for similar remarks.

10. The Condemnation Process, 1322–26

Once John XXII had the commission report in hand he would have been justified in moving directly to a condemnation, but he did not. Instead, the next official action known to us is the 1322 announcement that John is reserving final judgment on the matter for himself. Next we find him submitting discrete articles to individual theologians. There is no way of saying how many theologians were invited to comment. We can work only with what we have, and it is even difficult to say how many people are represented by what we have.

The Historical Context

Before examining our sources we would do well to consider the altered circumstances in which this second phase occurred. The Olivi process began while John XXII and Michael of Cesena were combining to crush the spirituals. By the time it ended, the pope and minister general would be less compatible.[1] According to one source, the trouble began in 1321 when a Dominican inquisitor branded as heretical the statement of a beguin that Christ and his apostles possessed nothing either individually or in common. When the Franciscan *lector* at Narbonne protested that the view in question had been promulgated in *Exiit qui seminat*, the inquisitor charged him too with heresy. Both appealed to John and the battle was on. Whatever value this anecdote may have, we know that John's mind was turning to the problem around this time. In March 1322 he issued *Quia nonnunquam*, which lifted the ban *Exiit qui seminat* had placed on discussion of its own contents. At Pentecost the Franciscan general chapter countered with encyclicals protesting that *Exiit* had been received into canon law and thus its decisions on poverty could not be abrogated. In December John retaliated with *Ad conditorem canonum*, which struck down yet another of *Exiit's* provisions. Whereas *Exiit* had insured Franciscan poverty by giving the papacy dominion over all goods used by the order, John revived the old argument—already used against the Franciscans by thirteenth-century opponents—that it was nonsense to say anyone except the order had dominion over whatever they consumed through use. Of course the Franciscans had claimed lack of ownership not only for themselves but for Christ and his apostles. In November 1323 John took care of that problem in *Cum inter nonnullos*, which declared the latter assertion heretical just as the Dominican inquisitor had done. Some modern scholars have suggested that John deliberately built a degree of ambiguity into his reversal of *Exiit*,[2] but it is hard to deny that his bulls had knocked the props out from under the Franciscan self-understanding.

During the same period John had been pursuing a long battle with Ludwig the Bavarian. By March 1324 he had announced that Ludwig would be excommunicated and denied imperial status unless he came to terms with the pope within three months. At Sachsenhausen during the same month, Ludwig issued a declaration reversing the equation, accusing the pope of heresy precisely because he had denied the same Franciscan poverty endorsed by seven of his predecessors. In July John did what he had threatened to do in March, and shortly thereafter Ludwig declared him a false pope. In May 1328 he took the logical step of replacing John with his own candidate, the Franciscan Peter of Corbara. By that point he had more Franciscans than Peter in his camp. In April Michael of Cesena, the minister general, summoned to Avignon the previous year, was accused of favoring heresy in the 1322 Perugia encyclicals. In May he, William of Ockham, and others fled the papal court, taking refuge with Ludwig. It had been a busy period for all concerned.

The Sources

We can now return to our sources for the second phase of the Olivi process. One manuscript, found at the Bibliothèque Nationale in Paris,[3] obviously presents the response of a single theologian, although it probably contains only a part of that response. It covers only the first two articles, but does so at some length. The author is unknown, and we will refer to the work simply as the *Allegationes*, according to the *incipit*. Whoever the author is, he renders several services besides the obvious one of saying what offends him about the two propositions. He tells us that the Franciscan order, after condemning the Apocalypse commentary at Marseilles, urged the pope to do the same,[4] and he tells us that eighty-two people already have died for defending Olivi's heresy. He is also our only source for what Olivi's defenders were saying at the moment.[5] Hardly one to underrate his enemy, the author announces that papal action is imperative because the Olivian heresy, now spreading within Europe and outside it, is more dangerous to ecclesiastical authority than either the Donatist or Waldensian errors, both of which it includes within itself.[6] He twice reminds the pope that elements of Olivi's thought are mirrored in Ludwig the Bavarian's Sachsenhausen Appellation.[7]

The other manuscript, at the Vatican Library,[8] covers all four questions but introduces them in a slightly different, briefer form, presenting less of Olivi's text. The author identifies himself at the end as "Francis, bishop of Florence."[9] Thus we know him to be Francesco Silvestri, bishop of Florence from 1323 to 1341.[10] Thereafter in the same manuscript, we find an extended passage from Olivi's Apocalypse commentary which turns out to be the same one at which the third question is aimed, and we find still another opinion on it. Whoever contributed it announces that he already has sent the pope his view on the matter in his response to "the third question sent to me." This comment, plus the juxtaposition of the opinion with the one on all four questions, leads Koch to conclude that Francesco is the author, while Pásztor argues more convincingly that we are dealing with still another theologian, who refers here to a document now lost.[11]

In essence, John XXII presented the theologians with four passages from Olivi's commentary and four questions concerning these passages. The questions were as follows:

1. Whether it is orthodox to say that the pontificate as given to Peter involved the apostolic and evangelical life; that only later, for useful and rational reasons, was it converted to a state of owning temporal property; that around the end of the fifth time it is so infected that it has become, as it were, a new Babylon; and that it will return to its original conformity with Christ.[12]
2. Whether it is orthodox to say that in the sixth period all the wisdom of the incarnate word and all the power of God the father will be seen, not only by simple intelligence, but by tactile and gustatory experience, as promised by Christ when he announced the coming of the Holy Spirit.[13]
3. Whether it is orthodox to say that the number of the elect is so established that if one should be corrupted, another would be

substituted lest the fabric of the supernal city should remain incomplete.[14]

4. Whether it is orthodox to say that blessed Francis is the revealer and (after Christ and his mother) highest observer of the evangelical life and rule of the sixth and seventh periods.

It is impossible to read these questions as in any sense a summary of the important issues raised by Olivi's commentary, since none of them explicitly mentions the most popular issue in the commission report and Catalan process, the destruction of the carnal church. Moreover, while there is no doubt about the importance of the first, second and fourth questions, the third seems almost ludicrously peripheral. Why, then, should John have submitted just these four? We will examine each in turn. The relevant passage from Olivi's commentary will be provided in the notes as each is introduced.

The First Question

The first question placed before the theologians contains, in the form reported by the *Allegationes*, all four of the elements listed above.[15] In the form considered by Silvestri, it contains only the first two elements and thus avoids Olivi's interpretation of the fifth and sixth periods.[16] Amazingly enough, the commission report does not include the Olivian passage targeted by this question. Thus, in submitting it to theologians, John was exploring one more suspect passage in the commentary. It proved worth his while. Silvestri's response finds Olivi's formulation wanting in two different ways. The first hinges on a rather marginal consideration and seems little more than a reservation about Olivi's wording. Olivi says that the "pontificatus Christi fuit primo stirpe vite evangelice et apostolice in Petro et aliis apostolis datus."[17] Silvestri protests that the pontificate was conceded to all Christians, not just to a discrete group. Peter eventually transferred his heredity to Clement, a Gentile, and did not feel bound to pass it on to one of the other disciples. Moreover, saying that Christ gave it to Peter and the disciples obscures the special place of Peter as head.[18] Silvestri's first and third sentences imply that his quarrel is with the idea that the pontificate was given to "Peter and the other apostles," which he thinks simultaneously too narrow and too broad; yet designation of Clement as a Gentile suggests that Silvestri is also dissatisfied with the word *stirps*.

So far the objection seems hard to take very seriously, but there is a serious issue buried within it. That issue emerges when Silvestri remarks that his point is proved by the fact that, when one of the faithful is elected pope or bishop, he is truly such without having to observe the apostolic life. "Otherwise no bishop could have any personal possessions, for that is an essential part of the apostolic life." Thus the first objection leads directly into Silvestri's second. He distrusts Olivi's assertion that the pontificate was altered to allow temporal possessions. This implies, he says, that the apostles had neither personal nor common possessions, which is heretical. The gospels, the book of Acts, and Paul's letters clearly say that they did. It is worth remembering that in November 1323 John XXII climaxed a long investigation by publishing *Cum inter nonnullos*, which proclaimed just this point. Silvestri seems to allude to this bull in the course of his attack.

The *Allegationes* attacks roughly the same elements in the first article but, since it includes more of the passage under consideration, has more material to work with. It too has difficulty with the word *stirps* and objects that the pontificate was given to Peter alone. As far as the commutation after Constantine is concerned, the author observes that if Christ originally ordained that the pontificate should be held by those without temporal possessions, there would have been no pontificate after Constantine, since neither the pope nor anyone else can change an ordination of Christ.[19] In other words, either the church has been without leadership for a millennium or Christ and the apostles had temporal possessions. The author predictably chooses the second alternative, citing *Cum inter nonnullos* and *Quia quorumdam* (1324). Later he adds *Gloriosam ecclesiam* as well.

Some people, the author notes, defend Olivi by saying that the commutation involves not the substance of the papacy but merely its way of life. He launches a barrage of counterarguments, three of which are worth mentioning here. First, the statement that Christ and the apostles had no temporal possessions is heretical in any case, because the Bible shows just the opposite. Second, this reading of Olivi would still credit him with the notion of commutation from a higher to a lower state, which the church does not sanction and which Olivi himself considers illegitimate. Third, Olivi plainly asserts that lack of temporal possessions *is* an essential part of the apostolic life. The author sees in all this an echo of the Waldensian, Donatist, and Manichaean heresies and an anticipation of the Sachsenhausen Appellation.

These judgments are not casually rendered. The author of the *Alle-*

gationes bases his interpretation not only on the specific passage given him but on other passages from the Apocalypse commentary, Olivi's Matthew commentary, and questions eight, nine, and fourteen of Olivi's *Questions on Evangelical Perfection*, all of which he cites.[20]

The Second Question

In the case of the second question, its relation to the commission report depends on whether one examines the version found in Silvestri or that found in the *Allegationes*. The commission report presents a long quotation from Olivi that includes the passage as considered by Silvestri and is precisely identical to the one considered by the *Allegationes*.[21] The commission finds no less than four heretical elements in it, including the statement, "Christ promised that when the spirit of truth comes, he will teach you all truth." The commission objects that Olivi's interpretation of that statement—he sees it as referring to the third age—is heretical because it suggests that the promise was not fulfilled at Pentecost.[22] Nevertheless, the commission passes no judgment on the earlier part of the passage given by Silvestri, in which Olivi speaks of knowing divine truth through gustatory and palpitative experience.[23]

That John himself thought that part worthy of attention is seen from a sermon he preached, probably sometime before the condemnation of Olivi's commentary. In it he attacked precisely these lines without naming the author, citing only "that evil, perverse and erroneous writing."[24] John saw Olivi's words as a denial of the limitations inherent in man's position as *viator*. Thus it touched upon a matter that seems to have been peculiarly important to him, one that led to his difficulties concerning the beatific vision.

Silvestri sees two errors in the passage. The first is essentially the one targeted in John's sermon: In predicting that all the wisdom of the incarnate word and all the power of God the Father will be known through palpitative and gustatory experience in the new age, Olivi is asserting that human beings will experience beatitude in this life. By saying this much, he errs in denying the need for faith and in suggesting that the infinite wisdom of God can be seen by finite minds within this finite world. Silvestri has no trouble finding passages like 1 Corinthians 13:9–13, 1 John 4:12, and Exodus 33:20 to support this criticism. He grants that special concessions were made to Moses and Paul, but only briefly. Olivi wishes to turn such exceptional knowledge into a general tendency of the new age. "He attributes to the entire sixth period of this life what was conceded transitorily to Moses and Paul as a special privilege." [25]

The second error in Olivi's statement is the same one already mentioned by the commission. Olivi seems to imply that Christ's promise to send the Holy Spirit is to be fulfilled in the sixth period rather than at Pentecost. Silvestri concludes that Olivi fits the reference in canon law to those pseudoprophets who, on the basis of their own conjecture and without any scriptural support, predict uncertain future events as if they were sure to occur. [26] He judges the statement under consideration to be false and erroneous.

The *Allegationes* presents a longer passage from Olivi that states the essence of the three ages in words taken largely from Joachim of Fiore, ending with the passage cited by Silvestri. It is, in fact, one of the most strikingly Joachite passages in the entire Apocalypse commentary. For the *Allegationes* it is reminiscent of the heresy of the Eternal Gospel, "in which it is said that there will be persons of some new religious order who will be given preference over all other orders in dignity and glory, and in whom the prophecy of Isaiah will be fulfilled." It also reflects the errors of those Tuscan rebels who fled to Sicily, an unsurprising connection since according to the *Allegationes* their views were in fact based upon Olivi's teaching. [27]

The author of the *Allegationes* objects to this passage for a number of reasons. First, the sort of vision anticipated in the sixth period implies that we will be able to dispense with faith and know the truth directly. Second, it reserves the gift of the Holy Spirit for the sixth period, ignoring the significance of Pentecost. Third, it suggests that spiritual brothers of the sixth period (i.e., those who follow the Franciscan rule) will receive the Holy Spirit more fully than did the apostles. Fourth, Olivi's notion of three ages, each appropriated to a member of the Trinity, divides the works of the Trinity in heretical fashion. The church recognizes only two *status*, those of the Old and New Testaments, and sees a single, undivided Trinity working in history, just as the church is single and undivided.

Here again the author of the *Allegationes* takes issue with Olivi's defenders. [28] They are reported here as saying that what is at issue is nothing more than a clearer vision of God's workings, not direct knowledge of God himself. There is, they say, nothing odd about God providing a bit more insight at a time of mass conversion. Moreover, the knowledge in question can be viewed as *gratia gratis data*, which does not imply that the recipient exceeds others in love and grace. The author replies that Olivi is obviously speaking of *gratia gratum faciens*. He thinks that denizens of the sixth period will excel all others both in knowledge and in love. Again, Olivi makes it clear that the sort of vision he anticipates does involve direct knowledge of God. The *Allegationes* also protests that, if the Holy Spirit is to be allotted on the basis of conversion needs, then the first period deserves a bigger share than the sixth. In addition, the author takes issue with specific elements in Olivi's idea of the coming great conversion.

To summarize the *Allegationes* in this way is to record particular aspects accurately while distorting the general emphases. The author returns continually to a single issue, Olivi's implication that those in the sixth period will surpass the apostles in spiritual gifts. The author finds this suggestion abhorrent because he sees it as an attack on the orderly descent of tradition, in which God gave knowledge of the Bible to the apostles and established in Peter a seat of authority for closer definition of that knowledge as it was developed throughout church history. He also rejects it because he views it as insufferable pride without basis in fact. He observes that over a century has passed since the days of Saint Francis, when Olivi says the sixth period began. In that time, no one in the Franciscan order or in any other order has come close to equalling the knowledge found in the doctors of the third period, or even of those like Anselm and Bernard in the fifth period, all of whom willingly acknowledged their inferiority to the apostles.[29]

The Third Question

When we arrive at the third question, we are beyond the point where the *Allegationes* can be used to supplement Silvestri, since the former contains only the first two questions; yet we do have a second source for this question, since it is considered in another response found in the same manuscript, immediately after Silvestri's reply to the four questions. Koch thinks that it too is by Silvestri, a claim hotly disputed by Pásztor. Here again Silvestri considers a more limited passage. He cites only Olivi's statement that "the number of the elect needed to complete the fabric of the supernal city is so preestablished that if one is corrupted through his own fault, another must be substituted so that the fabric will not remain incomplete."[30] The other judgment begins with what seems to be the theologian's marching orders, consisting of a transcription of Olivi's commentary on Revelation 3:11; a query about how to interpret precisely that part of it cited by Silvestri; and the words, "Reverend father, our lord wishes you to consider and write something about these things."[31] While the passage given here includes the same passage considered by Silvestri, it also bears within it a passage censured by the commission. In the latter, Olivi notes that, "just as the glory prepared for the synagogue and its pontiffs had they believed in Christ was transferred to the primitive church and its pastors, thus the glory prepared for the final church of the fifth period will be transferred because of its adultery to the elect of the sixth period. Thus in this book it is called Babylon the whore, to be damned around the beginning of the sixth period."[32] The commission sees these words as an attack on the present church.[33] Thus the passage given to the third, anonymous theologian overlaps with one censured by the commission, but it is not the censured part of it that the pope wants the theologian to consider. He is to pass judgment on a part of it ignored by the commission, the same part considered by Silvestri.

Silvestri begins by noting that, since the question of predestination is very complicated and theologians differ over it, he himself will say little. In fact, he says a great deal. He argues at some length that Olivi is right in saying the number of the elect is preset, but quite wrong in suggesting that one of the elect could possibly fall and lose his place to another. Such an idea is not merely wrong but "false and uncatholic."[34] Silvestri is, of course, quite right in taking exception to Olivi's statement. The real question is not why he tries to speak about such murky matters but why he spends so much time belaboring the obvious. Thus it is doubly amazing that, having done just that, Silvestri compromises his answer with an unexpected addendum. He has heard in logic classes, he says, that a hypothetical conditional proposition can be true even if its antecedent and consequent are false. For example, "If an ass flies, it has wings." "Thus perhaps it might be said that, considering the consequences and not the antecedent or consequent, this statement might be sustained, although it is not clear why he would want to speak in this way concerning a matter of faith, offering two categorical statements each of which is false, even though their consequences are true."[35]

This reply must have struck the pope as unsatisfying. The question now presented to the unidentified theologian can be read as John's response. The theologian is provided with Olivi's entire commentary on Revelation 3:11, then his attention is steered toward the same passage considered by Silvestri. He is explicitly asked whether it should be understood conditionally, as if it were his intention to say that, if one [of the elect should fall] through his own fault—assuming this to be possible, even though it is not—another would have to be substituted for him lest the fabric remain incomplete; or whether it should be understood modally, as if it had the sense that the number of the elect necessary to complete the fabric is prefixed in such a way that, if one should fall through his own fault, another must be subsituted.[36]

Apparently the unknown theologian is being asked to erase the pall of doubt left hanging over the matter by Silvestri. If so, he performs his task well. He begins with an ambiguous passage which seems to say that he does not see much importance in the question of whether Olivi's words should be taken conditionally or modally, because Olivi's sense and intention were always wrong anyway.[37] Shortly thereafter he appeals to canon law, Aristotle, Jerome, and Augustine in building an argument that one should read the *sancti* in a different way than one reads those suspected of heresy. The former should be treated to the kindliest possible interpretation. The latter should not. From this platform, he leaps to a conclusion which seems at best uncharitable:

> Because the aforesaid Brother Petrus Iohannis wrote many false, erroneous, and heretical things in his *Postilla super apocalipsim* (as is becoming plain to the whole church in the Roman Curia and elsewhere throughout diverse parts and nations of the world), I believe that the words of the aforesaid passage should be accepted and understood according to their perverse and corrupt sense, because whoever is at one time seen to be evil should always be considered such in that same genus of evil.[38]

Starting from this premise, the verdict seems a foregone conclusion: Olivi did mean to say that the elect could lose their election, and this sentiment contradicts the idea of divine certitude, "as I proved and demonstrated elsewhere in responding to the third question sent to me." Nevertheless, the author proceeds to make heavy weather of proving it again. He even allots some space to a rejection of the basic notion that the proposition would be true if taken as a conditional proposition along the lines of Paul's "If there is no resurrection of the dead, then Christ was not resurrected" (1 Corinthians 15:13). In the latter case the consequent follows from the antecedent necessarily, but in the former it does not. If one of the elect were, *per impossibile*, to fall, it would not necessarily follow that another impossibility must occur, namely that a *praescitus* must be substituted. "Thus this excuse is nothing." Moreover, the excuse "is founded in the snares of dialecticians, which are not so much snares as phantasms, that is, certain shadows and likenesses which immediately perish and dissolve." Sacred scripture deals with solid truths, not logical vanities. Along the way, the author makes extensive use of canon law. He concludes that it seems impossible to give Olivi's words any sound interpretation, "considering the aforesaid words themselves and considering the condition of the aforesaid brother Peter. And on this subject I have written a great deal elsewhere, which I have presented to Your Blessedness."

While it is not impossible that this anonymous writer could be Silvestri, it seems unlikely. He proceeds in a different way to a different conclusion, and his tone is dissimilar. Moreover, the two references to his previous contribution, far from confirming his identity as Silvestri, form the best argument against that identification. They simply do not fit Silvestri's comments.[39]

The Fourth Question

The fourth question is perhaps the most interesting of all: "Whether it is orthodox to say that Blessed Francis is the revealer of the evangelical life and rule to be propagated in the sixth and seventh periods and the highest observer of it after Christ and his mother."[40] Unfortunately Silvestri is our only source for it. Here we find a passage specifically addressed by the commission, and we find the commission levelling its fire at precisely the same idea Silvestri is later invited to consider. The commission report examines both the assertion later given to Silvestri (and presumably others) and Olivi's speculation concerning a possible resurrection. It finds the latter a "fantastic fiction" which Olivi would have been wiser to leave unmentioned, but its treatment of the former is relatively mild. Whereas in dealing with Olivi's exegesis of Revelation 10:1–3 the commission's solicitude for the apostles leads it to brand heretical the assertion that Francis is, after Christ, the first and principal founder of the sixth period, in the present case it says only that presentation of Francis as highest observer of the evangelical life and rule after Christ and his mother is, because of its apparent underestimation of the apostles, "temerarious, and we believe it to be false." Nothing is said about the idea of Francis as "renewer of the evangelical life and rule to be propagated in the sixth and seventh periods." There were, after all, two Franciscans on the commission.

Thus the fourth question may reflect a somewhat different concern than the first three. In the case of the first question, John was calling for consideration of a suspect passage which had been overlooked earlier. In asking theologians to consider the second and third questions, he was presenting passages which had been examined and censured by the commission, but he was focusing attention on hitherto undamaged statements within those passages, statements he viewed as bad theology. In posing the fourth question, he was inviting further comment on a statement that had been accorded negative comment by the commission, but in what John may have considered an unduly tentative manner. By 1324 he had little reason to be excessively solicitous about Franciscan sensibilities. Since the commission report, John had done little about the Olivi case, but in other respects he had been a busy man. He had launched a frontal assault on the Franciscan claim that the rule and life of the order was identical with that observed by Christ and imposed on the disciples. The Franciscans had reacted with anguish and with more objections than John cared to hear. By 1324 his theological advisors must have been aware that John would not object to seeing minorite feathers ruffled.

Silvestri begins cautiously. The passage, he observes, "contains some elements that are not lacking in the ability to provoke anxiety about dangerous error." When Olivi says that Francis is the revealer of the evangelical life to be propogated in the sixth and seventh periods, he "promises future events as if they were certain."[41] What was said in the second article about such conjectures applies here as well. In this case it is not only a matter of stating uncertain things as if they were certain, but of asserting improbable and even unbelievable things as if they were inevitable. The idea that the apostles observed the evangelical life and rule less fully than Francis did is one that "reason flees and probable belief casts aside." Again Silvestri refers to what was said in the second question, this time concerning the possibility of a more perfect state in the future.

So far, Silvestri has merely observed that the fourth passage seems to imply some of the errors already attacked in dealing with the second. He could stop there, he says, "but lest I seem to retreat from my earlier statement that some elements in this passage are not lacking in the ability to provoke anxiety about pernicious error, I shall speak the truth as my limited intelligence allows, for it is sinful to remain silent, especially in a matter like this one." By this time, the pope can expect that something really damaging is on the way. His expectation will not be disappointed. Silvestri suggests that Olivi's prediction concerning an apostolic life to be propogated in the sixth and seventh periods "implies clearly enough that there is still another gospel to come—and that is precisely the error condemned as heretical by the church in the time of [Pope] Alexander—for it follows that the law of Christ taught to us in the gospels is not perfect and thus cannot lead men to eternal life." This is, of course, "a manifest error and contrary to holy scripture."[42] Here again we find the suggestion that Olivi's commentary revives the heresy of the Eternal Gospel.

Silvestri now turns to another inherent difficulty. Perhaps someone will reply, he conjectures, "that the life of the evangelical rule to be propagated in the sixth and seventh periods is to be understood as the rule of the Brothers Minor that blessed Francis composed, and not a future new gospel." Such an objection "seems to be worth nothing." In the first place, it is nonsense to say that Jesus and Mary observed Francis's rule when they lived twelve hundred years before Francis wrote it. In the second place, the Franciscan rule is no more evangelical than the Augustinian or Benedictine rules. All of them observe the gospel counsels and precepts. If one should reply that the Franciscan rule is nevertheless more evangelical because it renounces common as well as personal possessions and the others merely renounce the latter, such a statement is false in one respect and heretical in another. It is false inasmuch as the Franciscans do have common possessions. They have houses, gardens, books, liturgical paraphenalia, and other things that they not only maintain but buy and sell. It is heretical inasmuch as the gospels, Acts of the Apostles, and *sancti* all clearly state that the apostles had common possessions. Olivi is not the only target here. Silvestri has entered into the running argument between John and the order on the nature of Franciscan (and apostolic) poverty. This fact is made all the more obvious by his decision to cite *Ad conditorem canonum* in support of his first point and *Cum inter nonnullos* to shore up his second.[43]

Silvestri now turns to the second part of the statement, the claim that Francis is the greatest observer of the evangelical life after Christ and his mother. He calls this idea "very absurd and erroneous." Later he terms it "blasphemous." It "is repugnant to the ears of the faithful" that Francis should be termed greater than the disciples and apostles. Nor can Olivi's opinion be salvaged by saying that the apostles are actually included in it, the members being implied by mention of the head, for by expressly including Mary he clearly implies exclusion of the apostles. Nor is it even legitimate to suggest an equality between Francis and the apostles. Biblical testimony—and Silvestri is more than ready to provide it—clearly states that the apostles were not only greater than Francis but greater than any succeeding saints.

This might seem enough to put the Franciscans in their place, but
Silvestri is not through yet. He goes on to argue that the martyrs, too, are
to be preferred to Francis, since it is a greater thing to achieve martyrdom
in desire and act than to achieve it in desire alone. Nor would he dare to
prefer Francis to Mary Magdalen. Anyone who did so would be "temerarious and insane, I would even say blasphemous." In fact, "I do not
doubt that many confessors were of no less merit than Francis, and no less
useful to the church." Who, indeed, would dream of comparing him with
Ambrose, Augustine, Gregory, or Jerome? Certainly Francis did great service to the church by instituting the Franciscan rule and order, but there
are other orders around that are no less useful. Thus it is "temerarious,
insane and blasphemous" to prefer Francis to all other saints.[44]

Silvestri's judgment seems a thoroughgoing repudiation of Franciscan
pretentions; yet hidden away in the middle of it is an interesting con-
cession. In the process of affirming the apostles' superiority, Silvestri cites
an array of New Testament passages praising them, noting that the Bible
says nothing similar about Francis. "And if in the material written about
him (*in gestis vel legenda eius*) some similar or even greater things are
found, it is pious to believe such writings, but not as if they were necessary
for faith or salvation, as it is necessary for salvation or faith to believe in
the truth of those things written in sacred scripture concerning the holy
apostles."[45] This comment is more important than its brevity might suggest, as we will see in a moment.

The Question of Accuracy

How well did these theologians read Olivi? Modern historians have
tended to assume that they did so very poorly. Edith Pásztor, the scholar
who has looked most carefully at these questions, argues that Silvestri neither understood Olivi's thought nor attempted to do so. She feels that
Silvestri's observations on the four questions are marginal, concerning
strictly juridical matters, without any attempt to look beyond to doctrinal,
historical, and ecclesiological dimensions. He offers no valid alternative to
Olivi's views on the situation of the church. He does not even bother to
investigate the context of the passages judged by him. The two men work
on entirely different levels. Silvestri's approach is formal and juridical,
while Olivi concentrates on essential questions of the entire church, outside any juridical formulation.[46] In dealing with Silvestri's reply to the

fourth question, Pásztor remarks that Silvestri simply lacks the sensitivity to appreciate the Franciscan spirit that motivated Olivi. His comments thus remain purely external when he treats matters like Francis, the order, and evangelical poverty.[47] The second writer in the Vatican manuscript, who presents an opinion on the third question, makes no better showing. Suspicious and hostile toward Olivi, he refuses to read the question in context, even though he has the entire passage before him.[48]

Such a complaint can hardly be made of the *Allegationes*. That writer reads the first article in context and sees its ecclesiastical implications. Moreover, he cites a series of other Olivian comments from the Apocalypse and Matthew commentaries and from the eighth, ninth, and fourteenth of the *Questions on Evangelical Perfection*. Yet Pásztor feels that he also misreads Olivi. In attacking the first article he continually sees Olivi's church of the fifth period as the Roman church and that of the sixth period as the spiritual Franciscans. In considering evangelical poverty he oversimplifies the Olivian position, omitting important qualifications.[49] In his judgment on the second question he misreads Olivi's view in a similar way, affirming, for example, that Olivi thought those in the sixth period would receive the Holy Spirit more fully than the apostles did.[50]

It is hardly surprising that the three theologians should show such insensitivity when the man who requested their help was equally insensitive. Pásztor remarks that Olivi's Franciscan profession of faith and eschatological vision "remained substantially extraneous, unappreciated, uncomprehended by the pope."[51]

There is much to be said for Pásztor's assertion that all three theologians misread Olivi, just as the commission before them had. It is true that they simplify his position, present what they see as valid inferences from his argument as if they were Olivi's own assertions, and anachronistically treat Olivi as if he were writing in the early 1320s rather than in the late 1290s. In the final analysis, however, it seems equally true that they generally see Olivi's drift and react to genuine differences between their shared view of the church and Olivi's, just as the commission did. They are essentially Augustinians in their view of church history. They feel that once the structure of church government was set and Pentecost had taken place, Christendom embarked on a course that would carry it through to judgment day. They do not expect the church to progress in a way that will dramatically change human knowledge, organizational structures, or the quality of everyday life. Olivi seems to expect just that. They think Christ will guide the papacy and keep it from betraying the gospel, while Olivi expects the pope to turn on the gospel by attacking the Franciscan rule in the near future. They think the apostles had possessions in common and so do the Franciscans, but Olivi thinks just the opposite. They think Francis is simply one more saint and that the character and existence of his order depends entirely upon papal approval. Olivi thinks Francis is the angel of the sixth seal who ushers in a new age, and the validity of his rule lies ultimately in the fact that it is uniquely the life and rule of Christ and his disciples. These are not minor differences. It is hardly surprising that John's theological advisors perceived them and, having perceived them, rejected them.

Nor is there much point in objecting that John's advisors failed to appreciate the spirit in which Olivi wrote, that they were insensitive to his Franciscan piety, as if they had somehow failed to recognize the *genre*. They were aware of the *genre*. They were dealing with a Bible commentary, an exegetical work. As such it fell within the purview of theologians. That is the significance of Silvestri's remark about Franciscan *legenda*. His point is essentially that the image of Francis as angel of the sixth seal is acceptable when encountered in Bonaventure's *Legenda maior*, as long as the reader acknowledges Bonaventure's intent. The Seraphic Doctor, Silvestri implicitly suggests, is offering a pious, devotional application of the passage, not its literal meaning, and the reader should accept his words accordingly. Olivi, however, is expositing scripture and, in the process, telling us what the passage really means. He wants to be taken seriously, and Silvestri is doing just that. Nor is Silvestri the first to do so. We have seen that, beginning with the anonymous initial consultant, those commissioned to examine the commentary attacked it not only because it seemed subversive, but also because it seemed out of step with the grand exegetical tradition inherited through Richard of St. Victor.

Notes

1. Lambert, *Franciscan Poverty*, 223–45, provides an excellent summary. Marino Damiata, *Guglielmo d'Ockham: Povertà e potere* (Firenze, 1978), 1:305–89 presents the story fully and intelligently.
2. Lambert, *Franciscan Poverty*, 237f.
3. Paris Bibl. Nat. lat. 4190, 40r–49v, cited hereafter as *Allegationes*.
4. See Chapter 9, note 28 above.
5. These defenders are described (40v) as *magni viri et docti*. Koch, "Prozess," 311f., argues that the *Allegationes* takes issue with another, milder opinion

submitted by Guilelmus Petrus de Godino, OP, cardinal bishop of Sabina, who was involved in the 1317–18 process against Ubertino da Casale, which itself involved Olivi's Apocalypse commentary. Koch suggests that Guilelmus was swayed by Ubertino's interpretation of the commentary. Pásztor, "Polemiche," 408, dismisses this view; yet we are then left with the problem of why the author of the *Allegationes* says (41r) he will not deal with a certain point because "ista blasphemia non fuit per dominum Sabinensem tacta nec excusata."

6. *Allegationes*, 40r.

7. Ibid., 40r, 44r.

8. Rome Vat. Arm. seg. XXXI, t. 42, 82v–91v, cited hereafter as Silvestri.

9. Silvestri, 88v.

10. On Francesco see Pásztor, "Polemiche," 391f.

11. Koch, "Prozess," 311; Pásztor, "Polemiche," 399, 405.

12. *Allegationes*, 42r, has all these elements, whereas Silvestri, 42v, has only the first two.

13. Thus Silvestri. *Allegationes* includes no explicit question but gives a much longer passage from Olivi outlining not only this much but his entire Joachite distinction between the three ages as found in *Lectura*, 229–31.

14. This article and the following one are taken from Silvestri, since the *Allegationes*, apparently mutilated, covers only the first two. The Rome MS actually deals with this article twice, leading to the debate between Koch and Pásztor as to whether we find one or two authors here.

15. *Allegationes*, 42r. The passage quoted is from *Lectura*, 51f.: "Consimiliter autem pontificatus Christi fuit primo stirpe vite evangelice et apostolice in Petro et apostolis datus, ac deinde utiliter et rationabiliter fuit ad statum habentem temporalia commutatus, saltem a tempore Constantini usque ad finem quinti status. Pro quanto autem multi sanctorum pontificum fuerunt regulares et in suis scriptis et in habitu sui cordibus preferentes paupertatem Christi et apostolorum, omnibus temporalibus ecclesie datis, pro tanto quasi usque ad duplum preeminuit primus ordo sacerdotii apostolici. Congruum est ergo quod in fine omnino redeat et assurgat ad ordinem primum, ad quem spectat iure primogeniture et perfectionis maioris et Christo conformioris. Ad istum autem reditum valde, quamvis per accidens, cooperabitur non solum multiplex imperfectio in possessione et dispensatione temporalium ecclesie in pluribus comprobata, sed etiam multiplex enormitas superbie et luxurie et simoniarum et causidicationum et ligitiorum et fraudum et rapinarum ex ipsis occasionaliter accepta, ex quibus circa finem quinti temporis a planta pedis usque ad verticem est fere tota ecclesia infecta et confusa et quasi nova Babilon effecta."

16. Silvestri, 42v. Silvestri considers only the following words: "Consimiliter autem pontificatus Christi fuit primo stirpe vite evangelice et apostolice in Petro et apostolis datus, ac deinde utiliter et rationabiliter fuit ad statum habentem temporalia commutatus."

17. *Lectura*, 51.

18. Silvestri, 82v.

19. *Allegationes*, 41v–42v. He makes the same point over and over in attacking six individual parts of the quotation. He does not attack the final part of the

Olivian passage dealing with the decay of the fifth period, but that is perhaps explained by his comment that the passage contains "sex errores seu hereses et una blasphemia falsa et detestabilis contra ecclesiam generalem et contra Romanam ecclesiam specialiter," but "quia ista blasphemia non fuit per dominum Sabinensem tacta nec excusata" he will say nothing of it except that it is false, defamatory, and likely to encourage disobedience toward clerics and laymen alike as well as lack of reverence toward the Roman church. For the "lord Sabina" see note 5 above.

20. *Allegationes*, 43r–43v, 44v.

21. It is equivalent to *Lectura*, 229–31: "Significatur etiam per hoc proprium donum et singularis proprietas tertii status mundi sub sexto statu ecclesie inchoandi et spiritui sancto per quandam antonomasiam appropriati. Sicut enim in primo statu seculi ante Christum studium fuit patribus enarrare magna opera domini inchoata ab origine mundi, in secundo vero statu a Christo usque ad tertium statum cura fuit filiis querere sapientiam misticarum rerum et misteria occulta a generationibus seculorum, sic in tertio nil restat nisi ut psallamus et iubilemus deo laudantes eius opera magna et eius multiformem sapientiam et bonitatem in suis operibus et scripturarum sermonibus clare manifestatam. Sicut etiam in primo tempore exhibuit se deus pater ut terribilem et metuendum, unde tunc claruit eius timor, sic in secundo exhibuit se deus filius ut magistrum et reservatorem et ut verbum expressivum sapientie sui patris. Ergo in tertio tempore spiritus sanctus exhibebit se ut flammam et fornacem divini amoris et ut cellarium spiritualis ebrietatis et ut apothecam divinorum aromatum et spiritualium unctionum et unguentorum et ut tripudium spiritualium iubilationum et iocunditatum, per quam non solum simplici intelligentia sed etiam gustativa et palpativa experientia videbitur omnis veritas sapientie verbi dei incarnati et potentie dei patris. Christus enim promisit quod, 'cum venerit ille spiritus veritatis, docebit vos omnem veritatem,' et, 'ille me clarificabit,' et cetera." The passage is heavily dependent on Joachim, *Expositio in Apocalypsim*, 84r–85v.

22. Commission report, art. 13.

23. Silvestri, 84r. The passage as Silvestri judges it asks whether that time (described by Silvestri as the sixth period rather than the third age) "non solum simplici intelligentia sed palpitativa et gustativa experientia videbitur omnis sapientia verbi incarnati dei et potentie dei patris, quia Christus promisit quod cum venerit ille spiritus veritatis docebit vos omnem veritatem."

24. Full sermon published in Pásztor, "Polemiche," 417–24, passage in question on p. 418.

25. Silvestri, 84v.

26. Silvestri, 85r: "Ad hoc etiam pertinet quod alibi dicit canon secundum tropologiam pseudo prophetas eos debemus accipere qui aliter verba scripturarum accipiunt quam spiritus sanctus sonat. Et eos divinos dicunt qui coniectura mentis sue incerta futurorum quasi vera pronuntiant absque divinorum auctoritate verborum."

27. *Allegationes*, 45v. The commission report does not draw connections between Olivi and the Eternal Gospel, but the Catalan process does so in art. 1, 2, 4, 35 and 41. The *Allegationes* also mentions the Catafriges (described by Augustine in the *Liber de heresibus*) and the Manichaeans.

28. *Allegationes*, 47r–49r.

29. *Allegationes*, 48r. Here again he cites the *Quaestiones de perfectione evangelica* in establishing Olivi's intention.

30. Silvestri, 85v: "Utrum catholice possit dici quod numerus electus ad implenda fabrica civitatis superne sit sic prefixus quod si unus per culpam suam curruat alterum oporterit substitui ne illa fabrica remaneat incompleta." See *Lectura*, 247.

31. Arm. XXXI, 42, 91v. The passage, from *Lectura*, 245–47, begins with the words "Tene quod habes," partway through Olivi's exegesis of Rev. 3:11, and extends all the way to "et finalis perfectionis ipsius," his final words concerning 3:12.

32. See *Lectura*, 246.

33. Commission report, art. 19.

34. Silvestri, 85v–86r.

35. Silvestri, 86r.

36. Arm. XXXI, 42, 91v.

37. Arm. XXXI, 42, 90r: "Ad premissa quesita rispondeo quod sive illa verba 'Notandum tamen quod per hoc verbum, etc.' sint intelligenda conditionaliter sive modaliter, quia in hoc nullam vim facio, semper sensus et intentio fr. Petri Iohannis, cuius illa verba esse censentur, fuit falsa et erronea ut mihi videtur, salvo semper iudicio vestre sanctitatis."

38. Ibid., 90r: "Et quia fr. Petrus Iohannis predictus multa falsa et erronea ac heretica scripsit in sua postilla super Apocalipsim, prout iam incipit innotescere toti ecclesie fidelium in romana curia et alibi per diversas mundi partes et nationes, secundum suum sensum perversum et corruptum, quia qui semel malus in eodem genere malitie, semper presumitur malus."

39. See the more extensive argument for this point offered by Pásztor, "Polemiche," 398–401.

40. Silvestri, 86v: "Utrum catholice possit dici quod beatus Franciscus sit evangelice vite et regule sexto et septimo tempore propagande revelator et summus post Christum et eius matrem observator." See *Lectura*, 416. Note that Olivi says *renovator* rather than *revelator*.

41. Silvestri, 86v.

42. Ibid. Silvestri supports his point with a barrage of scriptural citations.

43. Ibid., 86v–87v.

44. Ibid., 87v–88v.

45. Ibid., 88r: "Et si in gestis vel legenda eius legantur aliqua hiis similia vel maiora, credere talibus scripturis est pium, sed non de necessitate fidei vel salutis, sicut est de necessitate salutis et fidei credere vera esse que leguntur in scripturis sacris de sanctis apostolis."

46. "Giovanni," 97f.

47. "Polemiche," 406.

48. "Giovanni," 99

49. Ibid., 99–108.

50. Ibid., 108f. See *Allegationes*, 46r.

51. "Polemiche," 416.

II. The Significance of the Condemnation

Having come thus far, we might pause for a moment to look back over our route. It seems particularly useful to restate some earlier conclusions.

Olivi's Debt to Tradition

We have seen that Olivi can be located within a particular school of exegesis. It was, in fact, the dominant school at Paris in the thirteenth century, and was closely related to the mainstream of exegetical tradition extending back through Richard of St. Victor to Bede. According to this view, the book of Revelation is divided into seven visions, some of which cover the entire scope of church history. The second vision (the opening of the seven seals), the third (the seven angels with trumpets), and occasionally the first vision (the letters to seven churches) or even the fifth (the seven angels with vials), can be interpreted as miniature tours of church history.

It follows that church history itself is seen as divided into seven periods. There is a first period of persecution by the Jews; a second of persecution by the Roman empire; a third of heresy; a fourth of hypocrites; a fifth of the precursors of Antichrist; a sixth of Antichrist himself; and a seventh comprising the short interval between the death of Antichrist and the final judgment.

Up to a point, Olivi is representative of this school. He too divides the book of Revelation into seven visions and sees it as prophesying seven periods of church history. His periods are, on the whole, similar. Only the fifth, sixth, and seventh are different. Even here the change is very small, though very important. Other members of this school saw the fifth period as that of the precursors of Antichrist. Olivi sees it in somewhat similar terms. It is a time in which the church becomes big, wealthy, and powerful, but in the process becomes corrupt. By the end of the fifth period,

Olivi says, the church is corrupt from head to toe and has turned, as it were, into a new Babylon. We should take both of these images quite seriously.

When other members of this school deign to place themselves within the seven periods at all, they choose the dawn of the fifth period. Olivi places himself at the end of the fifth period, so late in fact that the sixth has been growing up within it for nearly a century. Others in this school see the sixth period as the time of Antichrist. Olivi thinks it *will be* that, but it is already a time of reform ushered in by Saint Francis. This reform is combatted by lingering elements of the corrupt fifth period. It will be combatted even more bitterly by the Antichrist, but the reform will eventually triumph, ushering in the seventh period of peace and contemplation. In other words, for Olivi the sixth period is a hinge of sorts on which all of later church history turns. It is organically related to the fifth period in much the same way it was for the other commentators. Antichrist in the sixth period is the culmination of a long decline already underway in the fifth period; but because Olivi also sees the sixth period as a time of reform, he can see it as organically related to the seventh period, which grows out of it. It takes little reflection to see the implications of this difference. Because Olivi places himself in the sixth period, sees Francis as founder of that period, and sees that period as one of renewal which will blossom into a seventh period of peace and enlightenment, he is more confident in his description of both the sixth and seventh periods. He knows what the new age will be like because it is already appearing around him.

This leads us to a second implication. Olivi's view allows him to project Francis, his rule, and his order into the book of Revelation in a way impossible for other commentators. The angel of the sixth seal is literally a prophecy of Saint Francis, and when Olivi exposits this verse he speaks not only of Francis but also of his subsequent followers. Francis's apocalyptic significance extends to encompass his rule and disciples.

This, in turn, leads to a third implication. Because Olivi places himself within a sixth period of renewal and turns the Franciscan life as he understands it into a criterion for recognizing the renewal and the new age produced by it, he is tempted to invest current Franciscan battles with heavy apocalyptic significance. Other commentators do not have this focus. Because they do not give the Franciscan movement major apocalyptic significance, their discussion of contemporary evil does not center on specifically Franciscan issues. They do locate the corruption to some extent. When they speak of contemporary failings, they are apt to mention *prelati*;

yet however much they may attack the *prelati* of their time, they prefer to avoid suggesting that the prelate of prelates, the pope himself, might be involved. Olivi's attitude is very different. The coming apocalyptic confrontation will be about issues that currently plague the order, particularly heterodox Aristotelianism and the practice of poverty. Moreover, Olivi takes the temptation of Antichrist very seriously. If it is to be the *dernier cri* in temptations, then the elect must face it without the support of familiar institutions, indeed opposed by these institutions. They must be prepared to defend theological orthodoxy against university masters, Franciscan poverty against Franciscan leaders, and both against the pope, or at least against the man who has usurped the papal seat in Rome. Such an expectation carries Olivi far beyond anything to be found in contemporary Franciscan Apocalypse commentaries.

We have seen that in some ways Olivi is closer to Saint Bonaventure than to previous exegetes. In the *Collationes in hexaemeron* Bonaventure places himself in the sixth period, describes it as a time of both renewal and Antichrist, and sees it as anticipating a seventh period of peace and illumination during which the church militant will be conformed to the church triumphant so far as possible. He also gives Francis a major role in the inauguration of the coming age. Thus Bonaventure, like Olivi, is in a position to invest current Franciscan problems with apocalyptic significance. These are important similarities. They suggest that to some extent Olivi's divergence from other Franciscan exegetes could be seen less as innovation than as a defense of the Bonaventuran view of history against the more traditional exegetical perspective. Seen in this way, Olivi becomes Bonaventure's most loyal disciple. Nonetheless, Olivi's thoughts on the impending temptation suggest that we cannot simply see him in this way. There is no trace in Bonaventure of Olivi's pessimism about future papal malfeasance. Nor does Bonaventure make Franciscan poverty a central issue as Olivi does. If Bonaventure seems deeply concerned about any single issue, it is heterodox Aristotelianism.

These are important differences, particularly when taken in combination. When he chose to agonize over heterodox Aristotelianism, Bonaventure picked an enemy that would soon be attacked by ecclesiastical authorities. Thus the Bonaventuran temptation of Antichrist never materialized. On the other hand, when Olivi forecast that the pope and Franciscan leaders would soon reject true Franciscan poverty—by which, of course, he meant his own notion of Franciscan poverty—he was offering a remarkably accurate prediction of what did in fact occur within two decades. Thus when Olivi completed his Apocalypse commentary and cast it out upon the Franciscan world, it floated just below the surface like a mine for close to twenty years until, in the year 1318, Pope John XXII ran straight into it.

The Significance of the Condemnation

That brings us to the condemnation. The most vulnerable elements in Olivi's Apocalypse commentary were the ones that separated it from other commentaries and from Bonaventure. These were, first, his willingness to take the poverty issue as it was currently being debated in his order and turn it into a criterion for determining whose side one was on in the great apocalyptic struggle; and, second, his prediction that those in positions of authority would be on the wrong side. The 1319 commission report, the Catalan process, and the individual theologians commented at length on these elements. Had they stopped there, they would have managed to condemn Olivi without touching the rest of his order; but they did not stop there. They went on to attack two other ideas. First, they rejected Olivi's view of Saint Francis as an apocalyptic figure heralding a new age. Second, they denied Olivi's identification of the Franciscan rule with the life observed by Christ and imposed on the disciples. In rejecting these two ideas, Olivi's critics extended the attack in a very significant way. One can see why they did so. They were concerned about safeguarding papal power. They saw that if Francis and his rule were literally apocalyptic events through which God had acted to restore the same evangelical life practiced by Christ and his disciples, then the pope had no more authority over the Franciscan rule than he had over the gospel. This was not exactly the standard view among John and his advisors. As far as they were concerned, the Franciscan rule, like any other rule, gained its legitimacy from papal approval and could be changed or abolished by papal decision. The point was such an important one that it was included in the sentence read to the first four spirituals burned at the stake in 1318.[1]

Unfortunately, by extending the attack in this way, the commission had moved from propositions held only by Olivi to ideas endorsed by other, more respectable Franciscans. That presented a problem. They had not been given a mandate to condemn the whole order. The obvious solution was to argue that Olivi and the rest were using the same words, but Olivi meant something different by them. This approach worked fairly well when applied to the image of Francis as an apocalyptic figure inaugurating a new age. Despite the unsettling parallel between Olivi and Bonaventure, one could legitimately argue that they were really saying different things. Here the necessary escape clause was provided by Francesco Silvestri. Silvestri suggested, in effect, that it was one thing for a preacher or hagiographer to make extravagant claims about Francis and quite another for a theologian to insist on them as the literal meaning of scripture. The implication was clear. Bonaventure's *Legenda maior* was orthodox, but Olivi's commentary was not. That was a relatively easy point for Franciscans to absorb. Extant Apocalypse commentaries suggest that by the early fourteenth century they had already come to much the same conclusion. The notion of Francis as angel of the sixth seal was seen as useful *pro collatione*, but Revelation 7 : 2 referred literally to Christ.

The adjustment would prove harder in the other area, identification of the Franciscan rule with the life observed by Christ and imposed on the disciples. Here too we find a case in which Olivi meant something different. The 1319 commission recognized as much. It distinguished between an unacceptable, Olivian interpretation and an acceptable one held by everyone else. Others proved less conciliatory. Silvestri, writing in 1324, did not even attempt to do with this problem what he had been so careful to do with the other one. He offered a blunt rejection of the proposition as all Franciscans understood it, not simply as Olivi understood it. Silvestri's way of dealing with the matter is evidence that the pope and the Franciscan order were already enmeshed in a battle over just this point. The dispute proved so nonnegotiable that, around three years after Silvestri wrote, the minister general of the order would find it necessary to flee from the papal court into exile.

The Condemnation and the Poverty Controversy

These observations inevitably raise a question that has fascinated historians for some time: how was the condemnation of Olivi's commentary related to John's assault on the Franciscan understanding of apostolic poverty? Viewed from a slightly different angle, it is the question of why the condemnation process developed as it did, with a flurry of activity in 1318–19 followed by apparent inactivity until around 1324. The most widely discussed theory, if not the most widely accepted one, has been Koch's argument that the condemnation process began as a weapon in John's attack on the spiritual Franciscans, and John's assault on the Franciscan view of poverty began as a weapon in the condemnation process. In brief, John saw in 1318 that condemnation of the commentary was a necessary element in his attempt to suppress the spirituals, since it was becoming— perhaps had long since become—an important ideological support for their protest. Thus he ordered the commission to do its work. On the whole, the commission did just what John wanted it to do, but he saw in its report evidence that a thoroughgoing condemnation of the commentary was hindered by what he viewed as a disturbing overlap with the accepted Franciscan self-understanding. The problem was clearest in the commission's reaction to article twenty-two. The commission recognized that Olivi's identification of the Franciscan rule with the life of Christ and his disciples was one of the linchpins of his thought, but it also realized that the identification was shared by the rest of his order and was apparently affirmed by *Exiit qui seminat*. The commission solved its dilemma by assuming that, whatever Nicholas III and Olivi may have meant, they must have meant different things. John was dissatisfied with such unclarity. He decided that, before he could complete the Olivi process, he must do something about the theory of Franciscan poverty. That is precisely what he did next. Only when he settled this matter did he turn back to the Olivi question.

Recent studies have been rather hard on Koch,[2] and some of their objections seem justified. There is something odd about the idea that the entire battle between John and the Franciscans over evangelical poverty should have been, in essence, a flanking movement in the war on Olivi. Moreover, as Thomas Turley rightly indicates, a substantial body of criticism (much of it Dominican) already had been directed against the Franciscan understanding of poverty by the time John read the commission report. While this criticism was understandably hesitant to attack *Exiit qui seminat* as well, the connection was hard to miss. There is even some evidence that John was attempting to secure a Franciscan change of heart on this matter as early as 1319.[3] Finally, there is the inconvenient delay between John's bulls regarding Franciscan poverty and the one condemning Olivi's Apocalypse commentary. If John's aim was to clear the deck for a condemnation of the commentary, why did he wait more than two years after *Cum inter nonnullos* before condemning it?

Nevertheless, unacceptable as Koch's explanation may be in its pristine form, it is attractive in a somewhat attenuated version. Whatever thought John may have given the matter of Franciscan poverty before he read the 1319 commission report, he could hardly have read article twenty-two of that report without recognizing that the problem lay not only with Olivi but with the entire Franciscan self-understanding and ultimately with *Exiit qui seminat*. Thus it is quite possible that the report encouraged him to redirect his gaze away from Olivi to the order and to *Exiit*. Once that alteration was made, his activities were no longer merely a function of the Olivi process. Still, it is not impossible that, in the interests of tidiness, he held up the Olivi process while this particular aspect of it was being settled.

In fact, after the flurry of activity in 1318–19, John's interest in Olivi may have waned. Long since dead, Olivi was of concern only insofar as he had a live following. In 1317 and 1318 John had moved resolutely against that following on several fronts. Perhaps in the period immediately after 1318, thinking that the spiritual Franciscans had been neutralized, he was less motivated to continue the offensive. He must have been aware that his victory was not a complete one. Shortly after the burnings at Marseilles, a number of French spirituals followed the example already offered by their Italian brethren and continued their defiance as fugitives. By the end of 1319 we find the inquisitor, Michel Le Moine, writing to the inquisitor of Tuscany with the announcement that certain of the friars who had abjured at Avignon have since returned to their error and are at large.[4] Better yet, we have a report of the farewell note some of them left behind.[5] They announce that they are leaving "not the order but the walls; not the habit but the cloth; not the faith but its shell; not the church but the blind synagogue; not a shepherd but a devourer." Moreover, they predict that after John's death "we and our companions who are now suffering persecution by Christ's adversaries will come forth and bear away the victory." The inquisition still had a great deal to do after 1318.[6]

Nevertheless, even with a righteous remnant of spirituals still in action, John may have felt little need at first to complete the Olivi process with a formal condemnation. Such a move would have had little effect on the rebels themselves, since they already had placed themselves outside ecclesiastical authority. Moreover, John had a great deal on his plate after 1319. He was edging toward confrontation with the leaders of the Franciscan order and with Ludwig the Bavarian. Why, then, should his interest have been rekindled after 1322? The answer is not entirely clear, but there are some possibilities. In the first place, he would have begun to realize that the spirituals were receiving a degree of lay protection in southern France, Spain, and Italy. While a condemnation of the Apocalypse commentary would hardly impress Franciscan fugitives, it might have some effect on those who aided and abetted them. At the same time, the growing problem with Ludwig of Bavaria began to assume Olivian overtones. The *Allegationes* explicitly acknowledges the similarity between Olivi's thought and the Sachsenhausen Appellation of May 1324. This connection must have given John additional reason to complete the Olivi process.

Nevertheless, if we follow Pásztor in seeing John's 1322 decision to reserve examination and judgment for himself as our first evidence of a new stage in the process,[7] it is dangerous to put too much weight on Ludwig and the Sachsenhausen Appellation as explanatory principles. Perhaps the real explanation lies in an inversion of Koch's theory. Once John attacked the Franciscan understanding of evangelical poverty and found the Franciscans loath to change their opinion, the Olivi process became a weapon in that struggle. A condemnation of Olivi's commentary, which offered that understanding in perhaps its most extreme form, seemed all the more attractive. John could now use Olivi against the order in much the same way the order had once used him against the spirituals. The renewed assault on Olivi could be used to underline the heretical implications of accepted Franciscan doctrine on evangelical poverty. These are questions that might be answered more satisfactorily if we had the condemnation, but we do not.

The Impact on Franciscan Exegesis: Pierre Auriol

Whatever role the condemnation may have played in the developing struggle between John XXII and leaders of the Franciscan order, it represented at the same time an attack on a specific piece of scholarly exegesis. One might ask how this attack affected subsequent commentaries. There are four relevant commentaries: those by Pierre Auriol (1319), Nicholas of Lyre (1329), Poncio Carbonnel (1329?), and Henry of Cossey (1333).[8] If we had only the first three, we might conclude that the Olivi process served as a profound cautionary tale for future exegetes. After reading Henry, we are not quite sure.

The most striking thing about Pierre and Nicholas is that they adopt the basic approach laid out by Alexander Minorita close to a century earlier, an approach that was virtually ignored during the second half of the thirteenth century. They see the Apocalypse as a successive narrative of church history. Pierre argues explicitly for the superiority of the Alexandrine scheme over other current strategies.[9] The intention of the Apocalypse, he says, is to predict "all the notable sufferings, changes, persecutions, and novelties occurring to the church, and not just the persecution under Antichrist." Given the magnitude of the task and the brevity of the text, why should God waste space repeating the same general pattern over and over? "It does not seem rational that what is said in chapter seven should refer to the end of the world, and yet at the beginning of the eighth we're back to the early church!"

There is no reason to assume that Pierre is being ingenuous when he defends his choice as hermeneutically superior, but neither should it pass unnoticed that he is writing in 1319, the same year his order condemned Olivi's commentary at the Marseilles general chapter and the papal commission submitted its damning report. One might ask whether Pierre was aware of these events and took them as a warning. What sort of warning, though? The view of the Apocalypse as seven largely recapitulative visions can hardly be termed Olivi's invention. Why would Pierre have seen it as something to avoid on Olivi's account? There is little evidence that he should have, but there is some. The Franciscan condemnation is unhelpful, since we do not know which specific aspects of Olivi's commentary were censured. If we consult the Florentine manuscript described by Koch as a partial list of the propositions condemned by the order, we find the same basic elements at which others directed their fire, but no particular interest in the recapitulative approach *per se*.[10] The commission report is more interesting. There is one passage which seems relevant, and it occurs in the first article. The commission begins by saying,

> The sevenfold division of the periods of the church, understood as he [Olivi] will explain it in the following articles—that is, that the sixth and seventh periods of the church are a notable advance beyond the first five, and thus they repudiate all those earlier ones as the church repudiated the synagogue—should be considered heretical. We consider it temerarious that he says the seven periods of the church are described in those seven visions of the Apocalypse, given the way he applies and exposits this idea.[11]

The commission is not attacking the traditional recapitulative approach, only what Olivi does with that approach; yet it is not impossible that its strictures made it easier for commentators moving in their immediate wake to question the traditional approach itself. The point is not simply that the commission report enmeshed the recapitulative approach in Olivi's errors and thus made subsequent commentators nervous about it, although that may have happened. It is also that the Olivi affair created an environment in which scholars were encouraged to look with fresh eyes on hermeneutical assumptions that had hitherto been taken for granted. Did it really do so, though? There is no way of knowing without more evidence than can be mustered at the moment.

Nor, in fact, should one be prepared to stake much on the notion that Pierre was influenced by the 1319 condemnation or the commission report in themselves. He took the master's oath at Paris in November 1318 and became provincial minister of Aquitaine in 1319, presumably after his Parisian task was completed. If we assume that his *Compendium of the Literal Sense of the Entire Holy Scripture* stems from his magisterial year at Paris—and his reference to the year 1319 in commenting on Revelation 20:7 seems to point in that direction—then he could have reached the Apocalypse late in the school year, late enough to have heard about the general chapter meeting at Pentecost.[12] Whether he would have heard about the commission report is uncertain, since we do not know when in 1319 it was completed. Nevertheless, all of these events would have come close enough together to make one wonder about the plausibility of either the condemnation or the report inspiring Pierre to seek a new approach to the Apocalypse. It seems more likely that the general atmosphere preceding them would have done so. As we have seen, there was enough agreement on the evils of Olivi's commentary to spare Pierre the tedium of waiting for the commission report in order to discover what it would say. As an intelligent, well-informed scholar, he undoubtedly knew what it would say, at least in general.

In any case, Pierre's decision to follow the progressive, Alexandrine reading of the Apocalypse rather than the more traditional recapitulative reading protects him from one set of dangers while exposing him to another. He avoids some of the latter dangers by eliminating Alexander's dithyrambic praise of the mendicants. At Revelation 20:5 he does echo in subdued form Alexander's reference to Francis and Dominic, but he expunges from his comments Alexander's invocation of the pseudo-Joachim *Super Hieremiam*, a less respectable document in the early fourteenth century than it had been in the mid-thirteenth. Moreover, whereas Alexander's exegesis of the last two chapters throws logical coherence to the winds and offers a sustained paean celebrating the mendicants, Pierre excises the mendicants from his treatment of the new Jerusalem, interpreting it entirely in relation to heaven.[13]

There were, of course, other dangers lurking in the Alexandrine approach. Its tendency to pair specific lines of scripture with concrete historical events might cause offense on more subjects than the mendicants. Pierre avoids these dangers, too, for he writes very much as a loyal son of the institutional church. The enemies are all external. They are the Jews, the heretics, the Greeks, the emperors who tried to limit the freedom of the church, and preeminently the Muslims. Following Alexander, Pierre concentrates heavily on Islam. By the nature of things, Islam cannot appear until 13:11, since Pierre, like Alexander, has barely arrived at the seventh century by that point; but once present, it dominates the narrative. Between 14:6 and 16:13, Pierre turns away for a moment to expatiate on the Franks, the perfidious Greeks, and the equally perfidious German emperors, but at 16:13 he picks up the interpretation of dragon and beast already developed in chapter thirteen and returns in force to the holy land for the first crusade. Everything from there to the end of chapter nineteen becomes a continuous narrative of Outremer. Chapter twenty turns briefly to the investiture controversy, and the dragon of 20:2 obligingly becomes the emperor for a moment, just long enough for the thousand-year imprisonment of the dragon to refer not to Islam but to the millennium after Pope Sylvester; but by 20:4 we are back in the Holy Land for Saladin's conquest of Jerusalem and the next four crusades, followed by Frederick II, Francis, and Dominic in verse 5.

In this respect Pierre is much like Alexander Minorita, who also maintains a lively interest in the Muslims; yet in some ways he has outrun Alexander's interpretation. Alexander, living in the early thirteenth century, could see the number 666 as a prediction of how long Islam would last, without having to live until his theory was tested. Pierre, writing in 1319, has to acknowledge that the period has expired. He observes that some Muslims feel they have exceeded the duration predicted by their prophets and are now living on borrowed time (*de gratia*), but others feel the 666 years should be begun from the reorganization of the faith and correction of the Koran that occurred after Mohammed's death, in which case they still have not expired. He himself, Pierre says, does not know what to think.[14]

Another significant effect of living over a half-century after Alexander is seen in Pierre's treatment of 20:7, when the thousand years elapse, the dragon is released, and Antichrist appears. For Alexander, this is the major text in dealing with the Antichrist. He dates the thousand years from the time of Pope Sylvester and places his election in A.D. 316. That gives him a more or less solid date for the arrival of Antichrist, 1316. It also gives him close to three quarters of a century between himself and that event, again enough to insulate him from the danger of unfulfilled expectations. Pierre, writing in 1319, is less fortunate. The thousand years have elapsed. Pierre observes that, on the basis of this interpretation, Antichrist must already be three years old. This inspires him with caution, and he suggests that the matter be left up to the Holy Spirit.[15]

Since the Antichrist arrives at Revelation 20:7, he can enjoy the company of Gog and Magog. Alexander recites Augustine's view at great length, gives equal time to the legend of fierce tribes penned up in the East by Alexander the Great, then develops a variation on that theory allowing for attack by godless peoples from the four corners of the earth. To this already heady brew he adds liberal doses of the Sybil and Hildegard of Bingen.[16] Pierre is more restrained. He eschews Hildegard and the Sybil but does remark that many identify Gog and Magog with the Mongols. The latter were enclosed beyond the Caspian Mountains by Alexander the Great, but in 1240 they broke out and have been running amok ever since. Pierre is obviously intrigued by this theory, but eventually he feels compelled to honor Augustine's insistence that Gog and Magog refer to the entire body of those following the devil, not to a specific people.[17]

Pierre has produced a remarkably safe commentary. In essence he offers a chronicle of the church and its struggles against its enemies. It is, he suggests, doing quite well against them at the moment. The church in question is clearly the Holy Roman Church presided over by the pope, not a small group of dissenters. It is hardly surprising that Pierre was made a Parisian master through the intervention of John XXII, or that he then proceeded from one honor to another, from provincial minister of Aquitaine in 1319 to archbishop of Aix in 1321.

Nicholas of Lyre

Nicholas of Lyre, writing in 1329, would have known not only about the 1318–19 processes but about the papal condemnation as well. He would also have known about Pierre, however, and could have opted for the progressive approach simply because it was currently being accepted at Paris as the exegetically superior interpretation. Nicholas presents a slightly altered version of the same basic interpretation found in Pierre. He too accords the Muslims a starring role in the great historical drama. Nevertheless, their part is somewhat changed by Nicholas's more skeptical read-

ing of Alexander. For example, he rejects as improbable any effort to see
the number 666 as pointing to the end of Islam, even if one counts from
the reorganization after Mohammed's death. Far from fading, Islam seems
to be prospering, as the extensive Tartar conversions to it suggest. Nicholas offers the alternative of counting backward instead, making 666 represent the time between Christ and Mohammed.

A major departure comes with his exegesis of chapter 17. He follows
Alexander and Pierre in reading the first crusade into chapter sixteen, but
he begins the next chapter with the announcement that he will exposit
Revelation 17:1–20:6 on the assumption that it refers entirely to past
events, then say what he thinks of that assumption. Thus he is able to
proceed with a double critique of Alexander and Pierre. On the one hand,
he is judging their interpretation and offering an alternate one on the
assumption that 17:1–20:6 refers to past events. On the other hand, he is
judging the assumption itself. The judgment is negative in both cases.
Nicholas finds three basic difficulties in their interpretation. First, his predecessors' consistent application of the text to the Muslims forces them
into interpretive inconsistencies. The beast with seven heads is seen as the
king of Egypt, yet we soon discover that one of its seven heads is the king
of the Turks. This leads to the second flaw: their interpretation proceeds
from a simplistic and often factually incorrect reading of history. A much
better historian than Pierre, Nicholas allows himself to observe that the
Turkish head on the Egyptian beast is not only exegetically inconsistent
but historically ironic, considering the actual relations between those two
powers. Earlier he gently corrects Pierre's notion of a great Islamic anti-
Christian alliance in the 1090s, observing that the Muslims were split until
the time of Saladin.

These two objections can be met at least partly by reinterpreting a
few passages, and Nicholas provides such a revision as he proceeds. In the
process, he manages to work the Mongols in at 20:4. Nevertheless, such
cosmetic surgery does little to meet Nicholas's third objection: by reading
everything to 20:7 as past history, his predecessors leave nothing said
about events between the present and the arrival of Antichrist. Pierre, of
course, already has faced this problem in his meditation on the possibility
of Antichrist as a living three-year-old, and has solved it by leaving the
matter to the Holy Spirit. Nicholas too invokes the Holy Spirit, but in a
slightly different way. He explicitly rejects the notion that the Antichrist
could already be born, and thus concludes that the events described from

chapter seventeen on might more wisely be placed in the future. That places them beyond the reach of mortals like himself. "Since I am neither a prophet nor the son of a prophet," he says, "I wish to say nothing about future events except what can be elicited from holy scripture, the saints, or the authentic doctors. Thus I leave exposition of this text to wiser men." He does, however, promise to let us know if God provides him with any additional insight.

Perhaps the most remarkable passage in the entire commentary comes near its conclusion, when Nicholas chooses to critique Alexander's interpretation of the heavenly Jerusalem as an allusion to the mendicant orders. "Although one might be able to maintain this interpretation in some mystical sense," he says, "I do not believe it can be defended in the literal sense." Nicholas's refutation, proceeding remorselessly through Alexander's point-by-point comparison, climaxes with the blunt observation that, whereas according to the Apocalypse nothing soiled or of abominable conduct will enter the heavenly city, "not all who enter [the mendicant orders] are unstained, nor do all who are good when they enter persevere in good, but many become apostates and the worst sorts of person."[18] He then quotes Augustine's remark that, while he has found none better than those who live well in monasteries, he has found none worse than those who live poorly in them.

The chasm between Nicholas and Alexander on this point reflects a series of differences between them. Certainly it bespeaks a difference in their exegetical styles. Nicholas is more hard-headed, more analytical, more concerned with avoiding confusion between different kinds of meaning. It also suggests a difference in personality. The skeptical, slightly sardonic attitude suggested by Nicholas's remark is seen elsewhere in his analysis of church history. Finally, it reflects a difference in historical context. Nearly a century of Franciscan infighting, some of it very unpleasant, separated Nicholas from Alexander. Between 1308, when he became a master of theology at Paris, and 1329, when he wrote the Apocalypse commentary, Nicholas had seen the spirituals and the community locked in a bitter dispute at the Council of Vienne; he had seen the spirituals and their lay supporters hunted down by the inquisition; and he had seen his minister general flee the papal court to set up a Franciscan government in exile under the aegis of Ludwig the Bavarian. Having witnessed all that, he understandably thought it a bit premature to speak of the New Jerusalem. Nevertheless, however disillusioned or sardonic Nicholas might have been, he was still quite safe. Like Pierre, he was given administrative as well as pedagogical duties. From 1319 to 1330, he functioned as provincial minister first of France, then of Burgundy.

Poncio Carbonnel

Poncio Carbonnel can be offered little more than recognition. His commentary, which Klaus Reinhardt dates somewhere between 1319 and 1329, exists in one manuscript containing not only the commentary but a brief defense of his methodology.[19] To date I have seen only the defense. Poncio begins by saying the Apocalypse "can be divided in such a way that, just as world history has seven periods, so church history has seven little periods (*etatunculas*)." He then lists them. The fifth, in Olivian fashion, is said to begin with Charlemagne, but the sixth is described in entirely negative terms as the time of Antichrist. Poncio seems to offer us a choice between two views of the seventh period, one containing at least the possibility of a space between Antichrist and judgment and the other explicitly denying that possibility; but that may be reading too much into his cursory description.

In any case, having laid out the recapitulative view, Poncio reports Pierre Auriol's criticism of it (without mentioning any names) and presents Pierre's progressive model. This too is scheduled for criticism, however, and here he seems in part to reflect Nicholas of Lyre, suggesting that this brief defense must have been written shortly after Lyre's commentary was composed in 1329. Poncio says that some people consider the model "very strained [*extorta*, Nicholas's word] in many places and neither consonant with the exposition of the *sancti* and authoritative *doctores* nor approved by the universal church." Thus he himself has chosen "to follow the exposition offered by the commonly approved *sancti*, ancient *doctores* and ordinary glosses, which I consider the truly literal one." For a division of the whole book, he refers the reader to Bede and Richard of St. Victor. This passage was printed in an eighteenth-century work which also includes a dedicatory letter to the archbishop of Toledo saying Poncio has chosen to use the words of the *Glossa*, Jerome, Augustine, Bede, Haimo of Auxerre, Richard, and others, adding nothing of his own.[20] These comments suggest that Poncio has produced a commentary so conservative that it leaps back over thirteenth-century mendicant exegesis, entrenching itself in earlier interpretations; yet mention of Richard suggests that he has not leaped all that far, while inclusion of Bede, Haimo, and Richard suggests that he endorses the recapitulative pattern. There is no way of knowing, however, until someone reads the entire commentary.

Henry of Cossey

The fourth exegete, Henry of Cossey, presents a much different picture. Practically all we know about him is that he was a lector at the Cambridge convent in 1325–26, then in 1330 was cited to Avignon along with three other friars to answer a charge of heretical preaching. It is impossible to say what happened next, but he is reported to have died in 1336 at Babwell convent, so he at least seems to have made it back to England.[21]

Henry's commentary shows that, however popular the progressive approach may have been at Paris, the recapitulative pattern was far from discredited in England. Neither was Joachim. In fact, Henry is, next to Olivi, the most Joachite Franciscan commentator whose works have survived. We have seen that other English Franciscans like John of Wales and John Russel cited Joachim on specific exegetical details but gave only scant attention to the thing that most intrigues modern readers, his theology of history. Henry is at one with the modern readers. Like Olivi he pays serious attention to the Joachite *concordia* of Old and New Testament history. He is careful not to commit himself to the Joachite perspective, or for that matter to any perspective. Normally he simply recites various alternate interpretations without attempting to argue that any one of them is correct. Nevertheless, it is hard to register the insistence with which he turns to the Joachite interpretation and the care with which he presents it without suspecting that Henry finds Joachim, if not an unquestionable authority, at least a highly plausible one.

Henry interprets all four sevenfold visions as miniature histories of the church, and his handling of the first four periods is in line with thirteenth-century Franciscan exegetical tradition. Like others, he sees the first three periods as characterized by consecutive battles between the apostles, martyrs, and doctors on the one hand and the Jews, pagans, and heretics on the other.[22] He echoes other commentators in singling out monasticism as characteristic of the fourth period. Most earlier exegetes described the central enemy of that period as hypocrisy or laxity, and so does Henry; yet he also speaks constantly of the Saracens, a subject that had been mentioned by some exponents of the recapitulative aproach but had been accorded comparable attention only by Olivi. The connection between Muslims, monks, and luxuriant hypocrites is a close one for Henry. He notes that the seventh-century Saracen invasion overran monastic establishments in the Thebaid,[23] and describes the fourth persecution as caused by "the hypocrisy and power of the Muslims . . . from the time of Justinian through that of Charlemagne."[24] He is willing to find evidence of Muslim hypocrisy in any number of places.[25]

His view of the fifth period is typical of Franciscan exegesis inasmuch as he speaks of the enemy as false Christians and precursors of Antichrist[26] and insofar as he alludes to lay persecution of the church during the investiture controversy.[27] His repeated references to the Patarenes[28] are dependent upon Joachim but nevertheless in line with previous minorite interpretation, which emphasized both heresy and laxity as characteristic enemies of the fifth period, when the devil utilized in concert all the weapons hitherto employed separately. In some ways, however, Henry sides with Joachim and Olivi against other commentators. Whereas most Franciscan exegetes seem to place themselves in the early fifth period at the latest, Henry, like Olivi, thinks the fifth period began with Charlemagne. Furthermore, he leaves the end of the period open, but in such a way as to make it unclear whether it has ended by his day. At one point he cites Joachim to the effect that the fifth period runs from Charlemagne to Antichrist,[29] yet at another he describes it as running from Charlemagne to Joachim. In the latter case he goes on to note that the period actually extended beyond Joachim, though we do not know how long.[30]

Henry's failure to clarify whether he is in the fifth or sixth period is rendered somewhat less important by the fact that, like the rest of the tradition, he links the fifth and sixth periods in a single battle against the reprobate beginning in the fifth period and climaxing in the sixth.[31] Nevertheless, in good Olivian style he identifies the sixth period not merely with the persecution of Antichrist, but also with a series of events leading up to that persecution, and portrays these events as having a positive as well as a negative side. The positive elements are those mentioned by Joachim and Olivi. The sixth period will feature a certain order "which is or will be."[32] This order will base its preaching on a *concordia* of the New and Old Testaments and will have the gift of *spiritualis intelligentia*, giving it the power to clarify obscurities in the Bible.[33] Its improved grasp of scripture will enable it to convert many Jews and others through preaching.[34] Henry does not explicitly link the new order with his own or even mention the Franciscans at this point, although he does so later.

Like Olivi, Henry is voluble concerning the negative aspects of the sixth period. It is important to remember that he sees the persecution as a continuation of the battle already being waged in the fifth period, and that he is heir to the widespread belief that the church in the fifth period will be plagued by a combination of the evils suffered separately in earlier periods. Henry's fifth period features a double threat: continuing conflict with nonbelievers outside the church, laxity and heresy within it. In enumerating these elements, Henry shows his debt to Joachim. He has inherited Joachim's interest in the Cathari and the investiture controversy.[35] Moreover, the major outside threat of the fifth period is that central villain of the fourth, Islam.[36]

In the sixth period, Antichrist's following will be composed of all these elements. Indeed, his supporters strike one as a French Foreign Legion of the reprobate[37] in which a motley variety of religious foreigners (Jews, Muslims, and pagans) are combined with nationals bearing bogus credentials (heretics and false Christians). In describing the resultant persecution, Henry mirrors the Joachite-Olivian approach. He constructs a scenario in which the political force that has guarded Christendom from external threat is gradually weakened by sin and eventually finds itself unable to withstand attack. At one point Henry refers simply to an attack "from the east," but in another he anticipates a fourfold attack by the Turks from the east, the Ethiopians from the south, the Moors from the west, and, from the north, "those who frequently war with the Germans."[38] Nevertheless, however many groups may be involved, the Muslims will play a central role. It is they to whom Henry continually returns when he envisions an outside threat. In his comments on complex images like the dragon and the beasts from land and sea (Revelation 13), the beast on which the whore rides (Revelation 17), and the four beasts in Daniel 7, Henry stretches them out over all of church history, yet inevitably sees their significance for the present as involving Islam.[39]

In his treatment of Islam, Henry flirts with the idea that the number of the beast reflects the number of years Islam will last, a view he associates with Innocent III. While Olivi too employs the number for that purpose, Henry seems to be reacting more to the use made of it by Alexander Minorita, particularly as critiqued by Pierre Auriol and Nicholas of Lyre. He cites as confirmation of the interpretation an astrological prediction by Albumassar that Islam cannot last longer than 693 years. Unfortunately, Henry observes, it is now 1333 and Islam has endured for 731 years. Some impious Muslims explain this situation by claiming that their religion has continued to exist through grace, while others say that the counting should begin not from its origin under Mohammed, but rather from its rebirth under "a certain successor." Since all of this seems uncertain, however, Henry thinks it might be wiser to rely more on the standard interpretation, which treats the numbers as letters spelling Antichrist's name rather than as years.[40]

While examining Olivi's view of the Muslims, we noted that his double use of them—they will destroy the carnal church and later, after a period of decline, play a central role in the persecution of Antichrist—may stem from chronological difficulties engendered by Joachim's concordances, although the sparsity of explicit references to concordance in his Apocalypse commentary makes this theory hard to prove. Henry too is less forthcoming about concordance than one might wish, yet he seems to face the same problem and solve it differently. He sees the slain and recovered head of Revelation 13:3 as Islam.[41] In dealing with Revelation 17:11 ("The beast which was, and is not, is an eighth but belongs to the seven"), he affirms that this beast can be identified with Islam, since it is powerful, then destroyed, then powerful again before finally being destroyed.[42] It is eighth because it comprises an eighth persecution, yet is one of the seven as well.

So far, Henry seems to be walking shoulder to shoulder with Joachim and Olivi. At this point, however, he faces the same set of alternatives already encountered by them, implicitly rejects the one they chose, and chooses the one they rejected. He identifies Islam's apparent destruction with Christian victories in the eleventh century,[43] and apparently views its recovery as a continuing phenomenon running into the present and beyond. Thus the successful attack on Rome and the persecution of Antichrist will be parts of a single event involving the revitalized Muslims. They will participate in an attack on Christendom that will lead directly into the persecution of Antichrist, or, more precisely, will be the opening of it. Henry mirrors Olivi in recognizing that the duration and success of Islam in themselves constitute a temptation. He comments that "many Christians, seeing so many people follow the Islamic sect, will say that God could never have wished so many people to be lost and so many of his faithful to be so hard pressed. Thus deceived, they will follow the beast."[44]

So far, Henry's persecution of Antichrist looks somewhat like Olivi's. The difference comes when one attempts to identify those false Christians who will act as a fifth column within the church. Henry avoids the problem. In fact, most of his concrete references tend to externalize the threat. This tendency is demonstrated by his treatment of the false prophets, who play such an important role in Olivi's scenario of ecclesiastical betrayal. Henry is not always consistent in explaining who these people might be—he can refer on the same page to "the Jews and false prophets," "the false prophets, that is, the Jews," and "the false prophets, that is, the tyrants or Saracens"[45]—yet the general drift of such phrases is clear enough. He studiously avoids any specific reference to support for Antichrist within the ecclesiastical hierarchy or the religious orders.

Like others before him, Henry anticipates a seventh period from the death of Antichrist to the final judgment, and describes it as a rest from persecution. He is prepared to believe that it will be an extended one. He follows Augustine in seeing the thousand years of 20:2 as a symbolic reference to the entire period from Christ to Antichrist, but remarks that according to some, the seventh period will be only one forty-eighth of the preceeding time. While Henry does not share the date of creation with us and is silent as to when Antichrist will be defeated, we can nevertheless assume that one forty-eighth of world history would add up to somewhat less than a century, but not much less.[46] It will end with the persecution of Revelation 20, involving Satan, Antichrist, Gog, and Magog.[47] Henry spends an inordinate amount of time on an examination of Gog and Magog as the peoples shut in by Alexander. In the process he neatly works in an extended treatment of the Tartars and a proud reference to the Franciscan missionaries sent to them by Louis IX. Then, presumably with regret, he announces that the interpretation is invalid and casts his lot with Augustine's view of Gog and Magog as all persecutors of the church.

Pierre, Nicholas, Henry, and Olivi

Pierre, Nicholas, and Henry resemble Olivi in some ways but differ sharply from him in others. Like Olivi, they are interested in interpreting the Apocalypse historically, although (like Olivi) they interpret it morally as well. They resemble Olivi in their preoccupation with the Muslims. This common concern is hardly surprising. All four lived in an era when Islam was doing quite well. In fact, it was doing ever better in relation to the Mongols as well as the Christians. By the time Olivi wrote, the Egyptian Muslims had checked what had earlier seemed an irresistable Mongol expansion and even reversed the flow. The Mongol Ilkhan's efforts to gain an alliance with the Christian West against Egypt had collapsed, the Muslim faith was making sustantial inroads among the Mongols, and Acre, the last Christian stronghold in the Holy Land, had fallen to the Muslims. Thus, while ignoring the Muslims would have been difficult for scholars who took Joachim of Fiore seriously—and Henry, like Olivi, did take him seriously—they did not need Joachim to remind them of Islam.

Nevertheless, Pierre, Nicholas, and Henry differ sharply from Olivi in other ways. In the first place, they largely avoid giving their own order the apocalyptic mission found in Alexander's exegesis of Revelation 20–22 or Olivi's exegesis of Revelation 7 and 10. Of the three, only Pierre works Saint Francis into the Apocalypse, and his reference is nothing more than a brief homage to Alexander's reading of the text. None gives the Franciscan order the sort of apocalyptic role celebrated by Olivi. Of the three, only Henry offers anything similar to Olivi's comments on the anticipated new order of the sixth period, and Henry not only says a great deal less but fails to tie what he does say to the Franciscans.

The second major difference between Olivi and the other three lies in the way Pierre, Nicholas, and Henry speak of Antichrist's minions. Their efforts at concreteness tend to externalize the enemy. They experience little difficulty in discussing Jews, Greeks, heretics, pagans, and especially the Muslims, but they find it hard to be specific about false Christians, that reprobate element subverting the church from within. They are successful in doing so only when invoking the investiture controversy, and they see that chapter as closed well before Antichrist's arrival. Olivi is all too voluble on the subject.

It is one thing to note these differences and quite another to say that they were a result of the Olivi process. Obviously the areas in question were important ones in the attack on Olivi, and it would be understandable if scholars working at the time of that attack were encouraged to avoid them; yet there is little point in suggesting that the condemnation caused exegetes to eschew positions they never would have held anyway. In differing from Olivi on these matters, our three commentators also diverged from some scholars who wrote before Olivi, but not from the majority of them. In granting Francis and his order an apocalyptic role, Olivi was not only Joachite but Bonaventuran; yet most exegetes of the late thirteenth century showed little interest in assigning the order an apocalyptic role in the sixth period as Bonaventure had. Some did emulate Bonaventure to the extent of reading Francis into their interpretation, but, as we have seen, even those who did so (except for Alexander Minorita and Olivi) lacked the hermeneutical assumptions that would have allowed them to see Francis as literally prophesied in the Apocalypse. They placed themselves in the fifth period and the angel of 7:2 in the sixth. By Olivi's time exegetes had embarked on the hermeneutical path that would make it easy for them to follow Francesco Silvestri's advice: pay homage to Bonaventure's identification of Francis with the angel of Revelation 7:2, but make sure you do not take that identification as the literal meaning of the passage.

Perhaps a more serious deviation from preceding exegesis is seen in the tendency of our three fourteenth-century commentators to externalize Antichrist's allies. This deviation is less surprising in the cases of Pierre and Nicholas, since the successive approach encouraged nothing similar to the "predecessors of Antichrist" read into the fifth period by devotees of the recapitulative approach. It is somewhat more problematic in Henry's case, since he follows the recapitulative approach and does allow for such predecessors; but even he makes little attempt to define them as they exist within the church. Several earlier exegetes were substantially less shy. While some Franciscan commentators like John of Wales might prefer to abstain from historical interpretation and seek timeless moral meaning in the Apocalypse, others were willing to draw from it a hard-hitting denunciation of contemporary evils within Christian society, lay and ecclesiastical. "Alexander" and Vital both devote considerable attention to contemporary ecclesiastical leaders, whom they accuse of leading others astray with their evil example.[48] Both also strike a passing, veiled blow at university instruction, commenting that they are entering a time in which falsity, subtlety, and novelty are valued more than Christian truth.[49] "Alexander" even manages to comment that the city of Rome is called a whore in Revelation 17:1 because of the sale of benefices, although his subsequent definition of "Rome" tends to deflect the criticism away from the Roman curia in particular toward bad prelates throughout the church.[50] Both spend much more time on the threats from within Christendom than on the external threats. Neither Vital nor "Alexander" goes as far as Olivi, but they both go further than Henry of Cossey. Henry could have drawn more from this tradition, but he did not. Perhaps he would have liked to do so, having had a brush with the hierarchy less than three years before he began the Apocalypse commentary. We cannot say, since we know little about Henry's inner thoughts or even about his encounter with the hierarchy.

Olivi's Enduring Significance

As the first century of the new Christian era moved toward its end, a man named John sat in exile on the island of Patmos and wrote furiously. The adverb is doubly fitting. He wrote tumultuously, by divine inspiration as he understood it; and he was a very angry man. In his Apocalypse, John described his world. It was one in which a small number of elect were being persecuted by a highly organized, wealthy, ungodly society. All of the institutions of that society were arrayed against the elect, but with God's help the righteous would endure and their persecutors would eventually be buried beneath their own collapsing institutions.

That vision was a hard one for thirteenth-century exegetes to share. They lived within Christian institutions and were protected, even rewarded by them. As certified intellectuals, they were members of the club. Their status as scholars was one sign of membership, and in most cases other symbols of acceptance would follow. They would become leaders within the order, bishops, perhaps even cardinals. Viewing their society from that perspective, they found it conceivable that the benevolent effects of that greatest of institutions, the Roman church, could be thwarted by corrupt scholars and *prelati* within or buffeted by heretics, Greeks, Jews, and infidels from without; but, since they saw the institutional church itself as a by-product of divine election, they found it hard to imagine that it could become so enmeshed in evil as to do the work of Antichrist.

A few people did imagine it, though. In the 1240s, the author of the pseudo-Joachim commentary on Jeremiah described a thoroughly corrupt institution that would soon be demolished by invaders. He saw the elect as a small, silent remnant hidden within the institution. From that seed a renewed church would spring in the days after the great desolation.

In the late 1290s, almost precisely twelve centuries after John wrote, Olivi too imagined it. He and the author of the Jeremiah commentary projected a remarkably similar scenario, at least in general outline; yet Olivi's Apocalypse commentary was so much more sophisticated that comparison between the two seems almost bizarre. Olivi was a dedicated intellectual and a dedicated Franciscan. As the former, he had mastered the stunningly complicated system known to us as scholasticism. As the latter, he lived within one of the most evocative legends in Western history. Olivi approached the Apocalypse with a complex theology and an equally complex mythology at his disposal. He put both to work and produced a commentary that was in some ways a typical thirteenth-century product, yet that in others came closer than any other contemporary commentary to capturing John's sense of his own situation on Patmos. Like John, Olivi saw himself as standing almost a century into the birth of a new age that would sweep away the old. Like John, he saw the old era as hanging on tenaciously. Olivi could not entirely accept John's alienation from contemporary institutions as his own, but he did the next best thing. He projected it into the near future. Olivi was not being persecuted as John was, but the *viri spirituales* soon would be. Like John, he knew that, however unequal the battle might appear, God's embattled elect would triumph, because the new era was on the divine agenda. Babylon would come crashing down and the New Jerusalem would descend.

Olivi's prospects for canonization were ruined in 1318 when his body was removed from its tomb at Narbonne and his cult suppressed. Perhaps his credentials should be reconsidered. He could be the patron saint of those who refuse to put their trust in institutions. Of course, however little faith Olivi had in current institutions, he had incredible faith in God's power to work outside them and despite them. His vision—of *viri spirituales* enduring persecution, then emerging on the other side of destruction to build the New Jerusalem—may be hard to accept, but it is perhaps his most important legacy to us, a legacy of hope.

Notes

1. Mansi, *Miscellanea*, 2:248–51. The inquisitor, Michel Le Moine, tells the condemned that no religious rule can be identified with the gospel, since the Roman church obediently submits to the gospel without correcting or confirming it, whereas all religious rules owe their legitimacy entirely to the Roman church. "Thus," he says, "the Roman pontiff would not violate the gospel and faith of Christ if he contradicted, changed or even abolished the [Franciscan] rule; nor is that rule identical with the gospel, but is instead a certain laudable way of life approved and confirmed by the Roman pontiffs and simply and absolutely subject to interpretation, alteration or any other sort of action on their part." His assertion is all the more striking when one considers that Michel himself was a Franciscan.

2. See the bibliographical references in Turley, "John XXII and the Franciscans," 80.

3. For Dominican criticism and papal efforts, see ibid., 80–87.

4. J.-M. Vidal, *Bullaire de l'inquisition française* (Paris, 1913), 38f.

5. It is cited in an anonymous document from the archives of the archbishop of Narbonne, published in Mansi, *Miscellanea*, 2:271f. The author says he found the spirituals' words in a letter sent by Michel Le Moine and read by the author in 1318. He also says the spirituals "transierunt ad gentes infideles."

6. For the subsequent history of the southern French spirituals see Manselli, *Spirituali*, chapters 7 and 8. For the Italian *fraticelli* see Decima Douie, *The Nature and the Effect of the Heresy of the Fraticelli* (Manchester, 1932), chapter 7 and, more recently, Clement Schmitt, "Fraticelli," in *Dizionario degli istituti di perfezione* (Rome, 1974–88), 4:807–21. On the limits of secular support for the Italian spirituals, see Giampaolo Tognetti, "I fraticelli, il principio di povertà e i secolari," *Bulletino dell'istituto storico italiano per il medio evo e Archivio muratoriano* 90 (1982/ 83): 77–145.

7. "Polemiche," 381, 386.

8. Petrus Aurioli, *Compendium sensus literalis totius divinae scripturae* (Quaracchi, 1896), 438–555; Nicholas de Lyra, *Postilla super totam bibliam* (Strassburg, 1492 edition reproduced Frankfurt/Main, 1971); Henricus de Cossey, *Lecturae in apocalypsim*, unpublished. I will cite Henry from MS Oxford Bodl. Laud. misc. 85, occasionally correcting it on the basis of MS Holy Name College 69, now at the Franciscan Institute, St. Bonaventure University. Folio numbers alone will refer to the former MS, folio numbers preceded by a "St.B" to the latter. Poncio Carbonnel's commentary survives in one manuscript, MS Toledo Biblioteca Publica de Toledo, Provincial 450. The commentary is at ff. 94–139 and is followed at ff. 139–41 by a defense of his methodology entitled *Expositio brevis vel divisio libri apocalypsis*. On this commentary see Klaus Reinhardt, "Das Werk des Nikolaus von Lyra im mittelalterlichen Spanien," *Traditio* 43 (1987): 342f., and Philip Krey, "Nicholas of Lyra: Apocalypse Commentary as Historiography" (doctoral dissertation, University of Chicago, 1990), 122–25.

9. *Compendium sensus literalis totius divinae scripturae*, 454–56.

10. MS Florence Laur. Santa Croce Plut. 31 sin. cod. 3, 175rb–175vb. There is, however, no strong reason to believe that this manuscript is a reflection of the condemnation at the Marseilles general chapter.

11. Mansi, *Miscellenea*, 2:258.

12. On the scope of the academic year see Hilarin Felder, *Geschichte des wissenschaftliche Studien im Franziskanerorden bis um Mitte des 13. Jahrhunderts* (Freiburg im Br., 1904), 369f.

13. *Compendium*, pp. 550–55.

14. Ibid., 505.

15. Ibid., 548.

16. *Expositio*, 450–58.

17. *Compendium*, 549.

18. Note, however, that in his *Postilla moralis*, completed in 1339, Lyra does acknowledge as the *moral* meaning of Rev. 7:2 that it signifies a preacher and can refer especially to Francis.

19. See note 8 above.

20. Vicente Manuel Castaño, *Noticia y defensa de los escritos del venerable y sabio minorita catalan Fray Poncio Carbonell* (Alcalá, 1790), 112–19.

21. The location of extant manuscripts supports this conclusion. For MSS consulted here, see note 8 above.

22. *Lecturae*, 75rb and elsewhere.

23. Ibid., 80ra.

24. Ibid., 96rb.

25. E.g., his exegesis of the white horse in Rev. 6:8 in ibid., 96va. See also 96rb.

26. Ibid., 75rb, 97va, 105vb, 135va (with missing word *precursores* supplied from St.B. 105v).

27. Ibid., 75rb, 142ra.

28. As in ibid., 105va–vb and 107va.

29. Ibid., 97va.

30. Ibid., 75rb. In this manuscript he says that it lasted until the year 1200 and longer, which would be the equivalent of his previous remark that it extended to the time of Joachim; yet in MS St.B, 47v, the date is 1300, which would mean that it extended at least into Henry's own lifetime. In either case, something similar to Olivi's overlap between the fifth and sixth periods may be implied.

31. Ibid., 108rb.

32. Ibid., 82va. His formulation reminds one of the passages in John Russel and *Vidit* cited in chapter 2, note 106, but they are speaking of the fifth period. Moreover, Henry anticipates a new order. His only uncertainty is whether it has appeared. Henry also honors the other option for the sixth period: at ibid., 114ra, he speaks of *two* new orders who will preach at that time.

33. Ibid., 82va–vb, 110va.

34. Ibid., 71ra, 110va, 113rb, 115ra.

35. Ibid., 75rb, 105va–vb.

36. Ibid., 97va.

37. Henry, 136ra, actually describes them as a legion of the damned, *militia hominum perditorum*. Whereas Olivi sees the various elements as united by a common commitment to carnality, Henry ascribes much the same function to luxury. E.g., ibid., 109rb.

38. Ibid., 108va, 136ra. The idea of an attack from the east is partially dependent upon Henry's acceptance of the idea that Antichrist will be from the tribe of Dan and born in the east (136ra, 141va); yet these are relatively unimportant factors. Far from playing any central role through a special relation to Antichrist, the Jews are simply one more group in the great Antichristian coalition.

39. See especially ibid., 120vb–123va, 135vb–136ra, 141va–143ra.

40. Ibid., 123ra–va. St.B., 95v, gives the date as 1331.

41. Ibid., 121rb–va.

42. Ibid., 112va–vb.

43. Ibid., 121rb–va.

44. *Lecturae*, 121va–vb.

45. Ibid., 109ra–rb. Occasionally the pseudoprophets are seen as false clerics within the church. E.g., see 136ra, where false clerics are alternately identified with the pseudoprophets and with the beast from the land itself.

46. Ibid., 102ra.

47. Ibid., 102ra, 153vb–154ra.

48. We saw that "Alexander" gives equal time to lay offenses. Dominican commentaries like *Vidit Iacob* and *Aser pinguis* are also significant in this respect.

49. Vitalis, *Expositio*, 77rb; "Alexander," *Commentarii*, 159. See also *Vidit Iacob*, 81vb.

50. "Alexander," *Commentarii*, 310f. *Vidit Iacob* has even worse things to say about Rome.

Bibliography of Works Cited

In the case of unpublished works, only those manuscripts actually cited in the text or notes are listed in the bibliography.

By Olivi

Petrus Iohannis Olivi. *De studio divinarum literarum*. In *Sancti Bonaventurae ex ordine minorum S.R.E. episcopi cardinalis Albanensis operum omnium Sixti V. Pont. Max. D. Ord. jussu editorum supplementum*. Trent: Typographia Joannis Baptistae Monauni, 1773, 1:24–49.
————. *Epistola ad Conradum de Offida*. In Livarius Oliger, "Petrus Iohannis Olivi de renuntiatione papae Coelestini V quaestio et epistola." *AFH* 11 (1918): 309–73.
————. *Expositio super Dionysii de angelica hierarchia*. MS Rome Vat. lat. 899.
————. *Lectura super Apocalypsim*. In Warren Lewis, "Peter John Olivi: Prophet of the Year 2000." Doctoral dissertation, Tübingen University, 1972.
————. *Lectura super Genesim*. MS Florence Bibl. Naz. Conv. Sopp. G 1 671.
————. *Lectura super Ioannem*. MS Florence Bibl. Laur. Plut. 10 dext. 8.
————. *Lectura super Iob*. MS Florence Bibl. Laur. conv. soppr. 240.
————. *Lectura super Isaiam*. MS Paris Bibl. Nat. nouv. acq. lat. 774.
————. *Lectura super Lucam*. MS Rome Vat. Ottab. lat. 3302.
————. *Lectura super Marcum*. MS Rome Vat. Ottob. lat. 3302.
————. *Lectura super Matthaeum*. MS Oxford New College 49.
————. "Petri Iohannis Olivi de renuntiatione papae Coelestini V quaestio et epistola." *AFH* 11 (1918): 309–73.
————. *Quaestiones de perfectione evangelica*, qq. 1 and 2. In Aquilino Emmen and Feliciano Simoncioli, "La dottrina dell'Olivi sulla contemplazione, la vita attiva e mista." *Studi francescani* 60 (1963): 382–445; 61 (1964): 108–40.
————. *Quaestiones de perfectione evangelica*, q. 8. In *Das Heil der Armen und das Verderben der Reichen*. Werl/Westfalen: Dietrich-Coelde-Verlag, 1989.
————. *Quaestiones de perfectione evangelica*, q. 9. In *De usu paupere: The Quaestio and the Tractatus*. Florence: Leo S. Olschki, 1992.
————. *Quaestiones de perfectione evangelica*, q. 16. In David Burr and David Flood, "Peter Olivi: On Poverty and Revenue." *Franciscan Studies* 40 (1980): 18–58.
————. *Questiones in secundum librum sententiarum*. Quaracchi: College of Saint Bonaventure, 1922–24.
————. *Quodlibeta*. Venice: Lazarus Soardus, 1509.

————. *Tractatus de usu paupere.* In *De usu paupere: The Quaestio and the Tractatus.* Florence: Leo S. Olschki, 1992.

OTHER APOCALYPSE COMMENTARIES

Alexander Halensis (?). *Commentarii in apocalypsim.* Paris, 1647. Also published in Bonaventura, *Sancti Bonaventurae ex ordine minorum S.R. E. episcopi cardinalis Albanensis operum omnium Sixti V. Pont. Max. D. Ord. jussu editorum supplementum.* Trent: Typographia Joannis Baptistae Monauni, 1773, 2 : 1–1037.

Alexander Minorita. *Expositio in apocalypsim.* Monumenta Germaniae Historica, Quellen, 1. Weimar: Hermann Böhlaus Nachfolger, 1955.

Anonymous, *Expositio in apocalypsim.* (Inc.: *Vox domini praeparantis cervos.*) In Aquinas, *Opera omnia.* Parma: P. Fiaccadori, 1860–62, 23 : 512–712.

Beda. *Explanatio Apocalypsis.* In *PL* 93 : 129–206. *Glossa ordinaria.* In *Biblia sancta cum glossa ordinaria.* Nuremburg: Anton Koberger, 1481.

Guilelmus de Militona. *Expositio super apocalypsim.* MSS Assisi 82 and 321.

Haimo Altissiodoris. *Expositio in apocalypsim.* In *PL* 17 : 937–1220 (as Haimo Halberstatensis).

Henricus de Cossey. *Lecturae in apocalypsim.* MSS Oxford Bodl. Laud. misc. 85; St. Bonaventure University Holy Name College 69.

Hugo de Sancto Caro (?). *Expositio super apocalypsim.* (Inc.: *Vidit Iacob in somniis.*) In Thomas Aquinas, *Opera.* Paris: Vivès, 1871–80, 31 : 469–661 and 32 : 1–86; Thomas Aquinas, *Opera.* Parma: P. Fiaccadori, 1860–62, 23 : 325–511; MS Oxford Bodleian 444.

————. *Postilla super apocalypsim.* (Inc.: *Aser pinguis.*) In Hugo de Sancto Caro, *Biblia Latina cum Postilla.* Paris, 1545.

Ioachim de Fiore. *Expositio in apocalypsim.* Frankfurt: Minerva, 1964 (reprint of Venice, 1527 edition).

Iohannes Gallensis. *Expositio in apocalypsim.* MSS Assisi 50, Todi 68, Florence Bibl. Laur. Conv. Sopp. 239 (Santa Croce 885), Breslau Univ. 83 (I.F. 78).

Iohannes Russel. *Expositio super apocalypsim.* MS Oxford Merton 122.

Matthaeus de Aquasparta. *Expositio super apocalypsim.* MSS Assisi 51 and 57.

Nicholas de Lyra. *Postilla super totam bibliam.* Frankfurt am Main: Minerva, 1971 (reproduction of Strassburg, 1492 edition).

Nicholas Gorranus. *In Acta Apostolorum et singulas apostolorum Iacobi, Petri, Iohannis et Iudae canonicas epistolas et Apocalypsim commentarii.* Antwerp, 1620.

Petrus Aurioli. *Compendium sensus literalis totius divinae scripturae.* Quaracchi: College of Saint Bonaventure, 1896.

Petrus de Tarantasia. *In Apocalypsim B. Joannis Apostoli Luculenta Expositio.* In Albertus Magnus, *Opera.* Paris: Vivès, 1890, 38 : 465–792.

Pontius Carbonell. *Expositio in apocalypsim.* MS Toledo Biblioteca Publica, Provincial 450, ff. 94–139.

Raymundus Rigaldi. *Distinctiones super apocalypsim.* MS Hereford Cathedral P 3.3 (XIV).

Richardus de Sancto Victore. *In apocalypsim Ioannis.* In *PL*, 196 : 683–986.

Vitalis de Furno (?). *Expositio super apocalypsim.* MSS Assisi 46, 66, 71, 358, Florence, Bibl. Laur. Conv. Sopp. 547 (Santa Croce 812). Most of work published in Bernardinus Senensis. *Commentarii in apocalypsim.* In *Opera.* Paris: D. Moreau, 1635, vol. 3.

OTHER WORKS

Abate, Giuseppe. "Memoriali, statuti ed atti di capitoli generali dei fratri minori." *Miscellanea franciscana* 33 (1933): 15–45; 34 (1934): 248–53; 35 (1935): 101–6, 232–39.

Adam Marsh. *Epistolae.* In *Rerum Britannicarum Medii Aevi scriptores* (Rolls Series). London: Longmans, 1858–82, no.4, 1:75–489.

Alatri, Mariano d'. "San Bonaventura, l'eresia e l'inquisizione." *Miscellanea francescana* 75 (1975): 305–22.

Amoròs, Leo. "Aegidii Romani impugnatio doctrinae Petri Ioannis Olivi an. 1311–12, nunc primum in lucem edita." *AFH* 27 (1934): 399–451.

———. "Series condemnationum et processuum contra doctrinam et sequaces Petri Ioannis Olivi." *AFH* 24 (1931): 495–512.

Analecta franciscana. Quaracchi: College of Saint Bonaventure, 1885–1941.

Angelo Clareno. *Epistole.* Rome: Istituto Storico Italiano per il Medio Evo, 1980.

———. *Historia septem tribulationum.* In *Archiv.*, 2:108–326.

Anonymous. *Allegationes super articulis.* MS Paris Bibl. Nat. lat. 4190, 40r–49v.

———. *Articuli abstracti de scriptis suis ab impugnatoribus.* MS Florence Biblioteca Laurentiana, Santa Croce Plut. 31 sin. cod. 3, 175rb–va.

——— (Guilelmus de Lauduno?). Critique of Olivi Apocalypse Commentary. (Inc.: *Ista sunt que in postilla fratris Petri Johannis super apocalipsim videntur esse heretica*). MS Paris Bibl. Nat. lat. 3381A.

Augustinus Aurelius. *De civitate dei contra paganos.* In *CCSL*, vols. 47–48.

Avray, David d'. "A Franciscan and History." *AFH* 74 (1981): 456–82.

Auw, Lydia von. *Angelo Clareno.* Rome: Edizioni di Storia e Letteratura, 1979.

Balduinus ab Amsterdam, "The Commentary on St. John's Gospel Edited in 1589 under the Name of St. Bonaventure." *Collectanea franciscana* 40 (1970): 71–96.

Baluze, Etienne. *Vitae paparum avenionensium.* Edited and emended by G. Mollat. Paris: Letouzey et Ané, 1914–27.

Bernardus a Bessa. *Liber de laudibus*, In *AF*, 3:666–92.

Bernardus Guidonis. *Practica inquisitionis heretice pravitatis.* Paris: Alphonse Picard, 1886.

Bihel, Stephanus. "S. Franciscus fuitne Angelus sexti sigilli?" *Antonianum* 2 (1927): 29–70.

Bihl, Michael. "Statuta generalia ordinis edita in capitulis generalibus celebratis Narbonae an. 1260, Assisii an. 1279 atque Parisiis an. 1292." *AFH* 34 (1941): 13–94, 284–358.

Bloomfield, Morton, and Marjorie Reeves. "The Penetration of Joachism into Northern Europe." In Delno West, ed., *Joachim of Fiore.* New York: Burt Franklin, 1975, 1:107–28.

Bonaventure. *Collationes in hexaemeron et Bonaventuriana quaedam selecta*. Quaracchi: College of Saint Bonaventure, 1934.

—— *Opera*. Quaracchi: College of Saint Bonaventure, 1882–1902.

Brady, Ignatius. "Sacred Scripture in the Early Franciscan School." In *La Sacra scrittura e i francescani*. Rome: Editiones Antonianum, 1973, 65–82.

Brooke, Rosalind. *Early Franciscan Government*. Cambridge: Cambridge University Press, 1959.

——. *Scripta Leonis*. Oxford: Clarendon Press, 1970.

Bullarium fransiscanum. Rome: Vatican, 1759–1904.

Burr, David. "The Apocalyptic Element in Olivi's Critique of Aristotle." *Church History* 40 (1971): 15–29.

——. "Apokalyptische Erwartung und die Entstehung der Usus-pauper Kontroverse." *Wissenschaft und Weisheit* 47 (1984): 84–99.

——. "Bonaventure, Olivi, and Franciscan Eschatology." *Collectanea franciscana* 53 (1983): 23–40.

——. *Olivi and Franciscan Poverty*. Philadelphia: University of Pennsylvania Press, 1989.

——. "Olivi, Apocalyptic Expectation, and Visionary Experience." *Traditio* 41 (1985): 273–85.

——. "Olivi's Apocalyptic Timetable." *Journal of Medieval and Renaissance Studies* 11 (1981): 237–60.

——. *The Persecution of Peter Olivi*. Philadelphia: American Philosophical Society, 1976.

——. "Petrus Ioannis Olivi and the Philosophers." *Franciscan Studies* 31 (1971): 41–71.

Burr, David, and David Flood. "Peter Olivi: On Poverty and Revenue." *Franciscan Studies* 40 (1980): 19–58.

Callaey, Frédégand. *L'Idéalisme franciscaine spirituel au XIVe siècle*. Louvain: Bureau du Recueil, 1911.

Castaño, Vicente Manuel. *Noticia y defensa de los escritos del venerable y sabio minorita catalan Fray Poncio Carbonell*. Alcalá, 1790.

Chartularium universitatis parisiensis. Paris: Delalain, 1889.

Chronica XXIV generalium. In *AF*, 3:1–575.

Corpus Christianorum, series latina. Turnhout: Brepols, 1954–.

Corpus scriptorum ecclesiasticorum latinorum. Vienna: Hoelder-Pichler-Tempsky, 1866–.

Damieta, Marino. *Guglielmo d'Ockham: Povertà e potere*. Firenze: Edizioni "Studi Francescani," 1978.

Daniel, E. Randolph. "A Re-Examination of the Origins of Franciscan Joachitism." *Speculum* 43 (1968): 671–676.

——. "Saint Bonaventure: Defender of Franciscan Eschatology." In *S. Bonaventura, 1247–1974*. Grottaferrata: College of Saint Bonaventure, 1974, 4:793–806.

Delorme, Ferdinand. "Diffinitiones capituli generalis Narbonnensis." *AFH* 3 (1910): 502–4.

Denifle, Heinrich. "Das Evangelium aeternum und die Commission zu Anagni." In *Archiv*, 1:49–142.

Denifle, Heinrich, and Franz Ehrle. *Archiv für Literatur- und Kirchengeschichte des Mittelalters*. Berlin: Weidmannsche Buchhandlung, 1885–1900.

Doucet, Ferdinand. "De operibus mss. Petri Io. Olivi Patavii." *AFH* 28 (1935): 408–42.

Douie, Decima. *The Nature and the Effect of the Heresy of the Fraticelli*. Manchester: University of Manchester Press, 1932.

Dufeil, M.-M. *Guillaume de Saint-Amour et la polemique universitaire parisienne*. Paris: Editions Picard, 1972.

Emmerson, Richard. *Antichrist in the Middle Ages*. Seattle: University of Washington Press, 1981.

Eusebius. *Ecclesiastical History*. In *Loeb Classical Library*. Cambridge, MA: Harvard University Press, 1942–49, vol. 53.

Felder, Hilarin. *Geschichte des wissenschaftlichen Studien im Franziskanerorden bis um Mitte des 13. Jahrhunderts*. Freiburg i. Br.: Herder, 1904.

Finke. Heinrich. *Acta aragonensia*. Berlin: Rothschild, 1908.

Franciscus Silvestri. Critique of Olivi's Apocalypse Commentary. Incipit: *In nomine domini*. MS Rome Vat. Arm. seg. XXXI, t. 42, 82v–91v.

Golubovich, Girolamo. *Biblioteca bio-bibliografica della Terra Santa e dell'oriente francescana*. Quaracchi: College of Saint Bonaventure, 1906–48.

Guillelmus de Militona. *Quaestiones de sacramentis*. Quaracchi: College of Saint Bonaventure, 1961.

Herde, Peter. *Cölestin V*. Stuttgart: Hiersemann, 1981.

Ieronimus. *Commentariorum in Hiezechielem libri XIV*. In *CCSL*, Vol. 75.

Ini, Anna Maria. "Nuovi documenti sugli spirituali di Toscana." *AFH* 66 (1973): 305–77.

Ioachim de Fiore. *Liber de concordia novi ac veteris testamenti*. Philadelphia: American Philosophical Society, 1983 (contains only books 1–4).

———. *Liber de concordia novi ac veteris testamenti*. Frankfurt: Minerva, 1964 (reprint of Venice, 1519 edition).

——— (pseudonymous). *Super Jeremiam*. Venice: Bernardinus Benalius, 1525.

Koch, Joseph. "Der Prozess gegen die Postille Olivis zur Apokalypse." *Recherches de Théologie Ancienne et Médiévale* 5 (1933): 302–15.

Krey, Philip. "Nicholas of Lyra: Apocalypse Commentary as Historiography." Doctoral dissertation, University of Chicago, 1990.

Lactantius. *Divinae institutiones*. In *CSEL*, vol. 19.

Lambert, Malcolm. "The Franciscan Crisis under John XXII." *Franciscan Studies* 32 (1972): 123–43.

———. *Franciscan Poverty*. London: S.P.C.K., 1961.

Lee, Harold, Marjorie Reeves, and Giulio Silano, editors. *Western Mediterranean Prophecy*. Toronto: Pontifical Institute of Medieval Studies, 1989.

Lerner, Robert. "An 'Angel of Philadelphia' in the Reign of Philip the Fair." In *Order and Innovation in the Middle Ages*. Princeton: Princeton University Press, 1976, 343–64.

———. "Antichrists and Antichrist in Joachim of Fiore." *Speculum* 60 (1985): 553–70

———. "Frederick II, Alive, Aloft, and Allayed, in Franciscan-Joachite Eschatology." In *The Use and Abuse of Eschatology in the Middle Ages*. Leuven: Leuven University Press, 1988, 359–84.

———. "Joachim of Fiore's Breakthrough to Chiliasm." *Cristianesimo nella storia* 6 (1985): 489–512.

———. "Poverty, Preaching and Eschatology in the Revelation Commentaries of 'Hugh of St. Cher.'" In *The Bible in the Medieval World*. Oxford: Blackwell, 1985, 157–89.

———. "Refreshment of the Saints." *Traditio* 32 (1976): 97–144.

Lewis, Warren. "Peter John Olivi: Prophet of the Year 2000." Doctoral dissertation, Tübingen University, 1972.

Little, Andrew G. "Statuta provincialia provinciarum Aquitaniae et Franciae (saec. XIII–XIV)." *AFH* 7 (1914): 466–501.

Little, A. G., P. Mandonnet, and P. Sabatier. *Opuscules de critique historique*. Paris: Librairie Fischbacher, 1903.

Madigan, Kevin. "Peter Olivi's *Lectura super Matthaeum* in Medieval Exegetical Context." Doctoral dissertation, University of Chicago, 1992.

Manselli, Raoul. *La "Lectura super Apocalypsim" di Pietro di Giovanni Olivi*. Rome: Istituto Storico Italiano per il Medio Evo, 1955.

———. *Spirituali e Beghini in Provenza*. Rome: Istituto Storico Italiano per il Medio Evo, 1959.

———. "La terza età, Babylon e l'Anticristo Mistico." *Bulletino dell'Istituto Storico Italiano per il Medio Evo e Archivio Muratoriano* 70 (1970): 47–79.

Mansi, Giovanni. *Sacrorum conciliorum nova et amplissima collectio*. Florence: A. Zatta, 1759–98. (volumes 14–31 published in Venice.)

———. *Stephani Baluzii Tutelensis Miscellanea*. Paris: Riccomini, 1761–64.

Mattheus de Aquasparta. *Sermones de sancto Francisco*. Quaracchi: College of Saint Bonaventure, 1962.

May, William. "The Confesson of Prous Boneta, Heretic and Heresiarch." In *Essays in Medieval Life and Thought*. New York: Columbia University Press, 1965, pp. 3–30.

McGinn, Bernard. *The Calabrian Abbot*. New York: Macmillan, 1985.

———. "The Significance of Bonaventure's Theology of History." *Journal of Religion Supplement* 58 (1978): 64–81.

Migne, J.-P. *Patrologiae Cursus Completus*. Series Latina. Paris: Migne, 1844–66.

Moorman, John. *History of the Franciscan Order*. Oxford: Oxford University Press, 1968.

Moynihan, Robert. "Development of the 'Pseudo-Joachim' Commentary 'super Hieremiam.'" *Mélanges de l'école française de Rome. Moyen Âge, Temps Modernes* 98 (1986): 109–42.

Oberman, Heiko. "The Stubborn Jews: Timing the Escalation of Antisemitism in Late Medieval Europe." *Leo Baeck Institute Yearbook*, 34 (1989): xi–xxv.

Oliger, Livarius. *De secta spiritus libertatis in Umbria saec. XIV*. Rome: Edizioni "Storia e Letteratura," 1943.

————. "Fr. Bertrandi de Turre processus contra spirituales Aquitaniae (1315) et Card. Jacobus de Columna littera defensoria spiritualium provinciae (1316)." *AFH* 16 (1923): 323–55.

Pacetti, Dionisio. "L'Expositio super Apocalypsim' di Mattia di Svezia." *AFH* 54 (1961): 297–99.

Papini, Niccola. *Notizie sicure della morte, sepoltura, canonizzazione e traslazione di S. Francesco d'Assisi.* 2nd ed. Foligno: Tomassini, 1824.

Pásztor, Edith. "Giovanni XXII e il Gioachimismo di Pietro di Giovanni Olivi." *Bulletino dell'Istituto Storico Italiano per il Medio Evo e Archivio Muratoriano* 82 (1970): 81–111.

————. "Le Polemiche sulla 'Lectura super apocalypsim' di Pietro di Giovanni Olivi fino alla sua condanna." *Bulletino dell'Istituto Storico Italiano per il Medio Evo e Archivio Muratoriano* 70 (1958): 365–424.

Paul, Jacques. "Hughes de Digne." In *Franciscains d'Oc.* Toulouse: Privat, 1975. 69–97.

————. "Le Joachimisme et les Joachimites au milieu du XIIIe siècle d'apres le temoignage de Fra Salimbene." In *1274: Année charniere,* 797–813. Colloques internationaux CNRS, no. 558. 1977.

Péano, Pierre. "Raymond Geoffroi, ministre général et défenseur des spirituels." *Picenum seraphicum* 11 (1974): 190–203.

Peck, George. *The Fool of God.* Tuscaloosa, AL: University of Alabama Press, 1980.

Pelegrinus de Bononia. *Chronica abbreviatum.* In *Tractatus Fr. Thomae vulgo dicti de Eccleston de adventu fratrum minorum in Angliam.* Paris: Librairie Fischbacher, 1909.

Petrus Comester. *Historia scholastica.* In *PL,* 198:1015–1720.

Potestà, Gian Luca. *Angelo Clareno.* Rome: Istituto Storico Italiano per il Medio Evo, 1990.

Pou y Marti, José. *Visionarios, Beguinos y Fraticellos Catalanes (Siglos XIII–XV).* Vich: Editorial Serafica, 1930.

Ratzinger, Joseph. *Die Geschichtestheologie des heiligen Bonaventura.* Munich: Schnell and Steiner, 1959 (English translation, *The Theology of History in St. Bonaventure.* Chicago: Franciscan Herald Press, 1971).

Reeves, Marjorie. "The Abbot Joachim's Disciples and the Cistercian Order." *Sophia* 19 (1951): 355–71.

————. *Influence of Prophecy in the Later Middle Ages* Oxford: Clarendon Press, 1969.

————. *Joachim of Fiore and the Prophetic Future.* New York: S.P.C.K., 1977.

————. "The Originality and Influence of Joachim of Fiore." *Traditio* 36 (1980): 269–316.

Reinhardt, Klaus. "Das Werk des Nikolaus von Lyra im mittelalterlichen Spanien." *Traditio* 43 (1987): 321–58.

Salimbene da Parma. *Cronica.* Bari: G. Laterza, 1966.

Schmitt, Clement. "Fraticelli." In *Dizionario degli istituti di perfezione.* Rome: Edizioni paoline, 1974–88, 4:807–21.

Schmolinsky, Sabina. "Expositio Apocalypsis intellectum historicum: Der Kommentar des Alexander Minorita im Rahmen der deutschen Rezeptionsgeschichte Joachims von Fiore." Doctoral dissertation, University of Munich, 1987.

Smalley, Beryl. *The Gospels in the Schools*. London: Hambledon Press, 1985.

———. "John Russel OFM." In *Studies in Medieval Thought and Learning*. London: Hambledon Press, 1981, 205–48.

Stanislao da Campagnola, *L'Angelo del sesto sigillo e l' "alter Christus."* Rome: Laurentianum, 1971.

Thomas of Celano. *Vita prima, vita secunda, et tractatus de miraculis*. In *AF*, 10:1–330.

Thomas of Eccleston. *Liber de adventu minorum in Angliam*. In *Rerum Britannicarum Medii Aevi scriptores* (Rolls Series). London: Longmans, 1858–82, no.4, 1:1–72.

Tierney, Brian. *Origins of Papal Infallibility*. Leiden: Brill, 1972.

Tognetti, Giampaolo. "I fraticelli, il principio di povertà e i secolari." *Bulletino dell'istituto storico italiano per il medio evo e Archivio muratoriano* 90 (1982/83): 77–145.

Töpfer, Bernhard. "Eine Handschrift des Evangelium aeternum des Gerardino von Borgo San Donnino," *Zeitschrift für Geschictswissenschaft* 7 (1960): 156–60.

———. *Das kommende Reich des Friedens*. Berlin: 1964.

Turley, Thomas. "John XXII and the Franciscans: A Reappraisal." In *Popes, Teachers and Canon Law in the Middle Ages*. Ithaca: Cornell University Press, 1989, 74–88.

Ubertino da Casale. *Arbor vitae crucifixae Jesu*. Torino: Bottega d'Erasmo, 1961 (reprint of Venice, 1485 edition).

Vidal, Jean Marie. *Bullaire de l'inquisition française*. Paris: Letouzey et Ané, 1913.

Wadding, Luke. *Annales minorum*. Rome: Rochus Bernabò, 1732.

Wessley, Stephen. *Joachim of Fiore and Monastic Reform*. New York: P. Lang, 1990.

Index

University of Pennsylvania Press
MIDDLE AGES SERIES
Edward Peters, General Editor

F. R. P. Akehurst, trans. *The* Coutumes de Beauvaisis *of Philippe de Beaumanoir.* 1992.

Peter L. Allen. *The Art of Love: Amatory Fiction from Ovid to the* Romance of the Rose. 1992

David Anderson. *Before the Knight's Tale: Imitation of Classical Epic in Boccaccio's* Teseida. 1988

Benjamin Arnold. *Count and Bishop in Medieval Germany: A Study of Regional Power, 1100–1350.* 1991

Mark C. Bartusis. *The Late Byzantine Army: Arms and Society, 1204–1453.* 1992

J. M. W. Bean. *From Lord to Patron: Lordship in Late Medieval England.* 1990

Uta-Renate Blumenthal. *The Investiture Controversy: Church and Monarchy from the Ninth to the Twelfth Century.* 1988

Daniel Bornstein, trans. *Dino Compagni's* Chronicle *of Florence.* 1986

Maureen Boulton. *The Song in the Story: Lyric Insertions in French Narrative Fiction, 1200–1400.* 1993

Betsy Bowden. *Chaucer Aloud: The Varieties of Textual Interpretation.* 1987

James William Brodman. *Ransoming Captives in Crusader Spain: The Order of Merced on the Christian-Islamic Frontier.* 1986

Kevin Brownlee and Sylvia Huot, eds. *Rethinking the* Romance of the Rose: *Text, Image, Reception.* 1992

Otto Brunner (Howard Kaminsky and James Van Horn Melton, eds. and trans.). Land *and Lordship: Structures of Governance in Medieval Austria.* 1992

Robert I. Burns, S.J., ed. *Emperor of Culture: Alfonso X the Learned of Castile and His Thirteenth-Century Renaissance.* 1990

David Burr. *Olivi and Franciscan Poverty: The Origins of the* Usus Pauper *Controversy.* 1989

David Burr. *Olivi's Peaceable Kingdom: A Reading of the Apocalypse Commentary.* 1993

Thomas Cable. *The English Alliterative Tradition.* 1991

Anthony K. Cassell and Victoria Kirkham, eds. and trans. *Diana's Hunt/Caccia di Diana: Boccaccio's First Fiction.* 1991

John C. Cavadini. *The Last Christology of the West: Adoptionism in Spain and Gaul, 785–820.* 1993

Brigitte Cazelles. *The Lady as Saint: A Collection of French Hagiographic Romances of the Thirteenth Century.* 1991

Karen Cherewatuk and Ulrike Wiethaus, eds. *Dear Sister: Medieval Women and the Epistolary Genre.* 1993

Anne L. Clark. *Elisabeth of Schönau: A Twelfth-Century Visionary*. 1992

Willene B. Clark and Meradith T. McMunn, eds. *Beasts and Birds of the Middle Ages: The Bestiary and Its Legacy*. 1989

Richard C. Dales. *The Scientific Achievement of the Middle Ages*. 1973

Charles T. Davis. *Dante's Italy and Other Essays*. 1984

Katherine Fischer Drew, trans. *The Burgundian Code*. 1972

Katherine Fischer Drew, trans. *The Laws of the Salian Franks*. 1991

Katherine Fischer Drew, trans. *The Lombard Laws*. 1973

Nancy Edwards. *The Archaeology of Early Medieval Ireland*. 1990

Margaret J. Ehrhart. *The Judgment of the Trojan Prince Paris in Medieval Literature*. 1987

Richard K. Emmerson and Ronald B. Herzman. *The Apocalyptic Imagination in Medieval Literature*. 1992

Theodore Evergates. *Feudal Society in Medieval France: Documents from the County of Champagne*. 1993

Felipe Fernández-Armesto. *Before Columbus: Exploration and Colonization from the Mediterranean to the Atlantic, 1229–1492*. 1987

R. D. Fulk. *A History of Old English Meter*. 1992

Patrick J. Geary. *Aristocracy in Provence: The Rhône Basin at the Dawn of the Carolingian Age*. 1985.

Peter Heath. *Allegory and Philosophy in Avicenna (Ibn Sînâ), with a Translation of the Book of the Prophet Muhammad's Ascent to Heaven*. 1992

J. N. Hillgarth, ed. *Christianity and Paganism, 350–750: The Conversion of Western Europe*. 1986

Richard C. Hoffman. *Land, Liberties, and Lordship in a Late Medieval Countryside: Agrarian Structures and Change in the Duchy of Wrocław*. 1990

Robert Hollander. *Boccaccio's Last Fiction: Il Corbaccio*. 1988

Edward B. Irving, Jr. *Rereading* Beowulf. 1989

C. Stephen Jaeger. *The Origins of Courtliness: Civilizing Trends and the Formation of Courtly Ideals, 939–1210*. 1985

William Chester Jordan. *The French Monarchy and the Jews: From Philip Augustus to the Last Capetians*. 1989

William Chester Jordan. *From Servitude to Freedom: Manumission in the Sénonais in the Thirteenth Century*. 1986

Ellen E. Kittell. *From Ad Hoc to Routine: A Case Study in Medieval Bureaucracy*. 1991

Alan C. Kors and Edward Peters, eds. *Witchcraft in Europe, 1100–1700: A Documentary History*. 1972

Barbara M. Kreutz. *Before the Normans: Southern Italy in the Ninth and Tenth Centuries*. 1992

E. Ann Matter. *The Voice of My Beloved: The Song of Songs in Western Medieval Christianity*. 1990

María Rosa Menocal. *The Arabic Role in Medieval Literary History*. 1987

A. J. Minnis. *Medieval Theory of Authorship*. 1988

Lawrence Nees. *A Tainted Mantle: Hercules and the Classical Tradition at the Carolingian Court*. 1991

Lynn H. Nelson, trans. *The Chronicle of San Juan de la Peña: A Fourteenth-Century Official History of the Crown of Aragon.* 1991

Charlotte A. Newman. *The Anglo-Norman Nobility in the Reign of Henry I: The Second Generation.* 1988

Joseph F. O'Callaghan. *The Cortes of Castile-León, 1188–1350.* 1989

Joseph F. O'Callaghan. *The Learned King: The Reign of Alfonso X of Castile.* 1993

William D. Paden, ed. *The Voice of the Trobairitz: Perspectives on the Women Troubadours.* 1989

Edward Peters. *The Magician, the Witch, and the Law.* 1992

Edward Peters, ed. *Christian Society and the Crusades, 1198–1229: Sources in Translation, including* The Capture of Damietta *by Oliver of Paderborn.* 1971

Edward Peters, ed. *The First Crusade: The* Chronicle of Fulcher of Chartres *and Other Source Materials.* 1971

Edward Peters, ed. *Heresy and Authority in Medieval Europe.* 1980

James M. Powell. *Albertanus of Brescia: The Pursuit of Happiness in the Early Thirteenth Century.* 1992

James M. Powell. *Anatomy of a Crusade, 1213–1221.* 1986

Michael Resler, trans. Erec *by Hartmann von Aue.* 1987

Pierre Riché (Michael Idomir Allen, trans.). *The Carolingians: A Family Who Forged Europe.* 1993

Pierre Riché (Jo Ann McNamara, trans.). *Daily Life in the World of Charlemagne.* 1978

Jonathan Riley-Smith. *The First Crusade and the Idea of Crusading.* 1986

Joel T. Rosenthal. *Patriarchy and Families of Privilege in Fifteenth-Century England.* 1991

Teofilo F. Ruiz. *Crisis and Continuity: Land and Town in Late Medieval Castile.* 1993

Steven D. Sargent, ed. and trans. *On the Threshold of Exact Science: Selected Writings of Anneliese Maier on Late Medieval Natural Philosophy.* 1982

Sarah Stanbury. *Seeing the* Gawain-*Poet: Description and the Act of Perception.* 1992

Thomas C. Stillinger. *The Song of Troilus: Lyric Authority in the Medieval Book.* 1992

Susan Mosher Stuard. *A State of Deference: Ragusa/Dubrovnik in the Medieval Centuries.* 1992

Susan Mosher Stuard. ed. *Women in Medieval History and Historiography.* 1987

Susan Mosher Stuard, ed. *Women in Medieval Society.* 1976

Jonathan Sumption. *The Hundred Years War: Trial by Battle.* 1992

Ronald E. Surtz. *The Guitar of God: Gender, Power, and Authority in the Visionary World of Mother Juana de la Cruz (1481–1534).* 1990

Patricia Terry, trans. *Poems of the Elder Edda.* 1990

Hugh M. Thomas. *Vassals, Heiresses, Crusaders, and Thugs: The Gentry of Angevin Yorkshire, 1154–1216.* 1993

Frank Tobin. *Meister Eckhart: Thought and Language.* 1986

Ralph V. Turner. *Men Raised from the Dust: Administrative Service and Upward Mobility in Angevin England.* 1988

Harry Turtledove, trans. *The* Chronicle of Theophanes: *An English Translation of Anni Mundi 6095–6305 (A.D. 602–813).* 1982

Mary F. Wack. *Lovesickness in the Middle Ages: The* Viaticum *and Its Commentaries.* 1990

Benedicta Ward. *Miracles and the Medieval Mind: Theory, Record, and Event, 1000 – 1215.* 1982

Suzanne Fonay Wemple. *Women in Frankish Society: Marriage and the Cloister, 500 – 900.* 1981

Jan M. Ziolkowski. *Talking Animals: Medieval Latin Beast Poetry, 750 –1150.* 1993

This book has been set in Linotron Galliard. Galliard
was designed for Mergenthaler in 1978 by Matthew
Carter. Galliard retains many of the features of a
sixteenth-century typeface cut by Robert Granjon
but has some modifications that give it a more contemporary look.

Printed on acid-free paper.

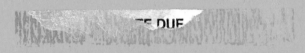